West Bengal in Perspective

West Bengal in Perspective

Politics and Governance

Amiya K. Chaudhuri

Maulana Abul Kalam Azad Institute of Asian Studies, Kolkata

SHIPRA

Rs. 950; US$ 47.50

ISBN: 978-81-7541-749-6

First Published in India in 2014

West Bengal in Perspective: Politics and Governance

Published by:
SHIPRA PUBLICATIONS
H.O.: LG 18-19, Pankaj Central Market, Patparganj,
I.P. Ext., Delhi-110092, Tel: 91-11-2223 5152, 2223 6152
Br.Off.: 4617/18, Ansari Road, Darya Ganj,
New Delhi-110002, Tel: 9650028065, 9810522367
E-mail: info@shiprapublication.com
www.shiprapublication.com

Acknowledgements

I am indebted to many named and mostly unnamed people, teachers, scholars and vibrant intellectuals belonging to social science and literature. The authorities of the Maulana Abul Kalam Azad Institute of Asian Studies helped a lot in providing me a Fellowship to undertake this project. I would fail in my duties if I do not particularly mention the help and encouragement I occasionally received from Dr. Hari Vasudevan, the former Director of the Institute and Dr. Sreeradha Dutta, presently Director of MAKAIAS. Professor Omprakash Mishra, Professor Suranjan Das, Professor Ashis Roy have always been generous to me. I am indebted to Professor Jayanta Kumar Roy, presently the Maulana Azad Fellow, who occasionally advised me to carry on my academic venture. I extend my sincere thanks to Sree Sandip Sarkar—the Librarian of this Institute. I must mention that the former Foreign Secretary Mr. Krishnan Srinivasan, Fellow of Maulana Azad Institute, frequently gifted me with very important books that really refreshed my energy as an academic. The other Fellows, my colleagues in my work place, also stood by me. Thanks to them all individually. I interviewed a number of Political Leaders from all parties, I put on record my thanks to them all. Last but not the least, my wife Dr. Manjusee Chaudhuri had to spend long hours in her loneliness at home helping me in my work in the office. My son Bushku and daughter-in-law Mimi, both working as Post Doctoral Research Associate, presently at Texas A&M University USA, helped in sustaining my spirit after my severe accident in early 2011 after which I suffered from occasional bouts of restlessness in working out the present Project. I extend my heartly thanks to D. Kumar of the Shipra Publications for his bringing out the book in a very short time. Opinions and mistakes, there might be many, are of my own only.

July 2014
Golf Green, WIB (M) 19/4
Kolkata - 700095

Amiya K. Chaudhuri
email: amiya_chaudhuri@yahoo.com

Contents

Abbreviations

AIFB	All India Forward Bloc
AITC	All India Trinamool Congress
BBC	Biplabi Bangla Congress
B Cong (R)	B Cong (Revolutionary)
B Cong	Bangla Congress Party
BJP	Bharatiya Janata Party
BLD	Bharatiya Lok Dal
BSP	Bahujan Samaj Party
CMP	Communist Marxist Party
Cong (O)	Congress (Organization)
Cong (R)	Congress (Requisition)
Cong (S)	Congress Socialist Party
CPI	Communist Party of India
CPI (M)	Communist Party of India (Marxist)
CPI (ML)	Communist Party of India (Marxist-Leninist)
DSP	Democratic Socialist Party
DSP(C)	Democratic Socialist Party (Congress)
FB	Forward Bloc
FB (M)	Forward Bloc (Marxist)
FB (R)	Forward Bloc (Ruiker)
FB (S)	Forward Bloc (Socialist)
GL	Gorkha League
GNLF	Gorkha National Liberation Front
HM	Hindu Maha Sabha
INC	Indian National Congress
INDF	Indian National Democratic Front
JAN	Janata
JD	Janata Dal
JKP	Jan Kranti Party
JKP/N	Jharkhand Party (Naren Hansda)
JMM	Jharkhand Mukti Morcha

JP	Janata Party
JS	Jana Sang
KMPP	Krishak Mazdur Praza Party
LF	Left Font
LSS	Lok Sevak Sangha
MUL/ML	Muslim Union League/Muslim League
PML	Party of Muslim League
PML	Progressive Muslim League
PSP	Praja Socialist Party/Pacifist Socialist Party
RCPI	Revolutionary Communist Party of India
RJD	Rashtriya Janata Dal
RSP	Revolutionary Socialist Party
SP	Samajvadi Party
SRP	Socialist Revolutionary Party
SSP	Samukta Socialist Party
SUC	Socialist Unity Centre
SUCI	Socialist Unity Centre of India
SWA	Swatantra Party
TMC	Trinamool Congress
WBSP	West Bengal Socialist Party
WPI	Workers Party of India

List of Tables

Introduction

The present study is not a theoretical discourse on the history of West Bengal. To continue the discourse only some remarkable historic moments are chosen. The approach is that of the derivation of political sociology—both empirical and normative or in other words the approach is that of political sociology. History in a bird's eye view, the sociological dimensions that have influenced the truncated history and its periodic political economy and electoral processes with democratic deficit all have been described and analyzed within the text. Democracy both in its form and contents in our plural society and the open political space as we share are of vital importance. Keeping in view this aspect, I have tried to proceed towards finishing the work. To write a proper history of West Bengal, one of the larger federal states, is being left to professional historians.

Certain common properties, either inherent or constitutionally contrived characterize the working of the process of state politics in historical moments in India and for that matter in several of the federal states. Achievement of good governance through democratic means for realizing political modernization and development objectives has been the coveted goal. Besides, the securing of equal opportunity and special provisions for deprived social groups and minorities as well find a special place in this overall objective. Whether and to what extent this objective and the values underlying it are or can be realized depends upon the way the political parties in India—both at national and regional levels, have conducted state affairs. Differential endowments in respect of political space and territorial size as also the magnitude and the density of population are, of course, important components. However, socio-political ethos in certain historical context, which differs from state to state, constitutes the most important factor in this regard. In West Bengal, anti-Congressism has been the mainstay of the Marxist political parties and other socialist parties. The politics of the break-away groups, and smaller parties from original Indian National Congress followed the footprint, though not always but occasionally though, throughout the history of the state since Independence. This has also been kept in mind. The refugees who had to migrate to West Bengal after Partition were mostly educated and the Marxists targeted them to side with the oppositions; their existential conditions and necessities made them susceptible to the leftist ideology and propaganda. It was easier for these parties to mobilize a large number of the refugees against the Congress government directly and through culturally mediated popular movements indirectly by showing cinemas and musical programmes depicting the miserable plight of the people uprooted from their ancestral homes and heaths. Refugee camps and colonies were built on the government lands and the lands left by the Muslims leaving for eastern Pakistan, during the period around the state capital Calcutta (now Kolkata) and many of the suburban areas including the districts of North Bengal. The actions of the Communist Party of India (undivided till 1964) were not so much to highlight and redress the miserable plight of the uprooted people from the erstwhile eastern part of Bengal as to gain political mileage and electoral gains. Successive election campaigns and electoral results of the state from 1952 to 1967 would prove the contention. It was widely felt that, instead of following the strict principles of federalism, the Central Government paid little heed to the regional socio-political mosaic and its legitimate demands and aspirations. The regional parties, particularly the CPI (M) since the split of the communist movement in 1964 and CPI, were contemptuous of other smaller parties particularly socialist parties and other local level parties. For opportunistic reasons, however, they did occasionally speak of some sort of a left unity highlighting the Communist thesis of United Front strategy. But historically they did not care to recognize the pragmatic necessity of establishing some sort of political equation between the powerful and the smaller parties in coalition making.

In West Bengal, specific politics revolving around the Marxist parties seems different from that of the other states. The Marxists very intelligently used their thesis without taking into account whether the perspective derived from the theory and practices of the Communist varieties elsewhere in the world would suit in the context of West Bengal in its socio-economic ground realities. The main Marxist Party in the state became restive because of their existential problems under a single party dominance in its socio-economic roots in the grassroots levels from the very beginning. To them, the single dominant party or, in other words, the Indian National Congress was a party of the elites whatever their social roots and composition was. A dominant party in a multi-party system in particular social and political space could not share and even provide democratic space with other parties, particularly with the Marxist and other varieties of the Left. The historical spaces in Bengal, therefore, suffered from democratic deficit. Starting from this view the left parties and various other parties with different orientations drew their conclusions as to what strategy they would follow in making and remaking the political history of West Bengal in subsequent phases.

The present study is a modest attempt to unfold the story of the state in different historical context that manifested in the electoral processes in West Bengal for more than last six decades. But all these factors, politico-historical processes were determined by the tortuous period of history—remarkable by itself. The history of Bengal during this period from 1937 to 1947 appeared to be very interesting path setting for socio-political realities of the uncertain and meandering course that began at the dawn of Independence after 15 August 1947.

1
Historically Remarkable but Politically a Tortuous Decade (1937-1946)

Leo Tolstoy after finishing his masterpiece in more than one thousand fifty pages took another fifty odd pages as epilogue to convey to his readers what history meant for him.[1] Incomplete knowledge of the demography and climate and its frequent changes in different periods of the year and, faulty planning of his objective to achieve or mistiming to carry out the mission was really the undoing of Napoleon. He had to retreat from his Russian invasion at the heaviest cost with loss of thousands of foot soldiers in the coldest winter in the Czarist Russian Empire. In his heart of hearts perhaps he realized for the first time that the word 'impossible' was still to be found in his dictionary. The greatest of the great masters had aimed at justifying elements of determinism in the making of history. He sought to find out the causal relationship of the then great moments of history, failing of which he talked about the design of nature that predetermined even the smallest events in the history of man.

But it is not beyond human wisdom to understand the apparent determinism. Thus Tolstoy continues, "Although the surface of the ocean of history seemed motionless, the movement of humanity was as uninterrupted as the flow of time. Various series of groups of men were joining together and separating; the causes were being prepared that would bring about the formation and dissolution of empires and the migrations of peoples."[2] Man makes history but any indiscretion on his part is visited with nemesis in the successive generations. That was what happened to Napoleon in France after his abortive war effort in Russia. Apart from larger issues in the ongoing process of history, even small events in the life of people create history.

Looking back at the colonial history of Bengal in the late 1930s, a very important fact is to be taken in consideration. It was just after the 1937 election under the Constitution of 1935. Finding no way out to construct a coalition with the Provincial Congress Party who had to have joined hands with the Muslim Leaguers. Even when Fazlul Haque at Lucknow proposed Pakistan Resolution in 1940 at the behest of Mohammed Ali Jinnah, Mr. Haque was not sure about the fate of the resolution. The Congress leadership at the centre did not agree to the proposal of Fazlul Haque to form a coalition government between the Krishak Praja Party of Haque and the Bengal Provincial Congress Party. Mr. Haque was not a Muslim League member or a Pakistan sympathizer. After 1937 elections in Bengal the Congress Party could have easily gone in for a coalition with the Party of Mr. Haque. Mr. Haque talked to several provincial leaders including Sarat Chandra Bose and others but failed to convince the Congress. Mr. Haque literally ran from post to pillar to prevent the Muslim League from spreading the design of Mr. Jinnah being in the dictating terms if in any form the Muslim League might be in power in Bengal. The central Congress leadership was too adamant to go in for a coalition in Bengal as elsewhere in the then United Province etc. In 1937 Jawaharlal Nehru was the Congress President. A resolution was passed in the working committee of the Congress to the effect that the provincial congress party would not enter into any coalition to form the provincial governments.

Again looking back, it is to be admitted that a few important Muslim Leaguers wanted the Congress to forge a coalition government in Bengal. To this effect the Muslim League leader Abdul Hashim mooted a proposal to Gandhiji. In reply Gandhiji told that he did not believe in coalition.[3] It was Nehru who piloted the proposal with Gandhi being present in the working committee meeting.[4] Possibly it was all at the "silent diktat of Gandhi" as perceived by people still living and could vividly recall the process of the history of Bengal[5] at that time. The attitude of the Congress may seem an absurdity in the context of the present day politics of coalition not only in India but also elsewhere in democratic countries of the world at large. Nehru never told what might have happened had a coalition arrangement made in Bengal between the Bengal Congress and the Krishak Praja Party led by Fazlul Haque. This arrangement could have debarred the Muslim League from getting such prominence as it did in the process of politics in Bengal. In the crucible of history any crucial element might change the entire course of history. The Congress Party's decision at that juncture was one of the determining factors that were not to be missed to understand the legacy of the decade before partition of Bengal. The Congress was perhaps overconfident about its strength and stance to fight against the colonial power on the one hand and the Muslim League led by Jinnah on the other. Ultimately Fazlul Haque, being promised by Jinnah to be made the premier, with his Krishak Praja, formed a coalition government with the Muslim League. This period of the history of Bengal from 1937 to 1946 Bengal Provincial election was very crucial to understand the later Congress-Muslim League's relation and political developments in the country that finally culminated in the vivisection of a more or less culturally cohesive subcontinent. If Fazlul Haque were allowed to form a coalition government with the Bengal Congress Provincial Party, it would have been difficult for Jinnah to pass a Pakistan resolution at Lucknow. It was actually a folly on the part of the central leadership of the Congress to leave Fazlul Haque to the lap of the Muslim League led by a determined Jinnah to gain Pakistan by means as the situations would demand to the advantage of his own self and the Muslim League.[6]

In fact due to the lack of farsightedness Jinnah began to preach what he actually did not believe in his heart of hearts that the Congress was a Party of the Hindus only. Possibly during a course of a difficult period of his political career, he had to choose either the devil or the deep sea. The Muslim Leaguers from the very beginning of the 1930s if not so much earlier, wanted Mr. Jinnah to be in their fold and the new messiah for the achievement of Pakistan. From then on in the late 1930s there was no looking back for incoming *Avatar* of the Muslim League. But it was a widely held opinion that Jinnah in his sick bed in the last days of his life expressed, "... had he been given another chance, he would have undone what he did as a charter of his acquired faith for the Muslim home land."[7] Mr. Jinnah as the President of the Muslim League gained total confidence among all sections of the Muslim Leaguers and played an important role immediately after the provincial elections of 1937 under the Federal Constitution Act of 1935. Mr. Jinnah by now overcame his ambivalence about the highest leadership of the Indian National Congress Party. He along with his party Muslim League vented their unhappiness and grievances against the Congress for its attitude and treatment with the Muslims in the provinces where Congress formed the government.[8] The Muslim League, Muslim groups and their leaders brought a few reports like Pirpur Report depicting and seriously alleging the Congress governments in the then British Indian provinces as pro-Hindu and anti-Muslim. In fact the period between 1937 and 1940 till the Pakistan resolution was piloted by Fazlul Haque was one of the far-reaching segments in the history of the partition making in India in general and Bengal in particular.

After Fazlul Haque, a number of governments came but all at the leadership of the Muslim League which engineered the "Great Calcutta Killing"[9] in August 16-20 in 1946 with S. Suhrawardy at the helm of affairs as the Premier (the Chief Minister in a Province as designated during the late colonial era at that time) of the British Province of Bengal. The political history of West Bengal in particular as we recounted on August 14-15 in 1947 and the Indian subcontinent in general, was as if providentially determined, when Jinnah exclaimed "the day of deliverance" when the Congress provincial governments resigned against British government's Second World War effort involving Indian people without consulting the Congress Party. At that point of time Congress singly, and people at large in India used to think that the INC represented the popular opinions of the country. The Muslim League leader Jinnah thought otherwise. Possibly it was his personal ego and the question of his identity as a great leader compared with Nehru, Vallavbhai Patel, Khan Abdul Gaffar Khan, Maulana Azad and above all Gandhi that impelled him with single minded determination, to carve out a portion of India to establish Pakistan—the holy place for the Indian Muslims. At that time Jinnah thought away the fact that large sections of much more Muslims would be staying in secular India than others that would leave for newly created Pakistan to be separated in two parts. Western part was to be populated by the up-country Urdu speaking Muslims including the Baluch and, the Eastern part was completely dominated by the Bengali speaking Muslims. A series of incidents that followed from 1939 are of far-reaching importance in making the history of the state. The conflict between Subhas Chandra Bose and Gandhi reflected the mind set of the elite circle or the middle order leaders in Bengal.[10] In 1938 Gandhiji himself asked his closer leaders to elect Subhas Chandra Bose as the Congress President for the year in Haripura Congress Session. Subhas had all round cooperation from different quarters. He was happy to carry through his pet agenda. He formed a National Planning Committee with a view to what the Congress would pursue a course of modernizing the industrial sectors and agriculture. With his consent Subhas Chandra appointed Jawaharlal Nehru as the Chairman of the Committee. It seemed in the process that in his over zeal Subhas Chandra might have alienated Gandhi. In a note to Vallavbhai Patel, Gandhiji had scribbled on a piece of paper and passed it on to Patel that Subhas might not be dependable as the Congress President in a Working Committee meeting at Sarat Bose's house in Calcutta, even though agreeing to elect Subhas Chandra to the topmost post of the Congress Working Committee as also the Congress Party. It is simple history now. In 1939 opposing the Congress Presidential candidate Pattabhi Sitaramiah foisted by Gandhi, Subhas sought reelection for the post in Tripuri Congress Session. The Leftist forces within the Congress massively supported him. He won the election with substantial majority but failed to constitute the Congress Working Committee (CWC). During that point of time nothing could be thought of without the concurrence of Gandhiji to form the Congress Working Committee. When approached by Subhas, Gandhi did not cooperate and asked him to form the Working Committee according to his choice. Vallabhai Patel, Jawaharlal Nehru and other heavy weight leaders kept quiet. Subhas quite dejected found no other alternative had to backtrack and resigned. He did not take the risk of constituting the CWC with other members of his limited choice. Subhas formed a new political party Forward Bloc (FB) in 1940. During this period, later on, he was put behind the bar by the British government for his attitude towards the imperialist war efforts as also for his perceptions about Soviet Russia on the one hand and the axis powers like Germany, Italy and later on Japan on the other. Due to his ailing health in jail, according to doctor's advice he was interned in his ancestral home at Elgin Road under the care of his elder brother Sarat Chandra Bose. On January 17th at the wee hour of night he left the country incognito, in company with Bhagat Ram Talwar alias Rahmat Khan in 1941. Subhas had to travel in the name of Md. Ziauddin. He reached Kabul and had to wait for quite a time to negotiate with the Soviet Embassy and other embassies. His first preference was to go to Stalin's Soviet Russia but ultimately Stalin's Russia failed him. As an alternative he would have to ultimately land in Hitler's Germany. He failed in his mission in Italy. Next he thought that Hitler would help him in fighting the British imperialism in India. The Fuehrer cold-shouldered but helped his journeying to Japan by submarine. In Japan, he took over the leadership of the Indian National Army (INA) founded by Rash Bihari Ghosh; Subhas Chandra formed Indian National Government in exile. He declared war against British government in India from Japan. As stated above that to carry on his brand of politics as against that of the Congress Party whose guiding force behind was Gandhiji, Subhas formed a new left oriented party Forward Bloc (FB) while he had to leave the Congress because of Gandhi's non-cooperation in forming the Congress Working Committee (CWC) as the second time elected President of the Party after 1939. But the Party he formed with a band of his dedicated followers was quite different from that of what we find today in West Bengal. Although the root of all varieties of Forward Bloc that grew in the later part of West Bengal's history after independence of the country and partition of Bengal drew its ancestry from what Subhas Chandra started in 1940. After Subhas Chandra left the country in 1941, the members of the Forward Bloc began infighting and broke into various factional blocks. In the later period during mid 1950s another faction of the Forward Bloc Ruiker, FB(R) fought the General Election. Later on, the former Left Front (LF) minister Ram Chatterjee formed another party namely Forward Bloc or FB (M). It was Marxist Forward Bloc that catapulted Pratim Chatterje to the ministerial rank in the LF government after the death of Ram Chatterjee. Even today's mainstream Forward Bloc claimed its ancestry in Marxist thought in the reformulation of the political thinking of Subhas Chandra. Perhaps paradoxically the present leadership of octogenarian Ashok Ghosh claims that they are Marxist also. Further many a leader of the FB like Ashok Ghosh and others, as they interpreted the political thought of Subhas Chandra, was oriented towards Marxism even from the beginning in the mid 1930s. There was another faction of the FB, which liked to designate itself as the Shubhasbadi Forward Bloc. It came into being as a result of difference of opinions with the present octogenarian state committee secretary Shree Ashok Ghosh or in other words it reflected simply inner party conflict as to the question of the retention of Shree Ghosh still as the state party secretary in spite of his age, failing health and unquestioning proximity with the leadership of the CPI (M).

In this Chapter, Subhas Chandra has come into our discussion in bolder focus simply because of his wartime activities in Far East and South East Asia and India in particular and the impact of his activities towards India's freedom struggle. Even after mid 1942, Gandhi's assessment of and attitude toward Subhas radically changed. British war cabinet led by the Prime Minister Churchill thought it absolutely necessary to have India's cooperation in the ongoing war effort. Churchill had no respect for Indian Congress leaders, was particularly contemptuous about Gandhi. Again, Churchill was very bitter about Gandhi. Churchill's hatred for Gandhi was well documented in history text. To him Gandhi was a "naked fakir" and disturbingly ugly to aristocratic perceptions of British middle class mind. Actually it was a subversive political game, so that he could politically finish Gandhi in the mind of the British people and here in India invoked suspicion in the minds of Indian Muslims led by Muhammed Ali Jinnah craving for a Muslims' holy home land, i.e. Pakistan. Reasons for the failure of Cripps Mission proved this point in the first quarter of 1942.[11] Winston Churchill's sense of possession of India as a British colony and, his recorded comments on Indian position and aspiration as perceived by its leaders including Gandhi at the helm to carry on a non-violent peaceful struggle against colonial domination, determined the Indo-British relations and the British war efforts till the end of the Second World War. Almost till the end of Britain's hold over India before independence Churchill was determined to keep India as the "Jewel of British Crown" that pitted him against Gandhi's struggle for national independence spanning a period of nearly forty years.[12]

It was a period of unprecedented situation both at home and abroad. Second World War started in Europe. British policy of appeasement of Hitler's Germany failed. Britain was directly involved in the war. After resignation of Chamberlain, Winston Churchill took over and formed a War Cabinet. Churchill's policy was to involve India in its war effort to confront the eastern front in containing Japan and save the entire South East Asia. But the British imperialist did not show the courtesy to consult the Indian nationalist leaders who were fighting a two-pronged non-violent war against the British government for independence and to keep the country together against the British intention to divide India in communal lines between the Hindus and the Muslims. Actually, Winston Churchill used to hate Gandhi. Churchill maintained his almost genetic hatred against Gandhi and his adverse attitude against the Indian leaders of the Congress Party even after his defeat in the general election in UK election 1946. After the general election the Labour Party leader Clement Attlee assumed the charge of the prime minister of Britain. In June 1947 he introduced the Indian Independence Act in British Parliament.

It is significant in this connection to note the observations made by Sir Winston Churchill the most successful wartime British Prime Minister in

Britain: "...power will go to the hands of rascals, freebooters; all India leaders will be of low calibre and men of straw. They will have sweet tongues and silly hearts. They will fight amongst themselves for power and India will be lost in political squabbles. A day would come when even air and water would be taxed."[13] Pankaj Mishra wrote a book review, recalling Churchill's deep-rooted anti India attitude against Indian national freedom movement. The review was published in *New Yorker* in August 2007. Mr. Mishra wrote, "...in the nineteen-twenties and thirties, Churchill had been loudest among the reactionaries who were determined not to lose India, 'the jewel in the crown' and as Prime Minister during the Second World War, he tried every tactics to thwart Indian Independence. He declared that he hated Indians and to quote him 'they are a beastly people with a beastly religion'. He had a special animus for Gandhi, describing him as a rascal and a 'half-naked fakir'. In a letter to Churchill, Gandhi took the latter as a compliment and claimed that he was striving for even greater renunciation."[14] So much so that Churchill in fact did not like to meet Gandhi during the Round Table Conference in London.

In this context it is pertinent to quote from Shirer, an American Journalist, "Churchill, the one Englishman of stature who had refused to see Gandhi in London during Round Table Conference. It was Shirer to know Churchill much better than many others. In 1935, inveighing against even the modest reforms a new Constitution for India he cried out, "Gandhi, and all he stands for, must ultimately be grappled with, and finally crushed!" when he became the wartime Prime Minister, Churchill would try to do just that—and fail. He would ultimately triumph over Adolf Hitler, but Mohandas K. Gandhi eventually would triumph over him—and gain all he stood for."[15] But Gandhi sincerely believed in the secular as well as the cultural ethos of the secular integrity and oneness of India. He proved himself even during the war in confronting British War Cabinet's proposal in the Cripps Mission in 1942 till the final outcome of the Cabinet Mission in 1946. Gandhi was pretty sure about the emasculation of the Britain's military strength after the war while Japan's partial invasion had already taken place in India. A shrewd politician within, Gandhi immediately realized the war ravaged British intention behind the Cripps Mission. He along with the Congress Party stalled the concept of a Constitution on the basis of the division of India in the line of having a constitution making body proportionately represented by the minorities, princely states and the Hindus. There was a proposal to be agreed upon by the parties about the secession of some provinces as also the insistence of Churchill that even in Indian democratic processes, the Defence Portfolio would always remain in the hands of the British authorities in India represented by the Commander in Chief. While facing the military reverses in the Asian front it was somewhat compelling for Britain to appease India in the form of certain short-term concessions contained in the Cripps Mission's proposals promising long-term concessions as thought out by the British establishment.[16] Mostly it was some sort of a dominion status for India within the framework of the Commonwealth of Nations. The Indian leaders of the Congress Party did not favour the proposals of the war cabinet led by Churchill and brought forward to India by Sir Strafford Cripps. Gandhi rejected the proposal by saying that it was a 'Post-dated Cheque on a crashing bank'. The objective of the Mission was to effectively involve Indian opinions in the British war effort. The question of conceding Independence was to be considered afterwards. British Government was not in a position to convince the Indian National Congress. The Muslim League followed a policy of wait and see, and the Communists were ambivalent. From the very beginning the Strafford Cripps had to face very difficult situations because of the attitude of the War Cabinet. Winston Churchill from the very beginning was against Gandhi. He thought of conceding Independence of India. Leaving behind British interests at the hands of Indian leaders and freedom fighters, was almost anathema to him.

The Congress Working Committee (CWC) dished out two suggestions. "First, an immediate change of the constitution, a point raised at the last moment and on that every one else has admitted to be wholly impracticable while the war is proceeding; and second, that they are prepared to enter a true national government with a cabinet of Indian leaders untrammeled by any control of the Viceroy or the British Government."[17] The agenda with which he came to India to convince important segments of Indian leaders left the country almost all of sudden.

It is also significant to note the following opinion, "(the) Cripps Mission failed because the Viceroy Wavell's stubborn predecessor Lord Linlithgo, and Churchill—the Prime Minister, undercut Cripps by their unwillingness to grant Indian desires for real, as opposed to potential authority."[18] On the penultimate day of his departure on April 12, Strafford Cripps wrote, "We have tried by the offer that I brought, to help India along her road to victory and to freedom. But for the moment, past distrust has proved too strong to allow of present agreement."[19] No doubt, Cripps Mission was possibly destined to fail because it had to deal with so many contrasting ideas and the components of Indian leadership. It might be that the British Government was more inclined to show its sincerity to sympathize with Indian people for their freedom struggle and solve Indian problems to the American war ally. Possibly it was a ploy of Churchill simply to befuddle the US opinions that would have liked real negotiation between Britain and India in regard to India's freedom. In concrete terms, some of the most important Indian opinion makers might have felt that Cripps had deceived them in the interests of British propaganda in the United States.[20] A simple explanation Menon indicated was that "there was no proper understanding between the Viceroy and Sir Strafford Cripps, nor between Sir Strafford Cripps and the British Cabinet. Sir Strafford Cripps had been over confident of 'selling' at least the interim proposals to the Congress but in their discussions both had reckoned without the Viceroy and His Majesty's Government. Four years later, in the course of his speech in the House of Commons on 12 December 1946, Churchill made it abundantly clear that his Majesty's Government had not been willing to support Sir Strafford Cripps to the extent to which he himself was prepared to go."[21]

It is absolutely clear from the statement made by Churchill after hindsight that the objectives of the British government at home were to involve the Indian parties in the ongoing war efforts promising something that would not come into fruition at least in the near future. Secondly, to divide Indian opinions but actually not to converge, in support of British Government's war against the Axis powers from Indian soils without having the least regard for Indian opinion. The imperial government thought that it would only ease the British war effort, in consonance with the American opinion as desired by Roosevelt about Indian struggle for freedom. Gandhi also knew as to what would be the fate of the half-hearted negotiations, as also the objectives of the Cripps Mission. He said, "It is a thousand pities that the British Government should have sent a proposal for dissolving the political deadlock, which, on the face of it, was too ridiculous to find acceptance anywhere. And it was misfortune that the bearer should have been Sir Strafford Cripps, acclaimed as a radical among the radicals and a friend of India. I have no doubt about his good will. He believed that no one could have brought anything better for India. But he should have known that at least the Congress would not look at Dominion status even though it carried the right of secession the very moment it was taken."[22]

Gandhi's statement above seems a bit naïve though he was as saintly a politician as he was shrewd and astute in his political articulations. The War Cabinet in Britain and particularly Winston Churchill might have chosen Strafford Cripps in the most difficult situation to serve the objectives of the war ravaged Britain and its national interests. Strafford Cripps was chosen as the interlocutor simply because of his radical image and as an India sympathizer. None other could have been a better bearer of the wartime British proposals. It was not that Cripps did not appreciate the British intent. Having the immediate interest and intent of the British wartime government in mind he did not hesitate to go a step further to accommodate Indian opinion. But he knew also the limited brief that British Government had given him. He might be a radical and have empathy with the Congress opinion makers but Cripps possibly realized the far more important national interests at the time when England was entangled with a devastating World War. To involve the United States as an ally it was far more necessary to show respect to the opinion of the American President Roosevelt who liked Britain to consult Indian opinion so that the allied forces could use Indian soil as one of the bases of the eastern front to manoeuvre and confront the Japanese war machine. Possibly to allay the apprehensions of the largest ally, the US, Strafford Cripps willingly carried the briefcase to India. From his latest statement after Churchill's statement as focused later on, the real intentions of the British Government certainly dawned on Gandhi. At last Gandhi made certain significant conclusions. Without depending upon anything or any power India had to settle its own chores. This final realization of Gandhi after Cripps Mission's manoeuvering in different sections of Indian opinions, ultimately determined the course of Indian history since the end of the Second World War. It might be assumed that the province of Bengal was foremost in the mind of the British War Cabinet. Its turbulent history of the past, Subhas Chandra Bose and his Indian National Army's presence in Japan and their probable military effort to enter India journeying through Manipur with the help of the Japanese were important factors to reckon with. India was nearer to Japan and Japan could use the Indian territory to fight its western enemies. Bengal was the abode of the revolutionaries and felt proud to hoist the leadership of Subhas Chandra the wartime ally of Japan. Therefore, to fight against Japan the British Government in India was keenly interested in Bengal's history, geography, demography, roads, waterways and other systems of communications. This would come in a bigger way in later part of this study. As stated above in this context, Gandhi's conclusion about the final outcome of the Cripps' Mission was extremely relevant in unfolding the course Indian policy making to proceed. He expressed, "…it is no use brooding over the past or British mistakes. It is more profitable to look within. The British will take care of themselves, if we will take care of ourselves. Our mistakes or rather our defects are many. Why blame the British for our own limitations? Attainment of independence is an impossibility, till we have solved the communal tangle. We may not blind ourselves to the naked fact. How to tackle the problem is another question."[23] The communal problem was during the freedom struggle in the 1930s and 1940s and still has been the bane of Indian politics. Actually this intractable problem arising out of the mindset of a few leaders at that point of time, sky high ambition and unsatiated desire for supreme power ultimately was responsible for the partition of the country. Jinnah because of his ambition and perceived rivalry with Jawaharlal Nehru was adamant. Nothing mattered to him except creating a "holy land" (Pakistan) for the Indian Muslims from 1937 till the Partition of the country in 1947. Nehru was also playing his power game, notwithstanding politically remarkable and saintly presence of Gandhi in the scene during the freedom struggle and a few months afterwards till he was assassinated on 30 January 1948. It appeared from the beginning of his negotiations with Jinnah on the one hand and the British Government on the other, Gandhi wanted to solve the communal problems before the independence of the country. He was very much concerned with communal problems particularly in Bengal. He did not want Bengal to be thrown into the communal morass as it appeared later on before the partition deal was almost settled during his visits to the riot torn the then eastern part of Bengal. He knew Fazlul Haque as a non-communal Muslim leader of the Krishak Mazdur Praja Party (KMPP). After 1937 election in Bengal Fazlul Haque was running from pillar to post in the Congress Party establishment in Bengal so that he could have formed a non-communal government in coalition with the Congress Party. But the Congress Working Committee (CWC) had already taken a decision that nowhere in the provinces the Congress would try and take part in coalition system. Having found no other alternative Fazlul Haque had to fall in line with the Muslim League in Bengal. It was almost to seal the fate of future Bengal, a Muslim majority province. Gandhi knew fully well as the other Congress leaders of Bengal and elsewhere in India that Bengal and Punjab were the most vulnerable. In politics and in the process of governance there can be no last word. Sensing vulnerability to rabid communalism of the aggressive Muslim League particularly in Punjab and Bengal and the Bengali Hindu sensitivities, Gandhi, the tallest among other leaders in the Congress Party might have made an exception in forming the KMPP and Congress coalition government in Bengal. But history flows as it is in the predetermined channel. Might be, Gandhi failed to convince other leaders of the CWP. But surprisingly no body finds any traces of his mind and written expressions in documents to this effect. The half hearted proposals of Cripps Mission were buried unceremoniously. Particularly in the Japanese selective bombing in Calcutta, an India friend Strafford Scripps's visit to India in that crucial time evoked sufficient interest in the minds of the Bengalis living both in Bengal and Delhi. In Delhi to the elitist Bengali circle it became a parlour talk about Japanese real intentions to drop bombs in Calcutta was to prepare for a bigger attack on India. A mutual distrust between the leaders of the Congress Party and the British Government in regard to Japan's advancement, was brewing fast quite visibly. It was a very interesting period. Niranjan Majumdar in a pen name *Jajabar* wrote a very contemporary novel *Dristipat,*[24] depicting a brilliant pen picture of the elitist people living in Delhi and were in continuous discussion about the imminent Japanese invasion of the eastern part of Bengal including Calcutta in India, Japanese bombardment in Calcutta and the future course of action to be taken by the Indian leaders in the larger context of the world war raging beyond the Indian border. Deep within the broader frame of military and political discussion as to what would happen in India and whether Japan had any chance to win, an enjoyable storyline ran all through. It was a remarkable novel that successfully covered the history of that transitional period including that of Bengal. A series of historical incidents took place in India after the unfortunate burial of Cripps Mission. The historic moments, that developed in India in the midst of ongoing national struggle were Gandhi's stiffened attitude towards British Government and his final moment to look at history, had its larger impact in Bengal. Initially Rajagopalachari was in favour of the creation of a separate state of Pakistan. This proposal was stoutly contested in the Congress circle. In the working committee meeting of the Congress on 29 April 1942 a resolution was passed unanimously. The resolution stated, "...that India's participation in the war was purely a British act and that not only the interests of India, but Britain's safety and world peace and freedom, demanded that Britain must abandon her hold on India." Finally, the Congress Working Committee, "called upon the people of India to offer complete non-violent non-cooperation to the invading forces and not to render them any assistance."[25] This was surely an historic moment. Before that Indian leaders never found Gandhi in such a state of mind. Gandhi from now on began writing a series of articles in his *Harijan* patrika almost every week urging the British authority to leave the country using a strong term, "Quit India" soon which would be the slogan of the people of India as well as a landmark socio-political movement never seen in a colonial country at that moment of time in history. Gandhi wrote: 'If the British left India to her fate as they had to leave Singapore, non-violent India would not lose anything. Probably the Japanese would leave India alone.'[26] In subsequent issues in *Harijan*, "Gandhiji referred to the conditions in which the people of India were living in a state of 'ordered anarchy'; if this ordered anarchy was to be replaced by complete lawlessness in India as a result of the withdrawal of the British, he was prepared to take that risk and could only hope that the people would evolve real popular order out of chaos."[27]

Seen in retrospect it appears in his several pieces that he was preparing the minds of the general public and giving clues to the top Congress leaders as to what type of resolutions were to be made in the Congress Working Committee subsequently. It was a clear indication that the Congress Party without getting embroiled itself with the British war effort in India should directly confront the British Government and would go in for a last mass movement in India. The ordinary people should be totally mobilized as far as possible. They should so prepare themselves that even in the absence of the top leaders who might be arrested and put behind the bar, the people could of their own must carry on the movement as the evolving situations might demand. This was possibly the prelude to the launching of the historic "Quit India" movement to seal out the fate of the British rule in India. It was quite uncharacteristic of Gandhi. It was at some cost because the Communist Party of India (CPI) came to play a negative role. The British Government lifted the ban on the Communist Party after nearly eight years. During this period the CPI used to work under the umbrella of the Indian National Congress. Soon the Party would be helping the British Government. Now the Party under the British patronage began the era of so-called *Jana Juddha* or people's war supporting the British cause of war in Europe and started campaigning against Japan's advance to the western front in India. As soon as Russia led by Stalin joined the allied forces, the allied power's war against the Axis power was perceived to be a People's War by the CPI. The party brought out a paper in the same name *Jana Yudhhdha* (people's war). To the Indian, mostly Bengali communists, it was now a war of the people of the country against western imperialist war by Stalin's Russia as one of the most important members of the allied power. The Party felt no qualms to go against the Congress in its nationwide call for non-cooperation of the British Government's war effort from Indian soil.

It requires for a thorough study of the history at that point of time after the Strafford Cripps Mission failed. The Congress under the informal (before that time Gandhi relinquished his primary membership of the Congress Party) but imposing leadership of Gandhi was preparing for a final show down to the British administration in India. There were further underlying considerations. The attitude of the leaders of the depressed classes, Hindu Mahasabha and Muslim minorities was not helpful for the cause of Independence without the vivisection of the country. Gandhi and other prominent leaders of the Congress Working Committee might have surmised that a call for a total mass movement, while the British government was at its final confrontation with the fascist regimes, might combine all the political forces to achieve Independence. And in the ongoing process of the mass uprising, the communal problems and issues constantly raised by the Muslim leaguer Mohammed Ali Jinnah might not be contained. But the fact was otherwise. Gandhi was keen to solve the emerging communal problems. He maintained his attitude all through even before his assassination at the hands of a Hindu fanatic. But his protégé Nehru and others though not communal had their own agenda to achieve power whatever might be the future geography of independent India. In respect to this point, one of the tallest leaders of the Congress Party, Maulana Abul Kalam Azad[28] had different viewpoints contrary to that of Nehru and others. On the other hand, Jinnah never recognized Azad as representing the views of the Muslims in India; he was simply a Congress leader, notwithstanding his being a Muslim by birth. Jinnah's relation with Gandhi was not that bitter as that of the Congress ideology of a non-religious or secular undivided Indian identity. Gradually Jinnah was becoming bitter after Strafford Cripps left the country. The Congress Party went forward to dish out resolutions that the British should leave the country immediately, even if freedom was not achieved by any means. To Gandhi no settlement of communal problems would be possible till the British regime ruled over Indian people. The argument of the British Government, that resistance to foreign invasion was essential, for Indian people to achieve freedom in near future. To the Indian leaders it seemed a British alibi to prolong their imperial stay further and further. Gandhi and the Congress Party took serious note of it. There was no looking back for the Congress. Therefore the Congress Working Committee took a decision to that effect in July 1942. For the Party there was no way out but for going in for future mass movements to reach out to the people in a bigger scale and dimension.

The All India Congress Committee later endorsed the decision. It was not an easy going for the top leadership. There was dissension among them but at the insistence of Gandhi, Nehru, Maulana Abul Kalam Azad and a few others, the other members overcame their ambivalence but some regional leaders like Chakavarti Raja Gopalachari went out. Sarder Vallavbhai Patel, Rajendra Prasad, Dr. A.N. Sinha and Gandhian Socialists like, Ashok Mehta and Jayaprakash Narayan, Usha Mehta, Aruna Asaf Ali and many others of the second rank and file came forward openly and very actively as well, to back the resolution and implement it at the final call. The Head of the Khaksar Tehrik Allama Mashriqi was expected to accept the resolution of 28 July 1942. Allama thought that the decision to go in for an all out movement might not be of any use to serve the purpose. To this effect he sent a telegram to Jawaharlal Nehru and many of the Congress leaders, stating, "I am in receipt of Pandit Jawaharlal Nehru's letter of July 8th. My honest opinion is that Civil Disobedience Movement is a little premature. The Congress should first concede openheartedly and handshake to Muslim League, the theoretical Pakistan and thereafter all parties unitedly make demand of Quit India. If the British refuse, start total disobedience."[29] In a sense this informal advice given by Mashriqi appeared to be prophetic in view of what happened later in the history of this decade. The defeat of the Axis power particularly Japan, the Indian National Army's abortive attempt to enter India through Manipur in inclement weather and unknown terrain, dangerous ground situations, failure of Cabinet Mission and ultimately through the inferno of riots and bloodbath, India had to be vivisected. Certain steps as transpired by the suggestions above by Mashriqi, such as exercise of far more discretion by the Congress leadership, to prepare ground to accommodate Jinnah and other leaders of the Depressed Classes might have peacefully resolved at least some of the problems India and Pakistan facing till today. Jinnah the sole spokesman of Pakistan during the period under consideration, reacted sharply to the Congress proposal for a nationwide non-violent mass movement.

The publication of the resolutions was greeted with a chorus of dissent. Jinnah made a statement, "The latest decision of the Congress Working Committee on July 14, 1942, resolving to launch a mass movement if the British do not withdraw from India is a culminating point in the policy and programme of Mr. Gandhi and his Hindu Congress of blackmailing the British and coercing them to concede a system of government and transfer of power to that government which would establish a Hindu Raj immediately under the aegis of British bayonet, thereby throwing the Muslims and other minorities and interests at the mercy of the Congress Raj."[30] Hindu Mahasabha asked their members not to actively extend their support to the movement to be undertaken by the Congress; a few other liberal Congress leaders like Sapru and Shastri also requested the top leaders to postpone the movement, for other reasons though. It was a fact that before taking the step there was not absolute unanimity in the Congress circles. Chakavarti Raja Gopalachari objected and left the meeting. Mashriqi's telegram to the Congress leaders was no doubt a landmark in its objective to soothe the feelings of Jinnah, was practically praiseworthy. But there was no certainty that if the passing the "Quit India" resolution had been delayed to bring all the sections of the people, particularly the Muslim minority led by Jinnah, would have succeeded. Looking in retrospect, Jinnah was unstoppable and he came to realize that the British Government would be encouraged to pay heed to his demand. The fall out of the Quit India move by the Congress rather indirectly helped the Muslim League. The demand for a separate state of Pakistan by Jinnah no longer weakened as a result of Quit India resolution. Muslim League acquired vigour and the Governor General Linlithgo began treating the Muslim League as at par with the Congress, although the Congress was the largest political party in the undivided India and had been fighting for the freedom of the country since 1885 in different ways according to the emerging situations. The "Quit India Movement" was declared; and a nation wide call to 'do or die' for the cause was given by Gandhi, on 7-8 August 1942. In a speech at Gowali Tank (later renamed *August Kranti Maidan*) Gandhi very poignantly told that it was the fight for the nation no matter what come it might. There was no looking back. The entire British administration in India got together and arrested the members of the Congress Working Committee. It did not spare even sympathizers and leaders at the district and local levels, under Defence of India Rules. In the absence of the top leaders on the scene, the public meeting was presided over by a not so prominent personality at that point of time, Smt. Aruna Asaf Ali. At that time Smt. Usha Mehta, a Congress prominent Socialist leader of Bombay (now Mumbai) took upon herself to start clandestine radio broadcasts from secret places to mobilize the public opinions in favour of Gandhi's clarion call to free the country from British yoke. Jinnah became furious. During the movement the Muslim Leaguers and their rank and file were conspicuous by their absence. The members of the Communist Party of India being influenced by the British Communist Party and as stooge of the Stalinist Soviet Russia as well, tried to stab the movement from behind and acted as British informers to unsettle the course of the movements. Even very ordinary supporters of the movement carried the banners of protest against continuing British rule any longer in India.

The later day historians of different persuasions might differ as to the impact of this outstanding event. To many of them British rule must come to an end because after the war the British hold over India became absolutely weak and government in Great Britain was not capable of holding the overseas colonies together. Added to their miseries were the INA trials—its impact not only on the Congress leaders and others but also commoners throughout the country. In the penultimate days, the British military authorities also lost control over the Indian soldiers. The naval soldiers' revolts that started in Bombay spread, in different places; and also in the minds of people it spread like wild fire. This indicated to the British Government in England to its loss of control over the Royal Indian Navy (RIN). The only option then to 'His Majesty's Government' was to leave India with dignity. Now, its concern was as to how it would keep India in an informal organization. That was how the concept of the Common Wealth of Nation came into being. There were others who believed that the factors stated above along with the impact of the 'Quit India' saga were extremely important and gave the signal to the British that they had to go.[31] But there were others who were prone to interpret that the Gandhian movements in general and the Quit India movement in particular was not that important to force the British leave this country.[32] An eminent historian of Bengal used to hold an extreme view about the impact of Quit India movement. *To him, there was however, no basis for the claim that Civil Disobedience Movement directly had led to independence (emphasis added).* There was an interesting story brought by the *The Tribune* published from Chandigarh. The story ran like this: "Which phase of our freedom struggle won for us Independence? Was it Mahatma Gandhi's 1942 Quit India movement or the INA army of Subhas Chandra Bose or the Royal Indian Navy Mutiny of 1946? According to the British Prime Minister Clement Atlee, during whose regime India became free, it was the INA and the RIN Mutiny of 1946 that made the British to internalize the fact that their time was out in India."

It has been still argued that when the leaders of the Congress were finally released, they came as tired and broken men both physically and intellectually. This allowed the British and the sectarian parties to press home for the advantages and negotiate better terms for them. An extract from a letter written by P.B. Chakraborty, former Chief Justice of Calcutta High Court, on 30 March 1976 was quoted here, "When I was acting as Governor of West Bengal in 1956, Lord Clement Atlee, who was the British Prime Minister in post war years was responsible for India's freedom, visited India and stayed in Raj Bhavan Calcutta for two days. I put it straight to him: 'The Quit India Movement of Gandhi practically died out long before 1947 and there was nothing in Indian situation at that time, which made it necessary for the British to leave India in a hurry. Why then did they do so?' In reply Atlee cited several reasons, the most important of which were the INA activities of Netaji Subhas

Chandra Bose, which weakened the very foundation of the British Empire in India, and the RIN Mutiny which made the British realize that the Indian armed forces could no longer be trusted to prop up the British. When asked about the extent to which the British decision to quit India was influenced by Mahatma Gandhi's 1942 movement, Atlee's lips widened in smile of disdain and uttered slowly, Minimal."[33] The campaign of Gandhi "came to an ignoble end about fourteen years before India achieved independence"[34]. During the First World War the Indian revolutionaries sought to take advantages of German help in the shape of war materials to free the country by armed revolt. But the attempt did not succeed. During the Second World War Subhas Chandra Bose followed the same method and created the INA. Hitler in Europe and Japan in Asia were fighting against Britain. None of these scored direct success. But a few would deny that it was the cumulative effect of all the three that brought freedom to India.[35]

History is the recorded chain of innumerable events. It is by and large true as observed in the statement made above[36]. If one deliberately or scornfully expresses that one event in the ongoing process of history had no impact upon the subsequent event or events, then it is simply regarded as opinionated. One can argue and analyze history according to one's own perspective that may not be accepted by others with different set of perspectives. History is the authentic records of the activities of leaders of men and materials, the interactions among men. Time and space, and the objective demands of the time in space that motivate the leaders in politics.

Totality of the events and subsequent actions and reactions rather than focusing on a particular action or reactions matter much in the understanding and analysis of the period in history. Therefore nobody can deny the contributions, motivated otherwise, of the processes of Indian National Congress's freedom struggles in different stages like making petition, prayer and persuasion, helping the British Government coming out successfully of the First World War, resorting to bringing the Indian masses to the political arena, Gandhian nonviolent and civil disobedience movements that led one to others till the Partition and the Independence of the country. Every leader of the Congress and other persuasions contributed his might to the final culmination, i.e. the independence of the country. But a few are also, except Gandhi and, Subhas Chandra in absentia, was responsible for the partition of a landmass of a continental size country into two States, 'Hindustan' and 'Pakistan'. Gandhi despite his religious practices really maintained his secular credential and tried even at the final stage to accommodate Jinnah in an undivided Indian identity.[37] Jinnah during the later part of his life till the approach of his final journey could not trust the Congress leaders. Perceived to many, Jinnah was out and out a westernized secular minded man in his personal life and breeding. He possibly had to succumb to the Muslim psyche of insecurity syndrome in a vastly Hindu dominated India and naturally he was getting impatient immediately to head a State as well by any means serving the purposes of a religion based Nation, i.e. Pakistan. Researchers in the contemporary history of Pakistan dug out some speculative opinions, assuming the matrix of the periods as they were, of the man of history that had Jinnah been alive for another five or six years he would have rearchitected the mindset and psyche of the Islamic Pakistan.[38]

Again getting back to the points that the 'Quit India' movement did play no part or a minimal role in booting out an alien power is to belittle the current and cross currents of the process of Indian history. It was perhaps the most remarkable period for the freedom struggle of an entire people at the penultimate days of their being dominated and dictated by an imperial power. The sections of people and a few political parties opposing the Indian National Congress frequently played unacceptable roles that had negative fallouts at that point of time, in the unfolding of the political process of contemporary society and politics in India and its several states as well. The impact of the 'Quit India' movement and Gandhi's call to the people to do or die was undeniable. Most of the historians who did not see or wanted to deliberately ignore the impact of this great event in pushing out the British imperialism from India were possibly not ready to recognize the contribution of Gandhi during the penultimate years of Indian struggle for freedom movement. Many of them had to migrate from the other side of the border and face great difficulty to reestablish themselves in the newly born West Bengal. Like many, most of the refugees and the historians coming from that side of the border in that point of time also blamed Indian Congress leaders like Jawaharlal Nehru and others including Gandhi who could not stick to his promise for an undivided and secular India. It was unfortunate for Gandhi that he and Khan Abdul Gaffar Khan, a genuine Gandhian (Frontier or *Simanta* Gandhi as he used to be called) of the North Western Frontier Province became absolutely lonely and frustrated in the Congress Working Committee where the decision of partition (as proposed by the British Government) of the country had to be endorsed. Indeed, INA movement and its partial entry into the north eastern state could not have gathered momentum but for Gandhi's attitude and his indulgence toward Subhas Chandra Bose. To Gandhi Subhas became a patriot of the patriots and to Subhas, Gandhiji was the Father of the Nation. Both of them kept aside their earlier assessments of each other. Gandhi in the eyes of the exile government of India and its head Netaji Subhas Chandra became a nation builder. Therefore, it was Gandhi's clarion call for Quit India and to achieve the purpose, people would become ready even to do or die. This was remarkable indeed. This was also the moment of history that brought the two points of view to converge for the main purpose for the future of India; or in other words two boldest men in Indian history for the first time came mentally closer together.

The historians of different persuasions may differ about the impact of the Quit India movement in hastening up the pace of independence in India. So far as the eastern part of undivided Bengal is concerned there was no denying the fact that Quit India movement had its tremendous impact almost all over the undivided Bengal. It had its imprint in different places also like Hazaribag; in Hazaribag jail in Bihar, Jayaprakash Narayan and others of his stature were detained. But the jail was too small to house him for long. Soon after his confinement he fled from the prison just to resort to greater movements outside remaining incognito. There were many other places, like Bhagalpur, rose to the occasions. The movement spread widely in Uttar Pradesh. In fact Balia from where Chandra Shekhar, one of the 'Young Turks' of that Congress Party, came to prominence, played his part importantly throughout the movement. The provincial Congress Party formed national government there and tried every tricks to oppose the Indian police under the British establishment. Exactly the same happened in Bengal. Under the leadership of Satish Samanta, Ajoy Mukherjee and Sushil Dhara all Gandhians at Midnapur opposing the police formed the national government on 17 December 1942 at Tamluk—a sub divisional town of Midnapur and hoisted or attempted to hoist the national flag as it was in that point of time, at the top of the government buildings including the police stations. They made several places inaccessible by the Indian policemen controlled by the British officers: the local leaders who were still outside the jail brought out several processions in different places in Midnapur and elsewhere. The police carried on inhuman torture among the agitators and on several occasions opened fire. But many of the people taking part in the movement were indomitable in their resolve to carry on the then Congress flag. On such an occasion, the policemen made barricade and opened fired against the unarmed people. But the procession went ahead without caring for the firing of the police. A few of the people dispersed to save their lives; then a frail lady took up the leadership at the front. She was Matangini Hazra who embraced the bullet and fell on the ground still holding the tri-colour high. She died the death of a martyr. Many more cases happened thereafter in different parts of the undivided Bengal.

Matangini Hazra is still alive in the hearts of freedom loving people as the courageous woman freedom fighter who gave her life for the final cause of a free nation during the Quit India movement in Bengal. The district of Midnapur was very special. The example of Sushil Dhara, Ajoy Mukherjee, Satish Samanta and particularly the martyrdom of Matangini Hazra inculcated the ideas in the minds of even very ordinary men of a free and national government and encouraged them to rise in revolt in different places of entire Bengal. Some of the examples were like Contai sub-division, Patashpur,

Sutahata, Nandigram, Mahishadal, Khejuri. At different places and in that point of times almost all the twenty eight districts of undivided Bengal like Maimansing, Rajshahi, Pabna, Barisal, Faridpur and many other places even in Muslim dominated Dhaka and Coomilla were agog with the supreme expectation. The people rose in protest individually and severally. As it began happening came down uncivilized police atrocities. Ordinary men were put behind bar; some beaten to death; women folks were assaulted and raped. The British idea of democracy and rule of law appeared to be of no value and use for the dominated people of India—the largest, brightest and the richest colony of the British government. It was a non-violent movement despite the fact that Gandhi in his last speech before being arrested uttered 'do or die' unambiguously. It was even quite different and probably nobler than the civil disobedience movement and Gandhi's fasting during the early 1920s. During this movement the irate mob attacked the police stations and killed a few policemen. For this Gandhi called off the movement and broke his fast. In Midnapur in 1942 several women were physically molested and raped; but they did not let loose any violent reactions.

In this connection the story told by Sushil Dhara[39] is remarkable and requires to be highlighted. During the last and final phase of the Second World War Gandhi, while he was fasting in Aga Khan Palace at Poona converted into a Jail, was released. Churchill's government feared that Gandhi might die there. Gradually the Great Britain's hold over her vast colonies particularly India for her prolonged and sustained movements against the British Raj was about to be crumbled. After the war an emasculated British government might not be able to confront people's adverse reactions not only in India but also of its other colonial spread elsewhere. After their release Gandhi and his team came to Midnapur to meet the people and leaders who made outstanding contributions to make 'Quit India' movement a grand success in terms of its impact in Bengal despite the Communists and other Muslim communities unmoved by Gandhi's call. While Gandhi was meeting masses of people a large number of women came to him and complained that they were inhumanly assaulted and raped by the British Indian police at the connivance and sometimes ordered by the higher-ups. Gandhi was terribly dismayed; he took a few minutes to gather himself and then told the women that the non-violent movements did not mean that the women did not have the right to self-defence, modesty and self-dignity. They might have confronted the marauders with whatever they had at their hands at that point of time—like kitchen knife and other useable larger spoons, *bonthi* (fish cutters), *lakri*—large wooden pieces used as fuel to cook with. On the basis of the facts that were gathered regarding the hellish terror the police let loose in the district of Midnapur a brilliant film *Biyallish* (42, depicting the inhuman treatment the police meted out to the agitationist; Bikash Roy the celebrated actor played the main role of the police officer) was made later. Possibly the film at that time might have been censored out. It was shown much later. From what Gandhi told the women gathered around, a new dimension of the meaning of Gandhian non-violence might be derived. Individual dignity and security, self respect and modesty must not be compromised even when individuals might fight against the adversaries in non-violent methods. Non-violent methods of protest did not preempt self-negation allowing others to hurl moral and physical indignities, most particularly to the women[40].

The 'Quit India' movement in different parts of Bengal is still remembered by the living older generations of people; there were many other movements like *Tebhaga* movement *(Andolan)* by the peasant communities against the landlords. The peasants and tillers of the lands should get three fourths of the produce they would grow and the landlords would be entitled to one fourth only.[41] The movement started in early mid 1940s in different districts of undivided Bengal. The political parties and the activists did not relent even after the Partition of Bengal. The movement started in undivided 24 Parganas and spread to undivided Dinajpur and other parts of the Province simultaneously with the national movements for independence. The Communist Party sabotaged[42] the national movement for freedom in favour of British government and acted as British agents or stooges against the 'Quit India' movement and caricatured Subhas Chandra Bose for his anti British stance. The Communist Party branded the 'Quit India' movement as the activities of the Fifth Columnist. The Party raised the slogan of *Janajuddha (*people war*)* to support the cause of the allied powers when Soviet Russia joined the war. Before Soviet participation it kept quiet and voiced vociferously against western imperialism. At that point of time the Party supported the proposal of dividing the country even to the extent of Balkanizing India on the basis of nationalities (Gangadhar Adhikari Thesis) for greater interest of the country. To serve this cause they dissuaded the factory workers or other labourers to go in for participating in any forms of *dharmaghat* (or strike). Seeing the activities of the Communists before and during 'Quit India' movement, the Pakistan proponent Jinnah chuckled at the Muslim League conference in Karachi in December 1943. Tottenham commented, "It will be interesting to see how People's War reacts to Jinnah's hand-off warning to the Communists."[43] The role played by the Communists during the 'Quit India' movement might have amused the Maxwell-Tottenham duo but it was really confusing to the intellectuals. Satinath Bhaduri and Subodh Ghosh two great Bengali novelists openly objected. Satinath Bhaduri in his novels very vividly pen pictured different characters in favour of the Congress movements at that period.[44] But the Communist Party to carve out a political space among the peasants not only supported the *Tebhaga* movement but also tried to carry over the movement till 1950s.[45] It was the first step in its way to undertake massive land reforms programmes by Siddhartha Sankar Roy's regime (1972-1977) and afterwards in 1977 onwards till 1987, when the Left Front came to power and stayed in power till 20 May 2011. In West Bengal in 1954 the Land Reforms and Land Revenue minister Shree Bimal Chandra Sinha, himself a big Zamindar at Kandi in Murshidabad district, piloted Zamindary Abolition Bill as a Cabinet Minister in the Council of Ministers of Dr. Bidhan Chandra Roy. He saw through its enactment very meticulously. Later on during the pre and post Partition era the leftists in their political and cultural programmes made the *Tebhaga* issue a single point agenda in their anti-Congress campaign, besides the Communists' own views about the nature of Indian state under the Congress regime. They tried to spread ideas and contents of the issues in different parts of Bengal. Several artistes like Chittoprasad, Salil Chaudhuri, and the musical groups like IPTA with few others and singers like Debabrata Biswas, Suchitra Mitra, Hemanga Biswas, Hemanta Mukherjee, poet like Subhas Mukhopadhyay, Arun Mitra, Samar Sen, Bishnu Dey, dramatist and theatre personalities Bijon Bhattacharjee[46], Shambhu Mitra, Utpal Dutta and an exceptionally talented film makers Ritwick Ghatak, belonging to leftist groups, helped spread the land issues and movements against the big landlords and the Indian bourgeoisie. But later on, many of them being disillusioned about the communist fundamentalism regarding arts, literature, music, etc., at least partially came out of the close party circle. Moreover, the party shackles that the communists had to wear compulsively, distanced the creative people from the party. Therefore these talented people went back to their original commitments to art, culture, literature, theatre and music.[47]

Taking up the cue again regarding the impact of the 'Quit India' movement in Bengal, it must be admitted that Bengal still shares the proud position in fighting the British regime even while the province had to face many other intolerable situations of Bengal famine, loss of communication chains and British made human atrocities. The 'Quit India' movement spread like forest fire in most of the 28 districts of undivided Bengal. Most surprisingly the young people even schoolboys were imbued with the idea of freedom, objectives of Subhas Chandra and other national heroes that participated in the movement. The elder boys even though they might not be in a large number used to come out from the schools in procession and discussed among themselves as to what were going to happen in near future as regards Gandhi's clarion call 'do or die' and Netaji's (Subhas Chandra Bose at that time already earned the acronym at the hearts of millions in India) objectives for leading the people to advance towards Delhi, the seat British power in India (*Chalo Delhi*) to regain the *Lal Killa* (the Red Fort),[48] as a symbol of freedom from British colonialism. Hem Chandra Chattopadhyay's and many more other stories about the local leaders were around. These leaders and people were the sympathizers of the movements. They had to go to jail during the end of

1942 to '44/45. The Headmaster, Hembabu[49] in a remote village in Faridpore whose wife at the time of his going to jail was carrying a third child, saw the face of this third child after he was released from the jail in 1945. This was the tale of a single village of Eastern Bengal district during the historic movement. Many more stories were to be found in the wrings of scholars, historians and in the works of the literateurs[50] and poets. As referred to above, it was never seen in the history of Bengal that so many young people, college students and even senior students of high schools were highly impressed by the course of the movement; they did not hesitate, or sometimes ignored their guardians to participate in this phase of the freedom movement. The means to carry on the movements were of no consequence, although they tried their best to be nonviolent until the situations indicated otherwise. In this connection an essayist, at that time a school teacher in Dhaka remembered, "The 'Quit India' movement had just started. A group of young revolutionaries came to our morning school classes at Dhaka Ranking Street and asked the upper class students to accompany them. Some of the teachers mildly objected. But that was of no avail to the departing revolutionaries and the students of the school. The school had to be closed immediately. The boys went to the other end of the Ranking Street where Uari Post Office was situated. Something might have transpired among them. In the next morning we found to our surprise that the post office was burning like hell. The police came and resorted to blank firing and began firing tear-gas shells. My father was a Station Master, a government employee of course, and, posted at that point of time at *Dholaiganje* Railway station in the nearest Dhaka outskirt. One day the revolutionaries attacked and looted the station and burnt everything out. Much later the station was renamed as *Gendaria.*"[51] Many more incidents of this type took place in different parts of Bengal. The students and even the labourers and peasants participated in damaging the railway lines and uprooting the electric poles in important points. This was not a solitary example of an important incident during those uncertainties, and periodic hiccups with pregnant expectations. Types of incidents described were not exhaustively documented.

It remains for a scholar or a genuine documentationist to unearth the memories of the people and their sentiment and near total involvement in anti-British movement during that time. It can be pursued through occasional notes jotted down by oral historians. The matters can be culled from written memoirs of the older generations also. The revolutionaries could not achieve in material terms but were successful enough to make their presence felt at least in Bengal. They could not carry on their immediate agenda because there were many other economic and socio-political factors they had to fight for. The then Bengal government was at the mercy of the non-Bengali members of the business communities and the nominated Englishmen members in the

Bengal Assembly where Congress Party could do nothing. And government was also coalitional one. Actually this was the period when the seeds of Coalition politics were sown that would flower during the late 1960s and 1970s.

In this connection it would be the fitness of thing to refer to Bengal Famine of 1943 or *Panchaser Mannantar* (it occurred in 1350 according to Bengali calendar) that might be compared with the terrible Bengal Famine that took place in 1776 or *Chchiattorer Mannantar*[52] even if it was not worse. Some of the pictures of the Bengal Fame (1943) that would tell the tales of their own are shown below.[53] It was a monstrous famine, the 20th century never saw before and after. It was a common sight that people emaciated to their bones with bowls at their trembling hands begging for the remains of the raw juice of rice (*Bhater Fyan*). The elderly people who were younger at that time, the novelist, poets and singers like, Salil Chaudhuri, Debabrata Biswas, who witnessed this worst of time in Bengal and experienced the impact of the great famine composed songs under IPTA banner and used to sing those pathetic lines and many other *durvikher gan* (song composed about the miserable plight of the victims of famine) which was in their tuneful voices leaving behind their trails for generation after generations: *"maron shiyore daladali kore ke ar banchibi bol, sonar bangla holo shasman"* (tr. death lurking large on your heads, who will live warring with one another, sonar Bangla becoming *burning ghat* or funeral places). The question of giving cooked food or stale rice did not arise because even the middle class families could not have procured right amount of staple food in the form of rice, vegetables, etc. Most families used to mix some kinds of *jowar, bajra* and some times *cheener (very small grains of food staff that are eaten by the wild birds)* with the rice. Particularly in rural areas, the middle class houses used these types of food staff during those days.[54] The rural Bengal began becoming gradually deserted. The village people used to live on cultivations and other odd jobs, streamed towards the nearest urban centres just to get minimum amount of eatables to survive. The urban centres were no better. The public distribution systems went dry because of scarce supply and hoarding by the business communities to help the British war effort by supplying the food to the military owned godown. People thronged together in front of the ration shops (*see* the picture attached) for hours together but to no avail. World War was raging. Many places in Bengal, Calcutta in particular, were the centres where British army had a near total control. And the army built up different centres of air raid precautions (ARP) to alert the people. These centres were still there even after India won freedom. The government, during expected Japanese raid in Calcutta, ordered total blackout in the city and elsewhere in urban areas just after the dusk. Without emergency no body was allowed to come out. The famine affected people had to take shelter on the pavements and other areas having overhead sheds without any food for the night. In the morning many dead bodies might have been seen here and there. Manik Bandyopadhyay in his stories and novels made out his points as did Bimal Kar[55] and Bibhuti Bhusan Bandyopadhyay about the great Bengal Famine. Bibhuti Bhusan's novel *Asani Sanket*[56] was filmised by Satyajit Roy. Mrinal Sen and others did also a great film Script named *Aakaler Sandhane.*

Starving Women Lining up for Government Doles and Handouts, in Calcutta

The above picture of the suffering people and sometimes their final end is just illustrative. There might be different explanations as to why Bengal suffered more than any other provinces in India. It was stated earlier that proper supply line of food did not work. The coalition government in Bengal was not sufficiently demanding what was the requirement in the province, in reasons of their coalition compulsions, and the design of the British government at home. Bengal was a rice deficit province. A large quantity of rice had to be imported from Burma (now Myanmar). The British army had to suffer terrific loses in Singapore and Burma's fall at the hand of Japan was almost imminent. A large number (but quite an unknown number because of lack of official statistics) of refugees began streaming into Bengal and the rice supplies dwindling for long during the period under consideration. The starvation death might be more than three millions or around. But it could not be conclusively proved because of the poor maintenance of data; the severity of the famine caused much official surprise although in a sense a representative government remained under the absolute supervision of the Governor of Bengal. "In a report transmitted to London by the Viceroy, the Governor of Bengal, Sir T. Rutherford, presented on 2 October 1943 a detailed account of the 'present food situation', including a lament about 'the dubiety of all availability statistics."[57]

The real focus more or less in this study is politico-historical discourse in the overall framework of political sociology. Therefore, there is no scope here to entre into a theoretical approach to and analysis of the great Bengal Famine that began earlier than only in 1943, as made out by the economists working on famine whether in India or China of 1959, as done by Sen and others. One editorial comment of a revolutionary monthly magazine (*Biplabi Patrika*) of that period was revealing.[58] It runs like this: For the last several months, food problem became acute and intolerable. The price of rice had been skyrocketing. The prices rose up to more than twice and thrice for some items even more than they were before. It was plain and simple robbery. The province lacked governance leaving the market to whims and greed of the traders and business communities to control. The system was sucking blood of the poor people, if continued, "…it would chew our skin and bones as well."[59] Now the time came for the suffering people to destroy the tormenters. Ridiculously, it was claimed, without evidence or calculations as the 1941 Census was not properly made, that one per cent or two per cent of the Bengal population ate much more than usual. But really their purchasing power rapidly increased because of wartime inflation and expenditure for the upkeep of the military establishments. Two thirds of the population went hungry. Among the population 10 per cent were very hungry. With half of this 10 per cent died of starvation and diseases.[60] The Central Government of British India was unwilling to send sufficient amount of food to Bengal despite having no food shortage as made out in many quarters. Due to the ongoing war situations in Europe and elsewhere, the British Government at home was unwilling to send food to India. The wartime Prime Minister Churchill did not want to believe that India required food import from external sources. A very cynical comment during that period was attributed to Churchill. The comment might be wrongly attributed to him or might not be. The alleged comment attributed to Churchill was, 'if so many people were dying because of famine, how it was that Gandhi did not die?' But there is a point to quote the comment for judging the attitude of the man who did not want to dismantle the British Empire so soon. Moreover the Conservative Party led by Churchill was defeated in the British Parliamentary election. The power went to the hand of the Clement Attlee. Clement was to an extent sympathetic to the cause of India. Secondly, perhaps Attlee did not mistake to realize that the days of colonial powers of Europe were numbered.

Again taking the cue from the paragraphs above it must be admitted that by the end of 1943 in Europe and as elsewhere in South and South East Asia, the war situations were looking brighter in favour of the allied powers. The possibility of shipping was not that dangerous as it was during the first and second phases of the Second World War. Thus the comment: in response to an urgent message by the Secretary of State for India Amery and Viceroy of India, Wavell to release food stocks for India. The wartime Prime Minister, Winston Churchill shot back a telegram to Wavell asking, if food was scarce, "why Gandhi had not died yet."[61] Initially during the famine Churchill was more concerned with the civilians of Greece who were facing the similar situations as those by the people of Bengal.[62] In India, particularly in Bengal, the British administration was following the "scorched earth policy."[63]

In this connection one can go through Lord Cherwell's memo to Churchill. He suggested to Churchill that the Bengal famine "arose from crop failure and high birth rate. He omitted to mention that the calamity, also derived from India's role of supplier to the British war;"[64] due to the man made famine for the cause of British war efforts in South East Asia and more than three million people died of hunger. The official figure culled out from the enquiry commission headed by John Woodhead was only one and a half millions. This was an absurd figure and one has no reason to trust it. Amartya Sen in his empirically made comparative studies of famines in Bengal in the early 1940s and China in the late 1950s wrote that the Bengal famine took a toll of around three million deaths.[65] In the late years of his career, Churchill used to hate not only the Congress leaders spearheading the Indian Freedom Movement but also to the poor and deprived ordinary people of India. It was absolutely undemocratic in the English sense of the term. But he was never ready to lose the "Jewel in the Crown" in the colonial empire of Britain.

In short a theory, though not directly perceptible by many, of the war cabinet headed by Churchill in Britain may be historically traced back. It still requires incisive and further research on this aspect of Bengal Famine exclusively. At that time the chief ministers were designated as Premier. It was the Syama/Huq (Syama Prasad Mukherjee and Abul Kasem Fazlul Huq) Coalition government in that point of time was ruling in Bengal. Sometimes in late 1943s on enquiry the Premier Huq Saheb (A.K. Fazlul Huq) came to know that hundreds of tons of rice and food articles were thrown in the rivers and the sea lest the articles should go into the hands of the invading Japanese soldiers. The Premier immediately asked for a written explanation from the then Chief Secretary. The result was unthinkable. The Governor John Herbert called the Premier to meet him at his earliest. Fazlul Huq met the Governor.

The Governor had a provocative argument with Huq. The final outcome was the resignation of Syama/Huq ministry and the Muslim League took over against which Fazlul Huq had to run from pillar to post as earlier he did also to save the ministry. Removing Fazlul Huq, the Governor Herbert invited the Nawab of Dhaka Khaza Nazimuddin as the Premier to form a Muslim League government in Bengal.[66] This Muslim League government was absolutely insensitive to the hunger and deaths by starvation of millions of people of Bengal during the historic Great Famine of 1943. The most important point to be noted was that this was the socio-historical turning point of the undivided Bengal and social vices that were inherited by West Bengal after the Partition 1947. The roots of vicious Hindu-Muslim divide, World's one of the greatest communal riots, lack of social morality and erosions of human values were the legacies of this particular period of undivided Bengal's history that were left behind.

Coming back again to this psychological trauma during the period under discussion may be of enormous interest to many a scholar. It was continuously emasculating Bengali strength of mind, nature and economic resilience. The Bengali culture socio-political, among the middle class, lower middle class and the poorer sections across the spectrum were distorted. The Secretary of the State in Britain, the Governor General of India, the Governor of the province of Bengal down to ordinary British officials, and above all the then coalition government of Bengal and Muslim League leaders[67] in the Bengal Legislature, down to a major chunk of British officials or nominated Members from Industry and business communities, were suspected to be involved. On 14 July 1943, Syama Prasad Mukherjee became outspokenly vocal in the Bengal Legislative Assembly and thundered, "The government was fiddling while the villagers in Bengal were crying for a morsel. He blamed the British administration in India fairly and squarely. But all the warnings were simply ignored by the government in both Calcutta and New Delhi".[68] Further, Ram Chandra Guha, a master of descriptive history, writing a review on Churchill's *Secret War* referred to above paragraph, commented, "Winston Churchill's dislike of India and the Indians has been known to scholars. But now, in *Churchill's Secret War*, we have, for the first time, definitive evidence of how a great man's prejudices contributed to one of the deadly famines in modern history. In her book Madhusree Mukherjee writes evocatively of how hunger and rebellion in rural Bengal was a product of cynicism and callousness in imperial London."[69] Opinions were many as to the exact causes of Bengal Famines, though. The Bengal Famine Inquiry Commissions (Whitehead Commission) were formed at the leadership of Whitehead. Several causes were highlighted, among them hoarding of food grains by business communities as also the military stockpiling came out in bolder focus. The Provincial Government was not serious enough to immediately tide over the difficulties. Only with the private initiatives taking help from various sources, makeshift arrangements were made to open *langarkhana* (improvised common kitchen to cook *khichuri*) simply to distribute this. The socio-economic situations the political unrest in the province was turning worse. So long a major section of middle aged and young people of Bengal expected a symbolical gain from Subhas Chandra and his INA's military advance to occupy the Andaman Islands, Moirang at Manipur and a considerable part of the forest areas in the north east like Kohima at Nagaland and Dimapur.

But by now it had become clear that Japan was going to lose the war. Gandhi, Nehru along with other Indian leaders of the Congress Party and others who participated in the Quit India movement as well were released from the jails. Historically, struggling leaders were ageing, physically tired and mentally not so well off as they were earlier, when they had to court arrest came out possibly to give in. Japan was defeated in the Second World War. The war was won by the allied powers on 9 May 1945. But to vaunt its supremacy to Allied Powers Britain, France, and China in general and Soviet Russia in particular, the United States of America dropped two Atom Bombs on Hiroshima and Nagasaki on August 6 and 9, respectively. The politics of symbolic hegemony of the super powers began. The Cold War between US and Soviet Russia was on the anvil but that was a different story not related to our focus. But there was no denying the fact that Sino-Russian relation and their ramifications and later the emergence of Communist China and its relations with many a Third World country, particularly India had had bearing upon the dynamics of Indian politics after independence in general and some of their sympathizers of Indian federal states and Marxist parties here and there in the states in particular. The British colonial power was also apprehensive of their capacity to retain their empire as it had been earlier after the devastating economic conditions during and after the war. The departure of the British colonial power from India and elsewhere, therefore, was simply a matter of time and final calculations as to be the modus operandi of leaving although the economic relations to be maintained.

It is therefore expected that the next histories would more or less take its meandering courses intercepted by the perceptions and the ambition of the leaders of national struggle for Independence in India since long. Indian political leaders of the Congress Party particularly those who mattered became restive and preparing themselves for the eventualities. After the war came to an end, the fate of Subhas Chandra Bose was uncertain. On the 24 August 1945 Domai a Chinese News agency, and possibly BBC News brought out an unconfirmed news that Subhas Chandra died of an air crash at Taipei.[70] It was neither officially declared nor confirmed by the falling government of Japan nor by the British governing agencies. Indian leaders like Nehru and a few others, but certainly not Gandhi who had to be publicly mute, were given to believe the unconfirmed story of Bose's death by air crash in Taipei. As soon as the alleged report of the death of Subhas Chandra came out in the press there was an electrifying though demoralizing effect was visible throughout the province of Bengal. To many it was unbelievable and to many others it was some sort of a conspiracy hatched by the British government. Some people also were eager to believe that Subhas Chandra himself went in cognito towards Manchuria to blunt the long and legal hands of the British government so that the government would find no trace of the most valiant freedom fighter of India.[71] Some are of opinion, claiming to have collected primary sources materials from Russian archives that Subhas Chandra was last seen in a remote place of the then Soviet Russia.[72] Wavell the Viceroy of India immediately before Mountbatten had "doubt" about the death of Subhas in an air crash.[73]

It has still been a raging controversy. The recent Report by Mukherjee Commission ordered by the NDA government unequivocally rejected the Air Crash Theory of Subhas Chandra's death on 18 August 1945.[74] But the present Second UPA government did not take any action on the Mukherjee Commission Report whatsoever.

Bose's adventurous saga has come in to a bigger focus simply to tell another story. The Bengali refugees who were to leave their places of birth had a deep rooted belief, had Subhas Chandra out and out a total secularist as proved by the composition of his INA brigade, been in India during the end of the War, the history of not only Bengal but also India would be different. These batches of refugees who streamed in West Bengal as poppers became disgruntled for living in colonies and ghettos. They bore a deep rooted dislike against Jawaharlal Nehru, even Gandhi and other Congress leaders.[75] For them Subhas Chandra could have proved a better Prime Minister. After leaving the Congress Party, Subhas Chandra in the early 1940s formed a new party of his own, i.e. Forward Bloc (FB). But the matter of the fact was that it had never made any dent in West Bengal politics till as one of the second major partners of the Left Front (LF) coalition in 1977. However Subhas Chandra episode his INA brigade and later on its trial in Red Fort was certainly a major event that most sentimentally influenced the radical Bengali psyche to do away with the British rule that enormously did harm to the people and their ways of life. By that time the Indians gradually became sure that the days of British rule in India were numbered; but how, when and in what ways the end would come, they were not sure about. The India hater Mr. Churchill had to give in. The British Parliamentary election was over and the reign was given to the Labour Party with Clement Attlee as the prime minister who was keen to transfer power at the hands of the Indian leaders at the earliest. The next very important step the Labour Government took was to declare that in 1946 the British Government were willing to end its rule over India. To that effect a

Cabinet Mission was sent to India. The purpose was to negotiate with the Indian leaders about the modalities of the Transfer of Power.

The mission consisted of three British cabinet ministers, Pethick Lawrence—the Secretary of State, Strafford Cripps—President of the Board of Trade and A.V. Alexander—the First Lord of Admiralty. They reached New Delhi on 24 March 1946. The summary of the Cabinet Mission proposal was: a two-tied federal plan which was expected to maintain national unity while conceding the largest measure of regional autonomy. There was to be a federation of the provinces and the states, with federal centre controlling only Defence, Foreign Affairs and Communications. Individual provinces could form regional unions to which they could surrender by mutual agreement some of their powers. For the unacceptability of the plan the next clause might have played a great role.[76] Jinnah was not very unwilling to accept the proposal as some historians were willing to believe. But one uncertain and off the cuff comment, at a period of great tension, by Jawaharlal Nehru possibly spoilt the moment.[77]

The Mission proposed there would be three groups of provinces—(i) Group A, was to include Madras, Bombay, United Province, Central Province and Orissa; (ii) Group B, would comprise Punjab, Sindh, North Western Frontier Province (NWFP) and British Baluchistan-predominantly Muslim majority areas; and (iii) the C Group, Bengal and Assam; at that time Assam consisted of all the seven north eastern states as they are at present. The division of Assam later on during 1960s was the result for the demand of ethnic and tribal identities of the people of the earlier greater Assam. This problem of the separation of territories for each of the ethnic and tribal people could never be completely solved that had been a lingering sore ever since. Further it was proposed that a Constituent Assembly would be convened of 389 members to draft a Constitution. The components would be 292 (members) from provinces, four from territories governed by the Chief Commissioners and 93 from Indian Princely States. These members of the entire component groups would draft the future Constitution of India. Most significantly, an interim government at the Centre consisting of representative of all the communities as also provinces would be installed on the basis of parity between the representatives of the Hindus and the Muslims.[78]

It appears from the beginning to the end, the British establishment was dead bent upon its programme to make a permanent division of the Hindus and the Muslims of this country. Cabinet Mission Plan was possibly a ploy to make India divided permanently on communal lines to keep the politico-economic interests of Britain even when they would leave the country. In this connection one can recollect some observations in the then Viceroy Lord Wavell's note for the Cabinet Mission, "I am very concerned about this, since if my understanding is correct, I consider that there has either been a reversal of policy which has been agreed, or that the assurance given to Mr. Gandhi is not entirely an honest one."[79] The essentiality clause was that to be a representative either as a Hindu or a Muslim within a group as a precondition was not revealed. Possibly the members of the Cabinet Mission was mandated to be secretive.

It is sufficiently clear that when Cabinet Mission Proposal was being prepared the Viceroy in India was completely in the dark. Wavell further observed, "I also wish to be clear as to our policy with regard to section 19(v) [*not within the quote 'grouping'*]. I understand from the press today that Congress may accept the statement of May 16th, provided that they are allowed to interpret the provisions of the statement in their own way, i.e. that the Provinces may elect to opt out of the sections in which they have been placed *before* those sections have been formed and have decided upon the matter. I take it that this cannot be regarded as an acceptance of the statement of May 16th, and that the Delegation will say so clearly."[80] Ultimately the Cabinet Mission was bound to fail; the reasons might be many; although the role of Nehru was highlighted by the interested sections as hinted above. But in retrospect, it would not be an overstatement that if the concept of grouping had been accepted, keeping in mind the communal sentiments that the British establishment began fomenting, and the Muslim majority provinces including Bengal and Assam. The fate of Bengal and Assam might have gone the way the East Pakistan had to go in forming Bangladesh separating itself from Pakistan in a bitter liberation war after the elections in 1970. Considering the present Indian socio-political situations in the age of coalition governments, rise of the regional aspirations, fragmentation of political parties the government's problems to tackle the insurgencies in the north eastern states have been enormous.

Maoist problems in more than 200 districts out of 600 odd districts and its external relations with Myanmar, China, Nepal and Bangladesh are tortuous. Looking at these countries' relations with insurgent groups within India, one might smell of something sinister in the British initiatives at that point of time. If it would happen what the British Government had wanted, India might have been Balkanized. None of the countries mentioned above and Pakistan as well as at present were democratic. Though Bangladesh and Nepal are democratic more often than not they are to suffer from some sort of democratic deficit because of their ethnic problems and political divide. After free and fair election in April 2008 the Nepalese political parties of different views were expected to draft Constitution with a mandated period of two years with a grace period of further six months. But it was not possible to maintain the period because of its inter party irreconcilability and ideological contradictions.

The democracy in Bangladesh is also running through difficult days. It shares the same geographic mass with India as also the eastern nearest neighbour of West Bengal. China has almost encircled India through its friendly countries, Myanmar, Nepal and Pakistan. If China is in a position to win over Myanmar, Nepal and Bangladesh in its relations with India in general and West Bengal in particular, China and Pakistan's objectives to Balkanize India[81] would be a reality. Therefore it had been really a good riddance that the Congress leaders did not accept the Cabinet Mission Plan as it was when Indian Independence was at the nearest distance. Then the Partition of the country for the second time within a span of 42 years of the same century on both the eastern and the western sides followed. It was a historical *repeat* indeed, but this time not in a farcical face but with enormous human cost with the ugliest communal face. An understanding with the British Government for an interim government in this country came to be agreed. It was a part of the Cabinet Mission proposal also. The same consisted of politicians of the undivided India. On 2 September 1946 the members of the interim government took the oath of office. "For the first time ever, the significant departments of state were to be run by the nationalist politicians rather than by toadies or bureaucrats. Although at that time nobody was entirely certain what this would achieve, in retrospect it is the most important moment in the demission of British authority—the more, in many ways, than the handover of the power in August 1947."[82]

The fact is very instructive to note from the Epilogue of the *Viceroy's Journal,* "Bevin and Alexander began to feel a John Bullish unwillingness to let the Indian empire slip from their grasp. But the Government could put forward no alternative to Wavell's proposals, (*Wavell proposed for a fixed date to transfer power to and established authority*, *emphasis added*), and they did not have the courage to tell him that they would look for another Viceroy who might think up something better."[83] Further, "Attlee assured Wavell that he had got what he wanted. What followed was a striking *reductio ad absurdum* of His Majesty's Government. They had rejected Wavell's demand for the fixation of a date and had decided to dismiss him from the post of Viceroy, only to find that his successor made exactly the same demand and would not to take office unless it was granted. So Attlee and his Government capitulated, and soon were quite happy to take credit for a decision that had, in fact, been forced upon them." Perhaps it was His Majesty's choice of the same Royal blood line. Louis Francis Albert Nicholas George Mountbatten 1st Earl of Burma (Mountbatten, in short) would soon take over in early 1947 to preside over the Partition of India and particularly the vivisection of Bengal, Punjab, and greater Assam, peripherally though. The paraphernalia to finalize the date of partition under Mountbatten's supervision would be 3 June 1948. But much earlier the Indian Independence Act (1947) was passed in British Parliament. He was the last Viceroy of India in 1947 and the first Governor General of the Independent India (1947-1948) from which the modern Republic of India would emerge on 26 January 1950.

Another landmark incident next is in the Provincial Legislature of undivided Bengal's Resolution to effect the decision of the partition of Bengal. The Bengal Legislative Assembly under British rule was held in between 17-23 March 1946. The earlier House was dissolved on 17 November 1945. The Party Position of the newly elected House was:

Table 1.1: Party Position (As on March 1946)

Muslim League	114
Progressive Party of Fazlul Huq	-
Krishak Praja Muslim Party	4
Congress	86
Hindu Nationalists	-
Hindu Mahasabha	1
Communists	3
Emarat Party	1
Kshatriya Samity	1
Schedule Caste Federation	1
Anglo Indian	4
Indian Christian	2
Europeans	25
Independents	8
Total	**250**

Source: BLA Records 1946.

The Bengal Legislative Assembly met on 14 May 1946 for the election of the Speaker and the Deputy Speakers. Looking at the party position it was clear that Bengal was a Muslim majority province and therefore the division of the province was a *fait accompli* as per the earlier political aspiration and demands of Muslim League led by Jinnah with almost helpless surrender of the Congress leaders except Gandhi in his loneliness to the decision of the majority party sitting in different places in the Legislative Assembly Building. The Congress party and a few Independents met in a session presided over by the Maharaja of Burdwan Uday Chand in the Lobby of the First floor of the Council Chamber. The Muslim Leaguers and few others sat in the Council Chamber of the House presided over by Mr. Nurul Amin.[84] The two meetings took place simultaneously in different venues in the same Building on 20 June 1947.

As per the decision of the Members and the statement made by the British Government, the undivided province of Bengal was partitioned into West

Bengal and East Pakistan. At that point of time the West Bengal Legislative Assembly was constituted with 90 Members including two nominated Anglo Indians. Nominally the geographic areas of the two sides were decided at the point of Independence but the actual geographical mass and demographic were surgically divided, 2/3 days after the declaration of Independence at the midnight (at the strike of 12) of 14 August 1947. Murshidabad was given earlier to East Pakistan and Khulna to India. On 17th of August the map was shown to be redrawn and Cyril Radcliff reversed the decision in regard to the fate of these two districts. Even the Punjab was vivisected after the Independence Day celebration on 14th August in Pakistan. And within a few days, Cyril Radcliff (a cartographer indeed!) left the country without any visible hassle within. Another significant observation is to be noted here. "The total impartiality was propagated by Radcliff and Mountbatten in the aftermath of independence, both maintaining that they were 'mutually most careful never to have any discussions about the boundaries'. However, according to Mountbatten's Deputy Private Secretary Ian Scott, the Viceroy attended a meeting of the Boundary Commission in Lahore on 22 July, and there was thus no question, as people like Ronnie Brockman and Campbell-Johnson maintain, that he kept himself aloof. This is not to suggest that Radcliff was corrupt or incompetent, but rather he took advice, as might be expected, from his client. As the historian Alastair Lamb put it, "there is simply no way that the Government of India would have allowed somebody with so little experience of India (*undivided Bengal included*, mine) to make the key decisions, Radcliff was barrister"[85] by profession to argue for the men interested in Indian problems in that moment of time.

Let us think back of the colonial historic-political scenario in the Indian Subcontinent and its great leaders like Gandhi, Jawaharlal Nehru and Jinnah among others. In the penultimate days of the Partition of India, the colonial power viciously bifurcating two of the larger Indian provinces—the Punjab and Bengal, to say the least was traumatic for the vast number of people. There were no reasons to misunderstand the role played by Jawaharlal, Patel and other leaders of the Congress Working Committee including Gandhi—prisoner of the circumstances in those days of the mid 1940s. The reasons of their own as also because of the historic churning of Indian social life in that point of time, the leaders could not or did not want to confront the messiah of the idea of Pakistan. The sad outpouring of the "Frontier Gandhi" Khan Abdul Ghaffar Khan to the Congress leader against the vivisection of India giving a burial to the principle of oneness of India and its secular ethos was a recorded fact in history. The brunt of the Partition had to be borne by these two provinces, Bengal[86] on the east and Punjab on the west. Of course the greatest impact was on Bengal for several reasons as West Bengal has been carrying on that unbearable legacy of the Partition of 1947 even today.

A very small unthinking and off the cuff comment or an eloquent silence on a very specific historic moment by the man in history or a simple gesture to wish away a possible solution may bring about situations that might have determined the fate of an entire generation or subsequent movements of history in its meandering course. In retrospect one may think of what transpired among the three leaders that Leonard Mosley narrated in his *Last Days of the British Raj*. In his last effort to stall the division of the country Gandhi was prepared to offer the Prime Ministerial chair in undivided India to Muslim League leader Jinnah. Possibly Jinnah was not unhesitant but Nehru's eloquent silence and leaving the room, finally helped Jinnah charting out his next course of action. Jinnah's had a political angle rather than his "belief of a two nation theory" that motivated him to create a state entirely at the final moments of his chequered career. His skin-deep faith in the theory of an exclusive Muslim homeland helped him immensely mobilizing the elite sections of the Muslim community in favour of a sovereign Muslim State of Pakistan. A new history began to unfold that culminated in the vivisection of the country and its aftermath. And this was the final and lasting offer to the people of Indian sub-continent that the British political establishment for their imperial interest was happy to leave behind. They never thought of the painful legacy to the truncated Bengal they were leaving behind where they had started nearly two hundred years ago.

To many a historian, the partition of Bengal on the eastern part of India was an inevitable fact of history as was Punjab on its western front. The problems of the west Punjabi refugees were fairly well tackled by the Indian leaders in Delhi. The idea of the exchange of population to a large extent between the two nations and divisions of properties appeared to be accepted. But these measures had not the chance to be effected in Bengal perhaps because of the misconceived notion and its practical implementation of the Nehru-Liaquat Ali Pact of 1950. The refugees from the Punjab got all sorts of unhindered opportunities. Moreover as an enterprising people they did not object to be dispersed all over the countries to be resettled. Because of their perseverance and the will to eke out a living with any job or situations available to them, the Sikhs and the Punjabi Hindus were fairly well rehabilitated. But in case of the East Bengali refugees the exact opposite happened for various reasons that would come up in relevant sections of this study. In the last century (20th century) the Partition of Bengal occurred twice. The first one was in 1905. The second Partition was made in 1947. In both the cases the British maneuver and bureaucratic machination in collaboration with the Muslim elites and their political organization Muslim League, worked behind. The British rulers to exploit the Indian market as also to be politically present in proxy in

Indian psyche wanted to communalize the country. In the first instance the colonial master did not succeed and the Partition was annulled within five years. But the communal seed between the two main communities—Hindu and Muslim they sowed, eventually came to fruition in the late 1930s and mid 1940s. The second Partition of Bengal was irreversible with its severe impact on the later history, geography, demographic, political economy, party politics, electoral process and the popular culture in the western part of Bengal subsequently designated legally as West Bengal. In the ongoing processes of history man always attempted to change its course wittingly or otherwise that helped evolve politics in its varied manifestations. The processes were reciprocal that influenced the management of economy of the state in a cultural perspective as seen in different developing but democratic countries in their development objectives.

Alongside the study of political history, governance and electoral process that have sustained the democratic polity is a part of political history in West Bengal which is starkly conspicuous by its absence in West Bengal's bordering state be it the erstwhile East Pakistan of the past or the present sovereign State of Bangladesh. East Bengal was renamed East Pakistan in 1956. Again East Pakistan rebelled against Pakistani military rule when the democratic rights particularly the right to retain the mother tongue—Bengali as one of the national languages was denied in early 1950s. The Bengalis of the eastern part were denied to form government with the prime ministerial office to Awami League, winning the largest number of seats to the Pakistan National Assembly after 1970 election. But in the process of the birth of a new nation *Bangladesh*, there came undesirable as well as unbearable demographic changes in West Bengal. This trend continued even long after the new entity Bangladesh—the bordering eastern neighbour of West Bengal and its political sovereignty became a settled fact.

The study includes several phases of the evolution of politics in West Bengal. Many other factors are to be brought in to bolder focus to appreciate the ongoing process of politics. There are several elements determining the politics that may appear to be temporal and contemporary. The demography, geographical location, financial viability of the truncated state, the skill of the government of the day to manage the economy, the part played by the opposition political parties in securing the responses of the government, the cultural ambience and the attitudes of the people, the influence of the popular culture on the evolving social movements, among other factors constitute the core of a genuine and unbiased account of society and polity in West Bengal we have been watching since Partition of Bengal in 1947. A modular representation in segments having a stitching thread within, all through might have been better, than a very simple narration of actual facts during the last sixty two years or so.

The Partition of Bengal and its socio-economic and cultural fallouts are the greatest historic event in the eastern part of India. The "Great Calcutta killing" in 1946 irretrievably disturbed the coexistence of the two main communities—Hindus and Muslims. In the penultimate stage this incident determined the fate of the two communities, which lived peacefully in the past except for certain stray conflicts occasionally. The events whether small or big during the early and mid 1940s were very important that left indelible mark in the subsequent history of the decades in the state of West Bengal which became a truncated one third of the undivided Bengal on 15 August 1947. But it had a population with insufficient economic resources to live on. Most of the industrial raw materials like jute and a considerable amount of paddy that used to feed the jute mills, rice mills, etc. went under the control of the East Pakistan government. Ultimately the jute mills and many of the manufacturing industries began getting sick on this side of the border. It was a horrible sight to remember the continuous influx of uprooted refugees—men women and children crossing the border in miserable conditions both in body and mind. The stream of refugees entered in to West Bengal from various points of the long borderline. Undivided Dinajpur received a large number of the displaced from across the border. Same happened in Coochbihar, Jalpaiguri, terrains of Duars, down south in Malda sharing the East Pakistan border with Bihar. The case was exactly the same with the then undivided 24 Parganas. Many people living near the border came by foot and other vehicles and even by ferry boats; but the people from far had to come by streamers and at points both by streamers and the rails. The longer railway routes were from Gaolanda, Faridpur via Kustia, Nadia and then 24 Parganas. Parbatipur to Sealdah route via *Poradah* station at the then larger Nadia district. It was the longest route to come to this side of the border from the then East Bengal; but there were points nearer to West Bengal from where people could enter their destination by road and water ways. The Gaolanda Sealdah line was divided at two points: Darshana railway station and Bunpur station; the land mass between Darsana and Bunpur was bisected, the former falling within East Pakistan and Bunpur in West Bengal, i.e. India or "Hindustan" (in Bengali language not in Hindi) to the perceptions of the Pakistanis. These were the two checking points on either side. The body search and material checking of people leaving to Darshana border station was inhuman and beneath human dignity. Men and women mostly in tattered clothes and hand bags or a few bundles or some of them carrying old rusted trunks containing some personal belongings were searched, and if doubts arose, which were rather normal always, in the minds of the Ansars (the self appointed guards belonging to Muslim fundamentalist), things would surely be forfeited. These were quite usual at that time and even in the presence of the authorized police and administrative officials.

There are more than 20 stations from Bunpur to Sealdah. There is another railway line which goes toward Krishnanagar from where a metre gauge line proceeds to Nabadwip and another broad gauge line to Lalgola in Murshidabad. A number of railway stations along the way were swarmed with refugees with tattered clothes who had to live in improvised shelters for the night with the thought that they had nothing to eat in the next morning. As time wore on refugee families occupied some portions of land around the railway stations where they alighted first in the long route. The government began giving some amount of doles but the amount was meagre; makeshift roof over their heads had to be built. How a family of 4/5 would carry on with such meagre amount. On the other hand men with immoral objectives were often seen in and around the shanties to allure the young women to resort to occasional flesh trade[87]. This continued for next 4 or 5 years. Many families during and after their transit to West Bengal found one or two of the girls missing. Moreover the sporadic riots were often seen in and around Calcutta till early 1950.

In New Delhi at midnight when the Prime Minister Nehru in a tremulous voice, reading out his "tryst with destiny" Gandhi was on a fast in *Hydar Manzil* at Beleghata in Calcutta to sensitize the people of both Hindu and Muslim communities to stop rioting against each other for humanity's sake. He was appealing to the governments of both West Bengal and the Eastern Pakistan to quell communal disturbances everywhere. Occasional curfew and even calling of the military to quell the riots and nab the rioters were almost the routine affairs in those days in Howrah and Calcutta. This happened because of the inner urge to take revenge for their miserable existence and others for their sense of deprivations even when they belonged originally to this side of Bengal. During those fateful three years (1947-50), it was a common sight that relatives and relatively known people of the incoming refugees waited with bated breath for the arrival or at least of the information of their relatives still living in East Pakistan. All the important stations on the route were full with unfortunate souls waiting for a handful of food distributed by the government agencies or by private initiatives. People had to wait hours together at the Sealdah station for the incoming trains just to search out the displaced men or the families from among the thousands arriving at the stations after hours of delayed arrival of the trains. Sometimes the police had to lathicharge or to burst teargas shells. Outside just in front of the old Sealdah station there was a huge space. Occasionally, to disperse the crowd in the space in front of the entrance of the gate, the police resorted to teargas shelling. A huge numbers of chappals and shoes littered all around left by dispersing crowd used to be found in the open space in front of the main Station. This was also a common sight in those days.[88]

Again to begin with, many of the women taking shelter in several railway stations had been raped[89] by the goons of a particular community and many disappeared during their stay in East Pakistan after August 1947. As also of the female members, Hindu families had to undergo inhuman treatment till they agreed to be converted to Muslim religion. Even some people with lower background or castes, mainly the Namasusdras, Charals, Myathors and Dalits had to be converted as a price for their staying in the country of their birth.[90] The parallel was seen by both the Muslim and Hindu women at the hands of the West Pakistani soldiers and the pro-Pakistani Ansar Bahini, Rajakar and Al Badar—the members of the Jamat-e-Islami after the 1970's Pakistan election where the Awami League led by Sheik Mujib. Mujibur Rahaman won the majority of parliamentary seats in both the West and the East over the Pakistan People Party (PPP) of Western part of the state backed by the military establishment in the Western Pakistan. The inflow of the refugees was incessant from 1947 to much after the Indo-Pak war in 1965. But during the Bangladesh movement nearly 90 million people belonging to both the Muslim and Hindu communities crossed over the border at different points. The Western Pakistani Military raped and massacred more than three million women and men in East Pakistan.[91] Just to seek shelter from their original home they were to be alert. The people and their Awami League leaders led by Sheik Mujib in absentia wanted to be assured by India for the recognition of Bangladesh. These hapless Bangladesh people in a stream thronged together to cross the border. This huge number arrived at this side of the border within a very short period. This sudden arrival of the compulsive migration, the demography of West Bengal had changed. The economy of Bengal went about nearly out of gear. However, after the Liberation War, many of the temporary migrants went back to Bangladesh but many mostly the Hindus stayed back to strain the already poor economic scenario of West Bengal. For shattered economic conditions due to the war of liberation during the last nine months (from 26 March, 1971 to 16 December, 1971) in Bangladesh many Muslim families also stayed back in West Bengal mingling with the Muslim populations in the border districts of undivided 24 Parganas, Murshidabad, Malda and undivided Dinajpur[92].

Even thereafter for economic reasons Muslims have been entering in to West Bengal every now and then to earn a livelihood. Clandestine border infiltrations by the Muslims and sometimes Hindus as well in this side of the border are long standing problems.[93] Life is also harder for the people living in the Enclaves on either side in general and Cooch Bihar-Jalpaiguri at North Bengal in particular. Although efforts are on now, to solve the problems which have been focused since mid 1950s after the Supreme Court case regarding the Berubaru Enclaves in North Bengal districts.

It is a massive displacement of people of the 20th century, not seen anywhere in the world so far.[94] Radcliff was in a hurry to divide the territory which was economically complementing each other of the two parts of the province of Bengal. It changed demographic scenario of the western part of undivided Bengal and impacted greatly on the existing society and economy.[95] At that point of time it was difficult for a cultural mix as we have been experiencing even today, between the original inhabitants of this part of Bengal and the incoming refugees across the eastern border of the state. During 1947 till 1955, more than four million Hindus migrated to India. Now at beginning of the new century (21st) the total number of the displaced persons would be around 20 million. The bulk of migration never stopped even after the matter settled down after the Indo-Pakistan war in 1965 and then in 1971. It was almost impossible to provide land and living for such a huge humanity within a geographic area that was just one third of the undivided Bengal. The first chief minister (called premier at that time till the Constitution came into force on January 1950) Dr. Prafulla Chandra Ghosh's tenure was very short and it was not possible to sort out all the problems faced by the new government. Yet he tried as best as he could. On 1st January Dr. Bidhan Chandra Roy took over. He was very sympathetic to the cause. He got a very good officer Shri Bimal Chandra Lahiry as the Refugee Rehabilitation Commissioner. With his sincerity of purpose Shri Lahiry allotted at least some slices of land to many of the refugee families in both the parts in North and South Bengal, and provided some amount of economic succour. Even the students were given stipend to pursue their higher studies. To complete the job Dr. Roy sent many families to the *Dandakaranya*, in several parts of Orissa and Madhya Pradesh. Dr. Roy wanted to send a large number of families to the Andaman and Niccobar Islands. This land was fertile and could have been a Bengali dominated state. West Bengal was deprived and the people from south, mostly Tamils and others occupied the space lost by West Bengal. This happened mostly by the over vociferous protest movements by the Communist Party of India (CPI). The Party was banned but when the ban was lifted the Communists launched a movement against the Roy government to the effect that the Bengali refugee families must be settled in West Bengal. This had a tremendous effect upon the refugees and also to the adverse economic repercussion on the state of West Bengal as a whole.

The business communities were keen to take the advantages of the fluid situation. They made their influence visibly felt in the political structure. Dr. P.C. Ghosh—a Gandhiite was chosen as the first chief minister but he had to resign. Under Gandhi's letter[96] to the Congress Working Committee member Dr. Prafulla Chandra Ghosh in West Bengal that a Minister sympathetic to the Marwari community (from Birlas) should be inducted in his Council of Minister. Dr. Ghosh was not in a mood to disobey Gandhi. But Dr. Ghosh wanted to have Shri G.L. Mehta[97] rather than a man groomed by and sympathetic to the Birla Group. Dr. Ghosh was at that time bent on eradicating corruption among the business community. A case of corruption was caught red handed. A Marwari businessman was selling wheat mixed with the inner white powder of the tamarind seeds. Rampant black-marketing was going on. The rationing system was almost out of control. Extreme food shortage followed. The Left politics was disruptive and quite rudderless. Being inspired by the earlier *Tebhaga* movements on behalf of the peasants, the Communist Party became ambivalent about the Congress taking over the reign of the state. To the Communists the definition of the nature of the Indian State did not change with the change of the colonial rule. To them the Indian Independence was 'sham' independence. They resorted to slogan mongering, "*ai azadi zhuta hai*," till they made up their mind to participate in the first democratic election in 1951-1952. Dr. Bidhan Chandra Roy became the next chief minister (after Dr. P.C. Ghosh's very short stint as pointed out earlier) who continued till his death on 1 July 1962. But these four years (1948-1952) were a nightmarish experience to any head of the administration. Dr. Roy with the help of his cabinet colleagues at home and at the Central level the Prime Minister Jawaharlal Nehru being a friend and admirer of Dr. Roy extended helping hand so that the Chief Minister could tide over difficulties of a "disinherited state."[98] Thus it was possible for Dr. Roy to tide over many difficult situations arising out of those tumultuous days after the Partition till the democratic elected government came to power in the early 1952. The Indian National Congress Party came to power under the leadership of Dr. Bidhan Chandra Roy in the Assembly elections 1952. He and his team won the 1957 Assembly election. Before his death in early 1962, Dr. Roy was always at the helm of the administration in West Bengal. He was a very successful Chief Minister. It was a decade of consolidation. To tackle successfully refugee problems, Dr. Roy took several steps. The leftist parties were in continuous conflict with government in regard to the places of settlement of the refugees and in their socio-cultural movements won the heart of the pauperized displaced people. The undivided Communist Party keeping aside their ideological dogma that parliamentary election and participation in parliamentary politics would not solve the fundamentals problems the people, did take part in the First General elections in India. In the Assembly elections they got 62 seats in the then Madras province, 42 seats in Hyderabad (presently Andhra Pradesh), 32 seats in Trivancoor Cochin (present day Kerala), and 28 seats in West Bengal Assembly. Before independence in 1946 election in Bengal, the Communist had only two seats. Watching the election results of Hyderabad after Telengana movements[99], West Bengal and Tripura, the Communist Party gained enormous confidence in their capacity as a political force in Indian politics, as the only anti-Congress political party from the very beginning, possibly they perceived. The Communist Party's first salvo against the government was in regard to the "one paise increase of the tram fare in 1953." During that period in July of the same year thirteen Tram Cars were burnt by the cadres of the CPI. The ordinary citizens of the state did not protest against such vandalism by a leftist party, but nobody except the politically interested persons about the prospect of the Communist Party in West Bengal, supported the wanton destruction of the public properties. After decades Dr. Ashok Mitra, the former Finance Minister of the Left Front government during the mid-1980s, wrote a Bengali Memoir (*Apila Chapila* in Bengali) referring to the incident and his happiness about this movement against Western Capitalist and Land Lord bourgeoisie supporting Congress Party. He referred to in his book that he became ecstatic because of what the CPI did, while he was a Ph.D student at The Hague.[100] West Bengal became a chronic food shortage state. The opposition parties led by the Communist launched a severe food movement during the mid-1950s. The agricultural problems were aggravated by natural calamities like the flood in 1959. Despite all these chronic problems, this was a decade of moderate economic take off. Industrializations began after the launching of the First and Second Five Year Plans. The abolition of Zamindari system, its fallouts, and its subsequent socio-economic impacts were remarkable. The implementation of State Organization Commission was also important during this decade. On the other hand, the opposition's demand for annulling the Bengal-Bihar merger proposal was respected by Dr. Roy after a by-election defeat of the Congress candidate. Dr. Roy was conscious of the acute housing problems of the middle class people. By attempting to implement the system of Panchayati Raj he got to the core of agricultural problems and the plight of the rural poor. Dr. Roy came to understand that the management of the political economy of the state was the real hazard. Almost at the end of the decade the cultural mix between the people of original western part of Bengal and the incoming refugees began taking a positive shape. Factionalism was not new in Congress politics.

In fact leadership conflict and factionalism has been germane in Congress politics since 1920s of the last century. Though the relation between the Chief Minister Dr. Roy and the Congress Chief in West Bengal as also a Working Committee member Atulya Gosh was cordial yet there was an undercurrent of conflict between the two. Later on it was decided that the Congress President Atulya Ghosh would be left alone in supervising the state Congress Party affairs but would not interfere in matters of administrative decisions which should be the exclusive preserve of the Chief Minister Dr. Roy.[101] Thus the second chief minister of the divided Bengal set the tone and tune of the Congress rule in the state for years to come till the Congress system faced the real challenges by a combination of the defector group of the Congress and the leftist forces combined.

2

Politics, Governance, Industrial Scenario of a Problem State

The time for the new Chief Minister Prafulla Chandra Sen was not easy. Food production was abysmally low due to occasional droughts and flood. Public distribution system was unmanageable. Despite stringent cordoning off systems between and among the districts, food procurement was not sufficient and rationing system came to near collapse. Sporadic food riots in different places across the districts were the order of the day and the left political parties wanted to utilize the situations to their political advantage when police opened fire against people participating in food movements. During this time because of the factional fight between the two warring factions of Hooghly and Midnapur, the Congress Party was almost vertically split. Ajay Mukherjee of Midnapur group left the party and formed his own party—the Bangla Congress. After the Indo-China Border War in 1962, the Communist Party of India on ideological question was split into two—the original Communist Party of India (CPI) and the Communist Party of India (M) or CPI (M). Both of them were at daggers drawn with each other. But in the next election the two groups of all the Leftist Political Parties formed two electoral fronts. After the election of 1967, under the leadership of Ajay Mukherjee and his Bangla Congress, for the first time in the History of West Bengal the Congress Party was defeated. In the defeat of the Congress government, the anti-establishment "radicalism" of past found its new appearance in a different garb. An expected social transformation, as it were, was on the cards.

Several governments on the basis of alliances among the political parties of different hues came to power. But none survived for a longer period of time. The first United Front (UF), Progressive Democratic Front (PDF), second United Front and then a very short lived Democratic Alliance government led again by Ajay Mukherjee. After first United Front government came to hold power another split occurred in the CPI (M). A new party, the Communist Party of India (Marxist Leninist) or CPI (ML) that did not believe in electoral and parliamentary politics launched a series of violent movements of individual annihilations. If violence can be an alternative vehicle of politics then the period may be designated as the "Violent Politics of West Bengal". The movement started at Naxalbari in North Bengal. It was actually a reaction against the UF's land reform minister Hare Krishna Konar's back track from his earlier promises regarding land question. Subsequently the Naxalites proliferated in different groups. They could not ignite the younger population. Their ideology was borrowed from the political game that Mao se Tung let loose during their Cultural Revolution in the mid-1960s in China. They wanted to spread out culturally but failed. During this period the education system was in a disarray. The Vice-Chancellor of a Calcutta based University (Jadavpur) was murdered and people of the street though afraid of their life and property denounced the Naxalite violence. A cultural transformation indeed! The cultural activities of the state came almost to a stand still. The economy of the state was in shambles.

In 1971 Bangladesh became independent from Pakistan. As the nearest neighbour due to the liberation movement in Bangladesh the demographics of West Bengal changed with a rapid pace. As a results of large number of influx, both Hindus and Muslims from East Pakistan (till Bangladesh to be recognized as a new nation), the economy of West Bengal was shattered. The socio-economic and demographic map of West Bengal irretrievably changed for the worse. More than nine million people had to take shelter on this part of the border. To feed such a large number of immigrants in an already crowded state was next to impossible without external help from international aid giving bodies. But the help was very meagre. India therefore, had no other alternative. Mrs. Indira Gandhi had to retaliate against Pakistan for its undeclared war and won the war on December 16, 1971. This was, therefore, the independence day of Bangladesh. Mrs. Indira Gandhi at that point of time required her Party to gain majority. With her image as the most powerful person and liberator of Bangladesh, she went in for parliamentary election in 1971 that won her nearly 2/3 seats in the *Lok Sabha* or the Lower House of Indian Parliament.

It was a psychological boost for the people of India the consequences of which were many.

Siddhartha Shankar Ray just utilized the three factors name: (1) Mrs. Gandhi's victory of Bangladesh war; (2) the electorate's disillusion about the left politics; and (3) depending upon the youth power. Ray proceeded aggressively for West Bengal Assembly election aligning with CPI. To the opposition party CPI (M), along with other left parties, the election of 1972 was totally rigged. There were grains of truth in their observations. Even the discerning people at that point shared the concern of the deliberate distortion of electoral process in Bengal. Ray and his Party won the battle but as perceived by many that the election was not free, but was unfair. To reiterate to the Left Political Parties, the 1972 Assembly election was totally rigged. The CPI (M) was badly mauled and won only 14 seats that were really unnatural. It did not participate in the legislative business for the next five years in protest but did not dare launch any popular movement. They appeared to be decimated both politically and socially. With the help of the elite police establishment, Mr. Ray destroyed the Naxalite presence in the state and brought about much needed peace in the state. He became infamous for his indiscretion but did what he had wanted to. During his period as the chief minister he encouraged his efficient and able ministers to enact certain legislations like the *Panchayat* Acts, the Land Reforms (Amendment) Acts, Calcutta Metropolitan Development Act or CMDA—in short many other progressive legislations. But unfortunately the Acts were not timely implemented first because of factionalism among his younger colleagues and later due to his involvement with the central leadership in implementing the infamous provisions of the Internal Emergency Act (1975) as per the relevant provision of the Constitution of India. This continued till March 1977 parliamentary elections. Freedom of speech and expressions was curtailed and press censorship enforced. As a consequence, the Congress's Assembly seats were reduced from 216 to 17 only in the Assembly election of 1977. During the whole period the CPI was always in tandem with the Congress both nationally and regionally. In West Bengal, the Congress and the CPI formed a pre-election political coalition named as Progressive Democratic Alliance (PDA). A document was signed by both the parties as how to run the PDA. But after the election the CPI did not participate in the Cabinet making. It was an informal but written understanding. They stood against the "fascist forces led by Jayaprakash Narayan" as they vented their spleen, but they themselves acted likewise. Democratic values and argumentations were given a good bye. The government of Mrs. Gandhi and her collaborators in the states by resorting to changing democratic institutional ethos for the sake of "discipline", wanted to bring about a cultural reorientation but ultimately failed miserably.

The Left Front (LF) is the combination or a political coalition (with a difference having surplus majority) based on the social reality at that point of time, has been ruling the state uninterruptedly for the last three decades till May 20, 2011. During Siddhartha Sankar regime the CPI (M) had to go in hiding because they feared that the PDA, particularly the Congress Party, might have brutally retaliated against the CPI (M) for what they had done during the UFs era in the late 1960s and early 1970s. All its front organizations like the Kisan Sabha, Student Front, Youth Organization and Trade Union were almost in hibernation. In the early 1977, Jayprakash Narayan brought all the opposition political parties—left, right and centrist together under a common umbrella to fight out the misrule of the Congress both at the Centre and the state levels. During Siddhartha Shankar regime the economic conditions did improve much in comparison to what it was seen during the late 1960s. The prices of food items were fairly under control. Inflation rate came down and SDGP was satisfactory. But the known leaders of the CPI (M) used to allege that the Congress leaders drove the CPI (M) people out of the localities and occupied their party offices quite forcibly.

After Jayprakash Narayan's clarion call to fight for and restore democratic governance, the CPI (M) had come forward in the open and gleefully agreed to be included in the Janata Party coalition during the parliamentary election in 1977. It was a grand victory for the rainbow coalition with a note that the CPI (M) was willing to be in the ramshackle Janata Party coalition from outside. It did not participate in the Janata Party government making at the Centre. But the political coalition in the state level of West Bengal broke down because of the negative attitude and overconfidence of Janata Party leader Prafulla Chandra Sen that the state Janata alone might win the Assembly election in June, 1977. This break down came as result of seat sharing formula of Shree Jyoti Basu. He wanted for the LF more than 120 seats in a House of 294. But Sen was in no mood to concede to the Left more than 80 to 90 seats in the Assembly.

Immediately the left parties except the CPI (initially though) could read the social reality of the state. Already even before the end of internal emergency a social coalition among all sections of castes particularly the Schedule Castes, Tribes other than backward castes and economic classes, were invisibly taking shape in favour of the left political parties. After the negotiation failed the CPI (M) with Jyoti Basu at the helm of the affairs stitched all the left parties except Socialist Unity Centre of India (SUCI), together to coalesce. A near permanent political formation came into being unlike its former incarnations i.e. of the two UFs in the late 1960s. Instantly a political coalition came up to fight the Assembly elections of 1977 against the Congress—CPI combine and the state Congress Party. The LF with the CPI (M) in the lead won Assembly election most comprehensively. The Janata Party was in a disarray and the Congress quite decimated. In a sense the people of West Bengal across the spectrum of castes class and communities had had an insecure sense of governance from the early 1960s to the late 1970s. To the ordinary people, both the Congress and the United Front (UF) governments appeared to be unresponsive to the needs of the time. Therefore, the people of the state wanted to repose their faith once again in the radical ideology (as the leftists still claim) that were people oriented in the apparent cohesiveness of the major left parties.

From now on there was no looking back for the LF. The first LF government and the left parties did not walk along the line of political vendetta as they had declared but verbally only. Within two years of their taking over, their objectives were to entrench themselves in the rural areas to reach the people irrespective of the caste, creed and community. This was the first step of the LF to build up a "social coalition" as had already been taking shape till then not perceived earlier. This coalition remained for two to three terms in support for the subsequent Left Front regimes. But after that, when incidents like the Marich Jhapi massacre in early 1979 and Bijan Setu killing of the Anand Margis innocent sanyasins by the CPI (M) on April 30, 1982 came to wider public notice, the CPI (M) completely a regimented party, had to resort to other methods for winning the popular elections in the state. Most possibly some sort of a social engineering in the electoral arena was used for many years. This perhaps helped the LF coming back to power again and again till 2006 Assembly elections in six phases. During this period the LF's two historic decisions were: (1) to complete the unfinished agenda of land reforms (enacted earlier by the Congress regimes) and *Operation Barga,* (2) Implementation of the *Panchayati Raj* legislation enacted by the previous government and calling for three tier *Panchayat* elections. In early 1980s the LF went in for elections of all the urban governing bodies i.e. Municipalities and Corporations. These three measures brought about enormous dividends that helped the LF government to continue for such a long period of time. As a result of fragmented opposition parties and their insignificant presence in the rural hinterland, no significant social and political movements against the existing political establishment in the state cropped up for the last several years till the days of Singur and Nandigram in late 2006 and early 2007, respectively.

Uninterruptedly the LF led by the CPI (M), the largest party in the Front, had been ruling the state with all the authorities at its command. During this time six Assembly elections, in 1987, 1991, 1996, 2001 and 2006 took place and except in 2001 election the CPI (M) successfully retained its surplus majority status in the Front. Theoretically defined, an ideal LF coalition was formed and led by the CPI (M) having 143 seats, i.e., five seats below the bench mark. Buddhadeb Bhattacharjee as the six-month-old chief minister was at the helm. From 1982 to 1987, till the Bofors scam against Rajiv Gandhi came up, the chief minister raised the bogey that at any time the Congress governments at the Centre first led by Sm. Indira Gandhi and then Rajiv Gandhi might take over the reign of the state government. It might be some sort of alerting as well as mobilizing the LF supporters, sympathizers, members and CPI (M)'s frontal organizations that penetrated most of the societal spaces in the state. During three parliamentary elections in 1984, 1998 and 1999 the opposition parties, the Congress, Trinamool Congress-BJP combine made some dent in the social arena. But it was next to impossible to break the oligopolistic political coalition led by the CPI (M) in West Bengal. However, belying the calculations of many and even beyond the expectation of the CPI (M), the LF won the 2006 Assembly election, with 235 seats. During this long period some outstanding events, some of them negative but mostly remarkable, came out in bolder focus. Jyoti Basu came to be regarded as a "guardian angel" according to his party colleagues and other interested political leaders of different regional parties, during the politically volatile time at the federal level. He was proposed to be the Prime Minister after the parliamentary election completely fragmenting the politics of that time. But his party vetoed the proposition. Not only to Jyoti Babu but to the discerning left oriented Bengali people at large, it was a "Himalayan Blunder" (in Jyoti Basu's own language). Secondly, the LF propped up the United Progressive Alliance (UPA)—a minority coalition government of the Congress Party from 2004 to the July, 2009—the LF which was supporting the UPA minority government of Dr. Manmohan Singh from outside, withdrew its support in July 2008 in opposition to the UPA government's signing the Civil Nuclear Treaty with the United States. The LF withdrew support on Nuclear deal and Indian American strategic partnership issues. But the UPA government survived till 2009 parliamentary election supported by the Samajvady Party (SP) and Bahujan Samaj Party (BSP) against the no-confidence motion brought by the BJP and the CPI (M) with its other LF partners.

Some of the decisions of the successive LF government raised ripples of protest by other left parties like the RSP, FB and even CPI and sometimes even within the front itself. The government ultimately had to retract. The social impact of many a decision was enormous, some of them are not positive though. It was really a feat on the part of the single majority party CPI (M) to stitch the coalition partners together even in the face of grave provocation. In course of time many of the important portfolios like Industry, Health, Housing, and *Panchayat* were taken over by the CPI (M) from the hands of the influential partners like the Forward Bloc (FB) and the Revolutionary Socialist Party (RSP). The coalition partners made occasional noises but could not get away. It was not the case when the Singur and Nandigram issues came to the forefront. The opposition parties and a considerable part of civil society and its several groups launched socio-political movements against the "pro-industrial policy of Buddhadeb Bhattacharya" depriving the poor peasants of their life and livelihood. They were very much dissatisfied by the way the governance of the state was run by the CPI (M) almost unilaterally. There were many law and order problems. Even the partners of the Front were in the dark regarding important decisions of the coalition government. Cracks and fissures within the front were visible. But till 2011 Assembly election, the political coalition of the LF government was very much intact. Finally when the LF government was badly mauled in April-May Assembly 2011 election, the left parties did not show any sign of falling apart.

Finally, many socio-cultural dimensions of the ongoing political process in the state over a period of many decades would be brought into a proper focus as the politico-historical discourse progresses. The socio-political space has appeared to be a mosaic of many hues to the observers. In course of the discussion special emphasis has also been laid on the political economy of development over years in this "problem state" of West Bengal

[1]

More than six decades is not a very short span in the working of a state government within the Constitutional scheme of a federal nation state. West Bengal falls somewhat in a different category because of its tortuous historic-political legacy that gave rise to leftist political ambience in many places in the state, if not the state as a whole. Each period of its working is sufficiently different from its earlier period. The actual processes of governance in different phases over the years were somewhat different from other several Indian states. This is not to state, of course that the governance was always responsive, good and transparent. Most of the time people found law and order problems sufficiently poor, the machinery of governance twisted and governance of political-economy quite opaque.

The growth of regional sentiments often overtakes the over-arching federal control system. Even the period of a single dominant party regime here is different from its earlier incarnation like the Congress system that we found during 1947-1966 and 1972-1977, not to speak of a predominant Left Front (LF) regime that have been taken over by a liberal democratic coalition system led by the Trinamool Congress Party with surplus majority since 2011. These peculiarities and uniqueness of the state politics of West Bengal are apparent.

Since 1989 after the defeat of Rajiv Gandhi government, six Parliamentary elections were held resulting in minority coalition governments in India. The Left Front (LF) gaining a seat share of 61, the largest ever in 2004 election, was claiming to be in a policy dictating terms to the minority United Progressive Alliance (UPA) coalition government at the Centre. The Left Front lionized itself. The Communist Party of India [CPI (M)] publicly bragged that the First UPA government was under its thumb rule. It won 253 Assembly seats—the largest ever in 1987. It was so in the context that the Congress Party won 16 Parliamentary seats in 1984 election. In terms of assembly segments it was supposed to win 112 seats. But 1991 elections deluded the opposition. Parliamentary and Assembly (the state poll was preponed) elections did not reflect the apparent reality. The Congress opposition won 43 seats only. In the light of what has been happening in West Bengal, electoral arena during the late 80s and early nineties was not that clean. The LF's electoral dominance particularly that of CPI (M) alone always in the state was puzzling. The Critics, Journalists and dispassionate academics attempted to dish out different reasons like electoral malpractices by the CPI (M) cadres and their sympathizer government employees—to be precise the members of the coordination committee[1], from the beginning of making the voter list[2] to the last stage of counting, inculcating a fear psychosis among the rural voters, assimilating people belonging to different layers of society in its party activities in exchange for jobs, prizes, moneys and many other allurements. As a result a sub-standard socio-political milieu was set in. The higher echelons of West Bengal bureaucracy either helplessly or willingly surrendered themselves to the dictates of the leaders of the Coordination Committee (a left oriented committee of government employees) of those who are closer to the Ministers belonging to the LF coalition government. As a matter of fact, political society in the State for the last three decades did not hesitate to envelop the civil society arena through their ideology as the Indian Marxists like to propound. They gleefully carried on according to their caprices and whims.

The questions that naturally arise are why politics of the state in West Bengal is moulded in the fashion at the hands of the Marxists as it has been until recently. Constitutionally Indian states as federal units have certain structural commonalities. How the state governments would act and maintain their relations with central government and the state governments with their adjacent neighbours involving common interests are well defined. With the passage of 73rd and 74th amendments of the Constitution, rural and urban governance have taken definite shapes and become the third tier of government in the mainstream of the major Indian states. This third tier of the government bears almost the same relations between the local and the state as that of the state and the centre. That means a federation within a Federation. The politics and governance of the local bodies is the concern of the state government and a recent phenomenon. It is interesting to note that politics of the local areas-rural and urban, particularly in a state like West Bengal is not autonomous as it should have been as per the Indian Constitutional design. Sometimes it is allowed to an extent by many of the other state governments in India. It cannot be explained away with the help of the centre periphery paradigm. The central government has to do nothing excepting occasional pumping of Central funds to the state governments for the pro-poor well defined Central government programmes. But how much to be channelized to the concerned areas and the prospective beneficiaries are determined by the state governments. The objective was to empower the rural people to participate in the process of economic development. The Left Front government by obliterating the distinction between party, government and the state, applied their thesis of democratic centralism as borrowed from the Leninist praxis, which appears to be contrary to the democratic ethos as understood elsewhere in Indian state including the alternate Marxist state of Kerala. Here the CPI (M) instead of going in for democratic decentralization opted for a model of its own, i.e. centralizing the process of decentralization (emphasis added) quite contrary to the concept, as envisaged by the Constitutional scheme in 1992-93 (73rd and 74th Constitutional Amendment Acts). Here one will find the differences as to how the state governments and the governance in India differ from that of the states. Political parties of the state, their objectives, implementations and, ideologies seem to play the most important role. In the wake of an enormous growth of regional, state and local parties, electoral process expected to be similar everywhere often get distorted. The processes of political parties and contents as well are more or less same reflecting caste, community, economic class and regional identities. But when hegemonic party within the democratic structure begins to predominate, the problems of governance become complicated politically, socially and economically. This is the situation that the people of Bengal have been facing for the last two decades if not more.

From this point of view the politics of West Bengal is conspicuously different from that of the other states. A coalition of so-called ideological parties led by the CPI (M) came up prominently in the mid-1960s. They had to follow a meandering course. The history was tortuous though tactical. The Marxist ideological parties were firmly saddled in West Bengal political scene till the Panchayat (their citadel of power and pasture for the last many years since 1978) elections. The year 2008 is actually the watershed of Bengal politics. The political commentators and the pundits begin to believe that after 2011 Assembly elections the 4th phase of the West Bengal politics is in the offing.

[2]

Certain common properties, either historico-culturally or constitutionally architected, characterize the working of the process of state politics in Indian states among other variants of politics in time and space. Achievement of good governance through democratic means for realizing political modernization over the time cannot be ignored; because the development objectives particularly economic progress has been the coveted and declared goal. Besides, the securing of equal opportunity and special provisions for deprived social groups and reducing gender bias, find a special place in these desired but overlapping objectives. Whether and to what extent these objectives and the values underlying them are or can be realized depends upon the way the political parties in India—national, regional and local—interact with political competitive spirit and, the ruling party or coalition of parties have conducted state affairs. In the interest of the people that the governing process should be simple and transparent as far as possible, meticulously worked out, little scope for discrimination and, responsive to the needs and demands of the citizens. Differential endowments in respect of political space and territorial size as also the magnitude and the density of population are, of course, important components. However, socio-political ethos, which differs from state to state, constitutes the most important factor. Besides past history and traditions, geographical location—nearer the centre or periphery, the terrain, changing demographics, the stage of political economy of development and the nature of the people and the incoming migrants are the most important variables that more often than not determine the politics of a particular state. In this respect the state of West Bengal is a very important state with many exogenous factors had to bear most of the constitutional features. But its peculiarities are many and immensely interesting. At the time of the Partition in 1947, it was economically as viable as its counterpart East Bengal. It was so to say a territorial division. It was just one third of the pre-partition Bengal Province.

The nitty-gritty of a well thought out division of a province, in their hurry both of the British imperial power and the then leaders of India are to be taken into consideration. The Partition of Bengal on the eastern side and Punjab on the western flanks of India was not on the same terms. To a greater degree the exchange of population in Punjab was agreed to. The rehabilitations of west Punjabi mostly Sikh populations were smooth and their less than fussy nature, capacity to quickly adjust to the northern Indian Hindi speaking people and for their hardworking nature it was not difficult for the Punjabi refugees to be rehabilitated and anywhere. The case was not the same with the East Bengali refugees. They wanted to be settled anywhere in West Bengal. The Communist Party also encouraged them not to leave for inhospitable terrain with different life style and language. In the making of partition, the human factors were most importantly ignored. As a result of riots and inhuman killings and gang rapes of Hindu women perpetrated by the fundamentalist Muslims in the newly formed East Pakistan and the prospect of the dreams of the Muslims for Pakistan being realized, millions of lower caste Hindus had to leave East Bengal to take shelter in West Bengal. These poor souls had to take temporary makeshift shelter in different railway stations, platforms and open spaces and marshy lands in and around greater Calcutta and a few districts of north Bengal as paupers. The conditions of the upper class Hindus were not as bad. They were mostly literate and many were highly educated. More than 4.5 million people began crowding the already crowded land areas of West Bengal. The processes of immigration had a tremendous socio-economic and cultural impact and repercussions—both negative and positive. The original inhabitants of the West Bengal people began to get hostile to an extent, because they thought that they would lose economically and would have to culturally contend with the refugees having peculiar linguistic orientations and life style. The people of the western part of Bengal had a feeling that their own lifestyle and economic activities would be dislocated and gradually thrown into political insignificance. But in positive terms, they were to gain because of the influence of the educated and more literate middle class and lower middle class people migrating to India. The sons of the soils of this part of

Bengal understood this later as they experienced and found as recorded in contemporary history.

The history of West Bengal can perceptively be classified into four general categories: a tortuous period for consolidating the emerging issues of a truncated state, politics of the Congress Party dominance and fragmented opposition parties, politics of aggrandizement, violence counter-violence, thereafter a politico-electoral movement, the reactions, and an oligopolistic politics based on real and sometimes a ramshackle social coalition. Each of the four periods of the disinherited state has been be subdivided having unique characteristics at times.

A Difficult Period for a Truncated State

The advisers with technical expertise did not properly think out different aspects, effects and negative human repercussions and economic dislocation that might happen due to an artificial partition of a Bengali speaking people having same historical origin. It was carved out just to provide the Muslims a territory, in the form of a state, i.e., the eastern part of Pakistan, where they overwhelmingly outnumbered the Hindus. The Radcliff used almost a surgeon's scalpel that vivisected the Bengal territory. It was less than rational and done in a hurry. After declaring the award he had to revise it within two days bringing Murshidabad in India, some portions of Malda, undivided Dinajpur and Khulna under East Pakistan. The problems of refugee rehabilitations and the politics of refugee rehabilitations was unrelentingly unleashed by CPI against the Congress government. The street fighting movements and activities of the Communist Party of India (undivided) and its politics to gain political mileage out of the miseries of the displaced persons and perceived "insensitiveness"[3] of both the central and state governments were the constant and serious propaganda planks. Dr. Prafulla Chandra Ghosh became the first Chief Minister in West Bengal after the Partition of the state of Bengal in August 15, 1947. But he could not stay in office for more than four months. The Bengal Provincial Congress Party was ridden with extreme factionalism. Dr. Ghosh was a Gandhian. But he could take the suggestion of Gandhi in regard to the allocation of the Finance portfolio to Nalini Ranjan Sarkar, who was closer to the Marwari lobby. At that time of excessive food shortage "a corrupt Marwari businessman"[4] was indulging in supplying spurious wheat—a very important and necessary scarce food item during those difficult days, to the market. It was brought to the notice of Dr. Ghosh who immediately took action. It irritated that particular Marwari lobby that compounded with Gandhi's recommendation for inducting Sarkar as the Finance Minister made Dr. Ghosh relinquish the office of the Chief Minister. Dr. Bidhan Chandra Roy took over in January 1948. To the Communist Party of India, Indian Independence was a sham. To them without economic equality, political independence was hollow having no real democratic contents or at best ephemeral: slogan mongering, like *e azadi jhuta hai, bhulo mat bhulo mat,* was the constant refrain. They used every opportunity to oppose any actions by the Congress Government in rehabilitating thousands of the hapless refugees in places like Andaman Islands and *Dandakaranya* outside West Bengal with insufficient habitable areas, in the already over populated territory of the truncated Bengal. The refugees were also unwilling to go outside the state having a common language spoken by all. Highlighting the cause and misery of the migrants, the undivided Communist Party CPI won the hearts of the refugees to a great extent. Later on the refugee population which began swelling in a big way till the early 1970s became the mainstay of the leftist ideological propaganda and crudely speaking, the vote banks of the Leftists particularly the Communist Party of India [later on the breakaway faction (CPI (M)]. The other activities of the CPI were to indirectly mobilize the suffering people by the leftist cultural organizations like the music circle such as Indian People Theatre groups (IPTA), Calcutta Choir, etc. They depicted the miserable plight and fate of the peasants before and after *Tebhaga Andolan (*movement for crop sharing formula*)* encouraged the peasant groups and middle class educated people. It had impressive records and the leftists reaped the harvest when the CPI decided to participate in the parliamentary democratic system in the very early 1950s. The socio-cultural movements by the Marxist intellectuals, left oriented artistes, theatre personalities, litterateurs, musicians had political impacts on a large section of people. The CPI exploited the situations. These socio-cultural groups always remained sympathetic to the cause of the Communist Party. When the parties could not directly communicate with the people, they took recourse to mediated or indirect mobilization through the socio-cultural activities and initiative of the people mentioned above. The theatre, films, music compositions depicting the unbearable miseries of the people at that point of time and space played a great role in focusing the contribution of the CPI. Thus, the Communist Party and the other left parties gained respectability and acceptance among the numerous displaced persons in the state and many other communities in the state that catapulted these parties to power in the late 1960s (the two United Fronts) and 1977 [Left Front (LF)]) till May 20, 2011. People's memories were not as sharp as they say. They forgot all about the role of the Communist Party in their support for the British war efforts, betrayal of the "Quit India Movement in 1942" abusing Subhas Chandra as a stooge of the fascist Germany and the "Quisling of Tajo" of Japan. The CPI's support of the Muslim Leagues' demand for self-determination on religious line were startling as also its support for a separate Gorkhaland in Darjeeling before Indian Independence on August 15, 1947. The newly formed interim governments, afterwards both at the Centre and the states, had to confront all this to consolidate itself before the first democratic elections in 1951-52 within the constitutionally accepted framework of universal adult franchise.

The first Parliamentary and Assembly elections in West Bengal were held in 1952. In those days till 1967 the Parliamentary and Assembly elections used to be held simultaneously. Therefore, the first period of the State Politics in West Bengal was the period of Congress Party Dominance. People reposed faith in the Congress for its past records. Its contribution to the national struggle was total and indisputable. But the moments of freedom were the worst in the history of Bengal. Sporadic communal riots were still going on. Gandhi began his fast at *Hydar e Manjil* now renamed as *Gandhi Bhawan* at Beleghata in the eastern flank of Kolkata. Gandhi appealed to the conscience of the two rioting communities. He was the unhappiest people's leader among the stalwarts who so long struggled hard for India's freedom from British colonial rule. During the inhuman riots in both sides of Bengal he traveled a lot and tried to bring back the sanity and normality among the people from ordinaries to the highest leaders. But in Bengal the results were not as desired.

Demographic characteristics were distorted. The areas with West Bengal were not enough to rehabilitate the displaced from eastern Pakistan. The people were to live in subhuman conditions. The doles given by the government were insufficient. The economy of the state was in disarray. There was no hope of immediate recovery. Major chunks of fertile and arable lands were given to the East. The raw materials like jute and other items that used to feed the large numbers jute industries along the side of the Ganges remained in the eastern part of West Bengal. With these resources the East Pakistan attempted to build up jute industries. West Bengal's industry and agriculture were yet to wake from the shock. The state was already burdened with enormous size of refugee populations in inhuman miseries from the late 1947. The general administrative structure and police administrations were to be trimmed up. The Chief Minister Dr. Bidhan Chandra Roy took up the helm with single-minded determination but the odds were heavy. The negative politics of the opposition parties and factionalism in the Congress stood in the way to progress and development. But he tried his best with the available quantum of help from his long time friend and colleagues in the Central government. The incoming stream of refugees never came to an end before the Passport system was introduced in 1952. It was really the most difficult or rather the worst of time in the initial history of West Bengal. The hapless millions crossing over the border could not enjoy the spoils of partition.[5] If it were really spoils, it had appeared later that the leaders or people with political clouts upholding the causes of the politics of refugees enjoyed the fruits and shared the political power for nearly three and a half decades.

The leadership profile of the leftist politicians bore and still bears the testimony to the facts that most of them came to this part of state and quite educated, and at least moderately well to do. More than 30 cabinet ministers out of 43 in the LF till 2011 were originally from the refugee communities from the other side of West Bengal border. At least their origin can be traced to the first and second generation of the displaced persons. This was true even in case of the higher party levels (in the CPI (M)'s state committee and the party state secretariat). Many of them are from the elite communities, belonging to the Brahmin, Kayasth, Baidya or upper layers of the backward castes, classes and communities.

Some of the early generation refugees are still living in the colonies; some are well settled in life during the LF regime for over three decades. These displaced people later on, for reasons of their own, posed a threat to the LF government. The left leaders' politics based on displaced persons and sometimes on their miseries paid the CPI (M) handsomely later in the mid 1960s in their desperate bid to marginalize the Congress in the power structure of the state. Ultimately the undivided Communist Party (CPI) even with two trends of thoughts working within, with different understanding of the nature of Indian State and character of the Congress Party, spearheaded the nationalist agenda through the dynamics of parliamentary democracy. How far it is real in case of the CPI (M) is yet to be explored.[6]

Congress Dominance, Fragmented Opposition

The first democratic elections were held in 1952. Both the Parliamentary and Assembly elections were held simultaneously throughout the country. The undivided Communist Party keeping aside their earlier views of pre-colonial state colonialism, consequences of decolonization, dependency of the third world countries and people's freedom to life and dignity in the "bourgeois democratic" elections, etc. ultimately participated in the Indian electoral process. By now the Congress Party had to reconcile with the parting of ways of the ginger groups. On the other hand, the other marginal groups as well that came out of the National Congress Party, forming parties of different hues were ready to contest the first general elections at various levels in the country.

The existence of multiple parties and the fragmented system have been shown later in this work that might have given an idea as to why the Congress Party was dominant and the fragmented opposition had to wait for long to realise the merits of coalescing in the electoral process to defeat the Congress. After the beginning of the LF regime, the number of political parties winning elections has been reduced to the advantage of the LF. In the meanwhile, the Indian National Congress (INC) underwent a few changes in nomenclature. It was clear that the popularity of the CPI (M) was on the wane, or in other words the anti-incumbency factor was working within even during the middle leg of LF regime.

It is significant to note that the CPI (M) led by Jyoti babu was reduced to 150 in 1996 and Buddhadeb began his journey with only 143 seats losing the absolute majority in the LF. From now on the politics of the state led by the CPI (M) took a new turn to regain the hegemony it enjoyed till the end of Jyoti Basu which brought back the LF particularly the CPI (M) with a bang during the regime of Buddhadeb Bhattacharjee. Dr. Bidhan Chandra Roy was a very able administrator. It was a difficult time and he had to steer through with the limited resources just after the independence. He never complained against the central leadership for its omissions and commissions. Centre-state relations and the controversy regarding inter-state commerce, the policy of freight equalizations, etc. were not brought into a broader focus, as they should have been. It was later raised by the left parties in their movements against the then Chief Minister Prafulla Chandra Sen during the 1960s and continuously from 1980s when Indira Gandhi came back to power after a short stint of Janata coalition regime led by Morarji Desai. Dr. Bidhan Chandra Roy was a national leader by his own right. He used to think he would be able to tide over all sorts of difficulties in local and national relations. He did his best in his policy options. The first step that he took was his policy of adopting the formulations of the State Planning Committee. The single minded objective was towards industrialization of the truncated state in all its several categories—heavy, small, manufacturing and cottage industries. To rehabilitate the unemployed youth belonging to the refugee families he introduced State Transport Corporation (STC). A large number of youths from the displaced poor people were given employment in different categories.

The Calcutta Tram Company owned at that time by the foreigners had still the control over the Tramways and its employees. The company with the approval of the government made a paltry increase of *ek paise* of Indian Rupee made of *64 paise* at that point of time (1953). It was really a time of a moderate inflation and income of the ordinary people was considerably low. The decision of the Company with the approval of the state government infuriated the Communist Party and other left parties. After participating in the democratic elections where they did not fare well; they could not make their presence felt in the Legislative House. Therefore, they wanted to focus on their politics in a big way in the streets. Street fighting, slogan mongering and propaganda in the nook and corner of the state were a routine occurrence. In a single day they burnt 13 Tramcars to ashes near and around Sealdah Railway Station in the early 1953. The government took control of the situation. This was the first disruptive major action of the leftists and their frontal trade union and student front, at the very beginning of the democratic process in the unhappy state of Bengal.

Building up of heavy industries and for that matter industrial regeneration was the priority of Dr. Roy. He attempted to modernize the Steel Industries in

Durgapur and Assansol. He made a modern township in Durgapur in Burdwan district. Durgapur Steel factories, DPL, Damodar Valley barrage at Durgapur to generate electricity. Measures of flood control mechanism were his contributions and achievements. For the same purpose he got to commission Mython barrage and water reservoir to generate electricity, and barrage on Mayureswari river, Tilpara barrage to help the peasant communities to get the irrigation water. Marurakshi Dam near Massanzore at Birbhum was also built up during the 1950s.

When the Planning Commission under the chairmanship of the Prime Minister Nehru introduced the First Five Year Plan Document according to Mahalanobis planning concept to build the heavy industries to lay the foundation of modern India, Dr. Roy immediately fell in line. His objective was to address the problems both of the industry and the agriculture. Building infrastructure capacity was the priority areas. He looked out for creation of employment opportunities in industry, agriculture and services sectors. Rural development and urbanization figured out in his economic thinking in those days.

Dr. Roy established Satellite Township like Kalyani and Salt Lake City and Durgapur (a little away from Calcutta) to provide housing facilities to the middle and lower middle classes near Calcutta. To supply milk to the cities and around he commissioned Haringhata Milk Project that during the 1980s became moribund. Digha Sea Beach in the eastern part of Midnapur was another dream project of Dr. Roy in his bid to enlarge the tourist industry. Dr. Roy was quite aware of the tourist spots in the state to increase potentials of tourism in the state to attract tourists from and around the states of India and foreign tourists as well. Many tourist bungalows in the hills areas of Darjeeling, Karshiang, Kalimpong and in plains in Durgapur, Massanzore and a few other places were built up for the tourists.

Let us look back to the manufacturing and small scale industries during Dr. Roy's time. He was intent to build up manufacturing industries, small scale industries and the cottage industries and to increase scope of the same and to maintain them as well which already existed in the state. Bellious Road at Howrah used be regarded as the Sheffield of Bengal for its small and manufacturing industries on either side of the road. Those were the thriving manufacturing companies mostly owned by private owners. These small industrial goods mostly lathe and sugar-cane crushing machines were very important items in the small industrial sectors in Bengal. The machines that were manufactured in these places used to be sent to Bihar, Uttar Pradesh and elsewhere in India. During the 1980s, Howrah manufacturing industries lost their glories and became the den of anti-social elements dealing with iron scraps. They actually survived with thieving and smuggling. At this point in time, the observers of political economy looked to a basic and very important fact. West Bengal used to contribute approximately eight per cent out of 23.10 per cent to the total income of India from registered industrial ventures in 1963. In 1959 the figure was 22.20 per cent. Thereafter the income generation was marginally increasing. Then the share of the state declined. It came down to 7.20 per cent in 1987-88. It was 6.70 per cent in 1989-90, 6.10 per cent in 1993-94, 3.4 per cent in 1998-99; a slight increase i.e. a gradual 4.30 per cent took thereafter. This was the registered industry's scenario in West Bengal in the beginning of twenty first century.[7] Along the river Hooghly on mostly the western side and some on the eastern bank there were very rich and revenue producing jute mills. These were mostly owned and run by private business houses and industrialists. After the partition the major quantum of jute and other raw materials that came from agriculturally rich East Bengal ceased to come to this side of the border. The Chief Minister did his best so that the working mills could be thriving. If the mills were closed, a large number of workers should have been totally unemployed. Dr. Roy wanted that such an industrial scenario could not develop. In the late 1950s, Dr. Roy introduced Panchayat Raj System after Nehru had introduced the system on the basis of Balwant Rai Mehta Report. It was intended to be an all India affair. It was unlike the Asoke Mehta Repot of 1978, a two, three or four tier arrangement as would be suitable for each state in India. Rural Development was the key element of Development Administration. The administrator should always be people-oriented which was exactly opposite to the old British system of governance by the administrators. The administrators should be the change agent and consider themselves as the servant of the public rather than the ruler of the people. Several posts in the lower tier of administration were created, like the Block Development Officer (BDO), Extension Officer (EO), and at the village level the Gram Sevak or Sevika. They were supposed to look after the development in block and village level. The objective was to involve the rural poor people in the process of development. The Gram Sevak or Sevika was to contact the villagers constantly and to help the people in their difficult times. Thus, it would help the administration to create employment opportunities in formal but mostly in informal ways. Dr. Roy also helped unemployed but healthy young people to enroll themselves as trainees in the military establishment at Barrackpur Military establishment in 24 Parganas (undivided till then). After Roy the next Chief Minister Prafulla Chandra Sen also attempted to give a new look to the industrial scenario and worked hard to that effect for the Jute Industry in Bengal. Later on because of political uncertainties and tumultuous political development the Jute industries began to be sick. It became extremely sick during the LF regimes. Possibly, this would give an indication as to how the picture of the political economy changed over the time after the death of Dr. Bidhan Chandra Roy in the very early 1960s (He died on July 1, 1962).

Actually, after the partition the new state was suffering from acute food shortages. Rationing system was still in place. But the procurement of paddy as levies was not adequate. Dr. Roy's Minister for the Department of Food, Shree Prafulla Chandra Sen introduced some sort of a cordoning off system so that the system of black marketing could be done away with or at best minimized. But it had its negative effect also. People in the state particularly the peasantry were dissatisfied. The Communists and others with vested interest exploited the situation and fomented the dissatisfaction among sections of the people. It had its salutary effect so much so that an efficient minister like P.C. Sen had to face defeat in 1957 Assembly election. However the Congress government brought back Shree Sen in a back door manoeuvre. He was elected in the second chamber i.e. Legislative Council and then was offered the Food Portfolio again. But the opposition members never forgot to retaliate against Shree Sen; the Left oppositions particularly the CPI and after the split of the Communist Party, the more militant group CPI (M) left no stone unturned to carry on slander campaigns against Prafulla Chandra Sen when he took over as the Chief Minister after the death of Dr. Roy in early July, 1962. He tried to carry on the unfinished agenda of Dr. Roy. The decade of the 1950s was terribly difficult for the government. The Leftists relentlessly carried out socio-political movements at the slightest opportunities. Zamindari Abolition Act was passed in mid-1950s. The Land Reform Minister Bimal Chandra Singh— a very big landlord having large estates on both side of the border had the spirit to come forward. He himself piloted the proposal in the West Bengal Legislative Assembly after Zamindari Abolition Constitutional Amendment was passed by the Parliament. He had also to look after the implementation as far as possible. The government had to face hassles regarding the paying of compensation, which ultimately resolved to an extent after the 4th amendment of the Constitution. The truncated state comprising only one third of Bengal had not sufficient fertile lands to grow rice. The famine situation appeared to be looming large. To tide over the difficulty Dr. Roy and the Chief Minister of Bihar Shri Krishna Singh mooted the idea of merging West Bengal and Bihar. The Communist Party incited people particularly in the urban centres of the state. In the meanwhile the Congress Party had to face a by-election in the North-West Calcutta. The Leftist opposition backed candidate Mohit Moitra defeated the Congress-backed candidate Ashok Sen — a brilliant barrister and a dedicated Congress stalwart. As a true democrat Dr. Roy took it for a referendum against his policy and abandoned the idea of merger. Dr. Roy wanted to make West Bengal as an economically viable state despite economic hardship after almost irreversible socio-political damages after partition. The state had to face chronic food shortages. Flood was a yearly routine despite having large dams to control flood and facilitate irrigations to boost up agricultural productions. As a result of a devastating flood in 1959 food production got down to all time low. A food riot began with the Communist Party at the lead. The police opened fire in different places. Many people had to suffer bullet injuries but there were controversies regarding the number of deaths. The CPI (M) claimed that more than 80 people died on the spot. But the Party was not in a position to verify the number.

To enhance capacity building for education it was Dr. Roy who changed the existing system and built up Higher Secondary Board that separated the school from the Calcutta University system. Attempts had been made to change and improve the examination process and procedures in the universities and the school board. He laid a good deal of emphasis on primary education and eradication of illiteracy from its existing conditions. The standard of higher education including medical and engineering improved; he energized all the existing medical and engineering colleges at Calcutta, Jadavpur and Sibpore at Howrah. During his period, Burdwan, Rabindra Bharati and other centres of Higher Education, i.e. universities were started with extraordinary teachers and scholars in the faculties of those institutions. Dr. Roy was also enthusiastic about the literary and cultural affairs of the state. He initiated before his death the 100th year of Rabindranath Tagore's birthday anniversary in 1962.

Satyajit Ray in the late 1950s was making his epoch film, *Pather Panchali*. But he had to face great difficulties in completing the film. It was through his Secretary Thomas, Bidhan Chandra Roy provided funds to complete the project. But unfortunately Satyajit did not acknowledge this gesture of Dr. Roy in public. Of course that was a different story altogether, but justify the generous nature of Dr. Roy.

During the Left Front (LF) regime of 34 years the number of colleges and universities multiplied but at the cost of merits and excellence. It was really a regime of mediocrities all around[8].

The period of the Chief Minister Prafulla Chandra Sen (P.C. Sen) was not administratively as remarkable but politically the period from 1962 to 67 was volatile and sometimes tumultuous, both from the perspectives of the State Congress Party and the Communist Party (undivided). The Congress Party was a coalition of different interests of the rural and urban communities consisting of different castes, classes and communities including the Muslim minorities and Other Backward Castes (OBCs). The castes, creeds and communities were under the command of the urban elite politicians and the rural people had to depend upon the congress rural gentries with considerable landholdings even after the zamindari system was abolished. In modern electoral parlance, this caste and community system of voting behaviour used to be utilized by the Congress Party, as it has been by the local and regional parties that are regarded today as the vote bank of different parties according to their orientations. This vote bank of the Congress was intact even during the elections in 1967. But the Congress had to kiss the dust because of extreme factionalism between the two groups: the Hooghly group led by the Congress President Atulya Ghosh and P.C. Sen and the Midnapore group led by Ajoy Mukherjee, Satish Samanta and Sushil Dhara. Actually groupism or factionalism was rampant in Congress politics even before the independence. Its intensity more or less depended upon the leaders of the party at the helm of both at the party as well as the top administrative levels. Even there was a conflict between Shri Atulya Ghosh the President of the state party committee and the chief administrative personality, the Chief Minister Dr. Roy. The controversy was later resolved by applying the parliamentary principle and process of separating the jurisdiction of the party and the government that would be elaborated later in this chapter.[9]

It was a period when the Leftists were divided in their assessment about the Chinese military advance to and aggression against India. The more radical elements of the Communist Party thought that a socialist country could not attack another country like India. Rather the first fire beyond McMohan line, still not recognized by China, was the handiwork of the Chinese armies. Even RSP, Forward Bloc and other smaller parties attacked the radical elements in the Communist Party of India. This paved the way for vertical split in the undivided Communist Party. This split of the party was almost inevitable. Since independence ideological debates among different leaders gradually began as regards to forms and contents of the Communism, its applications that were experienced in Soviet Russia, their world views and other peripheral questions. Possibly it was overdue since the mid-1950s. Of course factionalism in the Congress was rampant also during Dr. Roy's time but Dr. Roy made an arrangement with Atulya Ghosh that Ghosh would not interfere in any matter in regard to governmental administration. Dr. Roy also promised to make himself aloof from the day-to-day political domain as to be looked after by Shree Ghosh along with his coterie whatsoever as hinted above.[10]

This period was dogged by occasional floods and drought as also by skyrocketing inflation in consequences resulting from less than transparent governance. The public distribution system was not as speedy and efficient as it should be; or in other words it almost failed to deliver. Food articles were scarce. Sporadic food riots were the routine of the day during P.C. Sen's tenure of office. His government in the face of the street protests and agitations by the leftist political parties was almost unable to control the situation. The chief minister was requesting the people of the state to change their food habits. Instead of taking rice he suggested to take wheat and other chiefly available green vegetables and boiled green banana. The rice eating Bengalese particularly the well-settled refugees from other side of the border were infuriated. Food riots began in different places of Bengal. The police opened fire near Barasat. Nurul Islam a Muslim boy was shot dead by police firing. Ahoke Chatterjee, who was the Sub Divisional Officer (SDO) at that point of time at Barasat, was supposed to be responsible for police firing and was transferred to Calcutta in the Department of Weights and Measures. Actually in a conversation later on, while he was the Secretary in the Department of Education in the late 1980s, he expressed that for nothing he was tainted to be a desperado.[11] The Left political parties made a martyr of the boy and began a virulent political movement against an "unresponsive Congress government".[12] Secondly, the factionalism of the Congress grew to a new height. The veteran freedom fighter and much-respected Congress leader Shree Ajoy Mukherjee was expelled from the party and he formed his own party, Bangla Congress. The opposition parties took full advantages of these prevailing situations. It happened just before the fourth general elections in 1967. The Left party leaders worked hard for seat adjustments so that they could form a common front to confront the Congress, which had been split after Ajoy Mukherjee was expelled. The Left parties formed two fronts: ULF led by the CPI (M) and PULF led by the CPI. Bangla Congress fought alone and won a respectable number of seats (34) while the Congress won 127 seats. Together (161), they might have formed the government, as the benchmark was only 141. But Prafulla Chandra Sen and the then state Congress President Atulya Ghosh accepted the fractured verdict of the people. Really the mood of the people of the state was against the Congress government in the state. That was the mandate of the people. It was against Congress after Ajay Mukherjee was too humiliated to leave the Congress Party headed by Atulya Ghosh. But the opposition parties were not in a position to form the government because of inter-party rivalries. It was a hung Assembly never seen in West Bengal since independence. During this period Humayun Kabir came to play a big role in bringing about two warring fronts together with the help of Ajoy Mukherjee, Sushil Kumar Dhara and Satish Samanta, with their newly formed Bangla Congress a party with totally local orientation.

Politics Violence, Counter-Violence and, a Politico-electoral Reaction

Humayun Kabir of the Bharatiya Kranti Dal (BKD) was the architect of a coalition experiment in West Bengal in 1967. With Ajoy Mukherjee at the head, two Leftist blocks—one led by CPI (M) and the other by CPI came together to form United Front (UF) government. This second phase of West Bengal politics was extremely volatile. The opposition parties led by CPI and CPI (M) were yet to learn the culture of governance in parliamentary terms, least to speak about good governance. The revolutionary rhetoric of a Marxist variety in a parliamentary process gradually began to alienate the CPI (M) from other Left parties, and fissures and cracks developed within the CPI (M) itself. The Congress at the Centre was alleged to have conspired in this. Frequent visits of the Home Minister at that time fuelled the rumour that the Government of India under the leadership of Smt. Indira Gandhi might declare

Presidential rule to bring back the state Congress party to power. The Governor Dharmavira's internal report about the state might be of help to that effect. But it all appeared to be speculations by the Leftists.

Within a period of only four years from 1967 to 1971 West Bengal had to install four coalition Governments. The society was in turmoil. Law and security problems were never in such an abnormal state. Economic condition of the middle class and poorer sections of people was getting worse. Food productions were abnormally low. The main staple food was rice. Within a very short period the price of the rice jumped up to Rs. 5, while earlier it was between Rs. 1.50 or 2. Considering the purchasing power of the poor and even the lower middle class, this was an abnormal change that had never been seen since 1952. With the sharp rise of the food prices other items of eatable began rising. The leaders of the political parties were more interested to spread them horizontally. The income differential was high. Even the ruling class did not have the time to look at the political economy of the state.

Good governance implies sincerity of purpose and transparency on the part of the government to carry on the short term and long term policy administration. Policy decisions are to be formulated with a view to the welfare of the ordinary citizens. The implementation of the policy decisions are to be as quick and hassle free as possible. The bureaucracies (both civil and police) responsible for the job are to be people orientated. They should take it for granted that they are appointed not for over lording but to serve the people at large. Both at political and administrative levels transparency should be maintained in managing the political economy of each sector of governmental activities. During the first decade of independence tumultuous no doubt, yet governmental activities were more or less development oriented to a good extent. In view of the rapid and sudden changes of demographic, the end result was not sufficient as desired. Sometimes, it appeared that the government was unresponsive. There were political reasons also for this. The decades that followed during the mid-1960s were most volatile. For frequent flood and draught situations, economic productions, particularly food situations were worse. In many places food riots were almost regular occurrences. Law and order problems became endemic. Employment problems both in organized and unorganized sectors did not show any sign of improving.

Table 2.1 showed a partial picture of employment situation of both rural and urban sites in the state during 1951-81. The other sectors of economy health, literacy and income during the period were not very encouraging. Human Development Index was not available at that point of time. It came into the use only during the early period of 1990s. From that point of view, Table 2.1 is not comprehensive but just partial and illustrative only.

Table 2.1: Percentage of Rural-Urban Sexwise Workers among Total Main Workers (From 1951 to 1981) and Marginal Workers 1981 (in %)

	Sex	*1951*	*1961*	*1971*	*1981*	*1981**
Rural	Men	52	53	48	49	1.80
	Women	12	11	5	6	2.70
	Total	33	33	27	28	2.30
Urban	Men	61	55	50	49	0.9
	Women	9	5	4	5	0.9
	Total	41	35	30	29	0.9
Grand Total	Men	55	54	49	49	1.80
	Women	11	9	4	6	2.70
	Total	35	33	28	28	2.60

* Marginal Workers Percentage.

Source: Translated and Compiled by A.N. Basu, *Paschim Banger Arthoniti o Rajniti*, Nagarik Mancha, Calcutta, 1991.

It was a period of hopeless uncertainty and a phase of political aggrandizement. There were ideological differences among factions of the CPI (M). The extremists i.e. activists who used to oppose the party's participation in the electoral process were given the understanding that the law making body would be used to further the class struggle by taking over excess lands from the land owning classes. But the other group led by Jyoti Basu and the CPI (M) ideologue Hare Krishna Konar could not convince the extremist group led by Charu Mazumdar, Kanu Sanyal and Jangal Santal at North Bengal. After Hare Krishna Konar came back from North Bengal, to be precise Siliguri, the peasants led by the Charu Mazumdar and Kanu Sanyal started a revolt attacking jotdar and murdering people of dubious character and the class enemy as they perceived and even attempted to annihilate the ordinary police constables on duty. The first Naxalbari movement took its shape though in a ramshackle manner. The ultra-Leftist group still believed that adapting to a parliamentary path was a blunder. The CPI (M) leaders began influencing the police forces and wanted to use police administration and the general administrative machineries for their own party interests to root out the sporadic violence that began spreading in several parts of the state. Severe intra-party classes began. The CPI (M) with their party organization tried to spread horizontally to reduce the strength of the partners of the ULF and PULF coalition. A new party in the name CPI (ML) came into being challenging the hegemony of the CPI (M) in the UF coalition. Law and order in most part of the state was completely collapsed. The Bangla Congress, CPI and a few other parties were extremely disgruntled. On the advice of the governor Dharmavira President's Rule was imposed. The ordinary people and the toiling masses smelled conspiracy by the central Congress leadership in collaboration with the Bangla Congress Chief Ajoy Mukherjee, his lieutenant

Sushil Dhara and the state Congress leaders. Doubts in the minds of the people seemed not unfounded because of the frequent visits of the Union Home Minister Shree Gulzarilal Nanda in this state of turmoil. Jyoti Basu along with his party chief Promode Dasgupta was bitter and in a severe attacking mood. Political economy was in a disastrous stage at that point of time. Food prices were skyrocketing to an all time high of Rs. 5.00 a kilo (ridiculous as at present when the very low quality rice price rises to more than Rs. 20 per kilo!). Street fights, disturbances and slogan shouting by the Left political parties were rampant against Dr. Ghosh and the prevailing inflation. Dr. Prafulla Ghosh who was the Food Minister in the first UF regime with a group of breakaway members of the first UF formed the PDF government with the outside help of the Congress Party. But due to the peculiar politics of the Speaker Bijoy Banerjee the House could not function. The Speaker claimed in the House that he was having the key of the House and it was he who would decide whether the House would run or be under lock and key. Thereafter, the CPI (M) challenged the Governor Dharmavira's recommendations for President's Rule to the Calcutta High Court. But verdict of the High Court went in favour of the Governor acting in his discretionary power.

A second election took place in 1969 and the second UF coalition with the same parties came to power. This time the CPI (M) increased its strength (84 seats) that was by doubling its previous seat share. Again Ajoy Mukherjee was chosen to lead the coalition government although his Bangla Congress got quite a reduced number of seats this time around. There were currents and cross-currents among the parties. Every single party tried to enlarge its area of electoral influence. Particularly the CPI (M) was hell bent on dominating the political arena. The general administration and the police administration were almost completely over shadowed by the political dictate by the Deputy Chief Minister Jyoti Basu, an intolerant man, his party's State Secretary Pramode Dasgupta as also their party, CPI (M).

The second UF government could not stay more than 13 months in office. The Deputy Chief Minister Jyoti Basu and his party were dead bent on politicizing the general civil and police administration. The clerical staff of the government began insulting the Chief Minister Shree Ajay Kumar Mukherjee, even in the precinct of the Writers Buildings and around. A number of severe inter party clashes took places in different parts of the state. The CPI (M) leadership was trying to spread its organization to every corner at the cost of the other left parties of the UF coalition. The flash point was approaching at a quick pace. On the other side, the Naxalite violence started its salvo in the form of assassinating individuals, particularly the stray CPI (M) members and the police constables.

The second UF government was a victim of intra-party feuds and inter-party clashes. The Chief Minister Ajay Mukherjee and the Deputy Chief

Minister, Jyoti Basu were at loggerheads with each other, that was some sort of a cold war. The policy of the CPI (M) at that time was one of a policy of aggrandizement and attacking the opposing parties, be it the Congress or the partners of the UF. The flash point reached when the Chief Minister Ajoy Mukherjee reversed Jyoti Basu's order of transfer of a Gazol *Thana* officer at Malda. Some chosen IAS officers during those days helped Jyoti Basu carrying on his party objectives to politicize the upper echelons of West Bengal Bureaucracy.[13] The tension rose high and ultimately the Chief Minister declared a sit-in-strike at Karzon Park, against his own government and called it "barbaric and uncivilized".[14] The Chief Minister resigned on March 16, 1970. The second UF collapsed which infuriated the CPI (M). It called a state wise *Hartal* or strike on March 17, 1970 and unleashed unforeseen and most brutal attack and violence against the Congress Party leaders and their family in open day light at Pratapeswar Sibtala in the town of Burdwan. In Burdwan, a group of CPI (M) hoodlums led by Binay Konar, Khokan Sen alias Nirupam Sen, former Industry Minister till May 20, 2011, Manik Roy alias Anil Basu, all of them members of the state committee of the CPI (M) and many other cadre of the party, including a young SFI member who later on crowned a few government posts during the LF regime and ultimately retired as the Registrar of Jadavpur University, attacked the epi-centre of Congress activities—the house of the Sains.

It would be unfair if it is not mentioned here that Manik alias Anil Basu was the record vote getter from Arambag parliamentary constituency for many years. In a democratic system it may appear to many that it is almost absurd for a candidate to gain a margin of nearly six lakh votes defeating the main rival having his money deposit forfeited. The mob fury was severe and a select group as mentioned above speared the two Sain brothers and a youth Congress leader and two domestic helps. The Sain mother fainted; the sister and his one month old son were thrown into fire and like heroes, the marauders left the spot.[15] The eldest Sain brother Naba Sain who fled, later on was murdered by the hired killers of the CPI (M) within a year. During this period possibly the CPI (M) were trying to get back to their pet theory of class annihilation. The cadres of the party let loose a reign of terror threatening, that if necessary they would destroy Congress members and other opposition forces as they did in *Sainbari.* Simultaneously the Naxalite violence was in its peek. Instead of encircling the urban centres with the villages, actually they created an atmosphere of fear and insecurity in the minds of ordinary citizens. Both the CPI (M) and the Naxalities were at loggerheads and the latter were trying to eliminate CPI (M) cadres openly. None of the groups perhaps thought of the counter violence that might follow. Later during Siddhartha Shankar Ray regime before 1972 election, the CPI (M) helped the police identifying Naxalite dens[16] in Baranagar and Kashipur at Calcutta and around, killing more than 80 young Naxalites in a single operation on 12-14 August 1971. Afterwards the CPI (M) was cornered by the resurgent youth Congress activists and badly defeated by the Congress and won only 14 seats in 1972 election. This election was alleged to be rigged. There were grains of truth in the said allegation.[17] The CPI (M) boycotted the House for a period of five years. The CPI (M) cadres who were irresistible earlier during the period of 1967-69 till late 1971 had to face the Congress ire while Siddhartha Ray as central Minister for Education was holding the additional charge of West Bengal. They were afraid to confront the new Yuba Congress leaders like Priya Ranjan Dasmunshi, Subrata Mukherjee and others. These people were hell bent on retaliating as they suffered a lot at the hands of the CPI (M) cadres and members. It was a period of President's Rule in West Bengal. Dr. Asok Mitra in a public meeting as also within the House when the LF came to power in 1977, called the 1972 Assembly as the "House of Thieves" (*Chorerder Bidhan Sabha*).[18]

Again to take up the cue from Sain brother's murder, the then District Magistrate of Burdwan was absent from the town deliberately on that ill-fated day and the SP did not send the police to the place of the incident on time. By the goodness of an honest Naga police officer the police was ordered to reach the spot much later and arrested a few miscreants. Some were arrested but later let off free when the LF came into power in 1977. The case records were destroyed. The justice was never done till today. Even when Congress came to power in 1972 they did not take the matter; rather promoted some of the police officers and a top bureaucrat like Shri Tarun Dutta, an IAS officer, the then District Magistrate and the SP, Ramen Bhattacharya in Burdwan. Inter party clashes were in full swing. Unrecorded and clandestine murders were the order of the day. Satyajit Ray, in one of his remarkable films, "*Pratidandi*" (the storyline of was written by Sunil Ganguly), has depicted the period in a very sensitive ambience. The state as a whole was under Naxalite violence during this period.

After the failure of the two coalition experiments in 1967 and 1969, the Leftist forces went apart. The CPI (M) fought the election on its own in 1971 and bagged 113 seats in the Assembly but won nearly 35 per cent of the popular votes. This was the maximum percentage points of a vote share that CPI (M) alone garnered in comparison with its earlier records. This perhaps made the CPI (M) confident to propose for a social coalition that reflected later in arranging for political coalition (LF) with several parties in 1977. A government with the leadership of Ajoy Mukherjee joining Congress was formed in 1971 but it failed soon. This period was really a period of the "crisis of governance in West Bengal".[19] It was really the worst of time for the citizens of Bengal. They experienced enough of the politics of the Left. They were not only worried but mentally disgusted. Sensing the mood of the people it was not difficult to conclude that a change in the political atmosphere was all the more desirable. Siddhartha Shankar Roy by now a very powerful political leader of the Congress utilized the opportunities with a band of resurgent Yuba (Youth) Congress leaders like Priya Ranjan Das Munshi, Subrata Mukherjee, Kumud Bhattacharya, Lakshmi Kanta Basu and many others as stated above.

It was a time of complete political uncertainty. Due to Bangladesh crisis nearly nine million people both Hindus and Muslims crossed over to this side of the border. To feed and give shelter to such a large number of people in West Bengal, the government machineries were totally inadequate. The demographic balance of the state was disturbed. How to send back these displaced people after the birth of Bangladesh was also a great problem. Moreover like the Workers Party of Bangladesh, the CPI (M) in the state was of the opinion that India would not call back its soldiers from Bangladesh and might go in for an Indian colonial arrangement.[20] The CPI (M) used to spread the canard as a whispering campaign to attack Indian capitalism under the tutelage of Indira Gandhi.

After a good deal of wait and see policy, India had to intervene in the Bangladesh freedom struggle at retaliation of Pakistan's undeclared war with India on December 3, 1971. By now Smt. Gandhi had won the 1971 parliamentary election with a massive majority. Siddhartha Shankar Ray was the Minister for Education in her Cabinet. He was already given the additional charge to look after the political affairs of West Bengal. By this time the Shri Ray brought down the Leftist violence and consequent chaos let loose both by the Naxalites and the CPI (M). It was not a very good option but the youth Congress staff and police administration had to resort to some sort of counter violence to confront the Leftist violence and reduce the prevailing chaos in the state. The emergence of the Congress Party under the leadership of Siddhartha Shankar Ray with his young brand of youth leaders and being patronized by the then Prime Minister Indira Gandhi, was actually a political reaction against the political violence let loose by the CPI (M) and its break away factions. The youth Congress leaders during their student days in mid 1960s were heckled and sometimes treated shabbily by the organizational fronts of the CPI (M). Therefore, what these younger Congress leaders showed against the CPI (M) was but a political reaction. After the Congress came back to power, the younger leadership used even stronger arm tactics. Many a CPI (M) activists had to leave their original places. It was certainly not democratic but the CPI (M) leaders and members began bringing it constantly in their campaign against the Congress and the TMC in recent years. The CPI (M) in a more dangerous way was doing the same against the opposition parties. They captured village after village in different districts of the western belt of the state like, Lalgarh in West Medinipur, Bankura, Birbhum, Purulia and many other places to fulfill its well-designed political objectives.

During 1972 to the early 1977s, Siddhartha Ray's coalition government (PDA) with its partners CPI supporting the government from outside did enact certain people oriented legislations, like Panchayat Act, Building new administrative organizations like Comprehensive Area Development Project (CADP), Calcutta Metropolitan Development Act (CMDA) (now renamed KMDA after Calcutta was replaced by Kolkata recently), Housing Board to build government housing complexes for low and middle income groups. There were a few brilliant ministers in his cabinet like Bhola Sen, Ajit Panja, Kashi Kanta Moitra and many young talents. But factionalism within the Congress Party (*Nabha Congress* people used to say), was being encouraged by the Chief Minister himself to checkmate the rise and excessive ambitions of the younger ones. He even constituted an inquiry commissions against the *Bhusi Kelengkari* by Kasi Kanta Moitra—originally a socialist—and the corruptions of the younger ministers. Secondly, Siddhartha babu's name was sullied because of his association with pronouncements of the internal emergency declared by Indira Gandhi to retain her position as the Prime Minister. Siddhartha babu got many powerful politicians of the opposition, Rightists, Centrists and Socialists and Journalists, like Gour Kishore Ghosh, Barun Sengupta and others, sent behind the bars. Among the CPI (M) leaders, only one MP Shri Jyotirmoy Basu, was arrested from his Ballygunje house during the emergency. There was no denying that all this became the undoing the Congress in the country including West Bengal. An oligopolistic politics based on real and sometimes a ramshackle social coalition was propped up in this state.

In West Bengal, the Left Front Government which had been in power since 1977, again came back to power for the 7th time in a row in 2006 with a seat tally of 235 seats. The opposition parties could not provide any alternative political coalition or coalitions against the LF. During the last several years since 1989 the governments at the Centre were minority Governments i.e. Government without majority or sometimes minority coalition governments from outside by a major party. This type of Government is not new even in political system that is usually dominated by two major political parties.[21] The coalition governments are the norms in most other West European and smaller Scandinavian countries and even many a third world counties where proportional representations are incorporated in their constitutions. The LF coalition government sustains; how the LF coalition remained united despite frequent differences among the partners without any interruption for the last 34 years was really baffling. One explanation that claims validity was that the CPI (M) alone had the power to get absolute majority in all the elections, making other partners of the coalition superfluous. But the main partners never got away with the junior partner. Although in course of time, sine 1987 the CPI (M) took the major ministerial portfolios, like Industry, Health, Panchayat, Housing and Public Heath Engineering from the hands of the Revolutionary Socialist Party (RSP) and the Forward Bloc (FB). More often the CPI (M) took *expost facto* policy decision in their party secretariat then brought to the LF Committee. The partners made occasional noises but coalition partners here like other genuine coalitions elsewhere never left the CPI (M). If it were so, the Left coalition structure in West Bengal would have collapsed long back. It was like a political cartel like the activities of the economic oligopolistic structure in an imperfect political competitive situation in electoral arena (or in other parlance here it is taken for a market) in the state. Secondly, Jyoti Basu's managerial skill to contain the partners many a time saved the ugly situations. Even Buddhadeb and his important party colleagues were able to maintain the organization of the party-monolith till civil society movements of the Bhangar, Singur and Nandigram uprising began. These were all serious peasants' revolt when the government forcibly took away the fertile lands from the poor farmers to sell them in throw away prices to the national and international industrialists. They were more than willing to incorporate a programme of setting up Special Economic Zones (SEZ) in different parts of the state. In fact they already began the programme in the sector-V at Salt Lake City, Kolkata.

As stated above, in West Bengal a coalition arrangement with the CPI (M) as the surplus majority partner has been continuing since 1977. Only after 2001 Assembly election the dominant party CPI (M) lost absolute majority.[22] Actually, the CPI (M) has been holding majority seats in the Assembly all through in coalition with a few Leftist political parties and two factions of breakaway Janata Party (JP). The Communist Party of India (CPI) joined the Front in early 1980s. Even a Naxalite faction joined the Left Front political coalition as junior partner[23] without having a seat in the House. The undivided Communist Party carried on relentless movements in all fronts against the establishment and brought smaller opposition parties together. The politics of opposition was conditioned by several factors mainly geographical, economic and societal. West Bengal inherited a truncated state with a long borderline with Bhutan, Bangladesh and Nepal. The difficulties resulting from poverty, unemployment, underemployment and population growth and relentless propaganda against the Congress establishment gave them exceptional dividends first in the late 1960s and then again in late 1970s.

This is significant that a slight swing of 2 to 3 per cent of votes might have reduced the seats won by the LF since 1977 although it has been enjoying power due to a very low Index of Opposition Unity (IOU). The Congress Party was determined not to have any understanding with BJP direct or indirect through Trinamool Congress (TMC). Paradoxically, it was often found that in many of the panchayat bodies and some municipal bodies including Calcutta Municipal Corporation, there was clandestine understanding among the three parties that won them majority in those panchayats and municipalities.

In 2001 election the LF secured a total of 48.94 percentage points showed that the shares of the major partners of LF were 47.07 giving a 1.87 per cent points to the smaller partners like WBSP, SP, and FB (M). The Congress and Trinamool Congress combine secured only 38.92. The BJP's share of votes of nearly 11.50 per cent that it secured in parliamentary election in 1999 has been reduced to 5.19 per cent only. The LF's almost outstanding performance in 2001 Assembly election after its vote shares in 1999 parliamentary election, is very significant. Surprisingly the CPI (M) not only averted its decline but improved its position both in terms of seat shares and percentage points of valid votes cast. The BJP being slighted by the Trinamool Congress (TMC) when it severed ties with the NDA, mounted a sustained campaign against the party and wanted to defeat it even if voting in favour of the CPI (M) wherever it was possible.[24] The LF crossed over the hurdles it faced in the 2001 Assembly election having lesser number of seats as well as reduced percentage share of valid votes cast but in 2004 parliamentary election, the LF regained its positions in terms of vote shares. It proves the LF's extraordinary acumen for electoral management at a time when it was really difficult to tide over the difficulties of a stagnant situation or decline because of the incumbency factors. Due to vote-seat distortion natural for the First Past The Post (FPTP) system, the LF won 25 seats getting slightly more than 50 per cent of the valid votes; the Congress won six seats on the basis of its 14.56 per cent vote but BJP-TMC combine won only one seat while their vote shares were 29.10 per cent. It was to some extent the slight revival of the Congress but disaster for the Trinamool Congress due to a complete absence of seat adjustment to build up any alternative coalition of sorts. The relation between the Congress and the TMC was never very cordial. Once in 1997, Mamata Banerjee, the most promising and uncompromising Congress leader against the CPI (M), was defeated by the party electoral maneuver of Somen Mitra in the election of President of the state Congress organization. Mamata came to realize that many of the leaders were more happy having got loaves and fishes from the powerful state apparatus, than to fight against it. With the party as whole at her bidding, Mamata wanted to be the president of state party. Mamata was even ditched by the All India Congress Party Chief Sonia Gandhi by not coming to a pre-arranged meeting with Mamata Banerjee at the site of the Gandhi statue at Mayo Road. A Congress Committee meeting with Somen Mitra and other leaders were being held at Netaji Indoor Stadium, Sonia Gandhi to tie up the two warring factions gave an understanding that she would come to meet Mamata.[25] But at the appointed time Ajit Panja came out from the Stadium and told the gathering led by Mamata that Mrs. Gandhi would not meet them.

This was the beginning of solo journey of Mamata Banerjee with her trusted comrades. On January 1, 1998, Mamata formed her own party, Trinamool Congress (TMC), and within a short span of time TMC became the largest parliamentary democratic party in the state far outnumbering the age old Congress Party in the state. When all attempts to patch up with Congress went the wrong way, Mamata with some very important leaders like Ajit Panja, Sudip Banerjee and others broke away from the original Party.

The growth of population in the state and its density in comparison with other Indian states is abnormal. The quantum of its growth has greatly to contribute to the voting populations. No political party gives any attention to this serious problem, rather for political gains, encouraged the same even to the risk of abnormal demographic changes. Regular infiltration from beyond the border, mostly for economic reasons had been adversely affecting the economy of the state. Without exception, all the political parties, but mostly the ruling establishment, were in favour of allowing them the ration cards and voting identity cards.

The increase of voters in the state before each of the elections since 1977 has been phenomenal. There are several reasons for such increase in the number of voters. The fact is that this occasional bout of increase in the number of voters mostly went in favour of the LF coalition—quite contrary to the popular perceptions that larger voter participation usually go against the ruling establishment. The CPI (M) continued to have overwhelming support of these refugees[26] till the Parliamentary and Assembly elections in 1991. But during 1998 and 1999 Parliamentary elections, a different trend was found in the voting patterns in the refugee belts in and around Calcutta. The older generation of people among them was found to utter their disillusionment with Left Front Government. The CPI (M)'s relations with real estate middlemen and promoters associating anti-social elements working in tandem with lower level corrupt police officials alienated many of the erstwhile supporters of the so called Communists.

The newer generation of voters belonging to refugee families is a lot quite different. Culturally they are on a different plane from their predecessors. Most of them do not care for the "tedious propaganda" during election time as to how the leftists had to face the organized state repression during the early-seventies. History of sufferings of the people uprooted from the former East Pakistan and their miserable plight of living in makeshift refugee camps and urban shanties. These younger people have to face the brunt of unemployment and often suffer from a sense of existential purposelessness[27]. They also watch with contempt the life style of the political leaders and their association with promoters, contractors, men of the underworld and men of the shady character as well.

The political space, which was occupied by the Congress earlier, has been gradually taken over by the breakaway rebel Congressmen with Mamata Banerjee as the Chief of a newly formed Trinamool Congress Party (TMC) before the Parliamentary election in 1998. The Left Front has ruled West Bengal for long with the Congress party as the only opposition force. It has been, as if, perennially unable to really play an effective role as an opposition party to articulate the demands of people and make the present Government respond to the needs of all sections of people. *They are in a habit of voicing against the partisan attitude of the administrators in the fields of education, health, poverty alleviations, running local bodies like panchayats and urban civic affairs* (emphasis added).

To many people in Bengal the Congress Party has become a fortune-seeker and almost an appendage of the Left Front Government. The Central leadership also did not want to disturb the government of Jyoti Basu in anticipation of his support if necessary to snatch the governmental power from BJP-led Government or make an alliance to form a coalition after the election. The "*agnikannya*"[28] or firebrand leader of the Congress party, Mamata Banerjee, in the political process became the only focal point of anti-left movements and activities. Her capabilities to mobilize people's support from among the lower middleclass, women and the younger people of the state could not but be reckoned with. Mamata, after being expelled from the Congress Party, immediately formed her party, TMC. She made alliance with the BJP, before the 1998 parliamentary election. The TMC won seven seats conceding only one seat to the Congress. Surprisingly, the BJP, for the first time, won a seat (Dum Dum Tapan Sikdar from North 24 Parganas). The support of the younger generation of urban young voters, educated sections among the people and a large number of erstwhile displaced persons were behind the victory of the TMC and BJP combine. The BJP's rise in West Bengal was an "ominous" signal to the leftists — particularly the CPI (M) in 1998. The Dum Dum seat won by the BJP was a very important constituency. It was an area with a large concentration of refugee settlements, the upper and lower middle classes in Salt Lake and its surrounding areas. During this election it was reported in many newspapers and a section of the CPI (M) party leaders as well expressed that a large number of dissident CPI (M) members, with Subhas Chakraborty as their leader, helped the BJP candidate to win the prestigious Dum Dum seat to teach a lesson to the CPI (M)'s leadership in the district of North 24-Parganas and the heavyweight leaders of the CPI (M) Headquarters. In the election of 1999 the leadership of the CPI (M) left no stone unturned to win back. But the BJP consolidated its position with a larger margin of two seats.

It is true that emergence of BJP as a genuine political force can be traced back to 1989 parliamentary election. Before 1989 the BJP did not even get more than 5 per cent of votes, not to speak of winning a seat in the state. But in a massive rally the CPI (M) Chief Minister, Jyoti Basu, joined hands with BJP's Atal Bihari Vajpayee along with Viswanath Pratap Singh. To Viswanath Pratap Singh the single agenda was to defeat Rajiv Gandhi and dislodge the Congress and dislodge the Central Government. The CPI (M) and their leader Jyoti Basu were now constantly warning the people of West Bengal against the 'Hindu Communalism' of the BJP but never acknowledged the fact that they themselves for their electoral gains and to occupy a respectable political space at the national level were no less responsible for the rise of the BJP in the state. The change in the social composition and certain demographic changes in West Bengal in recent years combined with breakup of the Congress party resulting in the formation of Trinamool Congress, are also to be taken into account for the rise of BJP in West Bengal, since the parliamentary election in 1998.

Protest Movements against the Government Policies

Again to look back, the historical, cultural, demographic-cultural, social and economic factors have determined the politics in West Bengal. The state is unique in its political process. Protest movements by the radicals—particularly the Marxists and the variant of Maxims since Independence, the fallouts of the Partition and Indo-Pak Wars in 1965 and 1971 with consequent influx of thousands of refugees crossing over the porous border, demographic changes as a result of the influx of Muslims in search of work in the border districts of Dinajpur, Malda, Murshidabad, Nadia and 24 Parganas, unresponsiveness of the long-lasting Congress rule, the organizational weaknesses of the party are some of the many factors that have determined the politics of the state and consequently defined the orientation of the politics of the Left parties. There still other reasons. A large group of people left the Congress Party. During elections of 1952, many of them formed political party of their own and subsequently participated in the elections after elections. These political parties had certainly some social bases. But the party bosses of a large number of parties were unable to read it; or in other words they did not think of any coalition situation. They always fought the Congress in a very fragmented manner paving the way for the Congress Party to remain in power for such a long period of time.

West Bengal bearing the legacy of remarkable history, both politically and comically with a radical image is now, after partition, a truncated and weak state with a long line of porous border. It comprises a total area of 88,752 sq. kms with a population of 8,01,97,176 as per the Census Report 2001. The growth rate of population is more than 25 per cent during the decade 1981-19910. The decade between 1991 and 2000 has seen much larger growth of population than that of the previous decade. From the neighbouring countries like Bangladesh and Nepal, it is not difficult for Nepalese particularly the Bangladeshis mostly Muslims, to enter into India in a clandestine manner and settle in West Bengal with the help of political leaders and their parties. An abnormal increase in the number of voters is recorded in the border districts over the years.

Since 1977, the Left Front has been running the state uninterrupted. It is some sort of a record that a group of Leftist Parties, despite having love and hate relation with each other are maintaining the political coalition, which was actually the reflection of a *social coalition* that began crystallizing since the late 1970s. The moment this social coalition is disturbed, the Left Front will suffer a serious existential crisis. Actually, it is the critical political mobilization that the Left parties in opposition carried on in the social arena. Factionalism within the Congress in West Bengal, threw the Congress out power in 1967 after 17 years of its rule and then again in 1977 after a decade. The Left parties were able to capture power by focusing on, and propagating by dubious means against the corruption of Congress and its leaders. The Congress government failed to properly respond to the demands of the people as well. The third phase began with Siddhartha Sankar Ray as the Chief Minister. But this government after a period of initial stability was subjected to an extreme type of factionalism. The mainstay of this government was the young Congress leaders at that time. Siddhartha Ray to wanted keep his hold on Central government and show to Smt. Indira Gandhi, that he commanded the party singlehandedly. He, therefore, had to maintain dossiers against each of the young ministers in his cabinet. These naturally irritated leaders and they began distancing themselves from each other that ultimately divided the party in different factions. The Left parties on the basis of past experience of the late sixties came closer to each other. They formed a solid front and dominated the Bengal politics, economy and society for much over three decades from 1977 till May 20, 2011.

However, a political coalition arrangement that still has been continuing for the last 34 years is itself an achievement for the major Left parties. The credit largely goes to the CPI (M) and its capacity for electoral management, political mobilization—both direct and mediated, and organizational network, although the junior partners are often aggrieved over its "big brotherly attitude". After 1977 election victory, the Left Front came to realize that it had to spread out to the rural areas, which once were mostly the areas of influence of the Congress.[29] The panchayat raj legislation enacted by Siddhartha Ray Government was actually implemented by the first LF Government and received overwhelming response from rural Bengal. The LF Government also undertook a package of land reforms. The late Hare Krishna Konar wrote profusely in his party paper in the late sixties about the essentiality of the same. The government began distributing vested lands to the small farmers and marginal peasants through a process of *Operation Barga*. The LF Government has been successfully working on political development of the state and has "really brought about a change in the development of rural economy since 1977".[30] For such a long period of time for a "social democratic" party or a combination of parties to remain in power, with such little opposition either in the House or outside in the social plane, have its negative effects and pitfalls. Tensions grow within the party itself and organizational discipline and governmental activities begin to lose directions.

The opposition Congress Party despite its organizational deficiencies and individualized leadership began to acquire strength manifesting in the Assembly election in 1996. The rural areas for all these years were reserved, as it were for the combined left party coalition. The rural *jotedar* class switched over to the LF particularly after 1978 when the LF began to gain most of the panchayat bodies in all the three tiers. The ambitious local leaders of the CPI (M) began asserting themselves both socially and economically and culturally as well. The system of education level came under the domination of the largest partner CPI (M). The bureaucracy and the lower level authorities enforcing land reforms policies directly or indirectly helped the local party bosses to be the arbitrators of the destinies of the villagers. The local party committees and important leaders of the CPI (M) were seen to be the "dispenser of justice".[31] Enormous amount of money and materials in the name of rural development funds came in the hands of these leaders. Many of the rural poor who got lands could not cultivate them either for reasons of their own or for lack of agricultural or other material inputs, were compelled to sell out their lands. The local leaders in a clandestine manner purchased those pieces of land-mass or the local *jotedars* took away the lands for a pittance and hired the landless farmers once again to labour on their regained lands. With the nexus of the political leaders, lower level bureaucrats and land reforms enforcing authorities forming a "new class"[32] in the rural areas came to dominate socio-economic scenario of the rural hinterlands. The hierarchies of rich and middle class peasantries in the rural backyards helped them. This continued for over a decade, which ultimately resulted in the crack of the social condition that helped the Left parties together to garner their support base in the past. In this connection the following recent comment of a political analyst is relevant. "The bulwark of landless and poor peasants that they had built for the party's organization was badly breached by their creation of a new class of haves among the have-nots. So wide was the breach that they were unable to retain their traditional support base and allowed Trinamool Congress, a breakaway group led by Mamata Banerjee from the Congress in the eve of 1998 parliamentary election to make deep inroads into their strongholds either through persuasive or coercive skills." Actually the "alienation had begun much earlier. The panchayat pradhans and schoolmasters had antagonized their own comrades by institutionalizing nepotism".[33] The sign of alienation was seen in the Assembly election of 1996 when the Congress won 82 seats. The Congress was split in regard to the question of Pradesh Congress leadership. Mamata Banerjee was expelled from the party and formed her own outfit—Trinamool Congress (TMC). She made an understanding with the BJP. The Trinamool Congress fought the Panchayat election on May 28, 1998 independently. But an unwritten and invisible understanding was made among the anti-left forces including the Congress's dissatisfied supporters and a portion of BJP members at the local levels. For obvious reasons of organizational superiority and an element of fear psychosis[34] among the entire poor rural people, the Left Front won most of the *Zilla Parishad* seats and Panchayat *Samities* but had to feel a jolt in the third tier of the rural local *Gram Panchayat* levels. The Left Front had to lose many of the *Panchayat Samiti* seats and nearly a third of the *Gram Panchayat* seats. This is for the first time during the last twenty years that the leaders of the LF had to confront the reality that their hold over rural Bengal was not as closely knit as it had been. The social coalition that backed the pre-poll political coalition of the Left parties began indicating the first sign of fissures not only in urban areas but also in rural backyards where the fiats of the local CPI (M) leaders were the last words.[35] But it is often found that for a corporate body like political organization with modern gadgets to oversee and manage electoral process in each and every election at all levels was just a part of the political game

Industrial Policies of the Left Front Government

As stated earlier a large number of interest groups are backing the LF government. Sometimes individual members give vent to their dissatisfaction but on the question of a change of government they are afraid to disturb the *status quo*. The LF has been enjoying a massive support base in the rural backyards and most of the fringe urban areas at least till the Singur and Nandigram movements of the peasant communities. Different Interest groups viz. the *Kisan Sabha* [CPI (M) affiliated], the powerful Primary Teachers' Association, All Bengal Teachers' Association (ABTA), the West Bengal College and University Teachers Association (WBCUTA), the non-gazetted Police Association, *Ganatantrik Mahila Samity, Ganatantrik Lekhak Silpi Sangha, etc.* and above all the State Government Employees Co-ordination Committee and others are solidly behind the LF. Most of the commercial houses namely Bengal Chamber of Commerce, Bharat Chamber of Commerce, Federation of Indian Chambers of Commerce and Industries, and many others were quite sympathetic to the objectives of the LF. They were also afraid of aggressive trade union movements launched particularly by the Centre for Indian Trade Unions (CITU), affiliated to the CPI (M) as it did during its earlier UF incarnations in the late 1960s. A two-pronged strategy was perceptible in the politics of the LF. The LF was afraid of computer related systems but on the other hand it did not revive the tradionally large and medium sized industries like jute mills, pharmaceutical and manufacturing industries that were getting sick gradually over the period of time since late 1970s. The LF could not think of agro industries, the tea gardening and tea processing industries which were once the pride of West Bengal during the period of Dr. Bidhan Chandra Roy and then Prafulla Chandra Sen earlier in 1950s and till mid-60s. But gradually the support base of some of the organizations began cracking. The LF led by Jyoti Basu possibly was complacent in the context of what it did in working out to further the land reform programmes and Operation Barga. The effects were quite visible in the election results of panchayats. The ultimate fall out was that neither the agricultural systems nor the industrial scenario improved perceptibly during the LF era. The Chief Minister attempted overhauling the system and visited different Western countries including East European ones to invite foreign direct investment (FDI). In 1994 the LF Government restructured the West Bengal Industrial Development Corporation (WBIDC). The chairmanship of the corporation was given to Shree Somnath Chatterjee, a long time CPI (M) member and the MP. The WBIDC decided to acquisition lands for the prospective investors both non-resident Indian (NRI) and other foreign investors. Even after making some policy decisions and the urge to implement them, industrial scenario did not improve as they had expected. On the other hand, they allowed a horizontal spread of real estate business transactions and promoting business industries even in the premises of closed industrial locations. A new class of real estate promoters expanded its clutches throughout the state. In the name of urbanization they did not even spare the peasants. The CPI (M) resorted to acquire their fertile two and three cropped lands in exchange for a mere pittance. The scenario began deteriorating from semi urban to rural areas till it culminated in peasant movements in Singur, Nandigram, Rajarhat, Bhangar and even Nayachar, a newly formed soft island in the Bay of Bengal near the confluence of river Haldi in East Midnapore. Buddhadeb Bhattacharya and his Minister for Industry made several deals with Beni Santosha of Indonesia for building up Roads, Hotels and multiplexes and Chemical Hubs and Ratan Tata of Tata Group of Companies to start a Nano Car Factory. It was too much for the peasants and the rural lower middle class of people in the state. The main opposition TMC and its uncompromising leader Ms. Mamata Banerjee rightly capitalized these movements. During those movements, a section of the intellectuals, established people belonging to arts, culture, music, literature, Group Theaters and Bengali cinema artists raised their voice for a change of the guard in the state. Some of them went little further and supported Mamata Banerjee in her uncompromising campaign against the LF government led by the CPI (M). Many professors and sections of intellectuals, not belonging to the mainline socio-political activities, wanted even to make the CPI (M) irrelevant in Indian Politics. To them as revealed from various misdeeds and other facts of violence let loose by the leaders of the regime in different parts of the state and continuing ruthlessness of the CPI (M), the LF regime was out and out an "evil" that should be rooted out from the body politic of India.[36]

Actually two factors converged to focus on the democracy deficit in the state. First, the mandate for the CPI (M) in 2006 Assembly election rose from 143 seats i.e. below benchmark, to 176 and LF as a whole from 199 to 235 made Buddhadeb Bhattacharjee the CM too over confident to overlook the interest of the peasants. These communities were mostly of minority groups like Muslims, SC, ST and other so-called OBCs. In a state where tracts of cultivable fertile lands were scarce, the government should have taken sufficient care to acquire the same in the name of industrialization by modern technology which provided insufficient job opportunities required for a very large number of eligible unemployed. The cultivable lands bore the identification of the life and living of the peasants as it manifested in the peasants' movements in various places in the state. Secondly, Buddhadeb babu's idea of "developing capitalism to reach up to socialism" as he and his Minister for Industry, Sri Nirupam Sen, used to utter during those days of turmoil that began immediately after 2006 election victory, was infantile to say the least. Some utterances of the administrative head of the state against the opposition political parties, members of the civil society groups were atrocious. The police actions and barbarities against the villagers both at Singur and Nandigram were horrendous and absolutely unacceptable. The Calcutta High Court also disapproved the police actions, particularly at Nandigram. Other high-ranking colleagues of the party like Benoy Konar, Shyamal Chakraborty, Anil Basu and Md. Selim uttered languages against the TMC supremo Mamata Banerjee and important members of the civil society groups were almost slang and nearly "uncivilized".[37] The two factors mentioned above along with others determined the fate of the LF in 2009 and 2011. Over the last several years, particularly the last five years since September, 2006, the LF and more precisely the CPI (M) has been losing its hold over the Muslims, other backward castes, but not so much over the scheduled tribes and other deprived economic classes and the dalits. It was because of the LF's front policy of surreptitious land grabbing measures for the purposes of allowing to build up special economic zones (SEZ). For the first time, a number of civil society groups stood against the policy of the LF. This movement was further strengthened by the revolt of the poor peasants, mostly Muslims and other backward castes, landless labourers, *barga chachhi* (hired labourers from other places). The movements in different places gradually gathered momentum. The Trinamool supremo took advantage of the volatile situations. The provincial Congress and the BJP could not understand the ground reality and did not join hands with the Trinamool Congress for reasons of their own. Subsequently, the Congress could not but to have an electoral understanding with the TMC for their survival in the state. For, after the panchayat elections in 2008, the TMC was gaining all the by-elections in the state. There was seat adjustment between the TMC and the Congress in 2009 parliamentary election. The result was remarkable. The new combination brought down the seat share of the LF from 35 to 15 only. It had been a grave set back for the CPI (M) since 1977. Yet the Congress in order to prove its individual electoral strength did not go in for a seat adjustment formula in 80 Municipal seats in 2010 election, throughout the state, including the election of Kolkata Municipal Corporation. The result was an almost decimation of the Congress in the Kolkata Municipal Corporation election that made the Party again to join hands with the TMC in the Assembly election in 2011. This election was a disaster for the LF. The seat share of the CPI (M) came down from 176 to 42 only and the LF's total of 235 to 62 only. The CPI (M) became the poorer third while Congress Party increased its share from 23 to 42.

There are certain committed interest groups that have always been supporting the LF during the last 30 years. They have derived much benefit from the ruling front.[38] All through these long stints the LF and the partners have always been trying to expand their electoral bases as well as attempted to consolidate its position among the rural peasants almost giving them no succours, and the middle class service holders. As already stated, the front organizations of the parties, the teachers, students, non-teaching employees, businessmen, labourers—collectively and individually, small time industrialists always tried to hang around the major ruling party and front.

It is a common phenomenon elsewhere that the ruling party or coalition of parties after an innings or two in running the government is seen to suffer from anti-incumbency factor. In West Bengal the anti-incumbency factors were conspicuously absent and the ruling front rather enjoyed some sort of a pro-incumbency wave[39] till the panchayat elections in 2008. The decline of the LF actually appeared to be very clear after the results of the three-tier panchayat elections were declared. The fall of the LF was a matter of certainty. The CPI (M) tried every possible means to disturb the Congress—TMC seat adjustments in 2009 parliamentary election. But this time it miserably failed. The Left Front came into power in West Bengal in the wake of the Janata Party wave in 1977 immediately after Indira Gandhi lifted the "infamous, 25th June internal emergency" of 1975. Once the Front came, it began consolidating itself. It was expected by the political analysts and feared by the leaders of the LF that in the face of a challenge thrown by Mamata Banerjee, the Front might have lost the 2001 election—the most crucial for the last 24 years of the LF rule. But the final results proved otherwise. The only change that took place was that the CPI (M) had to lose its predominant hold over the Front. It could not, unlike five earlier elections, secure absolute majority. For the first time West Bengal was having a genuine coalition formation, although the CPI (M) was still the dominant party in the then coalition structure.

The situation, during the past several years and more particularly since 2001 Assembly Election, can aptly be described by the definition that West Bengal has been politically structured as a predominant party regime with smaller parties with ideological nearness has given rise to a political system of "consociationalism" to borrow the term from Ljjphart.[40] Despite having theoretical posture, the LF failed to be development oriented. The industrial scenario was bleak. Agricultural growth was stagnant. The employment situation was getting worse.

It is really puzzling, even in the face of so many odds, as to how it is possible for the LF to sustain itself in a very democratically conscious State— "without rabid caste considerations"[41] as is found elsewhere in other Indian states, and with an anti-establishment-prone people for such a long period of time. The one major factor that came to be easily recognizable had been almost the total absence of a viable opposition. The Congress Party was still unable to regain its social base and be got rid of the political trauma that afflicted it during the mid-seventies. There are other very important factors as analyzed by Atul Kohli in a very perceptive study.[42] The LF Government appears to maintain a popular image of responsible and radical governing coalition. Locally anti-Congressism and broadly a rabid anti-BJP political stance give it a distinct regional nationalist halo that helps it create a division among the opposition political parties. Finally, a perennially weak central rule is what the LF political establishment always desires. The objectives of the predominant CPI (M) in the ruling front as transpired from its party manifesto brought out during all types of elections — national, regional and local are supposed to inject certain amount of "redistributive justice" in the process of economic development and to remove rural poverty by restructuring rural local governments. But later the rhetoric of social justice appeared to be ephemeral. The rural bases of the ruling front earlier were sufficiently stable. The party or combination of the parties to capture political power in West Bengal must have the majority support of the panchayat bodies in West Bengal, which required a very well knit and hugely spread out party organization. This was the strongest point in favour of the CPI (M). The opposition parties appeared to be completely divided and inimical with each other as appeared during last four elections. But the situation radically changed in the three-tier Panchayat elections in 2008. In the Zilla Parishad election the LF was capable of retaining only 52 per cent but in other two tiers of Panchyat—Panchayat Samitis and Gram Panchayats its vote share came down to less than 48 per cent. The combined opposition particularly the Congress and TMC captured nearly 50 per cent share.

It is always found that the parliamentary election results more or less reflect the trends of West Bengal politics in terms of number of seats won by major political parties particularly the party or the combination of parties forming the government in the state. The voters like to use their votes in West Bengal with utmost caution and have some degree of discretion; they would make a distinction between electing the members of the state Assembly and the members of the Lok Sabha. The votes for the Lok Sabha were meant for political stability which would make sure that the country's integrity, diversities be maintained and the strategies, against fissiparous forces might not be jeopardized. The state government would be formed by the parties for meeting the proximate needs and demands of the people of the state. But a near total politicization pervaded in every stages of electoral process, the earlier distinction being obliterated.

The party or a coalition of parties in power has the privileges and the political hold to exploit the administrative machineries and the law and order maintenance authorities to its or their advantages. This is the reason for which the opposition parties are voicing the demands that the state elections should be made under President's rule or under a neutral authority in the state. The then Chief Election Commissioner Dr. M.S. Gill also in this connection emphasized the long-standing contention that what was required in the state elections was a neutral government in the run-up to the elections.[43]

The First Ever Challenge to the Left Front after Two Decades

When 1998 parliamentary election was held, the Congress Party in West Bengal was already split. Factionalism in Indian party system was not new. The Communist Party's split was sought to be explained in terms of their ideological moorings, something novel in the nineties. The CPI (M) was beset with factionalism in several district committees. This factionalism in recent times was not due to any ideological debates. After having enjoyed almost unopposed supremacy for long, some of the district leaders came into conflict with each other to increase their share of gains and influences both at the district and state committee levels. The continuous enjoyment of political power dictated them to increase the sphere of influences by means "fair or foul". The CPI (M) seemed to apply its Leninist principles that were diluted in its continued adjustment with and adapting to the parliamentary system of governance. Atul Kohli found that CPI (M)'s "parliamentary communism",[44] and "democratic centralism" made the party much more cohesive and disciplined than any other Indian political party. The largest national party, the Congress, on the other hand, appeared to have been suffering from perennial factionalism. The Congress Party's latest setback was about the question of the office of the Pradesh Congress Committee. The quarrel between Soumen Mitra and Mamata Banerjee came to such a pass that Mamata Banerjee had to run a parallel organization and ultimately was expelled from the party. The majority of the rank and file, particularly most of the younger people went out with her. Many of the Congress leaders overtly or covertly had the habit of enjoying some sort of patronage from the LF Government in terms of having Government housing land, Government-built flats, sons and daughters admitted in medical and engineering institutions out of chief minister's quota, etc. These leaders almost lost the confidence of the lower ranks of party workers. Mamata Banerjee formed her Trinamool Congress (TMC) and in no time appeared to become the symbol of anti-CPI (M) force in West Bengal. To her the one point programme was "to dislodge the authoritarian and corrupt CPI (M)" from power.[45]

The Idea of a Grand Alliance (Mahajot)

Mamata Banerjee floated the idea of a *mahajot* (grand alliance) of Trinamool Congress-BJP combine with the Congress party. The Left Front and its leaders became nervous. They began increasing their tempo of propaganda against the BJP about its "vicious Hindu communalism" and its patron Mamata Banerjee in West Bengal. The grand alliance or the *mahajot* appeared to the CPI (M) as a "conspiracy" and political "opportunism" on the part of the Congress.[46] The central and state leaders of the CPI (M) did not like Sonia Gandhi to go in for an alliance with Mamata Banerjee with BJP as her junior partner in West Bengal politics. Sonia Gandhi, who might have to depend on the left forces in some future plan of government formation in case the National Democratic Alliance (NDA) disintegrated, foreclosed the option. Secondly, the BJP with its "hidden communal agenda"[47] was the main political competitor of the Congress, as the second largest party it could not share the same socio-political space.[48]

Later in that year in a by-election the Left Front could not retain the Panskura parliamentary seat. The CPI (M) made it a prestige issue and used all sorts of epithets against Mamata Banerjee as a "symbol of bad politics and disruption."[49]

Objectives, Manifestoes, Issues and related Problems and the Campaign Style

It is to be generally noted that the objectives of the Manifestos though contextual remain more or less same for all the parties. The CPI (M) as the major partner of the LF declared before the election that the BJP government in its 13-month stint proved conclusively that the party was guided by the RSS. It believed in '*Hindutva*' and was committed to dismantle the 'secular democratic values' of the Indian Republic. The CPI (M) "stands against war and ultra-nationalism but for peace and patriotism".[50] The party stood against 'fascism' of the 'communal' forces and striving for 'democracy and secularism'. It was against "imperial expansionism" and stood for "national self respect". It was for 'economic self reliance' and fought all sorts of neo-colonial dominations'. The party promised to establish social justice against feudal and casteist exploitations. With a view to launching measures for social welfare, the party would fight against 'deprivation and secessionism'.[51] The TMC in its manifesto "pledged for emancipation of Bengal from the Marxist misrule".[52] The manifesto promised, among other things, a progressive move for alleviating the sufferings of the economically depressed, industrialization of Bengal, a comprehensive "package on priority basis for the minority, and for their socio-economic development and special reservation for the employment of women".[53]

Jyoti Basu spearheaded the campaign for the Left Front candidates. In many of the well-attended mass meetings he was the star attraction.[54] Jyoti Basu often in his usual style described the BJP government at the Centre as "uncivilized and barbaric". All these utterances might not sound pleasing to the discerning voters. Mamata Banerjee and her party leaders talked to the masses about the 'corruption' of the Left Front government and focused on the 'corrupt nexus between the CPI (M) and the real estate managers, promoters and men of questionable character'.[55]

By and large this has been largely continuing till the parliamentary elections in 1999 and 2004, Assembly elections in 2001 and 2006. It indicates the CPI (M)'s overwhelming organizational strength and superior "politico-electoral money and muscle power and management".[56] The recruits of the party leaders have been confined to the middle levels of society. A monolithic structure is subjected to stress and strains, which ultimately results in the politics of dissidence within. In the 1999 Lok Sabha election the CPI (M) received a jolt at the hands of the Trinamool Congress and the BJP combine. On the basis of evidence, particularly in the face of polarization between urban and rural voters, it can be concluded that the Trinamool's gain was based on negative votes and the rural base of the CPI (M) was not intact as it had been in 1998 and in previous elections.[57] In fact the 2001 Assembly election was a four-cornered contest. The other two fronts were Saifuddin's PDS, the NCP of Sharad Pawar and BJP.

The ultimate result was the victory for the LF for the sixth time, which was "quite unexpected".[58] Even to the leaders of the LF who had to almost reorganize the election machinery and fought the toughest battles in their own words with the back against the wall. The ultimate result appeared to be a little reduced mandate for the LF. The TMC and Congress combine anticipated that the larger participation of the voters would go in favour of the opposition parties. But they were bewildered to find the results. The anti incumbency factor did not work excepting that the CPI (M)'s seat share was reduced to

143 only. After some 24 years the LF became truly a coalition; it was all along was an oversized coalition CPI (M) always holding the surplus majority.[59]

The comparative figures of parliamentary elections in perspective have been taken into consideration. Even showing his clean image and appearing to be more honest than his predecessor Jyoti Basu, Buddhadeb could not redeem his pledge of giving a clean administration as proved by the result of 2001 election. But surprisingly the results of the 2006 Assembly election belied not only the expectations of the political analysts and discerning public but the LF partners also. The Left Front bagged 235 seats and won 50.12 per cent votes. If the matter was looked from other angle at least theoretically a paradoxical scenario appeared to the analysts. By fielding 294 candidates in the fray the LF won a total of 50.12 per cent votes in 2006. It was found, in a calculation on the basis of voting data and vote seat distortion because of FPTPS, that the winning candidates (235) of LF secured only 40.06 per cent. In the meanwhile Buddhadeb appeared to be a Brand Buddha Marxist *Bhadralok* image accepting the liberal parliamentary principles. He allowed himself to be packaged as a modern leader willing to fulfill the aspirations of the middle class and young first time voters. This might be his strong point in overwhelmingly winning the 2006 Assembly elections. His main rival Mamata Banerjee of the TMC did not care for the finer points of the changed circumstances of the newly emerging politics of the state. She did not care to package herself to be a leader acceptable to the most sections of the voters. Her single point of agenda was to remove the CPI (M) Government. She became popular but was no match for the organizational strength and acumen of the CPI (M). She was able to pull a massive crowd in her peculiar ways and sympathetic wavelength with the ordinary masses but was often unable to translate the voters' attention and love into actual votes in the ballot boxes.

Political Economy of Development

Thirty four years to be in power are not an ordinary phenomenon for a party or a coalition of parties in a democratic parliamentary system. This period of the LF for reasons for more than many is to be eked in democratic history. But it is only for their exceptional capacity to stay in office. Initially by introducing regular panchayat and municipal elections the CPI (M) earned wide approval and by the process it spread its political tentacles by means—fair and foul—throughout the state. It was able also to emasculate the opposition political parties. By introducing the Congress Party's earlier formulations since 1955 till Siddhartha Ray's regime (1972-77) of land reforms programme, the CPI (M) did follow a method of good policy implementation. But the reverse process began almost right from 1987. The party had to depend upon the bureaucracy at every level including all shades of interest groups. The growth process was perceptible but it was shady and for the benefits of the supporters of the CPI (M). At the completion of 20 years of the LF rule, the CPI (M) brought out a book, promising "Growth with Social Justice"[60] but it remained on paper only. The minority communities constituted 28.62 per cent[61] but not more than four per cent got government patronage in terms of low category services. The condition remained the same with the SC, ST and OBCs constituting a major chunk of population in the state.

Education system—literacy, primary education, secondary, higher secondary, college and university education— is worst affected. The government health sector is being deteriorated day by day. Rampant corruptions are detected in cooperative sectors. The government claimed excess production in agriculture and fish but the matter of fact was that large quantity of pulses, wheat and fish had to be imported from other states. The recorded unemployed exceeded more than 70 lakh and more than 55 lakh small and medium scale industries were shut down for long. Jyoti Basu formulated a new Industry Policy in 1994. But spending millions on foreign trips by the Chief Minister and his lieutenant Somnath Chatterjee as the chief of WBIDC, did not bring any tangible gains. Lack of electricity, arranging for potable drinking water, irrigation facilities as also the bad road conditions in most of the districts were the actual facts of life. More than 30 per cent of the population cannot earn Rs. 20 a day. Starvation deaths in remote villages of Purulia, Birbhum, Bankura as also in the tea garden areas of North Bengal areas were perennial. Even suicide death of the peasants for their debt burdens was not uncommon. Human development indices of different districts showed the conditions of the people in different areas of the state. The government experts observed the situations on the basis of the government generated data. The report was made in 2004. The West Bengal government's pre-budget Economic Survey 2009-2010 could not give any different stories. The conditions in respect of Human Development remained the same in March 2010.

A central organization, National University of Educational Planning and Administration conducted a survey. According to the report, the primary and secondary levels of education in West Bengal were very low and could be compared with only Arunachal Pradesh. Two generations of students became unworthy in the job market without the benefit of English learning for more than three decades.[62] Even in the mid 1960s West Bengal used to contribute 18 per cent of the industrial product to the GDP. But now it was only four per cent in the LF regime.

According to the incomplete Economic Review 2009-2010, the existing fiscal deficit of the state amounts to total of rupees one lakh ninty three thousand crores. Sector wise the figures remained: the small saving debt rupees sixty one thousand crores, and market loan rupees thirty one thousand crores, etc.

It all means that a child is born in Bengal with a debt burden of rupees seventeen thousand on his head.

The Parliamentary election in 2009 was an eye opener for the LF. Undemocratic utterances by the chief minister and many of his important party colleagues were uncalled for any parliamentary system. The chief minister and the Industry minister invited Salem of Indonesia for industrial ventures promising thousand acres of extremely fertile agricultural lands from the farming peasants in Bhangar, Singur, Nandigram Rajarhat, Nayachar, and Uluberia, etc. Peasants' revolts began though in a low key. Then the government made a secret contract with Ratan Tata of Tata group. Ratan Tata promised to set up a very cheap Nano car factory. For these purposes the government acquired by applying the 1894 Act, one thousand acres of a very fertile four cropped lands at Singur that could be regarded as "heritage land" mostly from unwilling peasants and some from the absentee landholders. The government declared IPC Section 144 and began walling the entire land area. This infuriated the peasants. They objected. The police opened fire and killed few protesters like Raj Kumar Bhool and others. The suffering peasants formed a "Jibon Jibika Krishi Raksha Committee". To teach a lesson to the adamant peasants the CPI (M) local committee secretary Shurhid Dutta and others got a protesting young girl Tapashi Malik raped and burnt alive. Mamata Banerjee and her Party TMC stood by the protestors. The main opposition leaders along with her colleagues were arrested and tortured in police station in Hooghly. She resorted to a 26-day hunger strike. By now the civil society groups comprising a part of the intellectuals, artistes, singers, theatre personalities joined in massive protest movements. The same thing happened in Nandigram. On the basis of a notice that more than thirteen thousand acres of agricultural lands were to be acquired to build a Chemical Hub, this time the protest became vociferous. The police and the CPI (M) cadres in police uniform opened fire on a quiet crowd—male female and children. Fourteen people were killed and many women were raped on 14 March 2007. The drama was again enacted during the first ten days of November 2007. On 14th November the civil society groups took out a silent protest March in Kolkata. Mamata Banerjee and the TMC by now garnered wide support from every corner. The government could not acquire the lands. Ratan Tata had to go. But he did not give up his land right from Singur. Rather very caustically he gave an advertisement in favour of the CPI (M) for the election of 2009. During this period, a few newspapers like *Dainik Statesman*, *Bartaman* and *Sambad Pratidin* played a very positive role. The election results of the subsequent three-tier panchayat, all the Assembly by-elections and the Parliamentary elections went against the LF

Actually all this has changed the colour of West Bengal state politics that the people particularly the younger lot have been watching for the last three and half decades. In the parliamentary election (Table 10), the CPI (M) got only nine seats. The party was reduced from 26 to 9. It became almost irrelevant in the prevailing politics of the states.

The LF particularly the CPI (M) had to face humiliating defeat in the state Assembly election in 2011. The party became a poor third having only 40 seats, even two seats less than the Congress Party (42 seats). It was a victory for the TMC and Congress combine. TMC won 184, SUC-1, Congress 42 seats, totaling 227 seats together. In terms of percentage points of votes TMC+ and Congress 49 and the LF a poor 41.

Since 2006 Mamata Banerjee has been pursuing a policy of consociationalism in her own style. She formed a coalition of different sections of the Left ideology oriented people, some 15/16 smaller social organizations and a few Left political parties keeping in mind her genuine pursuit for seat adjustment with the Congress. The political formation gave her almost unthinkable electoral dividends. After thirty-four years the anti-LF formation without BJP formed the government in West Bengal. As the new chief minister she really sought all sorts of cooperation in the process of governance from all parties, particularly the LF. Despite her continuous humiliation at the hands of the CPI (M) she never showed any vindictive attitude against her sworn political enemy CPI (M). Rather the chief minister earned accolade and parliamentary respect for her democratic reconciliation from the present leader of the opposition Dr. Surya Kantha Mishra.[63] The TMC-Congress coalition government just came into existence on 20 May 2011. Time is not ripe enough to make any judgement about its effectiveness. It is to be observed during the next several months as to how the chief minister Ms. Mamata Banerjee handles the affairs of the state, manages the coalition situations, and have been trying to desensitize the sagging morale of administration by her astute intervention.

In the making of partition human factors were ignored. As a result of riots and inhuman killings and gang rapes of Hindu women perpetrated by the Muslim gangs in the newly formed East Pakistan and before that the prospect the dreams of the Muslims for Pakistan being realized, millions of lower caste Hindus had to leave the East Bengal to take shelter in West Bengal's different railway platforms and open spaces and marshy lands in and around greater Calcutta and a few districts of north Bengal as paupers. The conditions of the upper class Hindus were not as bad. They were mostly literate and many are highly educated. More than 4.5 million people began crowding the already crowed land areas of West Bengal. The process had a tremendous socio-economic and cultural effect and repercussions—both negative and positive. The original inhabitants of the West Bengal began to be mildly hostile because they thought that they would lose economically and would have to culturally contend with the refugees having peculiar linguistic orientations and life styles. The people of the western part of Bengal had a feeling that their own lifestyle and economic activities would be dislocated and gradually thrown in to political insignificance. But in positive terms they were to gain because of the influence of the educated and more literate middle class and lower middle class people migrating to India. The sons of the soils of this part of Bengal understood this later as experienced and recorded in history.

The history of West Bengal can perceptively be classified into four general categories:

> a tortuous period for consolidating the emerging issues of a truncated state (1947-52), politics of the Congress Party dominance and fragmented opposition parties (1952-67), politics of aggrandizement, violence counter-violence, thereafter a politico-electoral the reactions (1967-77) and an oligopolistic politics based on real and sometimes a ramshackle social coalition (1977-2009 and onwards). Each of the four periods of the disinherited state may be subdivided having unique characteristics at times that would be pointed out for analytical purposes during the ongoing discourse.

A Tortuous Period for Consolidating the Truncated State

The advisers with technical expertise did not properly think out different aspects, effects and negative human repercussions and economic dislocation that might happen due to partition. It was carved out just to provide the Muslims a territory, in the form of a state, i.e., the Eastern part of Pakistan where they overwhelmingly outnumbered the Hindus. The Radcliff used almost a surgeon's scalpel that vivisected the Bengal territory. It was less than rational and done in a hurry. After declaring the award he had to revise it within two days bringing Murshidabad in India and Khulna in East Pakistan. The problems of refugee rehabilitations, politics of refugee rehabilitations unleashed by CPI against the Congress government, the other street movements and activities of the Communist Party of India and its politics to gain political mileage out of the miseries of the displaced persons and perceived "insensitiveness"[64] of both the central and state governments were the constant and serious propaganda planks of the CPI and other leftist political parties. Dr. Prafulla Chandra Ghosh became the first chief minister of West Bengal after the Partition of the country in 1947. But he could not stay in office for more than four months. The Bengal Congress Party was ridden with extreme factionalism. Dr. Ghosh was a Gandhian. But he could take the suggestion of Gandhiji in regard to the allocation of the Finance portfolio to Nalini Ranjan Sarkar, who was closer to a Marwari lobby. At that time of excessive food shortage "a corrupt Marwari businessman"[65] was indulging in supplying spurious wheat—a very important and necessary scarce food item during those difficult days to the market. It was brought to the notice of Dr. Ghosh who immediately took action that irritated that particular Marwari lobby. This compounded with Gandhi's recommendation for inducting Sarkar as the Finance Minister made Dr. Ghosh relinquishing the office. Dr. Bidhan Chandra Roy took over in January 1948.

To the Communist Party, Indian Independence was a sham. To them, without economic freedom, political independence was false: slogan mongering, *like e azadi jhuta hai, bhulo mat bhulo mat,* and opposing every actions by the Congress Government in rehabilitating thousands of the hapless refugees in places like Andaman Islands and Dandakaranya outside West Bengal with insufficient habitable areas in the already over populated territory of the truncated state by the undivided Communist Party won the hearts of the refugees. Later on the refugee population which began swelling in a big way till the early 1970s became the mainstay of the Leftist ideological propaganda and crudely speaking, the vote banks of the Leftists particularly the Communist Party of India (CPIM). The other activities of the CPI, by indirectly mobilising the suffering people by the Leftist music circle, Indian Theatre groups (IPTA) depicting the fate of the peasants before and after *Tebhaga Andolan* encouraged the peasant groups and middle class educated people. It had impressive records and the leftists reaped the harvest when the CPI decided to participate in the parliamentary democratic system in the late 1940s. The socio-cultural movements through the Marxist intellectuals, left oriented artistes, theatre personalities, litterateurs, musicians had political impacts on a large section of people. The CPI exploited the situations. These socio-cultural groups remained always sympathetic to the cause of the Communist Parties. When the Parties could not directly communicate with the people, they took recourse to indirect mobilization through the socio-cultural activities and initiative of the people mentioned above. The theatre, films, music compositions depicting the unbearable miseries of the people at that point of time and space played a great role in focusing the contribution of the CPI. Thus, the Communist Parties and the other Left parties gained respectabilities and acceptance among the numerous displaced persons in the state and many other communities in the state that catapulted these parties to power in the late 1960s (the two United Fronts) and 1977 till 2009 (Left Front). People's memories were not as sharp as they say. They forgot all about the role of Communist Party in their support for the British war efforts, betrayal of the "Quit India Movement in 1942", its support of the Muslim demand for self determination on religious line as also its support for a separate Gorkha Land in Darjeeling before Indian Independence on August 15, 1947. The newly formed interim governments afterwards both at the Centre and the states had to confront all this to consolidate themselves before the first democratic elections in 1951-52 within the framework of universal adult suffrage. The first Parliamentary and Assembly elections in West Bengal were held in 1952. In those days till 1967, the Parliamentary and Assembly elections used to be held simultaneously. Therefore, the first period of the state politics in West Bengal was the period of Congress Party consolidation. People reposed faith in the Congress for its past record. Its contribution to the national struggle was indisputable. But the moments of freedom was the worst in the history of Bengal. Sporadic communal riots were still going on. Gandhi began his fasting at *Hydar e Manjil* now renamed as Gandhi Bhawan at Beleghata in the eastern side of Kolkata. He appealed to the conscience of the two warring communities. Gandhi was the unhappiest man. During the inhuman riots in both sides of Bengal he travelled a lot and tried to bring back the sanity among the people from ordinary to the highest leaders. But in Bengal the results were not as desired.

Demographic characters were distorted. The areas with West Bengal were not enough to rehabilitate the displaced from eastern Pakistan. The people were to live in subhuman conditions. The doles given by the government were insufficient. The economy of the state was in disarray. There was no hope of immediate recovery. Major chunks of fertile and arable lands were given to East. The raw materials like jute and other items that used to feed the large numbers jute industries along the sides of the Ganges remained in the eastern part of Bengal. With these resources the East Pakistan attempted to build up jute industries. West Bengal's industry and agriculture were yet to wake up from the shock unburdened with enormous size of refugee populations in inhuman miseries. The general administrative structure and police administrations were to be trimmed up. The Chief Minister Dr. Bidhan Chandra Roy took up the helm with single-minded determinations but odds were heavy. The negative politics of the opposition parties and factionalism in the Congress were in the way. But he tried his best with the available quantum of help from his long time friend and colleagues in the Central Government. The incoming stream of refugees never came to an end before the Passport system was introduced in 1952. It was really the most difficult or rather the worst of time in the initial history of West Bengal. The hapless millions crossing over the border could not enjoy the spoils of partition.[66] If it was really spoils, it appeared later that the leaders or people with political clouts upholding the causes of the politics of refugees enjoyed the fruits and shared the political power for more than three and a half decades.

The leadership profiles of the Leftist politicians bore the testimony to the facts stated above. More than 30 ministers out of 43 in the LF cabinet are originally from the refugee communities from other side of the West Bengal border. At least their origin can be traced to the first or second generation of the displaced persons. This was true even in case of the higher party levels in the state (state committee and the party state secretariat). Most of them are from the elite community belonging to the Brahmin, Kayasth, Baidya or upper layer of the backward castes and communities.

Of the early generations of refugees, some are still living in the colonies, some are well settled in life during the LF regime for the last thirty-four years, posed a threat to the LF government for different reasons. The Left leaders' politics of the displaced persons and their miseries paid the CPI (M) handsomely later in the mid 1960s in their desperate bid to marginalize the Congress in the power structure of the state. Ultimately the undivided Communist Party even with two trends of thoughts working within with different understanding of the nature of Indian State and character of the Congress Party spearheading the nationalist agenda through the dynamics of parliamentary democracy. How far it is real in case of the CPI (M) is yet to be explored.[67]

Congress Party Dominance and Fragmented Opposition

The first democratic elections were held in 1952. Both the parliamentary and assembly elections were held simultaneously throughout the country. The undivided communist party keeping aside their earlier view of colonialism, freedom, elections, etc. participated in the electoral process. By now the Congress Party had to reconcile with the parting of ways of ginger groups and other marginal groups that came out of the Congress and formed different parties to contest the elections. The multi party and the fragmented system has been shown later in the essay that might have given an idea as to why the Congress Party was dominant and the fragmented opposition had to wait for long to realise the merits of coalescing in the electoral process to defeat the Congress. Table 2.1 shows the total and quite a large number of political parties that dominated the West Bengal politics till 1977. Till 1967 and thereafter in 1971 and 1972-77 Congress was absolutely dominant. After the beginning of the LF regime the number of political parties winning elections has been reduced to the advantage of the LF. In the meanwhile the Indian National Congress (INC) underwent a few changes in nomenclature shown in Table 2.1. It was clear that the popularity of the CPI (M) was on the wane, or in other words the anti-incumbency factor was working within for the leader.

It is significant to note that the CPI (M) led by Jyoti babu was reduced to 150 in 1996 and Buddhadeb began his journey with only 143 seats losing the absolute majority in the LF (Table 2.1). From now on the politics of the state led by the CPI (M) took a new turn to regain the hegemony it enjoyed till the end of Jyoti Basu which brought back the LF particularly the CPI (M) with a bang (Table 2.2), to be discussed later in this essay.

Dr. Bidhan Chandra Roy was a very able administrator. It was a difficult time and he had to steer through with the limited resources. He never complained against the central leadership for its omissions and commissions. Centre-state relations and the controversy regarding inter-state commerce, the policy of freight equalizations, etc. were not brought into a broader focus, as they should been. It was later raised by the Left parties in their movements against the then chief minister Prafulla Chandra Sen during the 1960s and continuously from 1980s when Indira Gandhi came back to power after a short stint of Janata coalition regime led by Morarjibhai Desai. Dr. Roy was a national leader also. He used to think he would be able to tide over all sorts of difficulties. He did his best in his policy options. The first step that he took was his policy towards industrialization of the state in all its several categories—heavy, small and manufacturing and cottage industries. To rehabilitate the unemployed youth belonging to the refugee families he introduced State Transport Corporation.

A large number of refugees were given employment. The Tramways had still been under the control of the Tram Company. The company with the approval of the government made a paltry increase of *one paise* (one cent in dollar terms) only. It was really a time of a moderate inflation and income of the ordinary people was low enough. The decision of the government infuriated the Communist Party and other Left parties. After participating the democratic elections where they did not fare well they attempted to make their presence felt in a big way on the streets. In a single day they burnt 13 tramcars to ashes near Sealdah Railway Station in the early 1953. The government took control of the situation. This was the first disruptive act of the Leftist at the very beginning of the democratic process in the unhappy disinherited state of Bengal. Industrial regeneration was the priority of Dr. Roy. He attempted to modernise the steel industry in Durgapur. He made a modern township there. Durgapur Steel factories, DPL, Damodar Barrage at Durgapur to generate electricity and flood control were his contributions. For the same purpose, he got to commission Mithon and Tilpara Barrage to help the peasant communities to get the irrigation water. Marurakshi Dam at Massanzore at Birbhum was also built up during the 1950s.

When the Planning Commission under the chairmanship of the Prime Minister Nehru introduced the First Five year plan according to Mahalanobis planning concept to build the heavy industries to lay the foundation of modern India, Dr. Roy immediately fell in line. His objective was to address the problems both of the industry and the agriculture. Building infrastructure capacity was the priority areas.

Dr. Roy established satellite township like Kalyani and Salt Lake City to provide housing facilities to the middle and lower middle classes near Calcutta. To supply milk to the cities and around, he commissioned Haringhata milk project which, during the 1980s, became moribund. Bellious Road at Howrah used to be regarded as the Sheffield of Bengal for its small and manufacturing industries on either side of the road. During the 1980s, Howrah manufacturing industries lost their glories and became the den of anti-social elements dealing with iron scrap thieving and smuggling. Actually after the partition the new state was suffering from food shortages. Rationing system was still in place. But the procurement as levies was not adequate. Dr. Roy's Minister for the

Department of Food, Shree Prafulla Chandra Sen introduced some sort of a cordoning system so that the system of black marketing could be minimized. But it had its negative effect also. People in the state particularly the peasantry were dissatisfied. The Communists and others exploited the situation and fomented the dissatisfaction among sections of the people. It had its salutary effect so much so that and an efficient minister like P.C. Sen had to face defeat in 1957 Assembly election. However, the Congress government brought back Shree Sen in a back door manoeuvre. He was elected in the second chamber, i.e. Legislative Council and then was offered the Food Department again. But the opposition members never forgot to retaliate against Shree Sen. The Left oppositions, particularly the CPI and after the split of the Communist Party the more militant CPI (M), left no stone unturned to carry on slander campaigns against Prafulla Chandra Sen when he took over as the Chief Minister after the death of Dr. Roy in early 1961. He tried to carry on the unfinished agenda of Dr. Roy. The decade of the 50s was terribly difficult for the government. The Leftists relentlessly carried out socio-political movements at the slighted opportunities. Zamindari Abolition Act was introduced. Though the Land Reform Minister Bimal Chandra Singh, was himself a very big landlord having large estates on both side of the border, but he himself piloted the proposal and its implementation. The government had to face hassles regarding the paying of compensation, which ultimately resolved to an extent after the 4th amendment of the Constitution. The truncated state comprising only one third of Bengal had not sufficient fertile lands to grow rice. The famine situation appeared to be looming large. To tide over the difficulty, Dr. Roy and the Chief Minister of Bihar Shreekrishna Singh mooted the idea of merging West Bengal and Bihar. The Communist Party incited people particularly in the urban centres of the state. In the meanwhile the Congress party had to face a by-election in the North-West Calcutta. The Leftist opposition-backed candidate Mohit Moitra defeated the Congress-backed candidate Ashok Sen — a brilliant barrister and a dedicated Congress stalwart. As a true democrat, Dr. Roy took it for a referendum against his policy and abandoned the idea of merger. Dr. Roy wanted to make West Bengal as an economically viable state despite economic hardship after almost irreversible socio-political damages after the Partition. The state had to face chronic food shortages. Flood was a yearly routine despite having large dams to control flood and facilitate irrigation to boost up agricultural production. As a result of a devastating flood, the food production got down to an all time low. A food riot began with the Communist Party at the lead. The police opened fire in different places. Many people had to suffer bullet injuries but there were controversies regarding the number of deaths. The CPI (M) claimed that more than 80 people died on the spot. But the Party was not in a position to verify the number.

To enhance capacity building for education it was Dr. Roy who changed the existing system and set up the Higher Secondary Board that separated the school from the Calcutta University system. He laid a good deal of emphasis on Primary Education and eradication of illiteracy from its existing inadequacies. The standard of Higher Education including Medical and Engineering, he energized all the existing Medical and engineering colleges at Calcutta, Jadavpur at Calcutta, and Sibpore at Howrah. During his period, Burdwan, Rabindra Bharati and other centres of Higher Education, i.e. Universities, were started with extraordinary teachers and scholars in the Faculties of those institutions. During the Left Front (LF) regime during those 34 years, the number of colleges and Universities multiplied at the cost of merits. It is really a regime of mediocrities all around.

The period of the Chief Minister P.C. Sen was not administratively as remarkable but politically the period from 1961 to 1967 was volatile both from the perspectives of the Congress and the undivided Communist party. The Congress Party was a coalition of different interests of the rural and urban communities. The caste creeds and communities were under the command of the urban elite politicians and the rural people had to depend upon the congress rural gentries with enormous landholding even after the Zamindari abolition

Politics of Aggrandizement, Violence, Counter-Violence, and Thereafter a Politico-Electoral Reaction

Humayun Kabir of the Bharatiya Kranti Dal (BKD) was the architect of a coalition experiment in West Bengal in 1967. With Ajoy Mukherjee at the head, two leftist blocks—one led by CPI (M) and the other by CPI came together to form United Front (UF) government. This second phase of West Bengal politics was extremely volatile. The opposition parties led by CPI and CPI (M) were yet to learn the culture of governance in parliamentary terms. The revolutionary rhetoric of a Marxist variety in a parliamentary process gradually began to alienate the CPI (M) from other left parties, and fissures and cracks developed within the CPI (M) itself. Within a period of only four years from 1967 to 1971 West Bengal had to install four coalition governments.

It was a period of hopeless uncertainty and a phase of political aggrandizement. There were ideological differences between factions of the CPI (M). The extremists, i.e. activists who used to oppose the party's participation in the electoral process, were given the understanding that afterwords the law making body would be used to further the class struggle by taking over land from the excess land owning classes. But the other group led by Jyoti Basu and the CPI (M) ideologue Hare Krishna Konar could not convince the extremists group led by Charu Majumdar, Kanu Sanyal and Jangal Santal at North Bengal. After Hare Krishna Konar came back from North Bengal, to be precise Siliguri, the peasants led by the Charu Majumdar and

Kanu Sanyal started a revolt attacking Jotedars and murdering police constable. The first Naxalbari movement took its ramshackle shape. The ultra-leftist group still believed that adapting to a parliamentary path was a blunder. The CPI (M) leaders began influencing the police forces and wanted to use police administration and the general administrative machineries for their own party interests to root out the sporadic violence that began spreading in several places. Severe intra-party classes began. The CPI (M) already tried to spread horizontally to reduce the strength of the partners of the ULF and PULF coalition. A new party in the name CPI (ML) came into being challenging the hegemony of the CPI (M) in the UF coalition. Law and order system completely collapsed. The Bangla Congress, CPI and a few other parties were extremely disgruntled. On the advice of the Governor Dharmavira, the President's Rule was imposed. The ordinary people and the toiling masses smelled conspiracy by the central congress leadership in collaboration with the Bangla Congress chief Ajoy Mukherjee, his lieutenant Sushil Dhara and the state Congress leaders. Jyoti Basu along with his party chief Promode Dasgupta was bitter and in a severe attacking mood. Political economy was in a disastrous stage at that point of time. Food prices were skyrocketing to an all time high of Rs. 5.00 a kilo (ridiculous as at present when the very low quality rice price rises to more than Rs. 20 per kilo!) Street fights by the Left parties were rampant against Dr. Ghosh and the prevailing inflation. Dr. Prafulla Ghosh who was the Food minister in the first UF regime with a group of breakaway members of the first UF formed the PDF government with the outside help of the Congress Party. But due to the peculiar politics of the Speaker Bijoy Banerjee, the House could not function. The CPI (M) challenged the Governor Dharmavira's recommendations for the President's Rule to the Calcutta High Court but the court order went in favour of the Governor acting in his discretionary power provided in the Constitution at that time.

A second election took place in 1969 and the second UF with the same parties with CPI (M) increasing its strength by more than double in this election again led by Ajoy Mukherjee and Bangla Congress with a reduced number. The Second UF government could not stay more than 13 months in office. The Deputy Chief Minister Jyoti Basu and his Party were dead bent on politicizing the general civil and police administration. The clerical staff of the government began insulting the chief minister even in the precincts of the Writers Buildings. A number of severe inter party clashes took place in different parts of the state. The CPI (M) leadership was trying to spread its organization to every corner at the cost of the other Left parties of the UF coalition. The flash point was approaching in quick pace. On the other side the Naxalite violence started its salvo in the form of assassinating individuals, particularly the stray CPI (M) members and the police constables.

The second UF government was a victim of Intra party feuds and inter-party clashes. The Chief Minister and the Deputy Chief Minister, Jyoti Basu was at loggerheads with each other. The policy of the CPI (M) at that time was one of a policy of aggrandizement and attacking the opposing parties, be it the Congress or the partners of the UF. The flash point reached when the Chief Minister Ajoy Mukherjee reversed Jyoti Basu's order of transfer of a Gazol *Thana* officer at Malda. Some IAS officers at that time helped Jyoti Basu carrying on his party objectives to politicize the upper echelons of West Bengal Bureaucracy.[68] The tension rose high and ultimately the Chief Minister declared a sit-in-strike against his own government and called it "barbaric and uncivilized".[69] The chief minister resigned on March 16, 1970. The second UF fell which infuriated the CPI (M) that called a state wise strike on March 17, 1970 and unleashed unforeseen violence against the Congress Party. In Burdwan a group of CPI (M) hoodlums led by Binay Konar, Khokan Sen alias Nirupam Sen, the present Industry Minister, Manik Roy alias Anil Basu, the record vote getter from Arambag Parliamentary constituency and many others including a young SFI member who later on crowned a few government posts during the LF regime and ultimately retired as the Registrar of Jadavpur University, attacked the epi-centre of Congress activities, the house of the Sain brothers. The mob fury was severe and a select group as mentioned above speared the two Sain brothers and a youth congress leader and two domestic helps. The Sain mother fainted; the sister and his one month old son were thrown into fire and like heroes left the spot.[70] The eldest Sain brother Naba Sain who fled, later on was murdered by the hired killers of the CPI (M) within a year. During this period possibly the CPI (M) were trying to get back to their class annihilation. The cadres of the party let loose a reign of terror threatening that if necessary they would destroy Congress members and other opposition forces as they did in *Sainbari.* Simultaneously the Naxalite violence was in its peek. Instead of encircling the urban centres with the villages, actually they created an atmosphere of fear and insecurity in the minds of ordinary citizens. Both the CPI (M) and the Naxalities were at loggerheads and the latter were trying to eliminate CPI (M) cadres openly. None of the groups perhaps thought of the counter violence that might follow. Later during Siddhartha Roy regime before 1972 election the CPI (M) helped the police identifying Naxalite dens[71] in Baranagar and Kashipur and killing more than 80 young Naxalites in a single operation on 12-14 August 1971. Afterwards the CPI (M) was cornered by the resurgent youth congress activists and badly defeated by the Congress winning only 14 seats in 1972 election. This Election was alleged to be rigged. The CPI (M) boycotted the House for a period of five years. Dr. Asok Mitra in a public meeting as also within the House when the LF came to power in 1977 called the 1972 Assembly as the House of Thieves ("Chorerder Bidhan Sabha").[72]

Again to take up the cue, the then District Magistrate of Burdwan was absent from the town on that ill fated day deliberately and the SP did not send the police to the place of the incident on time. By the goodness of an honest Naga police officer the police was ordered to reach the spot much later and arrested a few miscreants. Some were arrested but later let off free when the LF came into power in 1977. The case records were destroyed. The justice was never done till today. Even when Congress came to power in 1972 they did not take any serious action, rather promoted some of the police officers and a top bureaucrat Tarun Dutta, an IAS officer, the then District Magistrate and the SP Ramen Bhattacharya in Burdwan. Inter party clashes were in full swing. Unrecorded and clandestine murders were the order of the day. Satyajit Roy in one of his remarkable film, "Pratidandi" (the novel of the same name was written by Sunil Ganguly), depicted the period in a very sensitive ambience. The state as a whole was under Naxalite violence. During this period, after the failure of the two coalition experiments in 1967 and 1969, the Leftist forces went apart. The CPI (M) fought the election on its own in 1971 and bagged 113 seats in the Assembly but won nearly 35 per cent of the popular votes. This was the maximum percentage points of vote share that CPI (M) alone garnered in comparison with its earlier records. This perhaps made the CPI (M) confident to propose for a social coalition that reflected later in arranging for political coalition (LF) with several parties in 1977. A government with the leadership of Ajoy Mukherjee joining Congress was formed in 1971 but it failed soon. This period was really a period of the "crisis of governance in West Bengal".[73] Table 2 would show the party position with percentage points of votes won by each party. But it was the worst of time for the citizens of Bengal. They experienced enough of the politics of the Left. They were not only worried but mentally disgusted. Sensing the mood of the people it was not difficult to conclude that a change in the political arena was desirable. Siddhartha Sankar Ray by now a very powerful political leader of the Congress utilized the opportunities with a band of resurgent Youth Congress leaders like Priya Ranjan Das Munshi, Subrata Mukherjee, Kumud Bhattacharya and many others.

It was a time of complete political uncertainty. Due to Bangladesh crisis nearly nine million people both Hindus and Muslims crossed over the border. To feed and give shelter to such a large number of people in West Bengal, the governmental machineries were in adequate. The demographic balance of the state was disturbed. How to send back these displaced persons after the birth of Bangladesh was a problem. Moreover, like the Workers Party of Bangladesh, the CPI (M) in the state was of the opinion that India would not call back its soldiers from Bangladesh and might go in for an Indian colonial arrangement.[74] The CPI (M) used to spread the disinformation as a whispering campaign to attack Indian capitalism under the tutelage of Indira Gandhi.

After a good deal of wait and see policy, India had to intervene in the Bangladesh freedom struggle as a retaliation of Pakistan's undeclared war with India on December 3, 1971. By now Smt. Gandhi won the 1971 parliamentary election with a massive majority. Siddhartha Shankar Ray was the Minister for Education in her Cabinet. He was already given the additional charge to look after the political affairs of West Bengal. By this time the leftist political chaos let loose both by the Naxalites and the CPI (M) were brought down with a heavy hand by the police administration under the guidance of Siddhartha Ray. It was not a very good option but the youth Congress stuff and police administration had to resort to some sort of counter violence to confront the Left violence.

The emergence of the Congress Party under the leadership of Siddhartha Sankar Ray with his young brand of youth leaders and being patronized by the Prime Minister Indira Gandhi was actually a political reaction against the political violence let loose by the CPI (M) and its break away faction Naxalites during 1967 to 1971. The youth Congress leaders during their student days in mid 1960s were heckled and sometimes treated shabbily by the organizational fronts of the CPI (M). Therefore what these younger Congress leaders did against the CPI (M) was but a political reaction. After the Congress came back to power the younger leadership used even stronger arm tactics. Many a CPI (M) activists had to leave their original places. It was certainly not democratic but the CPI (M) leaders and members began bringing it constantly in their campaign against the Congress and the TMC. In a more dangerous way they were doing the same against the opposition parties and capturing the village after village in different districts of the Western belt of the state like Lalgarh in West Medinipur, Bankura, Birbhum, Purulia and many other places.

Siddhartha Ray's coalition government (PDA) with its partners CPI supporting from outside did enact certain people oriented legislations, like Panchayat Act, Building organizations of CSDP, CMDA (now KMDA), Housing Board to build government housing complexes for low and middle income groups. There were a few brilliant ministers in his cabinet like Bhola Sen, Ajit Panja, Kashi Kanta Moitra and many young talents. But on the factionalism, people used to say that was being encouraged by the chief minister himself to checkmate the rise of the younger ones. He even constituted an inquiry commission against the *Bhusi Kelengkari* of Kasi Kanta Moitra—originally a socialist, and the younger corrupt ministers. Secondly Siddhartha babu's name was sullied because of his association of the Internal Emergency declared by Indira Gandhi to retain her position as the Prime Minister. Siddhartha babu got many powerful politicians of the opposition, rightists, centrists and socialists, though not the CPI (M) ones excepting the MP Jyotirmoy Basu, and journalists like Gour Kishore Ghosh Barun Sengupta and others arrested. All this became the undoing of the Congress in West Bengal.

3
Electoral Politics: West Bengal

During the last two decades since the defeat of Rajiv Gandhi's Congress Government in 1989, eight parliamentary elections were held resulting in minority coalition or coalition governments in India. The Left Front (LF), gaining a major share of 61 parliamentary seats in 2004 election, was in a policy dictating terms to the minority United Progressive Alliance (UPA) coalition government at the Centre. The Left Front was almost in the driver seat in the UPA regime after its outstanding victory in Assembly election of West Bengal in 2006 by winning 235 seats — the largest ever since 1987. In 1977 election the LF astonishingly won 253 Assembly seats; it was so in the context that the Congress Party won 16 Parliamentary seats in 1984 election.

In West Bengal, the Left Front Government has been reigning since 1977. It came to power consecutively for the seventh time in a row. The opposition parties could not provide any alternative social coalition resulting in a political coalition or coalitions against the LF. During the last several years since 1989, the governments at the Centre were minority governments or minority coalition governments.[1] This type of government is not new even in political system that is usually dominated by two major political parties. The coalition governments are the norms in most of the West European and smaller Scandinavian countries and even many a third world country where proportional representations are incorporated in their constitutions.

In West Bengal, a coalition arrangement with the CPI (M) as the predominant partner has been continuing since 1977. Only after 2001 Assembly election the predominant party CPI (M) lost absolute majority.[2] Actually, the CPI (M) has been holding majority seats in the Assembly all through in coalition with a few Leftist political parties and two factions of breakaway Janata Party (JP). The Communist Party of India (CPI) joined the Front in early 1980s. Even a Naxalite faction led by Asim Chatterjee (later he fought Assembly election on a TMC ticket) joined the Left Front political coalition as junior partner[3] without having a seat in the House. During 1950s and 1960s, the undivided Communist Party carried on relentless movements on all fronts against the establishment and brought smaller opposition parties together as referred to in the previous chapter. The politics of opposition was conditioned by several factors — mainly geographical, economic and societal. West Bengal inherited a truncated state with a long borderline with Bhutan, Bangladesh and Nepal. The difficulties resulting from poverty, unemployment, underemployment and population growth as well as nearly 80 lakh refugee influx from the erstwhile East Pakistan were enormous. To tackle the problems through democratic means was an arduous effort for any democratic government. The situations were easy to be exploited by the opposition parties. The Communist Party did exactly the same particularly with the intractable problems of the millions of refugees that came across the border with no means to live on. The Congress Government with Dr. B.C. Roy as the Chief Minister wanted sincerely to settle the refugees in Andaman Islands and *Dandakaranya*. The Communist Party resisted the move and in the process won the hearts of the uprooted people from other side of the border. The refugees forcibly occupied many fringe areas of Calcutta and suburbs as also the habitable lands in the districts of North Bengal. The influx continued almost unabated for the next decade and a half. In the process they became a solid vote-bank for the anti-establishment opposition parties in general and the Communist Party in particular.

The growth of population in the state and its density in comparison with other Indian state is abnormal. The cause of its growth, to be discussed later, has greatly to contribute to the voting populations. No political party gives any attention to this serious problem, rather for political gains, encourages the same even to the risk of irrational demographic changes that may hurt the economy of the state seriously.

Table 3.1 shows the increase of voters (because the population has been increasing by leaps and bounds) in the state before each of the elections (1977-2011). There are several reasons for such an increase in the number of voters. These have been reasoned in course of the discussions that would follow. But the fact is that this occasional bout of increase of the number of voters mostly went in favour of the LF coalition—quite contrary to the popular perceptions that larger voter participation usually goes against the ruling establishment.

The CPI (M) continued to have overwhelming support of these refugees[4] till the Parliamentary and West Bengal Assembly elections in 1991. Gradually the displaced persons living mostly in different colony areas became disillusioned about the function and the corruptions among the members of the ruling elites. Still they did not get the *pattas* and other documentary evidence that they lived so long on the lands belonged to them. During the 1998 and 1999 Parliamentary elections, a different trend was found in the voting patterns in the refugee belts in and around Calcutta and the adjacent districts. The older people among them were found to utter their disillusionment

Table 3.1: Relative Increase of Voters before Each Election (1977-2006) (in %)

Year	Total Number of Voters	Relative Increase
1977	24942416	13.05
1980	29738146	19.23
1984	32955635	10.82
1989	39394265	19.54
1991	41407545	5.11
1996	45618922	10.17
1998	46836940	2.67
1999	47638728	1.76
2001	47668740	1.80
2004	47438520	–0.42
2006	48965140	3.12
2009	52241202	6.77

Source: Dilip Banerjee, *Election Recorder*, Star Publications, Kolkata, 2010, West Bengal (Revised Version) from Report of the Election Commission of India.

with the Left Front Government. The CPI (M)'s relations with real estate promoters, anti-social elements working in tandem with lower level corrupt police officials alienated many of the erstwhile supporters. West Bengal was watching a new generation of people from now on.

The newer generation of voters belonging to refugee families is a lot quite different. Culturally they are on a different plane from their predecessors. After such a long time Bengal is having a cultural mix among the young generations across the spectrum. The process of acculturation was meandering but for a purpose. The younger people do not care for the "tedious" propaganda during election period as to how the Leftists had to face the organized state repression during the mid-seventies, history of sufferings of the people uprooted from the former East Pakistan and their miserable lives in makeshift refugee camps. These young people have to face the brunt of unemployment and often suffer from a sense of existential purposelessness.[5] They also watch with contempt the life style of the political leaders and their association with promoters, contractors and men of the underworld and of the shady character.

The political space, which was occupied by the Congress earlier, has been gradually taken over by the breakaway rebel Congressmen with Mamata Banerjee as the Chief of a newly formed Trinamool Congress Party (TMC) before the Parliamentary election in 1998. The Left Front ruled West Bengal for long with the Congress Party as the only opposition force, feeble though. It has been as if perennially unable to really play an effective role as an opposition party to articulate the demands of people and make the present Government respond to the needs of all sections of people. They are in a habit of voicing against the partisan attitude of the administrators in the fields of education, health, poverty alleviation, running local bodies like panchayats and urban civic affairs. To a very large number of people, the Congress Party has become a fortune-seeker and almost an appendage of the Left Front Government. The Central leadership also did not want to disturb the government of Jyoti Basu in anticipation of his support in future if necessary, to snatch the governmental power from BJP-led Government or make an alliance to form a coalition after election. The "firebrand" leader of the Congress Party, Mamata Banerjee, in the political process became the only focal point of anti-Left movements and activities. Her capabilities to mobilize people's support among the lower middle class women and the younger people of the state could not but be reckoned with. Mamata, after being expelled from the Congress Party, immediately formed her Trinamool Congress Party (TMC). She made alliance with the BJP, before the 1998 parliamentary election. The TMC won seven seats conceding only one seat to the BJP. Surprisingly, the BJP, for the first time, won a seat. The support of the younger generation of urban young voters, educated sections among the people and a large number of erstwhile displaced people were behind the victory of the Trinamool and BJP combine. The BJP's rise in West Bengal, as perceived by the Leftists and the Congresswalas, was an ominous signal to the Leftists — particularly the CPI (M) in 1998. The Dum Dum, one seat won by the BJP was a very important constituency. It was an area with a large concentration of refugee settlements, the upper and lower middle classes in Salt Lake and its surrounding areas. During this election, it was reported in many newspapers and a section of the CPI (M) Party leaders as well expressed that a large number of dissident CPI (M) members with Subhas Chakraborty as their leader helped the BJP candidate to win the prestigious Dum Dum seat to teach a lesson to the CPI (M)'s leadership in the district of North 24-Parganas and the heavyweight leaders of the CPI (M) Headquarters at Alimuddin Street. In the election of 1999 the leadership of the CPI (M) left no stone unturned to win back. But the BJP consolidated its position with a larger margin of two seats this time around.

It is true that the emergence of BJP as a genuine political force in this state can be traced back to 1989 parliamentary election. Before 1989, the BJP did not even get more than five per cent of votes, not to speak of winning a seat. But in a massive rally the CPI (M) Chief Minister, Jyoti Basu, joined hands with BJP's Atal Bihari Vajpayee along with Viswanath Pratap Singh. To Viswanath Pratap Singh the single agenda was to defeat Rajiv Gandhi and dislodge the Congress from the Centre. The CPI (M) and their leader Jyoti Basu were now constantly warning the people of West Bengal against the 'Hindu Communalism' of the BJP but never acknowledged the fact that they themselves for their electoral gains and to occupy a respectable political space at the national level were no less responsible for the rise of the BJP in the state. The change in the social composition and certain demographic changes in West Bengal in recent years combined with break-up of the Congress party resulting in the formation of Trinamool Congress are also to be taken into account for the rise of BJP in West Bengal, since the parliamentary election in 1998.

Again to look back, the historical, cultural, demographic-cultural, social and economic factors have determined the politics in West Bengal. The state is unique in its political process and character. Protest movements by the radicals, particularly the Marxists since Independence, the fallouts of the Partition and Indo-Pak Wars in 1965 and 1971 with consequent influx of thousands of refugees crossing over the porous border, demographic changes as a result of the influx of Muslims in search of work in the border districts of Dinajpur, Malda, Murshidabad, Nadia and 24 Parganas, unresponsiveness of the long-lasting Congress rule, the organizational weaknesses of the party are some of the many factors that have determined the politics of the state and consequently defined the orientation of the politics of the left parties.

The dependence on micro surveys about limited social bases and other selective information, mainly governmental as done by some critics,[6] will not be enough to understand the politics and the political bases of the Congress Party and other opposition parties. Contrary to the observation of some critics, upper class people, a large number of scheduled castes, schedule tribes and the Muslims used to vote for the Congress Party. The rural *Jotedar* class barring a few in some districts like Burdwan was a vote-bank for the Congress.[7] Anticipating their doom after the Left Front came into existence in 1977 like the promoters in real estate business in urban areas and the contractors in both rural and urban areas the rural *jotedars* and urban upper and middle layers of peasants sided with the CPI (M) for their protection as they did during the Congress regime earlier. It was by and large common among the Muslim population to support the ruling establishment also due to their insecurity syndrome.

West Bengal is a truncated and porous border state as stated earlier. It comprises a total area of 88,752 sq. km with a population of more than 900 million as per the census report 2011. The growth rate of population is more than 25 per cent during the decade 1981-1991. The decade between 1991 and 2000 has seen much larger growth of population than that of the previous decade. From the neighbouring country, it is not difficult for the Bangladeshis — mostly Muslims — to enter into India in a clandestine manner and settle in West Bengal with the help of political leaders and their parties. An abnormal increase in the number of voters is recorded in the border districts over the years. Table 3.1 shows how the voters in West Bengal have been increasing since 1977 before each of the general elections.

The interesting feature of Table 3.1 is that within a span of nine years the number of voters in West Bengal went up by nearly 20 per cent. The reasons are many. The cross border illegal entry of a large number of people, Nepalese, Bhutanese but mostly Muslims has rapidly increased over the years. Once the then Home Minister, L.K. Advani, himself in a very guarded way admitted the fact.[8] Perceptually this is simply because of their religious minority status. The position had changed since the inception of the minority Government of V.P. Singh in 1989 and more rapidly after the *Babri-Masjid* demolition in 1992. There were riots in some places in West Bengal. But with deft handling of the problems by the Left Front government and with personal initiative of the Congress leaders specially Mamata Banerjee (at that time she was Youth Congress President in West Bengal), within a day or two the disturbances were quelled and brought under control. The incident hurt the psyche of the Muslim communities. The Left Front in West Bengal was partially successful in exploiting this situation in their electoral campaign in the state.

In West Bengal, the BJP and its predecessor Jana Sangh, has never been a serious political force. Its share of votes in any election — whether Assembly or Parliament — did not exceed six percentage points except in 1989 and 1991. And nor until 1998 did it win a single Parliamentary seat from the state. Leaving aside earlier elections, it won only one Assembly seat in 1977 as a partner of Janata Party and another Assembly seat in a by-election in the 1996 House.

Since 1977, the Left Front has been running the state government uninterrupted till 2006. It is some sort of a record that a group of Leftist parties despite having love and hate relations among themselves are maintaining the political coalition, which was actually the reflection of a *social coalition* that began crystallizing since late 1970s. The moment this social coalition is disturbed, the Left Front will suffer a serious existential crisis. Occasionally while some sort of a critical political mobilization that the Left parties in opposition carried on in the social arena, factionalism within the Congress in West Bengal threw the Congress out in 1967 after 17 years of its rule and then again in 1977 after a decade.

Analytically, politics in West Bengal is to be understood in its four different phases with definitive characteristics. The Congress dominated the first phase from 1947 to 1966. The Congress was able to continue because of total disunity among the opposition parties. The second phase beginning from 1967 to 1971 was characterized by chronic instability of all the subsequent governments as a result of inter party rivalries and often intra-party clashes throwing the state into a total chaos. The Left parties were able to capture power by focusing on, and propagating by dubious means, the corruption of its leaders and inability of the Congress government to properly respond to the demands of the people. The third phase began with Siddhartha Sankar Ray as the Chief Minister. But this government after a period of initial stability was subjected to an extreme type of factionalism. The Left parties, on the basis of their past experience of the late sixties, came closer together after the informal revocation of internal emergency in late December 1976 for the next democratic election. The point has already been touched on previously. The Left parties formed a solid front and came to dominate the Bengal politics, economy and society from 1977 onwards to the next 34 years.

Table 3.2 shows clearly that the Congress Party enjoyed absolute majority from 1952 to 1966. To the opposition parties the government led by the Congress was conservative. "Only the pressures of politicians and the groups they will lead for the Government to ameliorate the lot of the masses. Neither rational arguments nor petitions are likely to hasten Government action they believe, only mass activities, demonstration, *Hartal* (strike), civil disobedience and other expressions of mass-will, can force the Government to take action."[9] Table 3.2 also shows the total number of political parties that dominated West Bengal politics since 1952. After the beginning of the LF regime the number of political parties winning elections has been reduced to the advantage of the LF.

During 1950-1966 the opposition parties having failed to corner the government in the House brought politics to the streets. These included, among others, burning of trams and buses in the Calcutta streets, political mobilization against the proposal of Bengal-Bihar merger 1956, and violent food riots and movements in 1957, 1965 and 1966.

Humayun Kabir of the Bharatiya Kranti Dal (BKD) was the architect of a coalition experiment in West Bengal in 1967. With Ajoy Mukherjee at the head, two Leftist blocks—one led by CPI (M) and the other by CPI came together to form United Front (UF) government. This second phase of West Bengal politics was extremely volatile. The opposition parties led by CPI and CPI (M) were yet to learn the culture of governance in parliamentary terms. The revolutionary rhetoric of a Marxist variety in a parliamentary process gradually began to alienate the CPI (M) from other left parties, and fissures and cracks developed within the CPI (M) itself. Within a period of only four years from 1967 to 1971 West Bengal had to install four coalition governments. It was a period of hopeless uncertainty and a phase of political aggrandizement. The ultra-leftist group still believed that adapting to a parliamentary path was a blunder. The CPI (M) leaders began influencing the police forces and wanted to use police administration and the general administrative machineries for their own party interests.

The second UF government was a victim of intra-party feuds and inter-party clashes. The Chief Minister Ajoy Mukherjee and the Deputy Chief Minister, Jyoti Basu were at loggerheads with each other. The tension rose high and ultimately the Chief Minister declared a sit-in-strike near Curzon Park at Esplanade against his own government and called it "barbaric and

Table 3.2: Comparative Strength of Political Parties in West Bengal Assembly (1952-2006)

Year	*1952*	*1957*	*1962*	*1967*	*1969*	*1971*	*1972*	*1977*	*1982*	*1987*	*1991*	*1996*	*2001*	*2006*
NO. OF SEATS	238	252	252	280	280	280	280	294	294	294	294	294	294	294
Congress	150	152	157	127	55	-	216	20	-	-	-	-	-	-
Cong (R)	-	-	-	-	-	105	-	-	-	-	-	-	-	-
Cong (O)	-	-	-	-	-	2	2	-	-	-	-	-	-	-
INC	-	-	-	-	-	-	-	-	49	40	43	82	26	23
Trinamool Congress	-	-	-	-	-	-	-	-	-	-	-	-	60	30
Cong (S)	-	-	-	-	-	-	-	-	4	-	-	-	-	-
*Bangla Congress (BC)	-	-	-	34	33	5	-	-	-	-	-	-	-	-
*CPI (Undivided Communist Party till 1962)	28	46	49	16	30	13	35	2	7	11	6	6	7	8
*CPI (M)	-	-	-	43	80	113	14	178	174	187	188	150	143	176
KMPP	15	-	-	-	-	-	-	-	-	-	-	-	-	-
PSP	-	21	5	7	5	3	-	-	-	-	-	-	-	-
AIFB	14	8	13	14	21	3	-	26	28	26	29	21	25	23
*FB (M)	-	2	1	1	1	2	-	3	2	2	1	2	1	-
*RSP	-	3	9	7	12	3	3	20	19	18	18	18	17	20
*RCPI	-	-	2	-	2	3	-	3	2	1	1	-	-	-
WPI	-	-	-	2	2	2	1	-	-	-	-	-	-	-
*16, BBC	-	-	-	-	-	2	-	1	-	-	-	1	-	-
*17. WBSP	-	-	-	-	-	-	-	-	3	4	-	-	-	4
*18. DSP	-	-	-	-	-	-	-	-	3	2	1	2	2	1
*RJD	-	-	-	-	-	-	-	-	-	-	-	-	-	1
JANATA (JAN)	-	-	-	-	-	-	-	29	-	-	1	-	-	-
GL	-	1	2	2	4	2	2	2	1	-	-	-	-	-
SSP	-	-	-	7	9	1	-	-	-	-	-	-	-	-
SUCI	1	2	-	4	7	7	1	4	2	2	2	-	2	2

(Contd.)

Year	1952	1957	1962	1967	1969	1971	1972	1977	1982	1987	1991	1996	2001	2006
2ML	-	-	1	-	-	7	1	1	-	1	-	-	-	1
PML	-	-	-	-	3	-	-	-	-	-	-	-	-	-
CPI (ML)	-	-	-	-	-	-	-	1	-	-	-	-	-	-
Jharkhand (JKP)	-	-	-	-	-	2	-	-	-	-	1	1	-	1
27. Jana Sangh (JS)	9	-	-	1	-	1	-	-	-	-	-	-	-	-
28. Hindu Mahasabha (HM)	4	-	-	-	-	-	-	-	-	-	-	-	-	-
Swatantra (SWA)	-	-	-	1	-	-	-	-	-	-	-	-	-	-
INDF	-	-	-	-	1	-	-	-	-	-	-	-	-	-
SRP	1	-	-	-	-	-	-	-	-	-	-	-	-	-
LSS	-	7	4	5	4	-	-	-	-	-	-	-	-	-
FB (R)	1	-	-	-	-	-	-	-	-	-	-	-	-	-
GNLF	-	-	-	-	-	-	-	-	-	-	2	3	3	3
SP	-	-	-	-	-	-	-	-	-	-	-	-	-	-
FB (S)	-	-	-	-	-	-	-	-	-	-	-	1	1	-
IND/ OTHERS	15	10	10	9	11	3	5	4	-	-	1	7	7	4

Source: Compiled, Election Commission Report, West Bengal.

Note: *Indicates minor parties that fought elections with CPI (M)'s symbol. In the 1996 election the CPI (M) alone won 150 seats and in 2001 it won 143 i.e. below the benchmark.

uncivilized".[10] The Chief Minister Mukherjee resigned on March 16, 1970. Immediately the CPI (M) called a general strike on March 17. On this very day they brought out a big procession in Burdwan that culminated in a Congress supporters House. It was the house of Sain brothers. The CPI (M) marauders entered the house and carried on brutally murdering spree. It still has been infamously noted as "Sainbari Massacre" and into a bolder focus during the civil society agitation since September 2006.

The tattering UF government fell without delivering anything tangible to the people of the state. As a result of failure of the two coalition experiments in 1967 and 1969, the leftist forces went asunder. The CPI (M) fought the election on its own in 1971 and bagged 113 seats in the Assembly but won 35 per cent of the popular votes. This was the maximum percentage points of vote share that CPI (M) alone garnered in comparison with its earlier records. This time the Congress Party won 106 seats and secured more than 42 per cent of the popular votes. It was a very important point to reckon with that up to 1996, right from the first election in 1952, the percentage points of vote shared by the Congress always veered round 40 to 46 percentage points. This period was really a period of the "crisis of governance in West Bengal".[11] The period between 1967 and 1971 was a period of turmoil. Naxalite movements, and violence against land owners, merciless killings of innocent police men, retaliation against the CPI (M) cadres, CPI (M)'s enmity against not only congress workers but also against members of other Left parties, all these and other problems — administrative, social and political threw the state into a state of complete chaos. Economic conditions of the state and production in industrial units and agricultural outputs showed a downward trend. Siddhartha Sankar Ray at that time was the Central Cabinet Minister, in-charge of Education. In the beginning of the seventies Ray was given an additional charge to look after West Bengal affairs. The ordinary people of the state were really scared of the politics of the Leftists — extreme Left and that of the CPI (M) as well. It was a time when Bangladesh was liberated from Pakistan with the ultimate military help of India. During this period the CPI (M) in West Bengal clandestinely but in a sustained manner spread a canard that the Government of India would never call back its army from Bangladesh and intended to colonize the newly independent country. The Bangladesh Workers Party, sympathizers of the CPI (M) in India, in its party documents and other written materials, supported the ill-founded thesis of the cadres and members of the CPI (M).[12] Forming a pre-poll alliance — Progressive Democratic Alliance (PDA) with CPI — Ray fought the Assembly election on the crest of the popularity of Indira Gandhi, the real hero of Bangladesh war against the threatening USA, and along with an emerging group of youth Congress leaders, won the election with a thumping majority in the House. There was widespread allegation that the Congress and CPI Combine resorted to large-scale election violence and malpractices. The CPI (M), having won only 14 seats, boycotted the Assembly till the next election in 1977.

As a result of political stability, economic scenario began to be brightening. A few very important legislations — like the Calcutta Metropolitan Development Authority (CMDA), Housing Board, Metropolitan Development Authority and the Panchayat Act, etc. — were passed. Siddhartha Sankar Ray was not corrupt but many of' his younger colleagues could not claim that amount of transparency as was expected of young leaders. It was alleged that the new government was a regime of oppression. There was no doubt that the whole machinery of police administration was used ruthlessly to suppress the Naxalites. The CPI (M) activists — mostly those who were themselves used unbridled power, influence and other means like using administrative and state police machinery, were driven out. But unfortunately the new Chief Minister infused certain amount of groupism in his own brigade of young congress leaders and ministers and then instituted an enquiry commission headed by Mr. Justice Wanchu. The report never came out but the Chief Minister became very unpopular among his younger colleagues. By and large no serious "crisis of governance" irritated the people during this period.[13] The Ray government introduced a number of important legislations but had not the political will to implement them on time. The opportunity was actually utilized by the LF government when it came to power in 1977. During Siddhartha Sankar's PDA regime in West Bengal, the other left parties were quite inactive and, the leaders as well as the active party cadres of the CPI (M) had to be in the hiding. During the campaign of the opposition parties with Jayaprakash Narayana at the forefront, CPI (M) came out in the open with vigour. It was found that the party still maintained its well-knit and disciplined organization intact in its very moderate incarnation as compared to its present organizational clout. The CPI (M) along with other left parties like RSP, RCPI and FB was keen on a just seat adjustment with the Janata Party led by Prafulla Chandra Sen. The state leaders of Janata Party in the state particularly Prafulla Sen overestimated the strength of the newly formed Janata Party.[14] He did not want to concede anything more than 100 or if possible, less number of seats to the Leftists. The negotiation broke down. It was really a silent and continuous people's revolution during the period of 'internal emergency' in the mid seventies. A social coalition at the grassroots levels which was gradually coming up quite unobserved, found a better alternative in the politics of the Left parties. With a big majority, the Left Front won the election in 1977. The Janata Party had to eat the humble pie and the Congress was decimated. The Left parties maintained its strength for quite a time and only in 1996, the number of seats of the CPI (M) alone came down to 150. The political pre-poll coalition among the Left partners was intact. The factors that brought almost the major sections of people on the ideological as well as on the desirable plane of a social coalition appeared to be thinning out at least for the time being.

However, a political coalition arrangement that still has been continuing for the last 34 years is itself an achievement for the major Left parties. The credit largely goes to the CPI (M) and its capacity for political mobilization — both direct and mediated, and organizational network, although the junior partners are often aggrieved over its "big brotherly attitude". After 1977 election victory, the Left Front came to realize that it had to spread out to the rural areas, which once were mostly the areas of influence of the Congress.[15] The panchayat raj legislation enacted by Siddhartha Ray Government was actually implemented by the first LF Government and received overwhelming response from the rural Bengal. The LF Government also undertook a package of land reforms. The late Harekrishna Konar wrote profusely in his party paper in the late sixties about the essentiality of the same. The government began distributing vested lands to the small farmers and marginal peasants through a process of "Operation Barga". The LF government has been successfully working on political development of the state and has "really brought about a change in the development of rural economy since 1977".[16] For such a long period of time for a "social democratic" party or a combination of parties to remain in power with such little opposition either in the House or outside in the social plane, has its negative effects and pitfalls also. Tensions grew within the party itself, and organizational discipline and governmental activities began to lose directions.

The opposition Congress Party despite their organizational deficiencies and individualized leadership began to acquire strength manifesting in the Assembly election in 1996. The rural areas for all these years were reserved, as it were for the combined Left parties. The rural *jotedar* class switched over to the LF particularly after 1978 when the LF began to gain most of the panchayat bodies in all the three tiers. The ambitious local leaders of the CPI (M) began asserting themselves both socially and economically. The bureaucracy and the lower level authorities enforcing land reforms policies directly or indirectly helped the local party-bosses to be the arbitrators of the destinies of the villagers. The local party committees and important leaders of the CPI (M) were seen to be the "dispenser of justice".[17] Enormous amount of money and materials in the name of rural development funds came at the hands of these leaders. Many of the rural poor who got lands could not cultivate them either for reasons of their own or for lack of agricultural or other inputs, were compelled to sell out their lands. The local LF leaders in a clandestine manner purchased those lands or the local *Jotedar* took away the lands for a pittance and hired the landless farmers once again to labour on their regained lands. With the nexus of the political leaders, lower level bureaucracy and land reforms enforcing authorities forming a "new class"[18] in the rural areas came to dominate socio-economic scenario of the rural hinterlands. They were helped by the hierarchies of rich and middle class peasantries in the rural backyards. This continued for over a decade, which ultimately resulted in the cracking down of the social coalition that helped the Left parties coming closer together to garner their support base in the past. In this connection the following recent comment of a political analyst is relevant. "The bulwark of landless and poor peasants that they had built for the party's organization was badly breached by their creation of a new class of haves among the have-nots. So wide was the breach that they were unable to retain their traditional support base and allowed Trinamool Congress, a breakaway group led by Mamata Banerjee from the Congress on the eve of 1998 parliamentary election, to make deep inroads into their strongholds either through persuasive or coercive skills." Actually the "alienation had begun much earlier. The panchayat pradhans and the many rural schoolmasters had antagonized their own comrades by institutionalizing nepotism."[19] The sign of alienation was seen in the Assembly election of 1996 when the Congress won 82 seats. The Congress was split in regard to the question of Pradesh Congress leadership. Mamata Banerjee was expelled from the party and formed her own outfit—Trinamool Congress (TMC). She made an understanding with the National Democratic Alliance (NDA) led by BJP. The Trinamool Congress fought the Panchayat election on May 28, 1998 independently. But an unwritten and invisible understanding was made among the anti-Left forces including the Congress and the BJP at the local levels. For obvious reasons of organizational superiority and an element of fear psychosis[20] among the entire poor rural people, the Left Front (LF) won most of the *Zilla Parishad* seats and panchayat *Samitis* but felt a jolt in the third tier of the rural local *Gram Panchayat* levels. The Left Front had to lose many of the *Panchayat Samiti* seats and nearly a third of the *Gram Panchayat* seats. This is for the first time during the last twenty years that the leaders of the LF had to confront the reality that their hold over rural Bengal was not as closely knit as it had been even during 1960s. The social coalition that backed the pre-poll political coalition of the Left parties began indicating the first sign of fissures here and there not only in urban areas but also in rural backyards where the fiats of the local CPI (M) leaders were the last words.[21] But it is often found that for a corporate body like a political organization with modern gadgets to oversee and manage electoral process in each and every election at all levels, of the CPI (M)'s temporary set-back was just a part of the political game.

A large number of interest groups are backing the LF Government. Sometimes individual members give vent to their dissatisfaction but on the question of a change of government they are afraid to disturb the *status quo*. The LF is still enjoying a massive support base in the rural backyards and most of the fringe urban areas. Different Interest Groups viz. the *Kisan Sabha,*

CPI (M) affiliated, the powerful Primary Teachers' Association, All Bengal Teachers' Association (ABTA), the West Bengal College and University Teachers' Association (WBCUTA), the non-gazetted Police Association, *Ganatantrik Mahila Samity, Ganatantrik Lekhak Silpi Sangha,* etc. and above all the State Government Employees Co-ordination Committee and others are solidly behind the LF.

There are certain committed interest groups that have always been supporting the LF during the last 30 years. They have derived much benefit from the ruling front.[22] All through these long stints the LF and the partners always have been trying to expand their electoral bases as well as attempted to consolidate its position among the rural peasants and the middle class service holders. As already told, the front organizations of the parties, the teachers, students, businessmen, labourers — collectively and individually, small time industrialists always tried to hang around the major ruling party and the front.

It is a common phenomenon elsewhere that the ruling party or coalition of parties after an innings or two in running the government is seen to suffer from anti-incumbency factor. In West Bengal the anti-incumbency factors are conspicuously absent and the ruling front rather enjoys some sort of a pro-incumbency wave.[23] The Left Front came into power in West Bengal in the wake of the Janata Party wave in 1977 immediately after Indira Gandhi lifted the "infamous internal emergency" of 1975. Once the Front came it began consolidating itself. It was expected by the political analysts and feared by the leaders of the LF that in the face of a challenge thrown by Mamata Banerjee the Front might lose the 2001 election — the most crucial for the last 24 years of the LF rule. But the final results proved otherwise. The only change that took place was that the CPI (M) had to lose its predominant hold over the Front. It could not, unlike five earlier elections, secure absolute majority. For the first time, West Bengal was having a genuine coalition formation, although the CPI (M) was still the predominant party in the present coalition structure.

The situation, during the past several years and more particularly since 2001 Assembly Election, can aptly be described by the definition that West Bengal has been politically structured as a predominant party regime with ideological nearness that has given rise to a system of consociationalism politics to borrow the term from Ljjphart.[24] It is really puzzling, even in the face of so many odds as to how it has been possible for the LF to sustain itself in a very democratically conscious state — not vitiated by rabid caste and visible communal considerations as found elsewhere in Indian States, and more so with an anti-establishment-prone people for such a long period of time. The one major factor that came to be easily recognized had been almost the total absence of a viable opposition. The Congress Party was still unable to regain its social base and be got rid of the political trauma that afflicted it during the mid-seventies.

There are other very important factors as analyzed by Atul Kohli in a very perceptive study.[25] The LF Government appears to maintain a popular image of responsible and radical governing coalition. Its long standing anti-Central Government stance helps it to have almost a permanent cohesion among its ruling partners despite their occasional hiccups in regard to some of its important policy formulations dictated by the CPI(M). Locally anti-Congressism and broadly a rabid anti-BJP political stance give it a distinct regional nationalist halo that helps it create a division among the opposition political parties. Finally, a perennially weak central rule is what was always desired by the LF political establishment. The objectives of the predominant CPI (M) in the ruling front as transpired from its party manifesto brought out during all types of elections — national, regional and local — are supposed to inject certain amount of "redistributive justice" in the process of economic development and to remove rural poverty by restructuring rural local governments. Table 3.3 indicates that the LF's hold over the rural self-governing bodies will be illustrative before going into analyzing the Assembly election data over the years.

Table 3.3: Total Number of Seats Won and Percentage of Votes Polled by the Left Front and Opposition Parties (combined) in West Bengal in 3-Tier Panchayat Bodies

Parties	*Year*	*Gram Panchayat*		*Panchayat Samiti*		*Zilla Parishad*		*Total*	
		Seats	%	Seats	%	Seats	%	Seats	%
Left Front Total	2003	32,307	65.75	6,294	74.05	619	86.82	39,220	67.21
	1998	27,587	56.09	5,712	67.08	632	88.27	33,931	58.08
	1993	39,232	64.35	6,873	72.75	572	87.33	46,677	65.67
	1988	37,959	72.32	7,170	78.79	590	89.67	45,719	73.45
	1983	27,360	62.20	5,567	66.27	499	75.61	33,426	62.17
	1978	32,114	70.28	6,366	76.95	562	89.49	39,042	71.51
Total Combined Opposition Parties	2003	16,830	34.35	2,206	25.95	92	15.18	19,128	32.79
	1998	21,603	43.91	2,803	32.92	84	11.73	24,490	43.92
	1993	21,739	35.65	2,575	27.25	83	12.67	24,397	34.33
	1988	14,530	27.68	1,930	21.20	68	10.33	16,528	26.55
	1983	17,349	38.81	2,833	33.72	161	24.40	20,343	37.83
	1978	3,580	29.72	1,907	23.05	66	10.51	15,553	28.49

Source: Compiled, Directorate of Panchayat, Government of West Bengal.

Table 3.3 showed that the rural bases of the ruling front were stable for years at least till 2007. The people of West Bengal watched a different scenario after the Panchayat Raj election in 2008. LF.s seat share came down from more than 85 per cent to 52 per cent. The position of the LF in the Gram

Panchayat and the Panchayat Samiti almost nosedived to less than 48 per cent. It was really not auguring well for the LF in general and the CPI (M) in particular. The LF's vote share came down to 43 per cent while vote share of the combined parties went up to 57 per cent. It was a clear indication of people's angst against the CPI (M) and its the past activities and ruthlessness in the rural hinterland in Bengal.

The party or combination of the parties to capture political power in state, must have the majority support of the panchayat bodies in West Bengal which requires a very well-knit and hugely spread out party organization with a skill to continue social engineering as usual from 1982 onwards. This has been the strongest point in favour of the CPI (M). The opposition parties are a house divided and inimical to each other, as has been seen during the last seven elections—Assembly in 2001, Panchayat in 2003, Parliamentary in 2004, and the most recently concluded Assembly election in 2006. The weaknesses of the main two opposition parties appear to be established by a simple fact that the party cannot man even 2/3 of the total number of booths during any of the Assembly or Parliamentary election whereas the LF led by the CPI (M) used to put at least 3-5 polling agents in each of more than 51,500 booths as at present. This proves clearly the organizational strength and clout of the CPI (M) in the state politics.

Table 3.4 showed the positions of the parties in West Bengal Assembly since 1967. Some of the parties shown earlier subsequently went into oblivion at the advantage of the earlier two UFs and since then.

More important is the percentage points of the vote shares shown in Table 3.4. This is significant that a slight swing of 2 to 3 per cent of votes might have reduced the seats won by the LF. Actually it has been enjoying power due to a very low Index of Opposition Unity (IOU). The Congress Party was determined not to have any understanding with BJP direct or indirect through the Trinamool Congress. Paradoxically, it was often found that in many of the panchayat bodies and some municipal bodies including Calcutta Municipal Corporation there was clandestine understanding among the three parties, namely the Congress, somewhere with TMC and more surprisingly the BJP that won them majority in those panchayat bodies and municipalities. In 2001 Assembly election, the LF secured a total of 48.94 per cent votes. Table 3.4 shows that the share of the major partners of the LF was 47.07 giving a 1.87 per cent points to the smaller partners like WBSP, SP, and FB (M). The Congress and Trinamool Congress combine secured only 38.92. The BJP's share of votes of nearly 11.50 per cent that it secured in parliamentary election in 1999 has been reduced to 5.19 per cent.

The LF's almost outstanding performance in 2001 Assembly election after its vote share in 1999 Parliamentary election, is very significant. Surprisingly the CPI (M) not only averted its decline but improved its position

Table 3.4: Seats Won and Percentage of Votes Polled by Parties, Assembly Elections (1967-2001)

Party	*1967*	*1969*	*1971*	*1972*	*1977*	*1982*	*1987*	*1991*	*1996*	*2001*
CONG	127 (41.12)	55 (41.32)	105 (29.25)	216 (49.06)	20 (23.25)	49 (35.59)	40 (41.80)	44 (35.12)	83 (39.48)	26 (7.98)
B. Cong	34 (12.14)	33 (11.78)	5 (1.78)	–	–	–	–	–	–	–
CPI ('72-'77) with Cong	15 (6.17)	30 (6.99)	13 (8.42)	35 (8.33)	2 (2.62)	7 (1.81)	10 (1.72)	6 (1.75)	6 (1.75)	7 (1.79)
CPI (M)	44 (18.27)	80 (19.97)	113 (32.81)	14 (27.46)	177 (35.32)	174 (38.47)	188* (39.48)	187* (36.64)	150 (37.92)	143 (36.59)
RSP	6 (1.38)	12 (2.80)	3 (2.19)	3 (2.14)	20 (3.75)	19 (4.01)	18 (3.94)	18 (3.47)	18 (3.72)	17 (3.43)
FB	13 (4.43)	21 (5.01)	3 (2.90)	– (2.49)	26 (5.32)	27 (5.75)	26 (5.84)	29 (5.51)	21 (5.20)	25 (5.65)
BJP						– (0.61)	– (0.51)	– (11.37)	1 (0.34)	– (5.19)
TMC										60 (30.66)
Ind. & Others	75 (26.78)	82 (29.28)	43 (15.45)	12 (4.28)	49 (16.66)	18 (6.12)	12 (4.08)	10 (3.40)	16 (3.40)	16 (5.44)
TOTAL	280	280	280	280	294	294	294	294	294	294

Source: Reports, Election Commission.
Note: *indicates that the seats of a few minor parties that fought with CPI (M)'s party symbol are included in CPI (M)'s total.

both in terms of seat share and percentage points of valid votes cast. The BJP being slighted by the Trinamool Congress when it severed ties with the NDA mounted a sustained campaign against the party and wanted to defeat it even if voting in favour of the CPI (M) and its minor partners where ever it was possible.[26] Table 3.5 shows that the LF crossed over the hurdles it faced in the 2001 Assembly election having lesser number of seats as well as reduced percentage share of valid votes cast, but in 2004 Parliamentary election the LF regained its positions in terms of vote shares. It proved the LF's extraordinary acumen for electoral management at a time when it was really difficult to tide over the difficulties of a stagnant situation or decline because of reasons more than one including incumbency factors. Due to vote-seat distortion natural for first passed the post (FPTP) system, the LF won 35 seats getting slightly more than 50 per cent of the valid votes; the Congress won six seats on the basis of its 14.56 per cent vote but BJP TMC combine won only one seat (TMC) while their vote share together was 29.10 per cent. It was to some extent the slight revival of the Congress but disaster for the Trinamool Congress due to a complete absence of seat adjustment with the Congress to build up any alternative coalition of a sort.

Table 3.5: Seats and Vote Won by Parties in Parliamentary Elections 1996-2004 (in %)

Party	*1996*	*1998*	*1999*	*2004*
CPI (M)	21 (34.50)	24 (35.61)	21 (35.59)	26 (38.56)
CPI	2 (2.49)	3 (3.65)	3 (3.47)	3 (4.01)
FB	3 (3.40)	2 (3.32)	2 (3.45)	3 (3.66)
RSP	4 (4.74)	4 (4.51)	3 (4.25)	3 (4.49)
INC	11 (40.66)	1 (15.24)	3 (13.29)	6 (14.56)
TMC	–	7 (24.49)	8 (26.05)	1 (21.04)
BJP	–	1 (10.23)	2 (11.14)	– (8.06)
Ind. & Others	– (14.21)	– (2.95)	– (2.76)	– (5.62)

Source: Compiled. CEO's Reports, West Bengal.

It is always found that the parliamentary election results more or less reflect the trends of West Bengal politics in terms of number of seats won by major political parties particularly the party or the combination of parties forming the government in the state. Previously it was found that the electorate used to make a distinction between national parties, which were better equipped to look after the interest of the nation as a whole. The issues as thrown up by the parties in their campaigns on the basis of which elections were fought appeared to be different to the same electorates voting both for the assembly and parliamentary elections. Gradually this distinction became blurred and the state political parties made a big political issue as to how the government at the Centre always discriminated against the state government. This attitude has been found to prevail since her security guards murdered Indira Gandhi in 1984. But immediately after this ghastly assassination on a sympathy wave, the Congress Party in West Bengal got as many 16 parliamentary seats. This election was an exception and many Leftist politicians viewed that Rajiv Gandhi and his Congress Party on a rare sympathy wave fought the election. The Congress Party was also focused on the aspects of national security after the gruesome murder of the most powerful Prime Minister of the country while the Khalsa and other secessionist movements were rampant.

The voters like to use their votes in West Bengal with utmost caution and some degree of discretion; they would make a distinction between electing the members of the State Assembly and the members of the Lok Sabha. The votes for the Lok Sabha were meant for political stability which would make sure that the country's integrity, diversities be maintained and the strategies against fissiparous forces might not be jeopardized. The state government would be formed by the parties for meeting the proximate needs and demands of the people of the state. But a near total politicization pervades now in every stage of electoral process, the earlier distinction being obliterated.

The party system and its smooth working in a democratic framework should be based on competed ethos between or among them. This can be found in Britain; even it is true in bipartite activities in the US; so much so that it works in West European and other Nordic countries like Norway, Holland, Sweden, etc. where pluralities of the party system exist because of their constitutionally adopted proportional representation of the parties. Here no party can be enjoying absolute majority in the House. To reduce corruption the parties according to their political ideology and objectives work to create public awareness. Their activities more often than not appear to be transparent; a democratic political activity along with transparency in administrative culture is one of the fundamental focal points of good governance. At least theoretically these are the basics of people oriented government. But here particularly in West Bengal the totality of the political scenario is completely different. Fierce political enmity between or among them rather than socio-political rivalry based on democratic value system or lack of political competitiveness prevails since the mid-1960s. The party or a coalition of parties in power, has the self-made privileges and the political hold to exploit the administrative and the law and order maintenance machineries to its or their maximum advantages. This is the reason for which the opposition parties are voicing the demands that the state elections should be made under the President's rule or under a neutral authority in the state. The then Chief Election Commissioner Dr. M.S. Gill in this connection also emphasized the long standing contention that what was required in the state elections was a neutral government in the run up to the elections.[27]

Again to come back, an analysis of Table 3.5 shows the relative party positions in the parliament from 1996 to 2004. In a way this also proved our earlier contention that the people of West Bengal did not lose all hopes about the Congress as truly the biggest and stable national party. Before analyzing the parliamentary elections since 1989 till 2004 in their various ramifications in terms of campaign style, party manifestos and other related aspects, the election results of the few elections since 1952 are to be highlighted. The percentage point of votes shared by different parties are truly the reflections of the parties' acceptability to the electorates — particularly for the Congress on one hand and the opposition parties led by the CPI (M) on the other. Table 3.6 shows the comparative percentage point of vote shares of the parties over the years, of course, many of the parties later were merged with other parties in course of time and some went out of the race.

From 1952 to 1962 the vote shares of the Congress fluctuated between 39.25 per cent and 46.80 per cent, the maximum was 48.20 per cent only in 1957. From 1962 to 1996 the vote shares of Congress were between 46.80 per cent and 40.66 per cent. The minimum was 27.78 per cent in 1971 and 28.70 per cent in 1977. The vote shares of the CPI (M) in the Left Front coalition rose never beyond 39.81 per cent and that was only in 1980. When the CPI (M) fought parliamentary election alone in 1971 it captured a vote share of only 35.54 per cent.

There are other smaller six parties in the LF government. None of them have any representation in the Lok Sabha. The vote shares of 'Others' and the BJP were not inconsiderable. The 1991 and 1996 poll results showed a positive reduction of the share of votes of the Left parties to below the critical 50 per cent level. The *social coalition* indicated earlier seemed in danger but by the strength of its organizational networks, direct political mobilization and indirect societal mobilization the CPI (M) revived the LF's vote shares to 50.72 per cent in 2004 election. The BJP alone so long "untouchable" in West Bengal politics secured 12.20 per cent votes in 1991 and 7.20 per cent in 1996 but only 8.06 per cent in 2004. This was perhaps the fall-out of a sustained campaigning by all the parties against BJP after the *Babri Masjid* demolition in 1992 and Gujarat communal riot after Godhra train massacre in 2002. The scenario changed in two successive elections in 1998 and 1999 when BJP found a popular leader like Mamata Banerjee and her newly formed Trinamool

Table 3.6: Share of Votes of Parties and Alliances/Adjustment in Parliamentary Elections (1952-2004) (in %)

Year	*INC (%)*	*CPI (%)*	*JS (%)*	*FB (%)*	*RSP (%)*	*IND (%)*	*Others*	
1952	39.25	9.34	5.86	4.46	2.37	18.22	20.49	
1957	48.2	19.01	1.43	6.37	1.98	12.74	10.27	
1962	46.8	29.37	1. 05	6.32	2.59	6.06	7.81	
	INC (%)	CPI (%)	JS/BLD (%)	CPI (M) (%)	FB (%)	RSP (%)	IND (%)	Others
1967	39.69	9.14	1.39	15.65	4.83	2.03	11.23	16
1971	27.78	9.75	0.86	35.54	2.73	1.63	5.87	15.85
1977	28.7	5.86	21.47*	26.79	4.3	3.94	6.68	2.27
	CPI (M) %	CPI (%)	FB (%)	RSP (%)	BJP (%)	AITC (%)	INC (%)	IND
1980	39. 81	4.27	4,54	5.2	0.01	-	36.4	1.34
1984	32.24	13.63	3.7	4.15	0.36	-	43.23	1.71
1989	37.75	3.99	4.04	4.8	1.57	-	41.74	2.03
1991	35.38	3.7	3.67	4.52	12.2	-	36.36	0.96
1996	34.5	2.49	3.4	4.74	7.2	-	40.66	1.35
1998	35.61	3.65	3.32	4.51	10.23	24.49	15.24	1.04
1999	35.59	3.47	3.45	4.25	11.14	26.05	13.29	2.76
2004	38.56	4.01	3.66	4.49	8.06	21.04	14.56	5.62

Source: Parliamentary Elections in West Bengal (1952-2004), CEO, West Bengal.
Note: The votes of the smaller parties belonging to the Left Front were being usually transferred to the major parties like CPI (M), CPI, FB and RSP of the LF.

Congress (TMC) as its poll partner. The rise of Mamata Banerjee with her Trinamool Congress in West Bengal is a phenomenon in anti-CPI (M) electoral movements in the politics in West Bengal, first in 1998 and then in 1999 parliamentary elections.

The West Bengal Election Scenario

Immediately after the 'emergency', propelled anti-Congress wave in 1977 election, the Janata Party coalition came into power at the Centre. The LF in West Bengal led by CPI (M) alone having 17 parliamentary seats in West Bengal had the chance of consolidating itself in Indian politics. The LF with a total number of 55 seats in parliament was really a force to reckon with.

After a decade the LF, precisely the CPI (M), with its strength lent support to the Janata Dal of Vishwanath Pratap Singh to defeat Rajiv Gandhi and the

Congress Party in 1989 parliamentary election, the Front led by the CPI (M) came closer to the Bharatiya Janata Party (BJP) to support VP Singh in his virulent campaign against Rajiv Gandhi. This election was a watershed in Indian politics. This was substantially the beginning of a coalition era. Actually, it was a minority Government of V.P. Singh with outside support from BJP with its 88 members and the LF led by CPI (M) with its 55 members. V.P. Singh with his 131 Janata Dal members formed the government. The LF after a decade found a "friendly government" at the Centre after the Janata Party Government in 1977. As elsewhere in Indian states — particularly the Hindi belt — the election was fought on the main issue of Bofors scandal. The campaign style was extremely aggressive. The slogan coined by V.P. Singh was *"gali gali mey shore hyai, Rajiv Gandhi chor hai*" i.e. in every lane and bye-lane, the thief Rajiv Gandhi is there. The CPI (M) cadres painted Bofors canon on walls after walls and put Rajiv's face on the barrels of the canons. The Leftist's political slogan appeared always to be negative. The Congress Party's propaganda motif—"*mera desh mahan hai*" i.e. "my country is great" was rewritten by the CPI (M) as "*mera desh mahan hai, our Prime Minister chor hai*". A wonderful caricature nobody would doubt when mentioning the name of a corrupt politician! But the institution of the prime minister, the office of the chief executive of the nation was drawn and denigrated.[28] Corruption was not only a single issue in this election campaign, the Leftists raised their oft-repeated charge that the Congress if it came back to power would destroy the good work done so far by the successive regimes of the LF in the field of agriculture, industry, IT sectors and distort the institutional structures of the panchayat raj system in West Bengal. The poorer sections of the society would be deprived of their hard-earned dignity the LF claimed to have infused to them. The LF made severe propaganda that Rajiv Gandhi was trying to introduce elitist education policy and modern capital-intensive technology.[29] The LF quite effectively administered its well-orchestrated propaganda as it had done earlier focusing on their achievements particularly in the rural front. It tried to mobilize political opinions in favour of good things it claimed to have done, good things in the fields of education, health, unemployment allowances to the deserving youths, teachers' salaries, pension and enhanced pay and allowances to the government employees, better industrial relations. In short, they claimed to have dished out an alternative economic policy, and giving benefits to people engaged in the service sectors; above all, the LF regime claimed to have reversed the centre-state relations in favour of the state government.

When 1998 parliamentary election was held, the Congress Party in West Bengal was already split. Factionalism in Indian party system was not new. The Communist Party's split was sought to be explained in terms of their ideological moorings, something novel in the nineties, not exactly true though.

The CPI (M) was beset with factionalism in several district committees. This factionalism in recent times was not due to any ideological debates. After having enjoyed almost unopposed supremacy for long, some of the district leaders came into conflict with each other to increase their share of gains and influences both at the district and state committee levels. Many of the leaders at different levels, state, district, regional and grassroots levels were at loggerhead with the groups. The continuous enjoyment of political power dictated them to increase the sphere of influences by means "fair or foul". The CPI (M) seemed to apply its Leninist principles that were diluted in its continued adjustment with and adapting to the parliamentary system of governance. Atul Kohli found that CPI (M)'s "parliamentary communism",[30] and "democratic centralism" made the Party much more cohesive and disciplined than any other Indian political party. The largest national party, the Congress, on the other hand, appeared to have been suffering from perennial factionalism. The Congress Party's latest setback was about the question of the office of the Pradesh Congress Committee. The quarrel between Soumen Mitra and Mamata Banerjee came to such a pass that Mamata Banerjee had to run a parallel organization and ultimately was expelled from the Party. The majority of the rank and file, particularly most of the younger people went out with her. Many of the Congress leaders overtly or covertly had the habit of enjoying some sort of patronage from the LF Government in terms of having Government housing land, Government-built flats, sons and daughters' admission into the medical and engineering institutions out of the Chief Minister's quota, besides other means. These leaders almost lost the confidence of the lower ranks of party workers. Mamata Banerjee formed her Trinamool Congress (TMC) and in no time appeared to become the symbol of anti-CPI (M) force in West Bengal. To her, the one point programme was "to dislodge the authoritarian and corrupt CPI (M)" from power.[31] The CPI (M)'s propaganda that Mamata Banerjee's anti-communal stance against the BJP was a ploy to divide the opposition votes of the original Congress Party.

After the fall of the three Prime Ministers during the mid-1990s, people opted for a government that would provide at least a minimum amount of stability at the Centre. The regional parties—looking for asserting a real federal influence upon the Central government did not want to further experiment with a ramshackle structure subsisting upon the external support by the Congress on the one hand and the LF on the other. The BJP, in the process, with moderate Atal Behari Vajpayee as its leader, appeared to have gained confidence of the Leaders of several states and their parties excepting the Communists. Mamata formed an alliance with BJP at the state level assuring support to Atal Behari Vajpayee from outside. After the election BJP in West Bengal found a windfall gain. For the first time in the history of the state in recent years BJP won a parliamentary seat from Dum Dum defeating a veteran sitting member of the CPI (M). The Trinamool Congress (TMC) won seven seats and the lone Congress seat was won from Malda.

Table 3.7 indicates percentage points of vote shares by the BJP. The campaign against BJP as a Muslim "baiter" and "hater" by the CPI (M) did not work as expected by the LF.

Table 3.7: Vote Shares of Major Parties in West Bengal for Parliamentary Elections in 1998 and 1999 (in %)

Year	*Left Front*	*INC*	*TMC + BJP*
1998	47.09	15.24	34.72
1999	46.76	13.29	37.19

Table 3.7 shows that the Left Front's votes were reduced to 47.09 per cent in 1998 and 46.76 per cent in 1999 from more than 50 per cent in earlier elections. It was quite considerable in a competitive context when Trinamool and BJP combine was being gradually popular and the Congress's hold over its traditional vote banks around 40 per cent to 42 per cent over the years began shrinking. But Table 3.7 indicates that seat adjustment understanding as seen, many a local body would have thrown out the LF in the parliamentary election.[32] This calculation might have inspired the Trinamool to propound the idea of a grand alliance as happened in 1989 to throw out Rajiv Gandhi. Mamata Banerjee floated the idea of a *mahajot* (grand alliance) of Trinamool Congress-BJP combine with the Congress party. The Left Front and its leaders became nervous. They began increasing their tempo of propaganda against the BJP about its "vicious Hindu communalism" and its patron Mamata Banerjee in West Bengal. The grand alliance or the *mahajot* appeared to the CPI (M) as a "conspiracy" and political "opportunism" on the part of the Congress.[33] The central and state leaders of the CPI (M) did not like Sonia Gandhi to go in for an alliance with Mamata Banerjee with BJP as her junior partner in West Bengal politics. Sonia Gandhi, who might have to depend on the Left forces in some future plan of government formation in case the National Democratic Alliance (NDA) disintegrated, foreclosed the option. Secondly, the BJP with its "hidden communal agenda" was the main political competitor of the Congress, as the second largest party it could not share the same socio-political space.[34] Later in that year in a by-election the Left Front could not retain the Panskura parliamentary seat. The CPI (M) made it a prestige issue and used all sorts of epithets against Mamata Banerjee as a "symbol of bad politics and disruption."[35]

To derive benefit by supporting a coalition structure but absolving responsibilities, would not benefit the CPI (M) in the long-run. The party bosses realized the "historic blunder" of not allowing Jyoti Basu to head a congress backed minority coalition at the Centre in 1998. History repeated itself but with a comical gesture. This is perhaps the reason that Jyoti Basu, throughout the period of election campaign in 1999 and then in 2004 spoke to his audience that he was to go to Delhi and the party would have to take greater responsibilities. The points as to why the electorate would vote for a regional party if it shied away from the responsibility of governance could not be put under the carpet. As also to participate in the coalition government at the Centre had to be thoroughly thrashed out in the context of the observations that West Bengal is better administered than most other Indian states. Secondly, the questions were to be focused to judge the contention that "both at the elite and mass level CPI (M)'s support structure was relatively stable".[36]

By and large this has been largely continuing even till the parliamentary elections in 1999 and 2004, as also the Assembly elections in 2001 and 2006. It indicates the CPI (M)'s overwhelming organizational strength and superior "politico-electoral strategy and management and electoral engineering", as revealed later by Benechapra, Choto Angaria and Netaigram massacres to refer to only a few during and after the 2008 Panchayat elections. The recruits of party leaders have been confined to the middle levels of society. A monolithic structure is subjected to stress and strains, which ultimately results in the politics of dissidence within. In the 1999 Lok Sabha election the CPI (M) received a jolt at the hands of the Trinamool Congress and the BJP combine. On the basis of evidence, particularly in the face of polarization between urban and rural voters, it can be concluded that the Trinamool's gain was based on negative votes and the rural base of the CPI (M) was not intact as it had been before 1998 and in previous elections.[37] The analysis of several factors including the distribution of total votes polled in 294 assembly segments[38] in successive elections in 1998 and 1999 showed some cracks and fissures at various levels within the socio-political spaces both rural and urban levels of the LF. Under such circumstance the LF had had to face the electorates in the Assembly election 2001. It was a very crucial election for the LF. The social coalition that helped the LF to take over appeared to be sliding down and LF's vote shares were reduced[39] by nearly four per cent.

It is to be noted at the very beginning that electoral calculus, particularly in West Bengal, is puzzling to the political analysts and almost baffling to the newsmen when confronted with tightlipped voting populations, which were floating and noncommittal. The editor of a national News Daily wrote that Mamata Banerjee "is playing her cards well" and "she is a good grassroots politician and knows how to play the game" and exploit the prevailing political economy scenario during the LF regime during the past several years. "She can expect other Congressmen to follow but needs time to decide how many she can accommodate as candidates without upsetting those who have been with her steadfastly and allowing for Subhas Chakraborty to make his move."[40]

Ultimately, Subhas had to adjust himself with his party and finally deserted his rebel colleagues Saifuddin Chowdhury and Samir Putatunda and their new party, Party for Democratic Socialism (PDS). The caustic press criticisms, the aggressive postures of the Trinamool leader Mamata Banerjee — her confidence and the silent moods of the people and the sizes of the floating voters, the growing dissidence among the CPI (M) leaders and a portion of rank and files were well taken care of by the CPI (M).[41] Nearly six months before the May 2001 Assembly elections, the CPI (M) got the longest serving chief minister to retire on grounds of health. To refurbish the sagging morale of the administration and replenish the LF with a new-look, Buddhadeb Bhattacharya — the Minister for Home (Police) and Cultural Affairs in Jyoti Basu's Cabinet, was to take over. Buddhadeb personally appeared to be a changed man shedding off his earlier arrogance, and appealed to the people to vote for a change, for a reoriented better performing LF. The battle cry of Mamata Banerjee was to topple the LF government and bring about a change.

On the simple pretext of "Tehelka" episode, Mamata resigned from the Vajpayee Council of Ministers distancing herself and her party from (NDA). After a bitter bargain with the Congress leadership, in the process creating dissension among a section of her own party members and giving long rope to the Congress rebels and existing MLAs, entered into an alliance. The local leaders of the BJP — particularly Tapan Sikdar, M.P., bitterly attacked Mamata and appealed to the Bengal electorates to punish her. It appeared from public mood that people did not also like Mamata's hasty and a little immature action for a short term gain. Ultimately, the Trinamool and Congress combine had to lose 54 seats in the 2001 poll'; the independent presence of the BJP[42] in the fray undoubtedly played a part. In fact the 2001 Assembly election was a four cornered contest. The other two fronts were PDS led by Saifuddin, the NCP of Sharad Pawar and BJP. The ultimate result was the victory for the LF for the sixth time which was "quite unexpected"[43] even to the leaders of the LF who had to almost reorganize the election machinery and fought the "toughest battles" in their own words with the "back against the wall". The ultimate result appeared to be a little reduced mandate for the LF. The TMC and Congress combine anticipated that the larger participation of the voters (Table 3.8) would go in favour of the opposition parties. But they were bewildered to find the results. The anti-incumbency factor did not work excepting that the CPI (M)'s seat share was reduced to 143 only. After some 24 years the CPI (M) lost its surplus majority and the LF became truly a coalition, an oversized coalition all along though.[44]

Table 3.9 shows the number of seats and percentage share of votes won by the LF, TMC Congres combine and the BJP and others.

Table 3.9 shows that the LF was reduced marginally to 199 as compared with 203 in 1996. In view of political euphoria of TMC, the result of TMC +,

Table 3.8: Comparative Voters' Participation in Parliamentary Elections since 1977 (in %)

Year	*All India Average*	*Mean*	*West Bengal Average*	*Mean*
1977	60.50		60.02	
1980	56.09	60.28	70.07	77.36
1984	64.00		78.06	
1989	62.00		79.07	
1991	61.00		76.09	
1996	57.94		82.06	
1998	61.47		79.23	
1999	60.00		83.00	
2004	59.50		82.5	
2006	—		83.5	

Source: Compiled, Report, Election Commission.

Table 3.9: Result of the Assembly Election 2001 Percentage Share of Votes by Parties (in %)

Parties	*Seats Won*		*Parties*	*Vote share*	
CPI M)	143		CPI (M)	36.50	
FB	25	LF 199	FB	5.65	LF 48.94
RSP	17		RSP	3.43	
SP	4		CPI	1.49	
DSP	2		Smaller parties	1.89	
FB (M)	1				
TMC	60	TMC+ 86	Trinamool Cong	27.00	TMC + & Cong
Cong	26		Congress	12.00	39.00
BJP	0	BJP + 0	Others & Ind.	6.87	6.87 BJP + 5.19
		Independent & Others-9	BJP	5.19	= 51.06
Total	294		Total no of Parties	100.00	100.00

Source: Election Commission Report.

was unexpected. BJP and, the other combine of rebel CPI (M) leader Saifuddin's PDS plus Sharad Pawar's NCP (shown as others) got no seats. It was really a lost chance for the combined opposition parties. Due to the irreconcilable attitudes both on the part on the intra party deference Congress and to some extent the TMC, the incomplete alliance or better to mention as seat sharing formula did not work. Without presenting a viable alternative and trustworthy political formation with concrete policy proposals it was very difficult to destabilize the political coalition that so long gave a long rope to the LF regime and because of the vote division, the LF front appeared to be invincible in the 2006 Assembly election despite its misgovernance in different socio political spaces. Rather the LF bettered its position in the 2006 Assembly election. The opposition parties were in complete disarray. The Congress continued discussion with TMC for long to forge an alliance but at the last moment even at the intervention of Pranab Mukherjee, the idea of the TMC-Congress understanding did not materialize. On the other hand, the CPI (M) was overwhelmingly successful to keep its hold in all the districts (Table 3.10) and the social coalition particularly among the Muslims (28.62%), schedule castes (23.02%) and schedule tribes (5.62%) of the state. It won 235 seats sharing 50.12 percentage points of vote share. Actually the larger districts as also the entire western belt of Purulia, Bankura, Burdwan, Hooghly, Howrah, West Midnapur and this time in 2006 the two 24 Parganas contributed largely to the massive victory for the LF (Table 3.10)

Table 3.10: West Bengal Assembly Elections 2006 District-wise Party Position Constituency-wise with Percentage Point of Votes Polled

Districts	*Left Front*	*Congress*	*TMC*	*BJP*	*Others*
Cooch Behar	7 (49.32)	1 (12.65)	1 (24.55)	– (7.62)	– (5.86)
Jalpaiguri	11 (45.11)	1 (19.95)	– (15.55)	– (3.99)	– (15.40)
Darjeeling	2 (34.27)	– (13.84)	– (4.28)	– (2.02)	3 (45.60)
North Dinajpur	5 (39.20)	2 (40.05)	– (8.02)	– (2.00)	– (10.73)
South Dinajpur	5 (50.23)	– (12.27)	– (21.55)	– (10.83)	– (5.12)
Malda	7 (45.25)	4 (39.88)	– (5.10)	– (3.57)	– (6.20)
Murshidabad	13 (44.29)	3 (38.05)	– (2.56)	– (0.41)	3 (14.69)
Nadia	12 (49.49)	1 (11.80)	2 (33.80)	– (0.17)	– (4.68)
North 24 Parganas	24 (48.43)	– (8.75)	4 (36.61)	– (2.07)	– (3.50)
South 24 Parganas	21 (48.34)	1 (6.73)	4 (37.50)	– (0.90)	2 (6.53)
Kolkata	8 (44.99)	3 (17.68)	9 (30.70)	– (1.57)	1 (5.06)
Howrah	14 (48.21)	– (12.20)	2 (33.85)	—	– (5.74)
Hooghly	16 (50.96)	– (9.13)	2 (33.28)	– (1.65)	1 (4.98)
East Midnapur	10 (38.12)	– (3.29)	3 (44.02)	–	3 (14.57)
West Midnapur	17 (53.39)	2 (9.42)	– (24.16)	– (2.28)	2 (10.95)
Purulia	10 (49.85)	1 (16.82)	– (17.57)	– (2.05)	– (13.71)
Bankura	13 (57.02)	– (7.02)	– (25.90)	– (1.98)	– (8.08)
Burdwan	22 (56.98)	1 (10.61)	2 (24.26)	– (1.41)	1 (6.74)
Birbhum	10 (53.31)	1 (21.10)	1 (18.20)	– (2.03)	– (5.36)

Source: Compiled, Election Commission Report.

The Left Front bagged 235 seats and won 50.12 per cent votes. If the matter is looked at from the other angle, at least theoretically a paradoxical scenario would seem to the analysts. By fielding 294 candidates in the fray the LF won a total of 50.12 per cent votes in 2006. It was found, in a calculation on the basis of voting data and vote seat distortion because of FPTPS, that the winning candidates (235) of LF secured only 40.06 per cent.

The Assembly elections of 1996 were not encouraging for the CPI (M) having enjoyed an overwhelming predominance in the coalition structure with only 150 seats in the Assembly. In the intervening period the Chief Minister Jyoti Basu was concerned more with politics at Delhi than looking after the State politics and administration with whole-hearted attention. His oft-repeated comments about an elected NDA government led by the BJP at the Centre — "barbarous and uncivilized"[45] were not received kindly by the discerning audience. Even many of his colleagues in the LF felt a sense of uneasiness. His personal attack upon the most popular opposition leader as a "cheat" appeared to be unkind and personal. The economy of the state was in a bad shape and finally factionalism within the party was let loose. Two of the stalwarts—Saifuddin and Samir Putatundu and many a party activist left the party. Subhas Chakraborty, as usual, was undisciplined and in a state of "to be or not to be" about joining hands with Mamata Banerjee.

Buddhadeb Bhattacharya took over in November 2000. He immediately admitted certain defects in running the LF Governments. But Buddhadeb had to carry the legacy of his immediate predecessor. The 2001 election was not encouraging at all for him, because of the reduced number of seats he could garner. Buddhadeb appeared to be a Brand Buddha to a section of news media with a Marxist *Bhadralok* image having the "liberal parliamentary principles". He allowed himself to be packaged to be a modern leader willing to fulfill the aspirations of the middle class and young first time voters. These might be his strong points in overwhelmingly winning the 2006 elections. His main rival Mamata Banerjee of the TMC did not care for the finer points of the changed circumstances of the newly emerging politics of the state. She did not care to package herself to be a leader acceptable to the most sections of the voters. Her single point of agenda was to remove the existing LF Government. She became popular but was no match for the organizational strength and acumen of the CPI (M). She was able to pull a massive crowd for her peculiar ways and sympathetic wavelength with the ordinary masses but was often unable to translate the voters' attention and love into actual votes in the ballot boxes. In the penultimate phase of the Assembly election, to win over the Muslim votes which in a big way went against her Trinamool Congress because of her association with the BJP led NDA government, she left the Vajpayee Government on a flimsy ground of "Tehelka episode" as mentioned above and made an alliance before 2001 election with the Congress which she had earlier branded as a stooge of CPI (M). She left the Vajpayee Government in an inopportune moment. As a result she was benefited in neither way. On the other hand, the new Chief Minister was admitting that all was not well with the previous LF Governments. If he were given a chance he would try to bring about a "new Government and clean administration". He would be looking after creating necessary infrastructures in terms of making new roads and maintaining the older ones, communications, urging for more railway lines within the state, irrigation, bank loans to the 'would be self-employed', proper collections of state revenues, etc. He gave the impression that he quite understood the present scenario of industrial production that came down from 9.8 per cent in 1980-81 to 5.1 per cent in 1998-99. The export-import transit from Calcutta port fell down from 10 per cent in 1985-86 to four per cent in 1998-99. West Bengal holding the second position in industrial production in the 1960s, came down to the lowest level among the Indian states in 1999.[46]

Mamata and her team never formulated a socio-economic agenda for her party as criticized by the LF. Nor did she propound any plan for socio-economic redistributive justice for the poorer castes and communities. Moreover, by resigning from Railway Ministry, she lost the power to provide for thousands of unemployed young people. She was clamouring for a change of a "sloth Government" under both Jyoti Basu before 2001 and Buddhadeb before 2006 elections. She highlighted the "corruption and political bankruptcy of the CPI (M)". Along with her own party and the new ally — the Congress, she was complaining of the process of "political cleansing that the CPI (M) cadres with the help of a section of police and administration" let loose in different pockets in the western belts of Midnapur, Howrah, Hooghly Bankura and Purulia. But she was unable to do anything against it because of her organizational weakness. The proposition was true both during the elections in 2001 and 2006. Moreover all the opposition parties instead of thrashing out one or two viable alternative political formations were at loggerheads with each other. The message of the alliance in 2001 between TMC and the Congress did not reach out to the grassroots because it was too late. The workers of both the parties at different areas worked at cross-purposes. And lastly, actually the local party bosses helped to defeat their own candidates of their own parties because "their opinions and claims in selecting the candidates were ignored", as they furiously vented.

In modern day political and electoral system, party organization down below to grassroots level is more important than the popularity of a very "charismatic" leader. Mamata was yet to build it up. The middle class, the intelligentsia, the teachers of schools, colleges, universities, other establishments and institutions, some officials, bureaucrats and policemen, who were soft for Mamata Banerjee and her Trinamool Congress, appeared to prefer the *status quo* for some more years, watching Mamata's behaviour and listening to her "rabble rousing" speeches. That might also appear to be the reasons why the CPI (M) even losing its credibility to a great extent was able to sail through in the Assembly Election in 2006.

4
Coalition Politics: Making of Coalition

The electoral data of Parliamentary elections in 2004 and Assembly election in 2006 shown in the previous chapter indicate that the Left Front (LF) government of West Bengal was far more entrenched in power than it was in 1977. The LF government underwent only one change on November 6, 2000, when the former Chief Minister Jyoti Basu handed over the charge to Buddhadeb Bhattacharya. The LF government consists of political parties mostly of Marxist persuasions with the Communist Party of India (Marxist), CPI (M) as the pre-dominant partner. Despite occasional differences among them even on vital policy issues, the government never fell apart. It is an experiment among the major as well as the minor partners with the CPI (M) in the lead that seems to come off a long way from the United Front experiment in late 1960s.

The LF as a political coalition has been winning the Assembly elections with 2/3rd majority since 1977. It may appear quite puzzling to keen political observers as to how the same coalition structure can survive so long in a multi-party situation. The question is: Is it a system of "parliamentary communism"?[1] Are the left parties led by the CPI (M) simply using the most important political forum of legislature as a weapon to achieve a socialist revolution? The leaders of the CPI (M) preach exactly the same thesis to their party sympathizers and toiling masses. But they opine otherwise in private that this "theory is of little relevance" in the changed context. This, in a sense, reflects the CPI (M)'s strategy of retaining the regime and remaining at the center of power, as it did aggressively in the late 1960s.[2] The question is as to how a dominant Marxist Party in coalition with other left parties is adapting to a "bourgeois parliamentary system", but trying hard to stall the growth of a genuine parliamentary opposition and in the process making the ideology of "socialist democratic revolution" a mere political rhetoric. Jyoti Basu, the former Chief Minister smiled away the question saying, "Every point of view has its own merit".[3] In other words, the CPI (M), like any other party in this country, has quite fitted in the "bourgeois parliamentary system". In view of the unique stability of the LF coalition over the years, the questions that confronted us are: what is the nature of the LF coalition? Has it become a cartel of party oligopolies over the years? What stitches together the left parties for such a long period of time? Is it now the objective of the partners to cling to power to enjoy simply the benefits of offices? Are the social bases of the left parties any different from that of other major opposition parties? Is it the policy convergence, ideology or the compulsion to retain power that brings the parties together? Is it the political management of the coalition or the electoral engineering of the oligopolistic political market leader in the imperfect electoral competition that sustains the LF coalition? Do the micro studies of voter responses substantiate some of the hypothetical arguments? The questions are addressed, as far as possible, in the following pages.

Coalition Making

The experiment of the LF coalition has been out of power since May 20th 2011 to come through tortuously and, in the process, has to reinvent itself both ideologically and structurally. Coalition making is not something of a new experiment in West Bengal. It was even there in the colonial era from 1937 to 1947, as indicated in Chapter 1. But the politics that has been unfolding during the last three decades finds no parallel in the theories of coalition experiments elsewhere. The making of coalition by the same group of left parties is the reflection of societal politics or non-interfering politics of tolerance by people at large in the absence of any credible alternative political formations in the state. The position of the LF became further strengthened after the 7th Assembly election in 2006. The other left parties that participated were Forward Bloc (FB), Forward Bloc [Marxist] FB (M), Revolutionary Socialist Party (RSP), Revolutionary Communist Party of India (RCPI) and the Biplabi Bangla Congress (BB Cong). The Communist Party of India (CPI) was not a member of the newly emerging LF in 1977, because of its collaboration with the Congress Party both at the centre and the state. The Socialist Unity Centre (SUC) was also invited to join the coalition, but to maintain its "ideological purity undiluted", it did not join the coalition.[4] After 1982 Assembly election, the Janata Party (JP) was split into three factions. Two factions, the Democratic Socialist Party (DSP) and the West Bengal Socialist Party (WBSP) joined the LF governments. The CPI, Communist Party of India [Marxist-Leninist] CPI (ML), joined the LF political coalition, but after some time CPI (ML) left the Front. Looking in perspective, it might be mentioned that some other smaller parties were also participating in LF committee, although they did not have any legislative presence. The LF government promised to provide a "left radical alternative politics" to the people. The number of major partners, who really counted in the coalition, was really four. The pulls and pressure among them were negligible as compared with that of the UF in earlier times. Historically, existential compulsions brought back most of the left parties together. To "fight for democracy" after internal emergency, the left parties initially wanted to make broad based political coalitions with other rightist and left of centre parties. But that probable left-right-centre mix did not materialize. From the very beginning, the CPI (M) came to realize that to be in power, the other partners, irrespective of their minimum legislative numerical presence, should not be underestimated. The electorate did not vote for the CPI (M) alone to form the government. It was because of its larger presence both politically, organizationally and the fielding of more candidates that brought the CPI (M) finally as the dominant partner. E. Shreedharan made a cogent point in this regard while discussing the surplus majority coalition. This seat majority situation is dependent on the vote transfer of the CPI (M) to its smaller partners and, hence, a coalition is necessary if it is to get re-elected.[5] Electoral data since 1952, except during the revived Congress Party regime (1972-77) having pre-election seat adjustment with CPI, shows that the opposition parties — mostly Marxists as well as other left oriented parties always shared more than 50 per cent of the total votes cast in all the previous elections. This simple calculation was enough to put the left opposition parties together in 1977. Earlier, the ideological rigidities, socio-political angularities and political personal equation ignoring the chemistry of electoral process prevented them from coalescing. The left parties involved themselves in political movements against the ruling congress to spread a message for bringing into larger focus the insensitivity[6] of the Congress government and the exploitative nature of the ruling elites, particularly the Congress Party. But the CPI (M) and obviously other smaller left parties "never thought of forming a government of their own before 1977";[7] or even the attempt did not materialize.

The politics of coalition that the Left Front has been practicing since 1977 "is yet another manifestation" of certain "socio-political realities" obtaining in the state.[8] The polarization of political parties — ideological or on the basis of "social cleavages" reduces the options of alliances for the smaller Left Front partners to the minimum.[9] The coalition government in West Bengal during the late 1977s and onwards is in many ways different from that of other Indian states including the Marxist state of Kerala or even sometimes in Tripura, where government changes regularly between the two political formations. By now the LF coalition structure in the state appears to be institutionalized as obtaining in many of the West European and smaller Scandinavian countries.[10] Laver and Schofield refer to two models of coalition[11] viz., (1) The European Politics Tradition (2) The Game-Theoretic Tradition. From the first of the two categories, a vast number of data are available regarding the nature, objectives and ideology, nature and style of political bargaining, question of payoffs and the timing of party configurations to form the government. In Game Theoretic model, the numbers of political actors are not many.

The left parties, with the CPI (M) at the lead, wanted to have the "minimal winning coalitions."[12] The Left Front's initial calculation was similar to Riker's theorization as, "in social situations similar to n-person, zero-sum games with side-payments, participants create coalitions just as large as they believe will ensure winning and no larger".[13] The instant success was something that the CPI (M) initially did not expect during the period of bargaining the seat-adjustment, office sharing and political coalition making. To put policy perspectives and influencing policy inputs were the main objectives of the left parties rather than purely "office seeking motivations".[14]

Social divisions, political fissures, socio-cultural differences and ethnic cleavages unique to the country play decisive role in determining the process of coalition building. For better bargains and improved payoffs or resorting to policy options, the political actors may change partners and, thus, may set up a different configuration to form a new coalition government as found in Scandinavian countries. The undivided Communist Party of India and a few others, who voiced aloud earlier to incorporate constitutional provisions for proportional representations, fell silent subsequently.[15] Many of the developing countries constitutionally have incorporated proportional representations. Referring to the politics of Mauritius, Ramakrishna Sithanen[16] raised several essential issues of coalition formation – empirical and theoretical. The major considerations are: (a) important contextual determinants of coalition formation, (b) electoral system as a device for pre-electoral coalitions and post-election scenarios, and (c) coalition government in multi-ethnic societies.

Important dimensions of coalition government are conflict management and conflict resolution among coalition partners and political management of the coalition. The political actors strategize to maximize benefits, the distribution of which depends upon the numerical strength of each.[17] In that case and situation, the process and structure may seriously jeopardize the process of governance in countries like ours, as we often experienced during the late 1970s and then again from the late 1980s till date.

The theories of coalition governments based on empirical findings in European, Afro-Asian and Latin American countries for reasons of country specificity cannot be replicated. At political level as also in societal spaces, conflict situations continue to arise between the dominant CPI (M) and other partners individually or in concert, but the coalition governments in the state for the last three decades were not destabilized till 2011. It was because the partners despite having serious differences with regard to agricultural, industrial, health and educational policies had ultimately to fall in line by the *dictates of the CPI (M) (emphasis added)*. The coalition politics in West Bengal is a category by itself even when the LF government had to go.

The politics of a state is often redefined by the changing nature of socio-economic spaces and the entrenched cultural attributes of the people. It is a combination of several factors like history past and present, geography, fertility of landmass, environment, volume of population migration within regions, influx of displaced from outside the state. It depends also on the fact that different groups of people living in varied areas of the state and their cultural differences within. Historically, the truncated state of West Bengal has been a problem area since its partition in 1947 as stated earlier in this work. West Bengal is a border state; the porous borderline runs 4096 km along the territories of Bangladesh, Nepal and Bhutan. The state comprises a total area of 88,752 sq. km with a population of 9, 51,76,197. The density of population per sq. km is 903 and the male and female percentage being 51.72 and 48.28, respectively.[18] The characteristics of the land mass vary widely from that of the North Bengal districts to the Sundarban areas in the South Bengal and the alluvial mid-land regions of the state to the drought prone west. The cultural life of the people their folktales, folksongs, ethnic rituals in pockets of different districts, modes of social entertainments differ from one place to another. The environment and climate do also distinctly vary. These factors are no less important in tracing the political landscape and the voters' psyche Table 4.1 indicates religion-wise population break in the state.

Table 4.1: Percentage Distribution of Population by Religion in West Bengal

Hindu	69.10
Muslim	28.62
Christian	00.64
Sikh	00.08
Buddhist	00.30
Jain	00.07
Others (Religion not stated)	01.12

Source: West Bengal Human Development Report 2004, Kolkata.

Table 4.1 shows religion and caste-wise population distributions in different areas in the state. NSSO reports that the Muslim population is 28.62 per cent in 2004 (as quoted above in the Report shown above).

Table 4.2 shows district-wise percentage point of Scheduled castes, Scheduled Tribes and Muslim population.

The cultural attributes of a people, traditions, familial links and relations, social norms, mores and rituals of people of ethnic origin scattered in different regions of the state, linguistic differences and style of dialects have been found to be different from one region to another in the state. The state of economic development, occupational engagements and even the idiom of politics as observed in the past do also vary quite perceptively.[19] Economic class divisions overlapping the castes and religious divisions, play significant role in the

Table 4.2: % of Schedule Caste, Schedule Tribe and Muslims of the Total Population of WB and Each District of West Bengal

	Total. Population	*SC*	*ST*	*Muslims*	*% SC*	*% ST*	*% Muslims*
West Bengal	**80176197**	**18437555**	**4406794**	**20241541**	**23.02**	**5.50**	**25.25**
Burdwan	6895514	1860754	441832	1364133	26.98	6.41	19.78
Birbhum	3015422	889894	203127	1057861	29.51	6.74	35.08
Bankura	3192695	997408	330783	239722	31.24	10.36	7.51
Midnapore	9610788	1576337	798684	1088999	16.40	8.31	11.33
Howrah	4273099	658707	19168	1044383	15.42	0.45	24.44
Hooghly	5041976	1188881	212062	763471	23.58	4.21	15.14
24-Parganas (N)	8934286	1840397	198936	2164058	20.60	2.23	24.22
24-Parganas (S)	6906689	2218376	84766	2295967	32.12	1.23	33.24
Kolkata	4572876	274835	9810	926769	6.01	0.21	20.27
Nadia	4604827	1365985	113891	1170899	29.66	2.47	25.43
Murshidabad	5866569	703786	75953	3735380	12.00	1.29	63.67
Uttar Dinajpur	2441794	676582	124865	1156503	27.71	5.11	47.36
Dakshin Dinajpur	1503178	432660	242317	361047	28.78	16.12	24.02
Malda	3290468	554165	227047	1636171	16.84	6.90	49.72
Jalpaiguri	3401173	1233577	641688	369195	36.27	18.87	10.85
Darjeeling	1609172	258881	204167	85378	16.09	12.69	5.31
Cooch Behar	2479155	1242374	14246	600911	50.11	0.57	24.24
Purulia	2536516	463956	463452	180694	18.29	18.27	7.12

Source: *Economic Review* 2004-05, Government of West Bengal and Census Report of India 2001.

political process. Table 4.1 and Table 4.2 are very instructive to understand the caste and communal dynamic of politics in the districts and regions. Earlier, the Congress Party used to mobilize castes and communities directly through caste-community leaders. For the last several years, the CPI (M) and its front partners are doing the same thing very effectively, sometimes directly by the party and often by using a well-crafted method of mediated mobilization through myth, symbols and slogans. The observations have been substantiated to some extent by our field survey and field diaries.[20]

Sometimes, it is found in a few districts and regions that parties with contradictory political perspectives are participating in the running of the local governments.[21] It was simply the rural ethos and spirit of accommodation in village life that put different fishes in the same pool. It is interesting in this connection to note Glyn William's observations and ethnographical approach to get a clearer perspective in analyzing West Bengal's left politics at micro-levels.[22] The author refers to the works of Atul Kohli, Rudolf and Rudolf, Partha Chatterjee and a few others. Atul Kohli's observations of "crisis of governability" in connections with governance in India and several of the Indian states stood as a stark contrast in West Bengal till September 2006.

It was a successful coalition dominated all through by the CPI (M)-the politico-electoral market leader with a newly acquired sense of pragmatism and accommodation. Its style of political and electoral management became a model as never before.

It is also important for the present purposes to locate coalition dynamics at the regional levels in terms of seats won from each of the 19 districts by the political parties. Glyn's "style of works" in this respect can offer important insight when proper attention is paid to different geographies that political discourses create and inhabit.[23]

Arild Ruud's method is, to a large extent, political ethnographical as well as of 'oral history'.[24] He used his tools for detailed analysis of politics in selected villages. He chronicled the cultures — interaction within and around the society under the impact of "democratic decentralization". But, he stopped short of commenting on the recent mix of the liberal theory of democratic decentralization as institutionalized after 1992[25] and the Leninist formulations of "democratic centralism", and its socio-economic impact in a democratic State like India and its several constituent states. This study, in a significant way, may reflect the socio-cultural and political economy of the diverse populations of the state of West Bengal. A number of scholars, who in order to carry on micro level studies on democratic decentralization, selected a few *Panchayat* bodies only. The scholars mostly encapsulated their research findings in Western theoretical paradigms to highlight the politico-economic development of a Marxist state within a liberal democratic framework.[26] On the other hand, Bardhan and Mookherjee are clear and far nearer the ground realities in a broader sense. Their universe of study was larger, 80 bodies to be exact in comparison with that of the others'. The presence of the left parties' coalitions in rural Bengal was imposing, though political competition between the left coalition partners and the opposition parties in most places was conspicuously lacking, thus, not conducive to economic and political development. In this connection, the authors commented, "Land reform and implementation was highest in villages where local governments were more evenly contested between the Left and Rightist parties.[27] The LF coalition, through its rural local governance, took off well in the development process with political success during the early 1980s on the basis of the enactments made by the earlier Congress governments 1950s (B.C. Roy), 1960s (P.C. Sen) and the mid-1970s (S.S. Ray's), which were not properly implemented. The CPI (M), still sporting its ideological strap of "people's democratic revolution" resorted to its party objective of "democratic centralism", while making a public declaration of completing the process of "democratic decentralization". The local party leaders that increased by leaps and bounds enlarged their area of control and compulsively adapted to the "bourgeois liberal method" of combining the twin Western processes of development and political modernization. As expected, the centralized control by the party organizations spreads all over the districts in the state. In the last two decades, many of the CPI (M) leaders at local levels were seen to become the party incarnate. This was mostly felt in the disjointed western belts of Purulia, Bankura, Birbhum, Hooghly, Howrah and Midnapore.

However, the LF's massive presence in rural Bengal as indicated till 2008 *Panchayat* elections might have really ushered in a democratic socialist system to bring about redistributive justice as promised by the state committee of the CPI (M) in a volume, *People's Power in Practice.* It was not too much to expect that rural poverty and hunger would have been greatly alleviated had the promises even been partially fulfilled. But the folktales tell a different story. The fact of death by hunger and starvation in *Amlasole*[28] in West Midnapore, Belpahari and Jhargram, in tribal belts of Purulia, pockets of Nadia, Murshidabad, in tea-garden areas of Cooch Bihar, Jalpaiguri and the fringe areas of Dinajpur were not exaggerated. The facts were pathetic and beyond explanation after nearly three decades of uninterrupted leftist rule in rural Bengal. In many tribal and other undeveloped and underdeveloped areas, the local leaders either used to manipulate the data as published in newspapers and detected by the observers[29] of the Election Commission or did not care to distribute the "Below Poverty Line" (BPL) Cards to the deserving poor families. To alleviate poverty in the rural areas, the central government launched the programme of distributing daily necessities as rations at subsidized low price to the poorer people living under poverty line (32% in rural West Bengal while the national average was a little over 26%) on the production of the BPL cards to be issued by the state government. Observing the state of affairs, the Minister of Tribal welfare once lamented, "The local Panchayat leaders were squandering the central government funds meant for development to buy liquor and build club houses".[30] The LF government admitted that a total of 4612 villages had been marked as underdeveloped. In the last leg of their stay in office, the LF government persuaded the Central government for more funds to include four more districts over and above the six districts declared as the most backward economically in West Bengal. The poor people living miserably below poverty line approximated 4.6 million.[31] Table 4.3 indicated the level of rural poverty in state as compared with Indian average.

Table 4.3: Incident of Poverty in West Bengal, 1993-94 and 1999-2002 (Rural) (in %)

	1993-1994				*1999-2002*			
	Extremely Poor	*Very poor*	*Moderately poor*	*Poor below poverty line*	*Extremely poor*	*Very poor*	*Moderately poor*	*Poor below poverty line*
West Bengal	1.4	13.6	27.6	41.2	1.1	10.8	20.9	31.7
All India	2.0	14.7	22.1	36.8	0.8	8.2	18.3	26.5

Source: India Development Report 2004-05, New Delhi, 2005.

India Development Report 2004-05 also pointed out that some better-developed states, such as Maharashtra, Gujarat and West Bengal have a relatively higher share of poverty.[32] There were sections of people in the fringe areas of many districts, who had been underfed for months in a year for want of work in agriculture and industries, thereby becoming abysmally sick.

The phenomenal growth of the CPI (M) in the state was both a strength and weakness for the party. It appeared to the critics that to maintain its form of electoral dominance, it ignored the essential democratic contents. Ultimately, it failed to utilize the enormous social capital at its disposal for many years, for its partisan attitude. Consequently, the politics of the CPI (M) was seen to be sowing seeds of disaffection even among the major partners of the LF itself. The growth of the ultra-left Maoists, People's War Group (PWG), and resurrection of the Naxalite around the tribal and poorer western belt of the state was really a bad signal for the party and discerning to the people. The other movements like that of the *Kamtapuris*, Kamtapur Liberation Organization (KLO), for Greater Cooch Bihar Demand, separate Gorkhaland demand of the GNLF were frequent. All this indicated a sense of relative deprivation among the people concerned.

Politico-electoral management of the polity by any political party does not go hand in hand with the governmental management of the state economy.

The situation was not as gloomy in the late 1980s and even early 1990s as it was after 2006. Industries like iron and steel, motorcar, cycle, rubber, jute, manufacturing and engineering faced recession. The conditions of the tea gardens in North Bengal and the tea processing industries were alarming. The small and cottage industries had been ailing for the last several years. Agro-based industries were yet to be built up and encouraged for employment generation. Employment opportunities both in public and private sectors began hopelessly shrinking. Among the staggering unemployment of more than 7.23 million, there were a large number of educated unemployed that topped the list among all other Indian states before the LF regime came to a halt. It was a situation, where growth without employment syndrome still prevails after the change of regime after more than 34 years in the state. The government made a survey and found that the poverty stricken villages had spread all over the state.[33] In this context, the district-wise rank and position of the state in respect of human development indices were quite revealing as shown in Table 4.4.

This is the last and only Human Development Report 2004 that the LF government left behind till it stayed in power.

Table 4.4: Human Development Indices of District in West Bengal

Districts	*Health Index*	*Income Index*	*Education Index*	*Human Development Index (HDI)*	*HDI Rank*
Darjeeling	0.73	0.49	0.72	0.65	4
Jalpaiguri	0.61	0.38	0.60	0.53	10
Koch Bihar (Cooch Bihar)	0.50	0.41	0.65	0.52	11
Dinajpur	0.62	0.39	0.53	0.51	13
Malda	0.49	0.36	0.48	0.44	17
Murshidabad	0.57	0.29	0.52	0.46	15
Birbhum	0.53	0.27	0.61	0.47	14
Bardhhaman (Burdwan)	0.74	0.47	0.71	0.64	5
Nadia	0.65	0.41	0.66	0.57	9
North 24-Parganas	0.72	0.49	0.76	0.66	3
Hugli (Hooghly)	0.77	0.46	0.67	0.63	6
Bankura	0.67	0.26	0.62	0.52	11
Purulia	0.61	0.18	0.55	0.45	16
Midnapur (Midnapore-east and west together)	0.68	0.45	0.74	0.62	7
Haora (Howrah)	0.77	0.58	0.75	0.68	2
Kolkata	0.82	0.73	0.80	0.78	1
South 24-Parganas	0.71	0.40	0.68	0.60	8
West Bengal	**0.70**	**0.41**	**0.69**	**0.61**	**8***

Source: *West Bengal Human Development Report 2004,* Government of West Bengal, Kolkata.

The LF coalition regime did not confront effective anti-regime political movements for the last 30 years and failed to redeem many of its pledges. Yet the LF government coalition showed neither the sign of cracking nor likely to collapse in the foreseeable future till 2009, given the political party situations and the existing index of opposition unity (IOU) in the state. There were no trustworthy political contests in the state. The survey findings also pointed to the above observations.[34]

The scheduled castes constitute 23.02 per cent and scheduled tribes 5.50 per cent of the total population of the state. The West Bengal Human Development Report 2004 observes, "Among the minorities, the Muslims are the dominant section and they account for about 28.62 per cent of the total population of West Bengal."[35] The Report further explains, "It may be noted that these three categories, namely SC, ST and Muslim together account for more than half the population and these are the poorest groups in rural Bengal." These three groups constitute the majority of the electorate. The party or the coalition of parties, which is able to mobilize these groups politically, is surely to stay in power. That the Assembly elections in the state since 1977 till 2006 have been propping up the LF coalition, possibly reflects the castes, communities as also the class dynamics in the state despite its inefficient management of the economy.

The LF regime in West Bengal has been continuing for the last 34 years till May 2011. After 1982, the Front appeared to be sufficiently broad based by including CPI, two splinter groups of Janata Party (JP) i.e., DSP, WBSP. It started with a coalition of six parties in 1977; later on five other small local parties without any assembly representation are supporting the LF political coalition. One RJD member found a seat in 2006 WB assembly election in exchange for Lalu Prasad's minor seat sharing with CPI (M) in 2005 in Bihar. The only left party that did not join the LF was SUC because the party was actually "more Stalinist" than the CPI (M), was always conscious about its individual party political line.[36]

The LF coalition subsists because of the fact that this LF political coalition was the outcome of coalitions at different layers of society. Coalitions at the societal level or broadly termed as "social coalition", helped in bringing about the political coalition. The LF was in power in the absence of any other cohesive political formation of other parties. The predominant presence of the CPI (M) in respect of popular support, political articulations, organizational strength and legislative majority, was one of the main reasons for the regime stability. Several field surveys[37] and findings indicated that the upper, intermediate and lower castes in considerable majorities voted for the LF in subsequent parliamentary and assembly elections.

Since 1977, more than 60 per cent of the Muslims comprising a total of 25.25 per cent (or 28.62% in 2004, cited by NSSO) in the state supported the

LF. The people mostly Muslims, who had been continuously crossing over the porous border by stealth to search for economic subsistence, were patronized by the major political parties. Most of them constituted the support base of the ruling parties, because no other party had the proper resources to help them. Also, millions of refugees that came over to West Bengal both at the time of Partition in 1947 and thereafter in 1965 and 1971 continued to support the politics of the left parties. The Communist Party's sustained movements against the Congress government's policy of refugee rehabilitation earned the support of these pauperized uprooted people. But the recent politics of the refugees well settled in earlier colony areas in the urban fringes in the state recently began oscillating from the early 1990s.[38] But for organizational strength and political spread for various reasons, the CPI (M)'s erosion of vote-bank did not substantially affect the prospect of the Left Front's electoral fortune for such a long period of time.

The oft-quoted Bengali radicalism has become a cliché by now. But the slogan that central government's step-motherly attitude still cuts ice among the people of the older generations[39], even after the LF regime was replaced by another ramshackle political coalition with surplus majority of the TMC in 2011. During the UF regimes during late 1960s, the policy stance of the CPI (M) and its aim to have horizontal spread throughout the rural hinterland at the cost of other left parties were suspect. The CPI (M) alone, the vote share being as it were, would not be able to reach the benchmark in any elections in West Bengal. The left parties and their coalition led by the CPI (M) won the support not only of the well informed middle classes, but of a number of business and traders' communities, the rich and middle peasants in rural Bengal. The rich and middle peasants or *Jotdar* (big landholders) were terrified by earlier UF government's land grabbing programmes in the name of Land Reforms led by the then Land Revenue Minister Harekrisna Konar of the two UF governments. This time, the CPI (M) was circumspect and followed a policy of Land Reforms and "Operation Barga" quietly and in a phased and legal manner. The LF did have a successful *Panchayati Raj* experiment. The first *Panchayati Raj* elections in all its three tiers were held in 1978 and the LF won the elections at all the three levels. The winning spree had been continuing till the last election in 2003. The experiment of the rural self-governance through regular elections was another important factor for the consolidation of the LF in the rural hinterland. The LF won majority of the local body elections convincingly and made the first stride to have a total spread in all the five regions of rural Bengal. It seemed to be made through a deliberate "pro-poor" policy as also of a soviet style partocratic secularization programme among the racial, tribal, ethnic, religious communities and other societal spaces. The LF, particularly the CPI (M), proved its massive presence in the 116 Municipalities and six Municipal corporations in the state in that point of time. Consequently, over the years, the partners became weak in their barging power of office sharing. In earlier times, the partners of the LF, the FB and RSP were seen to be quarrelling with the CPI (M) regarding ministerial portfolio sharing and other office seeking claims. But the noticeable fact was that during any election — be it national, state or local — the partners of the front, putting aside their differences, came to depend on the organizational might of the CPI (M). They had to declare for their electoral existence, "We are to guard the unity of LF as the apple of the eye."[40] These parties, because of their region centric influences in the state, heavily depend upon the vote transfer from the CPI (M) in those regional constituencies.

To maintain the LF coalition intact, the CPI (M) appeared to go in for minor policy changes here and there. This indicated the coalition making and management skill of the CPI (M). The political style of "direct and mediated"[41] social mobilizations by the CPI (M)'s professional—occupational, educational and cultural front organizations always earned it wider support among the people. The CPI (M) with all its chain of committees — branch, local, zonal, district and the state had won over a number of societal spaces through a system of patronage. The West Bengal University and College Teachers' Association (WBCUTA), Primary Teachers' Association, All Bengal Secondary Teachers' Associations, Democratic[42] Writers and Artistes' forum, Left Students Union (SFI), Government Employees Coordination Committee, Government College Teachers' Association, the Peasant Organization, Women's Organization, Trade Unions, Union of Cooperative Societies, Women's Self-Help-Groups enjoying micro-credit facilities from the bank at the CPI (M)'s behest, always looked after the interests of the CPI (M) and the LF coalition, particularly during any election.[43] Before 1977, the leaders of the left parties never "imagined"[44] to form a government in the state by a single left party or a coalition of left parties.

Much has been written about Bengal's "radical politics". A number of justifications were enumerated for the Leftist rise to power in West Bengal and its consolidation.[45] It is debatable that the left parties with the CPI (M) in the lead have been on the crest of Bengal's proverbial "radical politics". But the leftist politicians are adept enough to cash in on their "anti-centre", "anti-establishment" stance, irrespective of the nature of the central government. Consequently the CPI (M) further strengthened its electoral bases in rural and semi-urban areas. Contrasted with other Indian states, caste and open communal politics find little space in West Bengal. Whatever may be the electoral strategy of most political parties, by and large the political games are played here in a politico-secular space. The law and order problems were comparatively well managed by the LF government. The policy decisions and implementation of the same by the government mostly depended upon the interactions between the government and the LF Coordination Committee at the state level. The urban, peri-urban middle classes and a considerable body of intellectuals were sympathetic to the politics of the left. It wanted to politicize the members of the staff of both the general administration and the police administration. The employees of the government undertakings, government aided schools, government aided colleges and even universities were mostly won over by the LF, by way of increasing salary packets and perks, etc.[46] The Chief Minister, Jyoti Basu allowed the non-gazetted police personnel to form associations in the very early 1980s. Indirectly, the higher echelon of the police forces was forced to fall in line with the dictates of the political establishment of the state.[47] The LF government even allowed its employees to go in for strike to fulfill their demands[48] and the political executive itself frequently supported the politics of *Bangla Band, Bharat Band* or *Chakka Jam* when directed against the "anti-people policies" or the "inconvenient Central Government". The Siddhartha Ray government brought about stability in the political process of the state after a tumultuous period of political aggrandizements by the CPI (M), particularly, that resulted in socio-political uncertainties. He contained the Naxalite violence, and tackled the problems of deteriorating law and order situations. It enacted certain important legislations like land reforms, a bill for *Panchayati Raj* system, urban slum development, housing boards, Calcutta Metropolitan Development Authority. But due to inner contradictions and factional infighting in the Congress Party, the government could not implement the decisions made in haste. At that time Siddhartha Ray, the Chief Minister, used to maintain dossiers against his entire young ministers. He even constituted an enquiry committee headed by Justice Wanchoo to go into the details of corruptions among his junior colleagues. That infuriated Subrata Mukherjee, Kumud Bhattacharjee, Lakshmi Kanta Bose and others. They went against their Chief Minister. This was the period when factionalism in its vicious form became endemic within West Bengal Congress party; although it was a glorious period for the youth congress wing of the party, the remnant of which continued for long. Even during the 1990s, it went unabated resulting in Ms. Mamata Banerjee's coming out of the mainstream Congress in the late 1990s. Prafulla Kanti Ghosh, Tarun Kanti Ghosh of Amrita Bazar Patrika and Shankar Ghosh — a historian, who wrote on national movements in India and Kasi Kanta Moitra were some of his senior cabinet colleagues. According to the political observers of the period, "Despite certain important achievements in a number of fields, there could not be seen a process of the beginning of a change in the socio-economic structure in the state."[49] Herein lay the tactical superiority of the LF regime. The LF government in the very beginning of its sustained innings realized that "government-led redistribution of wealth and sustained growth of agricultural output" could "potentially contribute much to the economic empowerment of the rural poor".[50] Social and cultural mobilizations are also two other mass-based programmes, which the CPI (M) has been carrying on since the beginning. In this connection, the comment made by Ruud that mobilization and maintenance of support from broad social groups was important. Indeed "social and cultural factors become crucial"[51] in the mobilization process for the local party leaders and representatives.

In short, it is still a general impression; the factors that greatly contributed to the stability of the regimes are: the programmes of land reforms, redistributing lands to the landless agricultural labourers and marginal peasants through *Operation Barga* and showing interest to bring about growth and equity with redistributive justice, garnering support of the migrant populations or refugees, introduction of *Panchayati Raj, Nagar Palika* system of local governance and the holding of regular elections in local bodies.

There are a few other contributing factors worth mentioning here. The Finance Minister, Asok Mitra, in the beginning of the first LF government, introduced unemployment allowances. The new government proposed to build up primary schools in every village of the state and appoint a large number of primary school teachers. The tradition of English teaching from the primary stages of the schools and the tuition fees up to the higher secondary levels were abolished. And lastly, during the 1990s, a scheme to eradicate illiteracy from every district of the state was launched. The government then engaged a large array of party cadres, educated sympathizers and sometimes only party activists for the purpose. All these programmes were addressed to the largest body of poor and lower middle class people. The CPI (M), before the 2006 Assembly election, implemented a policy of "self-help group" – women's cooperative organizations to produce homemade marketable consumables through micro-credit system, a recent step to emulate a success story in the neighbouring Bangladesh. This helped more than half a million rural families. But many of the policies and their implementations as seen in perspective were not fiscally sustainable[52] and a few of them were withdrawn later. But the messages hidden in those measures were loud enough for the consolidation of the CPI (M) in the state. In short, apart from garnering support among the teachers, students, unemployed youth, professionals, cultural workers, peasants and wage earners, the CPI (M) over the years built up a massive party organization with many other front organizations that continuously worked for the party in all sessions and at important points of time.[53] Tom J. Nossiter points out the reason behind the remarkable stability of the LF, "First the CPI (M) and the LF have succeeded in identifying themselves with Bengali resentment at what is perceived to be chronic central neglect of the difficulties of the state." The LF regime had always been focusing on this point and polishing the concept of Centre's neglect to finer shine. Nossiter further states, "Whatever deficiencies there have been in the performance of the LF, it is perceived as having a mission, discipline and leadership."[54] Many of Nossiter's observations might not stand the scrutiny of time, but the observations made during mid-1980s regarding "discipline and leadership" that helped the party in its electoral fight against disparate opposition parties in the state were valid. The larger opposition parties like the TMC, Congress and BJP even when electoral arithmetic indicated congenial, could not form an alternative coalition 2008-09. Even a perceptually viable alternative political formation would have been a catalytic agent in the political chemistry for the electorate; of course that happened much later, but in a ramshackle form. In such vacuum, the LF remained a better choice for the people, who valued the organizational discipline of the left parties.[55]

Coalition situation is seminal in the political process where multi-party system works unhindered. A few Indian writers have worked on the politics of coalitions and coalition governments in India both at the central and state levels.[56] The coalition models that have come up in developed European nations are institutionalized in the very working of their constitution. Therefore, the theories of policy pursuit models, office-seeking models, minimum winning models or large-sized coalition models based on strategy were of marginal theoretical applicability in West Bengal.[57] William Riker's Game Theoretic model was also not of any special relevance here. The coalition government experiments here had some particularities. The immediate past LF coalition in West Bengal was a category by itself. The dominant partner CPI (M) with absolute majority in the House never gave any public impression that other left parties in the coalition were disposable surplus members. Noticeably, after 25 years, when the Left Front became really a coalition government in 2001, the government did not show any sign of falling apart.

In the political process, the electoral market in the state has become imperfectly competitive due to the 'opposition parties' organizational weaknesses, verbal duels and trading abusive charges against each other. The opposition parties, because of their lack of organization, workable political understanding among themselves and inability to reach out to the grassroots had been gradually emasculated. The political arena is completely dominated by a cartel of LF political oligopolies. Table 4.5, although simply illustrative, indicated that the opposition parties got a little more than 50 per cent of total votes polled both in assembly and parliamentary elections in different years from 1996 to 2001. But it could not capitalize on the electoral arithmetic in subsequent elections by forging an alternative coalition in political terms and spaces.

During the 1960s, the *Panchayat* system was not streamlined and it became gradually moribund due to corruption resulting in a nexus between the politicians and the bureaucrats. About the congress government in the early 1960s, Myron Weiner said, "Only the pressures of politicians and the groups they lead will force the government to ameliorate the lot of the masses.

Table 4.5: % of Votes of the LF in Different Elections—Parliamentary, Assembly and Panchayat (3 Tiers)

Year	*Parliament*	*Assembly*	*Zilla Parisad*	*Panchyat Samity*	*Gram Panchayat*	*Average 3 tier Panchayat*
1998	47.09	-	-	-	-	-
1999	46.76	-	-	-	-	-[58]
2001	-	48.98	-	-	-	-
2003	-	-	86.82	74.05	65.75	75.54
2004	50.62	-	-	-	-	-
2006	-	50.12	-	-	-	-

Source: Compiled, Election Commission Reports and Panchayat Elections Reports, Government of West Bengal.

Neither rational arguments nor petitions are likely to hasten government action they believe; only mass activities, demonstrations, *hartals* (strike), civil disobedience and other expressions of mass will, can force the government to take action."[59] The observations might equally justify the political activities and the movements launched against the existing government by the Marxists. The opposition political parties, when they failed in their objectives to grill the government in the House, brought their anti-government movements out in the streets.

At this point, a short background note is necessary to understand as to how the governments have been changing over the years. Table 4.6 gives the picture of different governments over the years and the nature of the same.

It has been already shown earlier in this work the number of seats and the percentage points of vote secured by the parties. This is necessary to juxtapose Table 4.7 with Table 4.6 to better understand the strengths and weaknesses of the government by majority and the governments in coalition that were experienced in the state.

In fact, the Congress Party in the state was always faction-ridden between the Hooghly group and the Midnapore group. The one was led by the state congress president Atulya Ghosh and Prafulla Chandra Sen and, the latter was led by Ajoy Mukherjee. The Party was a coalition of different interest groups as well as castes and communities combine with leaders of their own.

However, the year 1967 is the watershed in the electoral politics of West Bengal. This is a historic period when politics of coalition government started in political term. The Bangla Congress gave a serious blow to the congress hegemony. Ajoy Mukherjee with his Bangla Congress was actually instrumental in ushering in a regime of coalitions in the state. Most of the left parties or groups of left parties were inimical to one another. The two communist parties, namely the CPI and CPI (M) seemed to be destroying each other.[60] These left parties fought the 1967 elections in two political

Table 4.6: Dates and Years of the Change of Governments with Parties and the Change of Chief Minister with Participating Parties (1947-2011)

Political Party, Nature of Coalition	*Chief Minister*	*Period*		*Participating Parties*
		From	To	
Single Party majority Congress System	Dr. P.C. Ghosh	August 15, 1947	January 14, 1948	Congress
	Dr. B.C. Roy	January 14, 1948	July 1, 1962	Congress
President's Rule	—	July 1,1962	July 8, 1962	
Single Party majority Congress System	P.C. Sen	July 8, 1962	March 1, 1967	Congress
1st UF	Ajoy Mukherjee	March 2, 1967	November 20, 1967	B. Cong., CPI (M), CPI, FB, FB(M), BKD, RSP, LSS, GL, BP, WPI, SUC, SSP, PSP, RCPI, three Ind. from unrecognized parties
1st Non-Marxist Minority Coalition led by P.C. Ghosh, Congress support from outside.	Dr. P.C. Ghosh	November 21, 1967	January 14, 1968	BKD, JKP, ML, Ind. & others totaling 14 defecting members supported by Cong. (127), from outside (Minority coalition)
2nd Non-Marxist Coalition with Congress led by P.C. Ghosh	Dr. P.C. Ghosh	January 15 1968	February 19, 1968	14 defecting members B. Cong, PSP, SSP, independents, etc. and the Cong. party with 127 members (coalition)
President's Rule	—	February 20, 1968	February 24, 1969	—
2nd ULF	Ajoy Mukherjee	February 25, 1969	March 19, 1970	B. Cong, CPI (M), BB Cong., CPI, FB, FB (M), RSP, SUC, LSS, GL, WPI, RCPI, PSP, SSP, BP, PML, Independents.
President's Rule		March 19, 1970	April 2, 1971	—

(*Contd.*)

Political Party, Nature of Coalition	*Chief Minister*	*Period*		*Participating Parties*
		From	To	
3rd Non-Marxist Democratic Coalition	Ajoy Mukherjee	April 2, 1971	June 28, 1971	B. Cong., Cong.(R), SSP, PSP, GL, ML,
President's Rule	—	June 28, 1971	March 19, 1972	—
PDA Coalition, CPI supporting from outside	Siddhartha Sankar Ray	March 19, 1972	June 21, 1977	Cong. (216), CPI (35) supporting from outside till mid June, 1974.
1st LF – 5th LF (Contd.)	Jyoti Basu	June 21, 1977	November 6, 2000	1977: 6-party coalition Govt., CPI (M), FB, FB (M), RSP, RCPI, BB Cong. since 1982: 9-party coalition Govt. CPI (M), FB, FB (M), RSP, RCPI, WBSP, BB Cong., CPI, DSP.
5TH (last six months) – 7th LF Coalition	Buddhadeb Bhattacharjee	November 6, 2000	May 20, 2011	CPI (M), FB, FB (M), RSP, RCPI, CPI, DSP, WBSP and 5 other smaller parties having no MLAs supporting the Govt. from outside as members of the LF political Coalition.
Trinamool Congress+ and Congress coalition	Mamata Banerjee	May 20, 2011	Continuing	Trinamool Congress, Congress, SUCI and 15 other very small parties and groups (contradictions between Congress and SUCI nevertheless)

Source: Dilip Banerjee, *Election Recorder* (4th Revised edition), Star Publishing, Kolkata, 2006.

Table 4.7: Seats won and % of Votes Polled by the Parties in Assembly Elections (1952-1962)

Year	*1952*		*1957*		*1962*	
	No.	*%*	*No.*	*%*	*No.*	*%*
Congress	150	63.03	152	60.32	157	62.30
CPI (Undivided)	28	11.76	46	18.25	49	19.44
KMPP	15	6.30	0	0.00	0	0.00
PSP	0	0.00	21	8.33	5	1.98
FB	14	5.88	8	3.17	13	5.16
FB (M)	0	0.00	2	0.79	1	0.40
RSP	0	0.00	3	1.19	9	3.57
RCPI	0	0.00	0	0.00	2	0.79
GL	0	0.00	1	0.40	2	0.79
SUC	1	0.42	2	0.79	0	0.00
JS (Jana Sang)	9	3.78	0	0.00	0	0.00
Hindu Maha Sabha (HM)	4	1.68	0	0.00	0	0.00
SRP	1	0.42	0	0.00	0	0.00
LSS	0	0.00	7	2.78	4	1.59
FB (Ruiker)	1	0.42	0	0.00	0	0.00
Independent / Others	15	6.30	10	3.97	10	3.97
Total No. of Seats	**238**	**100.00**	**252**	**100.00**	**252**	**100.00**

Source: Compiled, Election Commission Reports.

formations, the United Left Front (ULF) led by the CPI (M) and, the CPI led Progressive United Left Front (PULF). The ULF consisted of Revolutionary Socialist Party (RSP), Forward Bloc, FB (M), Workers' Party (WPI), Samyukta Socialist Party (SSP), Revolutionary Communist Party of India (RCPI), Socialist Unity Centre (SUC), the Bolshevik Party (BP) and a few individual centric smaller parties. The other formation, PULF led by the CPI was composed of Forward Bloc (FB), Praja Socialist Party (PSP), Lok Sevak Sangha (LSS), Bangla Congress, Kranti Dal (of Jahangir Kabir), an offshoot of BKD (led by Dr. P.C. Ghosh) and a few Independents. The electoral verdict was for a hung Assembly to provide opportunities for the three groups, the Bangla Congress, ULF and PULF to forge a coalition government for the first time in the state. The problem was to bring closer the two pre-election warring political formations, ULF and PULF. At the initiative of Humayun Kabir, a post-election coalition — United Front (UF) consisting of the ULF, the PULF and the Bangla Congress with other smaller parties and Independents, a government was formed with Ajoy Mukherjee as the Chief Minister. After a good deal of bargaining among the three groups, Jyoti Basu accepted the post of Deputy Chief Minister, holding the portfolio of Finance and Police Administration. The Congress was the largest single Party with 127 seats in the House. It did not stake its claim to form any coalition government with the help of Independents and others as feared by the ULF and PULF. Neither did it bargain with the Bangla Congress to form a coalition, offering the post of the Chief Minister to Ajoy Mukherjee. The other smaller parties and Independents as shown in Table 4.8 played very active role during the entire coalition era from 1967 to 1971

Table 4.8: Seats Won and % of Seats Won by the Parties in Assembly Election, West Bengal (1967-72)

Party	*1967*		*1969*		*1971*		*1972*	
	No.	*%*	*No.*	*%*	*No.*	*%*	*No.*	*%*
Cong (INC)	127	45.36	55	19.64	0	0.00	216	77.14
Cong (R)	0	0.00	0	0.00	105	37.50	0	0.00
Cong (O)	0	0.00	0	0.00	2	0.71	2	0.71
Bangla Cong.	34	12.14	33	11.79	5	1.79	0	0.00
CPI (M)	43	15.36	80	28.57	113	40.36	14	5.00
CPI	16	5.71	30	10.71	13	4.64	35	12.50
FB	14	5.00	21	7.50	3	1.07	0	0.00
FB (M)	1	0.36	1	0.36	2	0.71	0	0.00
RSP	7	2.50	12	4.29	3	1.07	3	1.07
RCPI	0	0.00	2	0.71	3	1.07	0	0.00
WPI	2	0.71	2	0.71	2	0.71	0	0.00
PSP	7	2.50	5	1.79	3	1.07	0	0.00
SSP	7	2.50	9	3.21	0	0.00	0	0.00
Gorkha League (GL)	2	0.71	4	1.43	2	0.71	2	0.71
SUC	4	1.43	7	2.50	7	2.50	1	0.36
PML	0	0.00	3	1.07	0	0.00	1	0.36
Jana Sangh	1	0.36	0	0.00	1	0.36	0	0.00
Swatantra	1	0.36	0	0.00	0	0.00	0	0.00
LSS	5	1.79	4	1.43	0	0.00	0	0.00
Ind. & Others	9	3.21	12	4.29	16	5.71	6	2.14
Total	**280 (100.00)**		**280 (100.00)**		**280 (100.00)**		**280 (100.00)**	

Source: Compiled, Election Commission Reports.

The first coalition structure was fragile. The major parties and their leaders did not like Jyoti Basu's handling of the police administration[61] and bureaucracy to the near total advantage of the CPI (M) alone. The Chief Minister, the leaders of the CPI and the FB became apprehensive. Intense politicking was let loose between the CPI (M) on the one hand and the CPI, FB and the Bangla Cong on the other. After the initial period, the Congress Party, both at the state and the centre, were trying to dislodge the first UF government.[62] Added to the problems were the inner ideological contradictions of the CPI (M) and the mounting food crisis. The CPI and then CPI (M) never had a cordial relation with Dr. P.C. Ghosh. Dr. Ghosh was severely criticized for failure of containing the crisis. Ajoy Mukherjee was closer to the leaders of the CPI and the FB because of their views about the intolerant and politically aggressive CPI (M). The state Congress till then was almost a mute spectator, but as alleged, the Central Congress government was not. Dr. Ghosh was disillusioned when the Congress Party stepped aside from its secret understanding with him to support his minority government from outside

However, the PDF coalition government of Dr. Ghosh with a thin majority, even in the second time, after the congress joined the coalition, was short lived. It could not transact any business in the House because of the Speaker, Bejoy Banerjee's "historic ruling of adjourning the House *sine die*".[63] Table 4.8 indicated that most of the partners of the first UF, except the Bangla Congress came back with larger strength. The Congress lost seats, but significantly increased its vote shares. The first UF government was formed after a post-election coalition. The second UF government was based on a pre-election coalition. The coalitions consisted of 14 parties. The uniqueness of the UF experiment was its political composition. The CPI (M), CPI, other Marxist parties, the centrist and left of center parties, all participated in the two governments. There were some innovations during the two UF regimes. The first UF government started with an 18-point common policy document and the second UF with 32-point policy programmes. A UF co-ordination committee was instituted to monitor the implementation of the policies. But in neither situation, the UF co-ordination committee could function as expected. While euphoria was calmed down, the leaders of the constituent parties discovered to their dismay the irreconcilable policy and other differences among them. The main objective of the government that suffered most in both the situations was governance. The "crisis of govern-ability"[64] defined the period of coalition governments in the 1960s. The most important issues that consumed the time, attention and goodwill among the UF partners were food, labour, education and, law and order situations.[65] The problems of the Naxalbari movements that were launched during the first UF government in 1967 plagued the internal politics of the CPI (M). Ultimately, the CPI (M) was split and a new Communist Party of India (Marxist-Leninist) or the CPI (ML) was formed on May 1, 1969. The law and order situations were beginning to deteriorate further. The industrial scenario was bleak. The labour unrest and industrial strikes were endemic. The labour minister, Subodh Banerjee of SUC used a method of Gheraos (confinement) as a political weapon to settle labour problems by pressure tactics on the industrial and business owners. There arose a very unseemly controversy between the Chief Minister and a few other leaders of UF for "partisan use of the police force and the administration".[66] Jyoti Basu from the very beginning wanted the police establishment to be under his total control.[67] All this vitiated the relation between the Chief Minister and the Deputy Chief Minister. The government employees sympathetic to the CPI (M) dared to insult the Chief Minister in the corridor of the Writers' Building — the central secretariat of the state government. The party was yet to learn the culture of governance, cultivate a sense of accommodation and the strategy of coalition building. The revolutionary rhetoric of the party and its hegemonic attitude began to alienate other major partners. The CPI (M)'s ideologue and minister for land revenue,

Harekrisna Konar started a programme of illegally taking over the excess and *benami* lands from the *Jotdar.* Sometimes, this programme had to be carried on by the application of the organizational machine of the party, while the police force was made to be silent spectators. The major partners perceived that the UF was in danger largely because of "CPI (M)'s sectarian move." They felt that "a collective drive was necessary to protect the Front's interest".[68] The Chief Minister sat in strike against the high handedness of the CPI (M) and drubbed his own government as "uncivilized and barbaric".[69] He resigned in disgust on March 16, 1970. The 2nd UF experiment had an indecent burial. The following day, the CPI (M) called a statewide (*Hartal)* strike. The law and order situation went absolutely out of control. The strikers, who were allegedly associated with the CPI (M), perpetrated a gruesome murder of "Sain brothers, members of the Congress Party in Burdwan town."[70]

On April 2, 1971 after another Assembly election, a 25-member non-Marxist Democratic Coalition Government with Ajoy Mukherjee as the Chief Minister was installed. The coalition partners were Bangla Congress, the resurgent Congress Party (R), SSP, PSP, Gorkha League (GL) and Muslim League (ML). This coalition with a bare majority in the House could not survive for more than three months.

The Congress Party was gradually gaining electoral ground. It was a period of revival for the party reflecting people's revulsion against the politics of aggrandizement and violence. Another government with Siddhartha Shankar Ray as the Chief Minister with pre-election seat adjustment (PDA) with the CPI came to power in 1972. The leaders of both the parties agreed upon the PDA coalition document in principle.[71] The CPI broke the PDA coalition in mid June 1974, but it neither played the role of opposition within the House nor without. In short, coalition government's pre-election, post-election and minority coalition and then again an informal post-poll coalition government making experiments were made in the late 1960s till early 1972s.

The Left Front Government's Continuous Presence

The partners of the LF formed a pre-election political coalition and won the 1977 election. The Congress Party was decimated and the Janata Party was a poor second. The CPI (M) won an absolute majority with 60.20 per cent of the seats in the House. The winning spree with absolute majority of the CPI (M) continued till the 1996 election.

Table 4.9 indicates the position of the parties in respect of their percentage points of vote and seat shares in the assembly over a period of the last three decades.

Table 4.9: Seats Won, % of Vote Share Seat Share of each Party [West Bengal Assembly Elections (1977-2006)]

Party	1977 (Total seat 294)			1982 (Total seat 294)			1987 (Total seat 294)		
	Seats Won	% of Votes	% of Seats	Seats Won	% of votes	% of seats	Seats won	% of votes	% of seats
CPI (M)	177	35.32	60.20	174	38.47	59.48	187	39.48	63.95
FB	26	5.32	8.84	27	5.75	9.18	26	5.84	8.84
RSP	20	3.75	6.80	19	4.01	6.46	18	3.94	6.12
CPI	2	2.62	0.68	7	1.81	2.38	11	1.72	3.40
FB (M)	3	0.51	1.02	-	-	-	1	0.19	0.34
RCPI	3	0.52	1.02	1	0.19	0.34	1	0.31	0.34
BBC	1	0.25	0.34	-	-	-	-	-	-
WBSP	-	-	-	2	0.37	0.68	1	0.18	0.34
DSPPC	-	-	-	-	-	-	2	0.02	-
CONG	20	23.35	6.80	49	35.59	16.67	40	41.80	13.61
TMC	-	-	-	-	-	-	-	-	-
CPI (M)L	1	0.09	0.34	-	-	-	-	-	-
MUL/ML	1	0.35	0.34	-	-	-	1	0.62	0.34
WPI	-	0.20	-	-	-	-	-	-	-
SUC	4	1.39	1.36	2	1.03	0.68	2	0.89	0.68
JK/JP	-	0.04	-	-	-	-	-	-	-
GL/GNLF	2	0.24	0.68	1	0.07	0.34	-	-	-
JAN	29	19.98	9.86	-	-	-	-	0.16	-
BJP	-	-	-	-	0.61	-	-	0.51	-
CONG (S)	-	-	-	4	4.05	1.36	-	-	-
JMM	-	-	-	-	0.01	-	-	-	-
BSP	-	-	-	-	-	-	-	-	-
JD	-	-	-	-	-	-	-	-	-
RJD	-	-	-	-	-	-	-	-	-
Ind and Other Parties	4	5.83	1.36	7	7.88	2.38	6	4.33	2.04

Source: Compiled: Election Commission Reports Governmentt of India.

Note: RCPI = Revolutionary Communist Party of India; BBC = Biplabi Bangla Congress; WBSP = West Bengal Socialist Party; DSP = Democratic Socialist Party; CPI (ML) = Communist Party of India (Marxist-Leninist); MUL = Muslim Union League; WPI = Workers Party of India; SUC = Socialist Unity Centre; JKP/N = Jharkhand Party (Naren Hansda); GL = Gorkha League; GNLF = Gorkha National Liberation Front; JAN = Janata; JMM = Jharkhand Mukti Morcha; JD = Janata Dal; BJP = Bharatiya Janata Party; BSP= (Bahujan Samaj Party); Rashtriya Janata Dal= (RJD).

Table 4.9 *(continued)*

Party	*1991 (Total seat 294)*			*1996 (Total seat 294)*			*2001 (Total seat 294)*			*2006 (Total seat 294)*		
	Seats Won	*% of votes*	*% of seats*	*Seats won*	*% of votes*	*% of seats*	*Seats Won*	*% of votes*	*% of seats*	*Seats Won*	*% of votes*	*% of seats*
CPI (M)	188*	36.64	63.61	150	37.92	51.02	143	36.59	48.64	176	38.68	59.86
FB	29	5.51	9.86	21	5.20	7.14	25	5.65	8.50	23	3.12	7.82
RSP	18	3.47	6.12	18	3.72	6.12	17	3.43	5.78	20	2.71	6.80
CPI	6	1.75	2.04	6	1.75	2.04	7	1.79	2.38	8	2.01	2.72
FB (M)	-	-	-	1	-	0.34	1	0.41	0.34	1	0.37	0.68
RCPI	1	0.30	0.34	-	0.29	-	-	0.13	-	-	-	-
BBC	-	-	-	-	-	-	-	-	-	-	-	-
WBSP	-	-	-	2	-	0.68	4	0.67	1.36	4	1.25	1.36
DSPPC	1	0.17	0.34	2	-	0.68	2	0.82	0.68	1	0.37	0.34
CONG	43	35.12	14.97	83	39.80	28.23	26	7.98	8.84	23	14.71	7.82
TMC	-	-	-	-	-	-	60	30.66	20.41	30	26.64	10.20
CPI (M)L	-	-	-	-	-	-	-	-	-	-	0.17	-
MUL/ML	-	-	-	-	-	-	-	-	-	-	0.04	-
WPI	-	0.03	-	-	-	-	-	-	-	-	-	-
SUC	-	-	-	2	-	0.68	2	0.82	0.68	-	3.01	0.68
JK/JP	1	0.51	0.34	1	0.40	0.34	-	0.02	-	1	0.26	0.34
GL/GNLF	3	0.32	0.68	3	0.44	1.02	3	0.52	1.02	3	0.50	1.02
JAN	-	-	-	-	-	-	-	-	-	-	-	-
BJP	-	11.37	-	-	6.45	-	-	5.19	-	0	1.96	-
CONG(S)	-	-	-	-	-	-	-	-	-	-	-	-
JMM	1	0.27	-	-	0.37	-	-	0.37	-	-	0.18	-
BSP	-	0.29	-	-	0.18	-	-	0.21	-	-	0.70	-
JD	1	0.67	0.34	-	0.29	-	-	-	-	-	0.10	-
RJD**	-	-	-	-	-	-	-	0.07	-	1	0.37	0.34
Ind and Other Parties	4	3.57	1.36	5	3.18	1.70	4	4.59	1.36	-	4.57	-

Source: Compiled: Election Commission Reports Government of India.

Note: **RJD, pre-electoral ally of LF in 2006.

In fact, the electoral votes were quite polarized between the LF on the one hand and the TMC and Congress on the other. The electoral data also pointed to the fact that political competitiveness between the LF coalition and other parties, namely the TMC, Congress, BJP and other smaller parties were quite imperfect. It also appeared that the localized individual centric parties in different regions of the state seemed in the process of being extinct.

Left Front Coordination Committee

The LF Coordination Committee was not an innovation. Actually, there was a UF Committee in the late 1960s. But this Committee could not function as expected. Therefore, from the very beginning, it was decided by the participating parties that the LF Coordination Committee should be a permanent body to monitor the activities of the LF government and would formulate policies. The leadership of the LF intended to institutionalize this committee as the main consultation mechanism.[72] The constituent parties wanted to build up LF committees in every district, but without any tangible success.[73]

In parliamentary elections also, the LF, particularly the CPI (M), was maintaining its massive superiority except in 1984.

Even today, the relations among the political parties, whatever may be their political ideology and socio-political bases and stance, is never cordial, as never found elsewhere in the country and the Western World as well. This phenomenon found in West Bengal since the late 1960s has become almost the rule rather than aberrations. The Assembly 2006 election results were an unexpected windfall for the CPI (M). The leaders[74] of the CPI (M) could not think of such a gain of seats from 143 to 176. In fact, Buddhadeb, during his first six months in office before 2001 election, could not stave off the political rot that was reducing the popularity of the CPI (M) for several reasons. He seemed to have faced a formidable alliance of the Trinamool Congress and the Congress. Mamata Banerjee of TMC left the NDA before 2001 election with a calculation to bank on the Muslim votes. But the TMC-Congress alliance at the last moment did not succeed as expected. During the next five years, Buddhadeb with his brand Buddha image, i.e. of a leadership package — a neo-liberal Marxist face, wanted to bring back the work culture of the employees and made a promise to rejuvenate the sick industries, set up institutes of Information Technology and other sunrise industries. It was, as if a dream, that Buddhadeb appeared to sell to the middle and younger generations by inviting internal as well as direct foreign investment (FDI), which he thought had enormous potential for growth with employment. He made a good rapport, which his illustrious predecessor appeared to despise, with the central ministers of the NDA government and the important BJP leaders. Paradoxically, to his predecessor Jyoti Basu, the BJP was a rabid communal party and its leaders were uncivilized. These were his public utterances. But the irony of the fact was that to save the interests of his son, Chandan Basu staying separately, he never hesitated to rub his shoulder with Atal Bihari Bajpai of the BJP in a clandestine manner. Jyoti Basu was in a habit of doing this even while the Congress Party was in power at the Centre. In contrast, Buddhadeb was keen to make certain important policy decisions with regard to Heath, Industry,

Table 4.10: Seats Won and % of Vote Polled by Parties in Parliament Election (1977-2004)

Party	*1977*	*1980*	*1984*	*1989*	*1991*	*1996*	*1998*	*1999*	*2004*
CPI (M)	17 (36.79)	28 (39.81)	18 (36.24)	26 (37.75)	27 (35.38)	21 (34.50)	24 (35.61)	21 (35.59)	26 (38.56)
CPI	0 (3.86)	3 (4.27)	3 (4.63)	3 (3.99)	3 (3.70)	2 (2.49)	3 (3.65)	3 (3.47)	3 (4.01)
FB	3 (4.15)	3 (4.54)	2 (3.70)	3 (4.04)	3 (3.67)	3 (3.40)	2 (3.32)	2 (3.45)	3 (3.66)
RSP	3 (4.15)	4 (5.20)	3 (4.15)	4 (4.80)	4 (4.52)	4 (4.74)	4 (4.51)	3 (4.25)	3 (4.49)
INC	3 (28.70)	4 (36.40)	16 (43.23)	4 (41.74)	5 (36.36)	11 (40.66)	1 (15.24)	3 (13.29)	6 (14.56)
TMC	-	-	-	-	-	-	7 (24.49)	8 (26.05)	1 (21.04)
BJP	-	-	-	- (1.57)	-	-	1 (10.23)	2 (11.14)	0 (8.06)
Janata Party and others Minor Parties	16 (22.20)	0 (9.78)	0 (8.05)	1 (6.11)	0 (16.37)	1 (14.21)	0 (2.95)	0 (2.76)	0 (5.62)

Source: Parliamentary Election in West Bengal (1952-99). *Chaturdash Lok Sabha Nirvachan, 2004*, CPI (M), *Pachimbanga Rajya Committee.*

Agriculture, Education, Infrastructures, and help building up of satellite townships in the state. On the other hand, Mamata Banerjee failed to change her leadership image and style to fit in the imagination of the people at large and, particularly, the youth between 18 and 23 — the new voters of the state.

Without an effective political formation with Congress and seat adjustments with BJP or a total combination of one to one seat adjustment with the Congress, BJP and other smaller parties, it was really impossible to confront a well-organized CPI (M) led coalition. But if such alliance would have been worked out, the hesitant major partners of the LF might have acted differently for being almost marginalized in respect of losing important portfolios and power to influence important policy decisions for the last several years. The emergence of Maoist and Naxalite violence and selective elimination of the CPI (M) leaders in Jangal Mahal, just at the western part of the state was another cause of concern for the CPI (M).

Much later, the problems of Jangal Mahal have been sufficiently contained by the next Chief Ministers in coalition with the state Congress Party. But this is a prolonged and different story to be unfolded later in this work.

The major political parties and their leaders always used to claim to be totally secular. But their electoral campaign in selected areas did not appear always to be so innocuous. But the fact that the civil society in West Bengal is still not fragmented in terms of castes and communities, like that of other Indian states including Kerala are quite perceptible.

Table 4.11: Caste, Community and Economic Class Base of the Political Parties in (%)

Caste and Community	*LF*	*TMC+BJP*	*Cong.*	*Others*
Upper and Intermediate	48.20	27.80	22.60	1.40
OBC and SC	55.40	22.40	20.70	1.50
ST	47.50	30.05	20.45	7.2
Muslim	65.50	14.50	17.80	2.20
Economic Class				
Upper	51.50	30.60	16.50	1.40
Middle	52.10	26.40	20.60	0.90
Poor	44.20	32.40	21.20	2.20
Very poor	47.5 0	31.50	19.40	1.60

Source: Field Survey Election, 2004 (UPIASI).

Table 4.11 indicated that the LF had a solid vote base among the Other Backward Castes, Schedule Castes and the Muslims. Significantly, the upper economic class and the middle class also supported the LF in a big way, opting for no-change in the established political order, as just before the *Panchayat* election in 2008. During the period from September 2006 and 2008, Mamata

Banerjee with her newly formed 17 smaller parties and groups coalition bumped into almost centre stage politics of West Bengal. Since 2009, the castes, communal and class equations went in favour of Mamata Banerjee, although the opportunistic upper and middle class did not favourably look at the change that was the writing on the wall. Mamata Banerjee became a phenomenon in West Bengal politics in 2009 and onwards.

Council of Ministers during the LF Regime

Jyoti Basu with his 29 member's Council of Ministers took over on June 21, 1977. The distribution of ministerial portfolios was such an initial hassle that the RSP, being dissatisfied, proposed to support the LF as a partner from outside. However, Jyoti Basu allotted a few important portfolios like Health, *Panchayat* and Rural Development, Public Works and PWD with Housing to RSP and Agriculture and Food, Industry, Education, Cooperative and Relief and Rehabilitation to FB. But as time went by, the CPI (M) began asserting its hegemony. The Front partners made occasional noises, but ultimately, they had to give in. The important portfolios like Industry, *Panchayat* and Rural Development, Health, Housing (separated from PWD) and Education were taken over by the CPI (M). The CPI (M) came out with an argument that it was necessary to lay particular emphasis to ameliorate the economic conditions of the backward sections of society.[75]

Table 4.12 indicates the caste and community representations in the council of ministers. Most of the members of the cabinet were of middle class background and majority of them are of erstwhile East Bengal origin.[76] During this period, only Jatin Chakraborty of RSP had to resign from the cabinet for bringing about a substantiated charge of "Bengal Lamp scam"[77] against Jyoti Basu's son.

During the new regime since May 20, 2011, headed by Ms. Mamata Banerjee, the ministerial caste and minorities composition of the council of ministers were more or less the same. Only a few more candidates from Muslim community were taken in the Council. Initially, when the Congress Party was in the coalition, it got a quota of five ministers among whom two ministers were from the Muslim community. But, after one and a half years, the Congress withdrew from the coalition as reaction against TMC's withdrawal of support from the Central coalition government. Subsequently, as the volume of workload increased, the new Chief Minister inducted 12 Parliamentary Secretaries enjoying the power of deputy ministers. The Chief Minister administered the oath to these Parliamentary Secretaries. This was a new innovation in West Bengal. But this system is still found in the Bihar Legislative Assembly. Therefore, it is not at all a new concept that can be found in the British Parliamentary system (Table 4.13).

Table 4.12: Composite Council of Ministers in LF: Percentage points classified according to Caste and Community (1977-2001)

Caste/Community	*1977*	*1982*	*1987*	*1991*	*1996*	*2001*
Upper Caste:						
Brahmin	11 (38.00)	19 (44.20)	9 (28.20)	14 (31.20)	20 (41.70)	16 (33.30)
Baidya	–	1 (2.30)	2 (6.20)	3 (6.60)	3 (6.30)	3 (6.20)
Kayastha	10 (34.40)	12 (28.00)	7 (21.90)	12 (26.80)	8 (16.70)	9 (18.70)
Aguri	1 (3.50)	1 (2.00)	1 (3.10)	2 (4.40)	1 (2.00)	1 (2.10)
Nepali	–	1 (2.30)	1 (3.10)	–	–	–
Other Lower Caste and OBCs:						
Maheshya	1 (3.50)	2 (4.60)	1 (3.10)	2 (4.40)	2 (4.10)	4 (8.40)
Namosudra Sodgope and Others	2 (6.80)	1 (2.30)	2 (6.20)	–	2 (4.10)	1 (2.10)
Mahato	–	–	–	–	1 (2.00)	–
Schedule Caste	–	1 (2.30)	3 (9.30)	4 (8.80)	4 (8.40)	5 (10.50)
Schedule Tribe	1 (3.50)	1 (2.30)	1 (3.10)	2 (4.40)	3 (6.30)	3 (6.20)
Others, Christian, Sikh	–	1 (2.30)	1 (3.10)	–	–	–
Muslim	3 (10.30)	3 (7.10)	4 (12.70)	6 (13.40)	4 (8.40)	6 (12.50)
Total	**29 (100)**	**43 (100)**	**32 (100)**	**45 (100)**	**48 (100)**	**48 (100)**

Source: WBLA Secretariat, Members List.
Note: Since 2004 as per the new Act, the composition of the council of Ministers should not exceed 15 per cent of the total number of the MLAs. Therefore, three ministers from CPI (M) and one each from RSP and Forward Bloc had to be dropped.

The legislative coalition of the LF since 1977 has never been tumbled. This is because of the dominant presence of the CPI (M) and, other partners' electoral dependence on the CPI (M). The RSP, FB and even CPI Members of the Assembly (MLAs) sometimes feel piqued and frustrated because of the "big brotherly attitude"[78] of the CPI (M) both within and without. But considering the social coalitions that had taken shape in different regions and

Table 4.13: % of Ministers from Each Party in Successive Seven Council of Ministers (1977-2006)

Year	*Number of Ministers with Percentage*					*Total*
	CPI (M)	*FB*	*RSP*	*CPI*	*Others*	
1977	20 (68.97)	4 (13.79)	3 (10.34)	–	2 (6.90)	29 (100.0)
1982	32 (74.42)	4 (9.30)	3 (6.98)	1 (2.32)	3 (6.98)	43 (100.0)
1987	22 (68.75)	4 (12.50)	3 (9.38)	2 (6.25)	1 (3.12)	32 (100.0)
1991	32 (72.76)	5 (11.34)	4 (9.10)	1 (2.26)	2 (4.54)	44 (100.0)
1996	33 (68.75)	5 (10.42)	5 (10.42)	2 (4.16)	3 (6.25)	48 (100.0)
2001	33 (68.75)	5 (10.42)	5 (10.42)	2 (4.16)	3 (6.25)	48 (100.0)
2006	32 (72.76)	4 (9.10)	4 (9.10)	2 (4.52)	2 (4.52)	44 (100.0)

Source: Documents, Government of West Bengal (1977-2006).

districts of the state, they never seriously vented their spleen in public to the LF's peril.

Table 4.14 in a synoptic way indicates the social, caste and community bases of the political parties during two Assemblies. This was more or less true in previous four Assemblies also.

The caste and community-wise composition of the Legislative Assemblies over the successive periods are shown in Table 4.15.

The Tables (15-18) indicate that the upper middle class, middle class, educated and middle-aged people had a dominating presence in all the successive Assemblies.

The Table 4.16 indicates an overwhelming presence of the political workers, teachers and lawyers in the House. The cultivators as a class had been decreasing that pointed to the class character of the Assembly.

Table 4.17 shows that the middle-aged members of two groups, 35-44 and 45-54 were the dominating force. This might mean that the Assemblies had been experiencing a moderate influence over the years.

Table 4.18 shows the presence of highly educated representatives, who naturally came from upper middle and middle class backgrounds.

Note: *The official and authentic data and other figures regarding the periods 2006-2011 and 2011 onwards are still not available to this date. (Emphasis given)*

Candidate Selection and Criteria of Selecting Individual Candidates

The higher leadership of each of the parties is not rigid in following the procedures that depend sometimes on extraneous calculations. But it is found that the left parties select their candidates more smoothly and earlier than other parties. The Congress and TMC make inordinate delay to finalize the lists. Fearing the public mood in 2006 election, the CPI (M) nominated 117

Table 4.14: Caste/Community Base: Party-wise Breakup of the Assembly (1996-2001) (%)

Caste/Community	**1996 (%)**						**2001 (%)**						
	CPI (M)	*FB*	*RSP*	*CPI*	*Others*	*INC*	*CPI (M)*	*FB*	*RSP*	*CPI*	*Others*	*INC*	*TMC*
Upper and Intermediate													
Brahmin	7.20	1.4	2.00	0.60	1.40	7.5	8.80	1.00	1.00	0.5	-	0.6	7.10
Baidya	1.00	-	-	-	0.70	-	0.60	-	-	0.3	-	-	0.80
Kayastha	7.80	1.0	-	0.60	1.20	5.4	6.80	2.70	1.00	0.6	1.60	1.4	3.60
Khashtriya	0.30	-	-	-	0.50	0.6	1.40	-	-	-	-	-	-
Aguri	0.60	-	-	-	-	0.8	0.60	0.60	-	-	1.30	-	-
Marwari	-	-	-	-	-	0.7	-	-	-	-	-	0.4	-
Lower and OBCs													
Mahishya	1.00	-	0.30	-	-	0.4	1.00	1.00	-	-	-	-	0.70
Bagdi	0.60	0.3	-	-	0.5	-	0.80	-	-	0.3	-	-	-
Barui	0.60	-	-	-	-	0.8	0.60	-	-	-	0.80	-	-
Sudra and Namosudra and others	7.50	0.3	0.60	-	0.25	2.7	7.20	0.30	0.30	-	1.00	1.4	3.00
Schedule Caste	12.50	1.4	1.40	0.3	1.10	2.7	10.50	1.70	1.30	-	2.60	1.0	2.00
Schedule Tribe	4.40	0.6	1.40	-	1.50	0.3	4.50	-	1.10	-	0.70	0.3	-
Community													
Muslim	5.10	1.3	0.30	-	1.30	6.4	6.10	1.40	1.00	0.3	0.20	0.3	3.40
Others													
Christian and Sikh	-	-	-	-	0.70	0.4	-	-	-	-	0.40	-	-

Source: WBLA Members lists and Who's Who and personal Interviews sometimes over telephone.

Table 4.15: Composition of the WB Legislative Assembly (1977-2001) Classified according to Members' Caste and Community

Caste/Community	*1977-82*		*1982-87*		*1987-91*		*1991-96*		*1996-01*		*2001-06*	
Upper and Intermediate												
Brahmin	66	19.73	50	17.01	55	18.71	60	20.41	66	22.45	62	21.23
Baidya	3	1.70	3	1.02	6	2.04	8	2.72	3	1.02	3	1.03
Kayastha	48	17.35	32	10.88	60	20.41	53	18.03	48	16.33	56	19.18
Marwari	2	0.00	2	0.68	2	0.68	2	0.68	2	0.68	0	0.00
Kshatriya/Aguri	4	1.70	8	2.72	9	3.06	5	1.70	4	1.36	9	3.08
Lower and OBCs												
Maheshya/Mahato	15	5.10	30	10.20	20	6.80	9	3.06	11	3.74	17	5.82
Bagdi	2	0.68	5	1.70	3	1.02		0.00		0.00		0.00
Barui	4	1.36	4	1.36		0.00		0.00		0.00		0.00
Sudra, NomoSudra and Others	45	15.31	35	11.90	20	6.80	42	14.29	40	13.61	30	10.27
Schedule Caste	54	18.37	55	18.71	55	18.71	57	19.39	58	19.73	58	19.86
Schedule Tribe	19	6.46	31	10.54	21	7.14	16	5.44	18	6.12	17	5.82
Muslim	34	11.56	37	12.59	42	14.29	40	13.61	43	14.63	39	13.36
Others, Christian, Sikh	2	0.68	2	0.68	1	0.34	2	0.68	1	0.34	1	0.34
Total	**294 (100.00)**		**294 (100.00)**		**294 (100.00)**		**294 (100.00)**		**294 (100.00)**		**292 (100.00)**	

Source: Compiled, WBLA Secretariat Documents.

Note: The Data of 2006 are yet not available.

Table 4.16: Members of the Legislative Assembly Classified according to Occupational Background (1977-2001)

Occupation	*1977-82*		*1982-87*		*1987-91*		*1991-96*		*1996-01*		*2001-06*	
	No.	*%*	*No.*	*%*	*No.*	*%*	*No.*	*%*	*No.*	*%*	*No.*	*%*
Political and Social Worker	72	24.91	111	38.95	107	36.64	119	40.48	111	38.14	100	34.01
Teacher	82	28.37	82	28.77	98	33.56	98	33.33	104	35.74	106	36.05
Lawyer	30	10.38	19	6.67	21	7.19	13	4.42	13	4.47	19	6.46
Cultivator	42	14.53	16	5.61	19	6.51	17	5.78	14	4.81	5	1.70
Businessman	11	3.81	10	3.51	13	4.45	11	3.74	17	5.84	18	6.12
Landholder	1	0.35	10	3.51	9	3.08	12	4.08	7	2.41	14	4.76
Trade Unionist	24	8.30	13	4.56	4	1.37	4	1.36	3	1.03	3	1.02
Medical Practitioner	15	5.19	10	3.51	9	3.08	10	3.40	9	3.09	6	2.04
Writers, Journalist and Artist	3	1.04	3	1.05	0	0.00	0	0.00	0	0.00	2	0.68
Farmer Zamindar	0	0.00	1	0.35	1	0.34	0	0.00	0	0.00	0	0.00
House wife	0	0.00	0	0.00	0	0.00	1	0.34	2	0.69	2	0.68
Engineer, Technologist Consultant	0	0.00	0	0.00	0	0.00	1	0.34	1	0.34	2	0.68
Serviceman	9	3.11	10	3.51	11	3.77	8	2.72	10	3.44		
Total	**289**		**285**		**292**		**294**		**291**		**294**	
Total No. of MLAs	**294**		**294**		**294**		**294**		**294**		**294**	

Source: A.K. Chaudhuri, *Legislative Control over Public Administration (1993)*, *Members List, Who's who*, personal Interviews. Note: The data of 2006 are not yet available.

Table 4.17: Members of the West Bengal Legislative Assembly Classified according to Age Group:1977-2001

Age Group	*1977-82*		*1982-87*		*1987-91*		*1991-96*		*1996-01*		*2001-06*	
	No.	*%*	*No.*	*%*	*No.*	*%*	*No.*	*%*	*No.*	*%*	*No.*	*%*
25-34	32	11.59	17	6.16	24	8.25	16	5.44	6	2.06	7	2.38
35-44	98	35.51	74	26.81	61	20.96	67	22.79	74	25.43	50	17.01
45-54	73	26.45	104	37.68	118	40.55	118	40.14	103	35.40	102	34.69
55-64	58	21.01	59	21.38	58	19.93	67	22.79	80	27.49	102	34.69
65 and above	15	5.43	22	7.97	30	10.31	26	8.84	28	9.62	33	11.22
Total	**276**	**100.00**	**276**	**100.00**	**291**	**100.00**	**294**	**100.00**	**291**	**100.00**	**294**	**100.00**
Total MLAs	**294**		**294**		**294**		**294**		**294**		**294**	

Source: A.K. Chaudhuri, *Legislative Control over Public Administration* (1993) *Members List, Who's Who,* Personal *Interviews*. The Data of 2006 are not yet available.

Table 4.18: Members of the West Bengal Legislative Assembly classified According to Educational Background (1977-2001)

Educational Background	*1977-82*		*1982-87*		*1987-91*		*1991-96*		*1996-01*		*2001-06*	
	No.	*%*	*No.*	*%*	*No.*	*%*	*No.*	*%*	*No.*	*%*	*No.*	*%*
Below School Final	43	15.47	45	16.07	36	12.24	36	12.24	28	9.69	24	8.19
Under Graduate	73	26.26	86	30.71	82	27.89	84	28.57	76	26.30	72	24.57
Graduate	87	31.29	94	33.57	109	37.07	111	37.76	122	42.21	132	45.05
Post-graduate	70	25.18	52	18.57	63	21.43	58	19.73	58	20.07	59	20.14
Above Post-graduate	5	1.80	3	1.07	4	1.36	5	1.70	5	1.73	6	2.05
Total	278	100.00	280	100.00	294	100.00	294	100.00	289	100.00	293	100.00
Total MLAs	294		294		294		294		294		294	

Source: A.K. Chaudhuri, *Legislative Control over Public Administration (1993), WBLA Members Lists, Who's Who,* and Personal *Interviews*. The data of 2006 are not yet available.

new faces against the old guards having reservations against them. This was a rewarding decision that 105 won among the 117 fielded for the CPI (M) as revealed in the final results of 176 as against 143 in 2001 election.

Table 4.19 shows the institutional methods of selecting the candidates for elections

Table 4.19 is interesting. The party leaders were asked to tick the importance and contextual relevance of the criteria of selecting individual candidates in order of preference.

Table 4.19: Procedure of Selecting Candidates (Parliamentary and Assembly) of Important Parties

Recommended and approved by	*CPI (M)*	*FB*	*RSP*	*CPI*	*CONG*	*TMC*	*BJP*
Block Committee	–	–	–	–	Applications accepted	–	–
District Committee	Names submitted	Names submitted	Names submitted	–	List of Applications prepared	Applications accepted	List prepared
State Committee	List prepared and approved	List approved	List approved	List prepared	Final list for approval	List prepared	–
Central Committee/ Politburo	Finally approved if, necessary	–	–	Approved if, necessary	–	–	–
Central Election Committee	–	–	–	–	–	–	Finally approved
Parliamentary Board	–	–	–	–	Finally approved	–	–
Working Committee	–	–	–	–	–	Finally approval if necessary	–

Source: Field survey. Interview, secretaries of the state committee of the parties.

Table 4.20: Criteria of Selecting Individual Contesting Candidates (Parliamentary and Assembly)

Party	*Ideology*	*Loyalty to Party*	*Loyalty to Leader*	*Winn-ability*	*Perfor-mance and acceptability to constituency*	*Age*	*Corruption free*	*Resourceful*	*Others*
CPI (M)	2	1	5	3	4	6 (b)	9	7	8 (M+W)
FB	1	2	5	3	4	8 (a+b)	7	6	9 (M+W)
RSP	1	2	3	4	5	8 (a+b)	6	7	9 (M+W)
CPI	3	2	6	1	4	5 (b)	8	7	9 (M+W)
CONG	4	3	2	1	5	6 (a+b)	7	8	9 (M+W)
TMC	4	3	1	2	8	6 (a+b)	5	7	9 (W+M)
BJP	3	2	5	1	7	8 (a+b)	4	6	9 (M+W)

Source: Field survey Interview.

Note: Numerical (1 to 9) indicates order of preference. Age indicates (a) Young (b) middle-aged and (c) above 65. Others indicate (M) man and (W) woman.

Significantly the LF in general and the CPI (M) in particular substantially gained in 2006 election by fielding new and young faces replacing many of the old guards. A hypothetical situation might arise if major political parties including others had combined together to offer a new political equation. But politics is not only electoral arithmetic only. The political chemistry that mattered most was a combination of a few common objectives, issues, possible policy reorientations and ideological nearness among the parties as far as possible. This was where the opposition parties failed and the left parties were always in advantageous position till the Parliamentary election in 2009. But as indicated in earlier chapter, the danger signal for the LF perceptively sounded already in the three tiers *Panchayat* elections held in 2008.

In course of arguments with and comments of the important party leaders and other knowledgeable people who had seen the behaviour politics of West Bengal and the leadership profiles, a number of hypotheses came up. To address the problematic, available documentary evidences as also the opinions of very important state and national level leaders were studied in this work. The caste, community and economic class bases of the political parties appeared to be very important in forging any coalition, be it that of left variety or of the rightist ones. The social bases and people's support of the parties or coalition were almost overlooked by the Congress leadership in earlier Congress regimes from 1952 to 1967 and then during the period from 1972 to 1977. The parties' policy of economic development, class differentiation and particularities of the state, and their influence on them, the problems of splits and mergers, tensions among coalition partners, the stabilizing factors, and social coalition to political coalition gradually became prominent features among political players. The importance of allocative justice and egalitarian policies, and the fiscal sustainability of some of the policies came to be recognized, particularly since 1977 by the LF. But because of LF's prolonged stay in office for more than 34 years, its policy focus towards the rural backyard got diluted. The missing thread has been taken up by the new regime of TMC coalition led by Ms. Mamata Banerjee after her long political battle with CPI (M). Earlier, the Congress Party made seat adjustment with the TMC and its other smaller partners; but soon after, the Congress left the coalition and its state level leaders began criticizing the TMC and its supreme leader to some extent unjustly. Mamata never asked the Congress Members of Cabinet to leave. She simply broke away from the Congress coalition at the centre on the plea that she could not agree with some of the policy decisions of the UPA-II led by the Congress coalition at the Centre; it was her breaking point against the Congress leadership, particularly the last straw on the camel's back when the Central government allowed the total entry of the Foreign Direct Investment (FDI) in multibrand retails.

It is yet to be seen what happens to the state party of the Congress and how far it would be able to manage the emerging situations; in the last *Panchayat* elections (2008), it did not totally fail to maintain its wavelength with the masses in the rural backyard of West Bengal. Finally, the people's responses with regard to their assessment of the last leg of the LF coalition and importance of its policies were empirically studied in another study.[79] The responses were not totally negative, but not encouraging either, particularly unfruitful industrial venture and land policy of the LF. Peasants of Singur at Hooghly and then Nandigram in East Midnapur were gradually becoming restive. The local people, along with the TMC, launched serious movements against agricultural land policy of the LF. It was instantly supported by Mamata Banerjee; side by side, groups of civil society came forward in perfect sympathy with the poor peasants and other agricultural labourers from various parts of the districts brutalized by the CPI (M)'s goondas and supporters at the behest of the important local party leaders. But all this happened after 2006 at the third quarter of the year when Buddhadeb and his Industry Minister, Nirupam Sen made a secret contract with the Tatas receiving 997 acres of heritage agricultural land to build up a small car (NANO) factory. This is the story that would be unfolded later in this study.

Finally, the figures as shown earlier in the chapters in different Tables indicated that the coalition structure, processes, policies and electoral style in West Bengal format, both in its societal and political spaces, appeared to be entrenched till the end of 2006. The LF partners, particularly the CPI (M) as the leader, at least, acquired a sense of accommodation as an essential element for coalition management and culture to mature. The other opposition parties, the Congress Party and then the TMC, even in the face of electoral decimation, fail to realize the potential of the coalition culture-attitude, and the politics of coalition making. The two most important political parties, the Congress and the TMC might have their own compulsions in that context when the central minority coalition government of United Progressive Alliance (UPA-I) led by the Congress was formed after 2004 with the support of the LF from outside. But the greater issues and strategically important considerations were involved in the political calculations of the CPI (M) and to a lesser extent by the partners of the LF.

A number of factors contributing to the stability of the LF government have been enumerated elaborately above. The initial attempts were the follow up of the land reform programmes and 'Operation Barga', setting up of a system of rural self-governance and regular elections, civic administrations in urban and peri-urban areas through the civic body elections. The primary support bases of the left parties were the refugees from the East Pakistan as described earlier in this work. These groups of refugees, later on during mid-

1980s, began oscillating because of their still unresolved problems in the colony areas. Surreptitious acceptance by the local party leaders of the infiltrators, both Hindus and the Muslims as the citizens, from across the borders made good the loss.

The left party leaders and other parties including the BJP in case of the Hindus only, do not publicly admit the fact that the caste and communal influences in electoral politics mattered heavily. But oral history and empirical findings and electoral data point to the fact that the LF was privileged to receive support of lower castes, schedule castes and schedule tribes. The Muslims supported the Congress at the Centre and LF in the state in a big way. The urban and semi-urban middle classes were already sympathetic to the causes of the left parties, particularly the Communists. Significantly, the urban and rural upper classes, contrary to the expectations of the CPI (M) in the initial phases of the LF, appeared to contribute to the might of the LF regime. The agricultural and industrial stagnation began during Jyoti Basu regime in mid 1980s although agriculture growth, food and industrial production to an extent, except the power situation in the state, were not totally insufficient till the mid-1980s. Basu toured several Western countries sometimes with his comrade Somnath Chatterjee, the then chairman of the West Bengal Industrial Development Corporation (WBIDC) to invite Foreign Direct Investment (FDI) or investments in any other forms; but in terms of concrete results, he did not succeed as expected.

Buddhadeb Bhattacharya made a promise of providing a more developed and new look of the Left Front government. Bhattacharjee, in order to invite foreign direct investment (FDI), which his party at the federal Centre was trying to stall, paradoxically invited industrial groups like Salem of Indonesia and captains of information technology (IT) and at the beginning of the 7th LF regime, the Tata group, Jindal, Ambani, Japanese Mitsubishi and other prospective investors, promising them thousands of acres of vantage lands and other facilities on subsidies. The party went even to the extent of ignoring the opposition not only of the front partners like the RSP, FB and CPI, but also of his own cabinet minister for Land Revenue, Abdul Rezzak Molla. The coalition partners, particularly the RSP and FB and even CPI were seen to murmur that food production would suffer as a result of acquiring agricultural lands and then leasing them out to neo-industrialists. To silence them, the LF Coordination Committee *authoritatively persuaded* them. The opposition parties like TMC, SUCI and some other fringe left parties, were opposing the move, but not without a message to the electorate that they were not against industrialization.

It appears that the CPI (M) has been maintaining two faces together. They were nursing two constituencies as it were, for two different objectives.

It is CPI (M)'s tactical move to critically support the UPA-I government at the Centre for enjoying larger payoffs without shouldering direct responsibility and, hobnobbed with other friendly state governments if possible, and other state parties to forge a third front in future. It is significant to note the utterances of Anil Biswas, the then Secretary of the State Committee, "We hate capitalism, but invite national and foreign capitals for the economic development of West Bengal."[80] The Minister for Industry, Nirupam Sen told in the same vein and asked the Trade Union (CITU) leaders of the country not to tread the path they used to do earlier against the industrialists. In the name of industrialization, according to sections of the ambivalent hard-liner CPI (M), as also the partners of the LF, the government was indulging in joint collaboration with local investors, promoters and some national business communities. The internal and foreign industrialists were being allured for building up satellite townships in Rajarhat, Howrah, Durgapur and South 24 Parganas, motor bike factory at Uluberia in Howrah, small car factory at Singur in Hooghly, factories in rural areas of Durgapur and Midnapore on the fertile agricultural lands forcibly acquired from the peasants on a pittance. The LF partners RSP, FB, CPI opposed the proposals to acquire cultivable two-cropped or multi-cropped lands. To them and others as well, industrialization for development does not mean building up of township, gyms, health clubs, multiplexes and shopping malls for upper classes and upper middle classes in a less developed country.

The path of growth, without sufficiently creating employment opportunities in high-profile industrial ventures, may be counterproductive. Acquisition of thousands of acres of multi-cropped fertile lands from the peasants to lease out to the internal or foreign industrialists and companies in different areas of the state evoked bitter protests by all the opposition parties. In fact, the present land acquisition method of the CPI (M) has brought the disparate opposition parties including the Jamaat-e-Ulema Hind — a near secular socio-religious Muslim organization together to form a common platform to resist the land acquisition move. At that point of time, even the front partners were opposing the CPI (M)'s move against land grabbing indirectly by government sponsored agencies, like West Bengal Industrial Development Corporations (WBIDC). For the first time during the last 30 years, a large number of peasants cutting across party lines stood in revolt against the government move in many places of the state. The political compulsions of the partners of the LF to cling to power and share the payoffs put them in a dilemma. A few years back, the LF partners, FB and RSP opposed to accept Mackinsay Report for reforming agriculture in the state. The CPI (M) itself opposed tooth and nail against accepting conditional financial grants of the World Bank and IMF. The CPI (M) now had no hesitation to accept consultancy services of the DFID and UNDP to go in for inviting foreign investment and accepting loans for urban renewal of the state. The voices of the LF partners have become almost muted even when the CPI (M) was falling in tune with the UPA-I government for its policies of neo economic liberalization, disinvestment and privatization. The propositions that CPI (M)'s co-operation with the Congress at the Centre and electoral fight in the state against the Congress Party might have damaged the CPI (M)'s position in West Bengal and would impact its concept of left consolidation were not clear enough even to them. The CPI (M)'s ideological strategy and its nature of coalition building might help indicating that its Marxist concept of coalition is very different from the coalitions that one usually comes across in West European models of coalition — be it European Politics Tradition model or of Riker's Game Theoretic model.

The models of coalition found in developed West European countries, Scandinavian and even less developed countries do not quite fit in the model that have been in vogue in West Bengal for the last several years under the dominance of the CPI (M). During the last few years, the CPI (M) as a well-organized political party almost became a corporate giant, a political oligopoly as it were from political economy perspective. The party's propaganda machineries were well orchestrated. It brings out daily Newspapers, Journals, and pamphlets and starts TV channels as also computer networks through which electoral information and data from every corner of the state are available. It maintains election cells in the central party and daily Newspaper offices. The party regularly brings out numerous books and reports on electoral data. All this adds to the exceptional stature of the party as well as the indispensability of the CPI (M)'s help for the partners of the LF. This makes easier for the party to smoothly manage the political coalition that has been working uninterrupted since long. The coalescing LF partners, whatever might be their occasional hiccups and muted opposition as regards the unilateral policy formulations by the CPI (M) and the nature of governance at different levels, had no other options, but to cling to the "big brother" for political power and office-sharing objectives. The CPI (M)'s massive organizational presence and influence over the major societal spaces became the real cobbling threads. And finally, the CPI (M) dominating LF coalition became all the more powerful having sensed it's all India spread in collaboration with the UPA-I government at the centre. It also began to rope in other parties at that in the fold of the NDA, except the Trinamool Congress. After being sufficiently entrenched in West Bengal as a predominant party without any alternative till 2011, whatsoever, it had possibly been once again enthused with the Leninist's cause of championing the United Front of the Second Communist International and its resurrection in line with Georgi Drimitroff's concept of the United Front of parties and social forces.

In the process, the CPI (M) transformed the Left Front into an oligopolistic cartel of a political coalition, because the electoral market place in West Bengal was very imperfect without having any possibilities of an alternative coalition of opposition parties that appeared to be trying to destroy one another. On the other hand, the LF government with left orientation, forgetting their earlier enmity with one another that vitiated their existence of a loose coalition during the late 1960s. But their late incarnation as a perfect left coalition from 1977 to 2006 was a perfect reality as seen in Table 4.21. Their spread throughout the state in each of the 19 Districts was shown in Table 4.21. A large number of the upper and middle class elites of the state and the intellectuals beyond the state were in a habit of praising the LF coalition for its democratically electoral victory over such long period of time. Showing the spread of LF all over the state (as shown in Table 4.21), they began questioning the contention of the skeptics that such thumping victories by any political formation could not be achieved without electoral engineering and deft political management. Now it came to light to the people that the CPI (M) was not electorally that honest. Even the LF, particularly the CPI (M) and its party state secretary, were nervous about the results of 2006. They did not expect this time that the LF would get 235 seats. They appeared to be a bit nervous as seen from the statements in television and many other newspapers. Even the party secretary Biman Bose could hardly believe that their tally might cross 180 seats, although the voting per cent exceeded 82 per cent. It was generally believed that higher percentage point of voting generally goes against the ruling party as a result of incumbency factor. The Election Commission was very strict and arranged for phase wise voting. It was a five phase voting instruction. And the opposition, the TMC, Congress and other opposing parties became very hopeful that after such a long innings, this time the LF was going to swallow some bitter pills. The results went otherwise giving the opposition parties less number of seats. Thereafter, Buddhadeb Bhattacharjee began bragging, "We are 235 and they are only 30." Really this time, the TMC won 60 seats and the Congress only 23. The utterances were made not only by the Chief Minister and other ministers, but surprisingly by Nirupam Sen, the industry minister and other heavy weight party leaders, like Binay Konar, Shyamal Chakraborty, Gautama Dev. Anil Basu, Susanta Ghosh, Dipak Sarkar, to name only a few, began to use very objectionable words not only against Mamata Banerjee and her Party TMC, but against the members of the Civil Society Groups. These were too much to be tolerated. Silently, ordinary people from different professions extended support to the movement to bring about a change in the existing political regime in West Bengal. Therefore, the results of the 7th Assembly elections as shown in Table 4.21 indicated both the strength and weakness for the LF as a whole, and most particularly the CPI (M).

Table 4.21: West Bengal Assembly Election 2006: District-wise Party Position of Each Party in (%)

Districts	*Left Front*	*Congress*	*TMC*	*BJP*	*Others*
Cooch Behar	7 (49.32)	1 (12.65)	1 (24.55)	– (7.62)	– (5.86)
Jalpaiguri	11 (45.11)	1 (19.95)	– (15.55)	– (3.99)	– (15.40)
Darjeeling	2 (34.27)	– (13.84)	– (4.28)	– (2.02)	3 (45.60)
North Dinajpur	5 (39.20)	2 (40.05)	– (8.02)	– (2.00)	– (10.73)
South Dinajpur	5 (50.23)	– (12.27)	– (21.55)	– (10.83)	– (5.12)
Malda	7 (45.25)	4 (39.88)	– (5.10)	– (3.57)	– (6.20)
Murshidabad	13 (44.29)	3 (38.05)	– (2.56)	– (0.41)	3 (14.69)
Nadia	12 (49.49)	1 (11.80)	2 (33.80)	– (0.17)	– (4.68)
North 24-Parganas	24 (48.43)	– (8.75)	4 (36.61)	– (2.07)	– (3.50)
South 24-Parganas	21 (48.34)	1 (6.73)	4 (37.50)	– (0.90)	2 (6.53)
Kolkata	8 (44.99)	3 (17.68)	9 (30.70)	– (1.57)	1 (5.06)
Howrah	14 (48.21)	– (12.20)	2 (33.85)	–	– (5.74)
Hooghly	16 (50.96)	– (9.13)	2 (33.28)	– (1.65)	1 (4.98)
East Midnapore	10 (38.12)	– (3.29)	3 (44.02)	–	3 (14.57)
West Midnapore	17 (53.39)	2 (9.42)	– (24.16)	– (2.28)	2 (10.95)
Purulia	10 (49.85)	1 (16.82)	– (17.57)	– (2.05)	– (13.71)
Bankura	13 (57.02)	– (7.02)	– (25.90)	– (1.98)	– (8.08)
Burdwan	22 (56.98)	1 (10.61)	2 (24.26)	– (1.41)	1 (6.74)
Birbhum	10 (53.31)	1 (21.10)	1 (18.20)	– (2.03)	– (5.36)

Source: *Election Recorder*, Star Publishing, Kolkata, 2006.

5

Politics of Trinamool Congress and Formation of a New Coalition

A Real Threat to Dislodge the Left Front

Certain common properties, either inherent or constitutionally contrived, characterize the working of the process of state politics in historical moments in West Bengal. The achievement of good governance through democratic means for realizing political modernization and development objectives should be the most coveted goal. Besides, the securing of equal opportunity and special provisions for deprived social groups find a special place in this overall objective. Whether and to what extent this objective and the values underlying it are or can be realized depends upon the way the political parties in India — both national and regional, have conducted state affairs. However, socio-political ethos, which differ from state to state in India, constitutes the most important factor. In West Bengal, anti-Congressism has been the mainstay of the Marxist political parties. Many of the refugees, who had to migrate to West Bengal after Partition, were educated[1] and very carefully the Marxists targeted them to side with the oppositions; their existential conditions made them susceptible to the leftist ideology and their continuous propaganda against the Congress Party, both at the Centre and the state. To the refugees, the state government led by the Congress was not providing them sufficient space in life and living.

Refugee camps and colonies were built on the government lands and the lands left by the Muslims during the period around the state capital, Calcutta and many of the suburban areas including North Bengal. The actions of the Communist Party of India (undivided till 1964) were not so much to highlight and redress the deplorable condition of the uprooted people from the erstwhile East Pakistan as to gain political mileage highlighting the cause of the refugees. Successive election campaigns and electoral results of the state by the left parties from 1952 to 1967 would prove the contention.[2] It was widely felt that, instead of following the strict principles of federalism, the Central government paid little heed to the regional socio-political mosaic and its legitimate aspirations.

For opportunistic reasons, however, the Communists always did speak of some sort of a left unity highlighting the Communist thesis of "United Front"[3] strategy. But they did not care to recognize the pragmatic necessity of establishing some equation between the powerful and the smaller parties in coalition making. In West Bengal, specific politics revolving around the Marxist parties seems different from that of other states. The Marxist very intelligently used their thesis that West Bengal was discriminated against both politically and economically by the central government. The Marxist regime exploited both the situations: When the Central government was strong, it raised the bogey of discrimination and in the case of a friendly but weak Centre, its demands for autonomy of regional parties[4] met with success. In July 2008, the LF (with its 61 MPs in the Parliament) withdrew support from the United Progressive Alliance (UPA-I) government. It opposed the Indo-US Civil Nuclear Agreement. But the minority UPA-I government survived, because it received support from the Samajwadi Party (SP) of Mulyam Singh Yadav with 38 MPs, while Mayawati and her Bahujan Samaj Party (BSP) did not oppose the No Confidence Motion. The CPI (M)'s political calculation was to further emasculate the Congress at the state level in West Bengal and Kerala. At that point in history, they thought it prudent to distance the LF from the Congress with a view to enhance its image as Caesar's wife, more honest and people oriented in their traditional bastions, West Bengal and Kerala. Holding its strategy very close to the chest, the CPI (M) wanted to carve out an exit route in view of their future course of actions to maintain their electoral hold in Bengal. They did not like to give up even an inch to the Congress and the Trinamool Congress (TMC) in state politics. Rather, they did everything possible to keep the Congress and the TMC at loggerheads with each other since 1998. But this time, the middle class, several groups of civil society, the refugees living still in the colonies, the Muslims and the Scheduled Castes and Tribes, the mainstay of social coalition that sustained the LF so long, appeared sternly to turn their back against the LF, as very partially discussed at the end of the previous chapter.

In retrospect, it appears that the LF led by the CPI (M) did loathe sharing the responsibility when the UPA-I government at the Centre had unwittingly committed mistakes. It was uncharitable for the highest leadership of the CPI (M) to say., "The UPA coalition government survives on the LF's support. Therefore, if we want them to stand up or sit down, they must do that."[5] Actually, the people largely in West Bengal did not like this neo Bengali Marxist vocabulary.

The LF led by the CPI (M) had to withdraw support from the UPA government perhaps for tactical reasons. They would have to go in for parliamentary election next year in 2009 to save its most important red bastion. If it had made the decision earlier, it would have been wiser. Its support base had already begun to erode because of its contradictory positions: a pragmatic support for the Congress at the Centre and, throwing electoral challenges to the Congress Party in West Bengal. The main opposition party, the TMC, made a sustained campaign against the Congress Party as team 'B' of the CPI (M) in the state after its split from the Congress in 1998. The CPI (M)'s duplicity in supporting Congress at the Centre, and at the same time, fight against the Congress at the state, was ridiculous to the people at large. Some of the left leaders thought that the LF should have withdrawn support much earlier to tidy up the home turf in West Bengal. Its failure to do so was amply reflected in 2009 election result.

The middle class people, possibly for reasons of their past history, are in the habit of thinking that they are uncompromisingly radical.[6] The communists and the ever increasing band of supporters considered themselves to be superior species because of their ideologically congruent socio-political and economic perspective. They believed to think that politics was guided by a superior political objective as compared to other political parties. More often than not, they claimed that the LF led by the CPI (M) stood for the poor and was more democratic and people oriented. They also claimed that the caste and communal divides that are paramount in other Indian states are absent in West Bengal. However, a close look reveals this idea to be a myth as confirmed by their mode of selecting candidates at all the levels. The life styles of leftist leaders at all levels have undergone sea change since 1977 and they began behaving like the elites of society since long. This elite mentality has percolated down to the most leaders down below. Instead of perceiving society in terms of caste and communal distinctions, the left oriented Bengali social groups would like to divide it into two classes — *bhadarlok* (elite)[7] and *chhotolok* (subaltern). They take it for granted that the subaltern or the *chhotolok* can, with subtle electoral engineering and political manipulations, be brainwashed by continuous verbal outpourings. Possibly they ignore that the rise of the *chhotolok* class (in economic terms) at certain historical junctures is a predestined fact of social evolution. To the upper and middle class elites, Mamata Banerjee and her party TMC appeared to represent the rural subalterns. They failed to realize that soon after the Assembly election in the state in 2006, she would be able to mobilize the rural masses on the basis of their fear against the government's land acquisition and special economic zone (SEZ) related industrial policies. Unchallenged for such a long period in the electoral politics, Buddhadeb Bhattacharjee, like his predecessor Jyoti Basu, was encouraged to obliterate the democratic distinction between the party and the administration. He proceeded to think in terms of total equation between the party run state and the civil society. According to Ross Mallick,[8] this government put party interest above the people. No other Indian state, not even Kerala, another CPI (M) bastion, is guided by such a mind-set. As he says, "Given this record of failed reforms, non-reforms, and regressive policies, the question remains as to how such a singularly unsuccessful government was able to achieve the world record for being the longest ruling democratically elected Communist government in history."[9]

And, finally, the LF's focused tirades against the Central government's discriminatory attitude and actions, whether real or ephemeral, meant for popular consumption, had been habitual. They also claimed that people's rights to equality, life and liberty were better ensured in West Bengal than anywhere else. But the fact of the matter was that the CPI (M)'s organizational dominance in Bengal, particularly in the rural hinterland for the last three decades, alienated even its important partners, the Revolutionary Socialist Party (RSP) and the Forward Bloc (FB). The CPI (M)'s policy prescription and its implementation of recent land and industrial policies[10] kept them in the dark. The question then arises as to why the partners of the LF, despite their sense of deprivation of real political power, still clung together. An important minister belonging to RSP gave the answer: "It is simple electoral arithmetic and, to a great extent, of certain politico-electoral compulsion. If any of the major partners come out of the left fold, the result would be disastrous not only for any individual partner, but the LF as a whole. The CPI (M) would also suffer a political paralysis for years to come."[11] The people still remember that the three leaders, who had a hand in massacring the *Sain brothers*, in Bardhhaman on 17 March 1970,[12] the day after the second United Front fell, are actively alive and leading the CPI (M) from the front. The Chief Minister, Ajoy Kumar Mukherjee, while demitting office characterized his own government by saying "that the second United Front government led by him was uncivilized and barbaric." [13] He repeatedly pointed out to the partisan use of the police administration to serve the party interest by the then Deputy Chief Minister, Jyoti Basu. Another instance of the LF's total indifference to the wellbeing of the people they claimed to serve is provided by the tragic case of the refugees settled in Marichjhapi — an Island near Sundarban at 24 Parganas. The earlier refugees came over to *Sundarban from Dandakaranya,* where they were originally settled over in the arid areas of Madhya Pradesh and Orissa. They built up a colony at Marichjhapi. The CPI (M) committee of refugee organization went to the island and asked them to take the membership of the CPI (M). They refused and the government retaliated harshly. The CPI (M) government stopped the supply of drinking water and food and committed the sin of murdering more than two thousand innocent refugees by burning their hutments and sinking their boats while fleeing. The CPI (M) brutally pounced upon the refugees on 15th and 16th May, 1979 led by the SDO of the undivided 24 Parganas along with an array of police personnel. The CPI (M)'s hoodlums joined the forces. The Island was totally vacated on 31st May, 1979. An inhuman, rather barbaric action was meted out to the refugees, who wanted to live in small piece of West Bengal of the CM Jyoti Basu in his reincarnation. This left an indelible dark spot on the history of the first phase of the LF government in West Bengal.[14] These were meticulously documented by several private individuals.[15] Next were the *Bijan Setu* (the Ballygunje Station Flyover) murders in which 17 Sanyasins (including a woman) were burnt alive by the CPI (M) hoodlums.[16] The *Bantala* incident at South 24 Parganas was gruesome; however, the Chief Minister, Jyoti Babu took no serious note of it and commented: "These are nothing extraordinary; occasionally it may happen."[17] Perhaps acting on a rumor, the criminals protected by the CPI (M) attacked the World Health Organization (WHO)'s car that was returning from a village health centre. Anita Deyan, an officer and another lady of the same rank were returning to Calcutta. In their way back, both the ladies were stripped naked and raped by the lumpen elements of the CPI (M). Anita Deyan was brought dead to the Nilratan Sarkar Medical College. The other lady was brought back to Calcutta seriously wounded and mentally traumatized, unable to speak about the incident.[18] The driver of the car was mortally wounded, unable to speak and fought with death in the SSKM hospital for a few days, but ultimately succumbed. All this raised the question whether the people of West Bengal had reconciled themselves to the atrocities caused by the LF supporters and activists. The stories describe above are mentioned earlier. The gruesome nature of such politically motivated crimes, the facts have been reiterated above. However, they never confronted this reality.

The question, which should have stirred the earlier generations of the ever-protesting Bengalis, has been piquantly answered by a scholar, "Bengalis have adjusted remarkably well with the reality. They have opted to coil up and seek comfort in pursuing the simple art of making money."[19] Another gruesome incident, which occurred at Khandua, Arambag in Howrah, involved the CPI (M) resorting to its semi-fascist method of politically controlling the entire western belt of rural West Bengal. It was some sort of political cleansing. Atrocities like these paved the way for the overwhelming victory of the LF in elections after elections, particularly since 1987.[20] Actually, the objectives of the CPI (M) were to gag the voices of the opposition in rural Bengal. As years went by, the electoral malpractices of the CPI (M)'s local leaders took a new turn. At least in 30 to 40 booths, things were very intelligently managed by CPI (M) activists often resorting to terror tactics in and out of the polling stations against the opposition polling agents. It was sheer terror letting loose around the areas of the villages by local leaders of the CPI (M), days before polling day. For fear of life and social boycott, the opposition voters had to follow the CPI (M)'s diktat.[21] This had been continuing for a long time. In 1991 elections, a group of Congress supporters voted for the Congress candidate. After the result was out, the CPI (M) activists attacked the villages; burnt some of the houses and chopped off the hands (hand was the election symbol of the Congress Party) of a few voters, who supposedly had voted for the Congress candidate.[22]

On 21 July, 1993, the police barricaded a Youth Congress procession led by its President Mamata Banerjee to symbolically encircle the Writers' Building. When the younger restive activists attempted to cross over the police barricade, the police fired indiscriminately without heeding to the police manual. Thirteen people were killed on the spot and many more injured. Thereafter, the police fired at the procession of the Socialist Unity Centre (SUC) near Curzon Park. One person was killed and a few others suffered heavy injuries. Mamata Banerjee, while still a Youth Congress leader, was mercilessly beaten near the crossing of Hazra Road by the CPI (M) cadres, while protesting against a *bundh* called by the CPI (M). She had to be hospitalized with serious head and abdominal injuries for quite a long time. Such attacks on Ms. Banerjee were mounted frequently even while she was in the Congress as a Central Minister. She formed her own party, Trinamool Congress (TMC) formally on 1 January 1998 after a hitch with the state Congress leadership. The then Chief Minister never ordered for any inquiry, in a parliamentary system, it is always mandatory. The police officers, who ordered to open fire, did not heed to the police regulation that in such cases, the presence of judicial magistrate is mandatory also. The CPI (M) led either by Jyoti Basu or Buddhadeb Bhattacharjee never cared for the parliamentary niceties, rather they ordered for judicial enquiries for all the alleged wrongs done in Siddhartha Shankar Ray's government during 1972 to 1977. After the regime change, Mamata Banerjee, the new CM, set up a few Judicial Commissions to unveil the murder of innocent Congress members and supporters on the fateful day of July 21, 1993.

The land reforms, with which the LF is credited for long and rightly so, but only initially, came to a halt in 1986. In fact, a reverse process started by 1988. The *Panchayat* system as spearheaded by the LF was in fact to spread its tentacles to the remotest part of the rural areas, became by now all "Political *Panchayat*,"[23] and was totally centralized politically and administratively by the surplus majority party, the CPI (M). The power at all the three tiers of the *Panchayat* came to be concentrated in the hands of the local and regional committee leaders. The urban bodies and their extended areas around urban conglomerate are controlled by the central party apparatchik at district headquarters. By providing muscle powers to the leaders and money to the interested politicians, *Jotdar* and the urban real estate promoters began to rule the roost with the connivance of the party. Scholars from abroad, who studied the functioning of *Panchayat* bodies under the LF government, eulogized the LF government for its good work in rural areas.[24] However, D.

Bandyopadhyay and Nirmal Mukerji[25] and Pranab Bardhan and Dilip Mukherjee[26] were down to earth in their assessments. Even those, who had benefited most from the patronage of the government, could not believe the extent of the erosion of democratic values and corruption among the LF functionaries at different levels. What had helped the CPI (M) maintain its hegemonic dominance almost all over the state, was the policy of terrorization in most of the rural hinterlands and distribution of largesse to the aspirant elite sections, including the government employees, trade unionists, rich peasants and teachers of all categories. The higher echelon of the government officials and high-ranking police personnel, who could not think beyond status quo, were happy and tension free for the reason[27] that the oppositions were too emasculated to throw any challenge to the ubiquitous CPI (M) regime. The successive LF governments were particularly impatient and often vindictive against the opposition TMC. But by virtue of her hard labour and political honesty, Ms. Mamata Banerjee emerged as a charismatic mass leader. To the popular perception, she was the only uncompromising main opposition political leader to challenge the "social fascist party i.e. the CPI (M)"[28] and the "misrule of the LF government."[29] Once the chief minister, Jyoti Basu, refused to meet Ms. Banerjee — a Central Minister at that time, when she went on a deputation to seek justice for a deaf and raped victim by the CPI (M) cadres. She sat in waiting in front of the Chief Minister's chamber. The police evicted her forcibly and put her in the Lal Bazar jail. The police released her at the dead of night without any protection en route to her way home.

Such behaviour from a high ranking police officer and ordinary constables became a regular feature during the last 34 years of the LF rule. Misbehaviour with women by the CPI (M) leaders, their constant ridicules and frequent ill treatments encouraged the police administration heckling the endeared Mamata Banerjee to the oppressed people of the state.[30]

Ms Banerjee began her fight for *Maa, Mati, Manush* (mother, earth and men) during Singur land acquisition incident. It was a magical symbol and a slogan that helped the underprivileged Scheduled Castes, Scheduled Tribes and the minority Muslim community at large to rally behind the Trinamool Congress. Ms. Banerjee was prepared to stake even her life to fight against the "undemocratic fascist regime of the CPI (M)."[31] She fasted for twenty-six days against the acquisition of the multi-cropped 997 acres of fertile agricultural lands of the suffering peasants of Singur acquired by the government agency, West Bengal Industrial Development Corporation (WBIDC) for the Tatas. Meanwhile, brutal killings took place at Nandigram by the police and the CPI (M)'s hired killers in police uniforms, which was characterized by the Governor of the state, Gopal Gandhi, as "spine-chilling violence."[32] A very organized civil society group took up the cudgel and played a very important role to expose the "fascist method of the Buddhadeb

Bhattacharjee regime"[33]. After these two serious incidents for three long decades, the people began shedding off their fear and came out in the open to seek a "change of the CPI (M) regime."[34]

Against this backdrop of the explosion of the desire for change, the parliamentary election was held in 2009. The results of the election were absolutely "demoralizing for the CPI (M) after years of its control in all aspects of life in the state."[35] The social coalition that paved the way for the LF was the product of a reality prevailing in the beginning. From the very beginning, LF began to vaunt its superiority as a party with progressive ideology and vision. Demonstrating showmanship, the LF began propagating that only it could give good governance to the people since only Marxists of their brand understood the "nature of Indian State"[36] and its political economy. They claimed that they were better able to pursue political economy of development.[37] The Chinese development pattern, rather than US and Western economic institution's imperialistic model, would safeguard the sovereign decision-making process and serve Indian interest better,[38] the CPI (M) propagated. But the leaders always deceived the people knowing it well that it was not possible until and unless the Marxists of the West Bengal variant were able to guide the total decision-making process of the government of India

The withdrawal of CPI (M)'s support from the Congress-led UPA government was inevitable in view of their electoral compulsions in West Bengal and Kerala. Had it been earlier, they could have put across a message to the state electorate that they were really against the Congress both at the Centre and the states. Fighting against the Congress in the state and giving support to the Congress at the Centre was sheer "political duplicity"[39]. The Congress Party in the state was also gradually losing its electoral credibility while the TMC was coming out bolder as the most successful and, uncompromisingly, the only opposition party to the CPI (M)'s one-party "misrule."[40] It was clear to the discerning public as well as to a large percentage of ordinary public that the CPI (M)'s single agenda was to cling to power by repeatedly raising their voices against "the menace, the communal BJP."[41] The result, in fact, became counter-productive.

While in 2004, the LF won 61 parliamentary seats from all over the country, while it was able to retain only 24 seats in 2009 parliament election. The results of the 2009 parliamentary election were a rude shock to the CPI (M). In 2004, the CPI (M) alone in West Bengal had won 26 seats and CPI, RSP and Forward Bloc (FB) had three seats each in a total of 35 seats. Getting a total six seats — from Darjeeling (1), South Dinajpur (1), Malda (1) and three from Murshidabad, the Congress Party was, in actuality, reduced to a regional party of the north and a part of the east (Murshidabad). The TMC had a poor parliamentary presence with only one seat of Ms. Banerjee from

South Kolkata constituency. In terms of vote share, the CPI (M) received 38.56 per cent, CPI 4.01 per cent, RSP 4.49 per cent, FB 3.66 per cent, Congress 14.56 per cent, TMC 21.04 per cent, BJP 8.06 per cent, Independent, Janata and other minor parties got 5.62 per cent. This poor showing by the LF in 2009 was not so much a shock to other partners like the CPI, RSP, and FB as it was for the CPI (M). The CPI general secretary openly criticized the "big brother" CPI (M) for the electoral debacle.[42] So did other partners for the miserable electoral performance of the LF, particularly in the southern, eastern and middle parts of West Bengal. This was what exactly happened also in the *Panchayat* (2008), Parliamentary (2009) and then recently in the 16 Municipal elections (2009). In these Municipal elections, the LF was able to retain only three boards, losing previously held nine. The LF retained the Siliguri *Mahakuma Parishad* (Sub-divisional Board), with a margin of one seat only. Because of local factionalism in the Congress, the TMC-Congress coalition did not work well in this case, although in the *Panchayat* election, this newly formed coalition gave a serious jolt to the LF not only in Siliguri sub-division, but in most of the districts of north Bengal too.

Anti-incumbency factors did not work and no traces of stagnancy in the percentage point of vote shares of the CPI (M) could be discerned in 2004. It was something that could never have happened in any other state of India. Over the years, the voter's turnout 'was the highest in the state with the average being 79.5 per cent and sometimes nearly 82 per cent. To the Marxists, this abnormal voter turnout was due "to the ideological contribution of Marxist parties in educating the rural people in the state."[43] Many a discerning people argued that this had been happening because of the absence of a viable political alternative and, more importantly, of the organizational machineries and electoral management of the CPI (M). This doubt proved right in later years, when many a heinous crime perpetrated by the CPI (M) leaders like Anil Bose of Arambag, Susanta Ghosh of Garbeta fame and Tapan, Sukur Ali's criminal activities during the elections, came to light after the LF regime came to a halt in May 13, 2011.

However, even in this era of coalition making, the Index of Opposition Unity (IOU) was found to be absent or almost negative, save in 2001 Assembly election, when the TMC and the Congress made a pre-election makeshift seat adjustment. Many other smaller parties including a few left parties fought the election with no understanding with bigger parties like TMC and the Congress whatsoever, against the LF monolith. These were only a few reasons among many that went in favour of the LF. The upper class, middle class and the poorer sections in the state could not trust the opposition parties warring with one another. By showing muscle power and parading motor bike riding hired goons with AK 47 rifles in the back, a fear psychosis was instilled in the minds of the rural people by the CPI (M). The LF has, over the years, entrenched itself in rural Bengal through the villages, block and district level *Panchayat* bodies, left parties won a large measure of acceptability among the people. But all this continued only up to 1987. Thereafter, the system of governance in West Bengal began a downward slide.

Some interesting features become discernible if Human Development Indices of the state as a whole and several districts are studied. The more underdeveloped the districts in respect of health, literacy, income and education, the more the LF won in election after election. It appears that the CPI (M), always claiming to be the party of the toiling masses, was adept enough to electorally dominate the docile poor fellows. It is already noted above that, over the years, the CPI (M) resorted to political cleansing in the rural areas of north Bengal districts and districts like Burdwan, Bankura, Purulia, Hooghly, Howrah, and west Midnapore or, in other words, the entire western belt of Bengal. These western districts account for more than 70 Assembly seats. Arambag at Hooghly, Keshpur, Garbeta, Ghatal and Jhargram at West Midnapore were out of bound for the opposition parties. Even during the 2009 parliamentary election, when there was a tornado of change sweeping over Bengal, the CPI (M) cadres did not allow the civil society groups to enter their electoral territories in those places.[44] One opposition TMC supporter, who hoisted a flag on a tree in Keshpur, was murdered[45] for ignoring the diktat of the CPI (M). Even TMC candidates could not campaign in Keshpur, Garbeta at Midnapur, Arambag, Goghat and Pursura Assembly segments in the district of Hooghly.

Almost a repeat electoral performance by the LF was seen in 2006. The LF won 235 seats polling 50.12 per cent of votes. The single majority party in the LF, CPI (M) alone won 172 seats. It was as if there was a quantum jump from 143 in 2001 to 172 in 2006 as shown above. The CPI (M) tried often to electorally emasculate the other Front Partners, but did not dare to discard them totally for its own safety. The opposition, as a whole, secured 49.88 per cent of votes polled. The TMC got 30 seats, the Congress 23, SUC two and Others five only. Disunity among opposition parties was, therefore, a positive gain for the LF.

The Election Commission of India has to work with the help of Chief Electoral Office of the state; this means inducting the state government employees as necessary for the conduct of the elections during the process of election from notifications to declarations of the end results. Even the central observers often remain under the surveillance and control of the Returning Officers and other high-ranking district officials. The attitude of the administration under the political control of the CPI (M) failed to instill confidence and trust in the minds of the voters and the public at large. It was sheer fear of life, feeling of losing property and dignity that made the rural people at all levels — middle, lower middle and the poor people to succumb, for different reasons, to the superior power and electoral management strategy of the CPI (M) in the past several years.

The *Panchayat* elections in 2008 were, however, held in a different context of massive social protests, as the apogee of some sort of a social churning since 1977. The seats won by the LF in each of the elections before 2008 were overwhelming in all the three tiers acquiring more than 55 per cent of votes.[46] But this time, the vote share of the LF was 52 per cent in *Zilla Parishad* and 47 per cent in *Panchayat Samitis* and *Gram Panchayat* taken together.[47] This indicated a danger signal for the LF. Another ominous sign for the CPI (M), just before the 2009 election, lay in the loss of two seats with the largest ever vote margin in any election. The results reflected the adverse mood of the people, a phenomenon unthinkable to the CPI (M) before. A genuine challenge was faced by the CPI (M) this time; civil society groups, encountering the "fascist face of the LF,"[48] vigorously campaigned against the CPI (M)'s perverse use of administration, police forces and electoral machineries. Concerned civil society groups frequently appealed to the people at large to ponder over the atrocities carried on by the CPI (M) against the peasants at Singur in Hooghly, Nandigram at east Midnapore and Lalgarh in west Midnapore. The civil society group sent deputations to the State Election Commissioner, Shri Ashok Gupta, Chief Electoral Officer, Police Commissioner and other concerned authorities, but without any results. Being backed by Buddhadeb Bhattacharya's camp followers — literati, poets, TV serial artists, cinema actors, small time directors and other professionals — the CPI (M) mounted severe verbal attacks against important personalities of protesting civil society groups and resorted to character assassination of the protestors. But all this became counter-productive. In the process, the ordinary rural people overcame their fear psychosis that they had been suffering from because of the "ferocious"[49] presence of the CPI (M)'s organizational network and state terror in rural hinterlands.

The 2009 parliamentary election results reflected the mood of the majority of the people. Each of the partners of the LF, FB, RSP and CPI lost one seat each against three seats they had won in the 2004 election. The greatest loser was the CPI (M); it won only nine seats. The decline in the percentage share of its votes was shattering for the party. Even while the CPI (M) had contested the Assembly election alone in 1971, it received nearly 35 per cent of total valid votes cast. Its vote shares increased over the years crossing sometimes more than 39 per cent. But this time, it received a humiliating 33.10 per cent.

Despite the continued political dominance of the LF in each of the several elections in the past, economic development in the state has been low as compared to many other Indian states; with industrial and unemployment situations worsening since 1991.[50] More than 55 thousands medium and small industries have been shut down since the mid-1980s. During the last several years, the state of political economy was bleak and fiscal deficit of the state stood at a staggering 1, 65,000 crores. And yet, on the floor of the Assembly, the state finance minister juggled with statistical figures and depicted, year after year, rosy pictures about the next fiscal situation.[51] Strangely, people remained complacent during elections. Many language newspaper reporters smelled something abnormal in the election observer, Afzal Amanulla's secret report to the Central Election Commission, which did not make the report public. Eminent newspaper reporters reported that the CPI (M) (I)'s success lay in their use of organizational network for a politico-electoral-engineering and election management strategy in the past. In the 2009 election, the LF was able to retain its electoral superiority in the districts of North Bengal and the western belt of the state from Purulia down to West Midnapore. In these areas, the CPI (M)'s organizational clout and oft-used method of electoral management did not fail them. Electoral figures indicated that the FB won the Cooch Behar seat just by getting 44.66 per cent votes, because the Bharatiya Janata Party's (BJP) share of votes (5.52%) cut into the vote share of the main opponent. In North Bengal, the LF won three seats from Cooch Behar, Alipurduars in Jalpaiguri and Balurghat in South Dinajpur. Even in 2009 election, when the LF had to face a severe challenge from the Congress and TMC (+) coalition's seat adjustment, the CPI (M) was able to retain its earlier hold, but with reduced percentage share of votes. In most of the constituencies as revealed, the margin of victory for the CPI (M) was alarmingly reduced.

The Left Front, in spite of occasional hiccups among its partners, has been winning the Assembly elections with overwhelming majority since 1977, seven times in a row till 2006. Barring communist regimes like in China, the then Soviet Russia, Cuba, etc., the government of a majority party or even of a coalition of several parties has never survived for such a long period. Is it, it can be asked, due to the fact that the CPI (M) functions in a parliamentary system? Or is it simply using the most important political forum of Legislature as a weapon to achieve a socialist revolution? The hardcore leaders still attempt to dish out publicly the same version of the thesis of socialist revolution in a different language. It does not matter whether the party sympathizers, cadres, promoters, contractors and other clients,[52] enjoying benefits from the LF government helped it in the manner it wanted. Like the unalloyed older generation of the Marxists, Buddhadeb Bhattacharya and Nirupam Sen, the minister in charge of Industry, like to propagate that socialism and socialistic development cannot be achieved at a go. The development of capitalism is the need of the day; socialism is to wait till the development of capitalism is complete; this is a new formulation, at that point in time, they were in power, to which the Chief Minister and Minister of Industry have to stick to. The Marxist chief minister and Industry minister, Nirupam Sen, did not mince words about their theoretical position focusing on achieving rapid industrialization at any cost. In his hour-long interview with the author, Jyoti Basu, the former Chief Minister and the senior most member of the Politburo of the CPI (M), simply smiled away the question about establishing 'socialism' in a bourgeois parliamentary democracy. He did not even think of a "parliamentary communism."[53] He, of course, took rather a pragmatic view of supporting the party's "confused theoretical stance."[54] But, he asked the party bosses to think twice to take over very large chunks of fertile agricultural lands at Singur for establishing a small car factory[55] on such a huge tract of fertile land.

Surprisingly, the opposition parties, particularly the main opposition, TMC and the Congress Party began gaining substantially in subsequent elections after *Panchayat* elections in the first quarter of 2008. After 32 years, the Guardian constituencies, where they used to elect their own representative of the School Managing Committee in different districts, the LF candidates were defeated and demoralized. In colleges, the Student Federation of India (SFI), the student front of the CPI (M), found it tough to confront opposition candidates in different institutions. It seemed baffling even to the left oriented people. The exercise of unbridled power, using 'power brokers', promoters, contractors and land mafias in both rural and urban areas resulted in rampant corruption in the party. Leaders from top down began to be a degenerated lot.[56] It was difficult to cope with or overcome the emergent situation without antagonizing land mafias, contractors, promoters and other middle class clienteles. Paradoxically, the State Committee Secretary of the CPI (M), Biman Basu[57] mildly expressed the same characterization about the present clienteles of the CPI (M). The Chief Minister, Buddhadeb Babu himself said, "Money is flowing around. From this springs wrongdoing and sin."[58]

When the land scam at Rajarhat in North 24 Parganas for the construction of Vedic Village (a luxury health resort of not very good repute) and New Township project came out in public, a commentator wrote, "The present Chief Minister is paying the price for the greed and sins of Jyoti Basu and Pramode Dasgupta."[59] In fact, never before in history of the state such a great land grabbing fraud, involving politicians, administrators, business tycoons and political party-backed musclemen and land mafias, took place. However, it was only the tip of the iceberg. It involved fifteen thousand acres of fertile agricultural and marshy lands. The fertile lands and marshy areas were the sources of livelihood for thousands of peasants, fishermen and lower middle class people. Corruption of such a dimension at the highest level and highhandedness on the part of the politicians of the ruling party might have later influenced the election of the Municipal Corporation of Siliguri.[60] The result of the parliamentary election in 2009 was heavy blow that the CPI (M) never experienced after 1977.

Siliguri is popularly regarded as the second capital of North Bengal. It is the gateway to foreign countries on the north, southeast, on the one hand, and south Bengal through the "chicken neck," on the other. That is why the area is a strategically very important and sensitive too. It is the business hub of the entire Northeastern region of the country. The Gorkhaland issue, created by the shortsightedness of the CPI (M) in the mid-1980s was still unresolved even in 2011 during the LF regime. Without the support of the hill people of the three subdivisions of Darjeeling, no party could win the Darjeeling parliamentary seat. In 2009, the BJP candidate, Jaswant Singh, won the seat backed by the Gorkha Jana Mukti Morcha (GJMM) at that point of time. The opposition Trinamool Congress was trying to capitalize on the LF government's land policy. The LF failed to take into account the serious problems of hunger and starvation among the tea garden workers.[61] The CPI (M) leaders, including the LF government minister for urban affairs, Ashok Bhattacharya, acquired a large tract of moribund tea gardens, land for cinchona cultivation areas around Darjeeling. These tracts of the land were given to promoters to build shopping malls, multiplexes and housing complexes.[62] The people of Siliguri retaliated through ballot against this policy of the LF in the municipal election immediately after the parliamentary election. The Siliguri Municipal Corporation's election in all the 47 wards was a moral victory, and electoral booster for the opposition Congress and the TMC coalition. It won 30 seats (Congress 15, TMC 14, and one supported by both the parties, actually a rebel TMC man). In 2004 election, the opposition won only 11 seats and the LF bagged 36 seats. This time, the LF managed to get only 17 seats [CPI (M) 15, RSP 1, and FB 1]. It was really an electoral debacle for the CPI (M). This meant that the seat adjustment between the Congress and the TMC did not prove ineffective. That meant a danger signal for the LF for 2011 Assembly election. This time, the CPI (M) might have to confront the biggest ever challenge to its earlier electoral superiority. The opposition coalition replaced the LF from the seat of power by getting nearly two per cent of votes more than the LF. The CPI (M) led LF's propaganda plank was about "development" of the entire North Bengal areas[63]. The coalition of the opposition parties was exploiting the "wave of change" raised by the civil society groups and the poor peasants, who lost their agricultural lands in different places and had to face a precarious livelihood. Elections evinced the mood of the people and their silent, but almost decisive verdict that swept the southern, eastern, and three other districts.

After the defeat in Siliguri Corporation election, the top leaders of the CPI (M) were trying to put up a brave face. To them, a defeat by a margin of slightly more than one per cent vote was nothing remarkable.[64] This indicated that the central and local parties' bosses were wielding swords for cross purposes completely keeping aside 'the possibilities of the rise of alternative political forces in their own LF fortress. The partners of the LF were not as loyal as they were even before 2004, not to speak of the beginning of the 21st century. The CPI (M) was still under the delusion "Banglar Mati Durjay Ghanti" (Bengal under the LF led by the CPI (M) was an unconquerable fortress). The people were the same in their perception as they had been for long.

They like to believe that there was sufficient scope for a dignified come back in the next major elections. Many of their statements were based on a flawed electoral logic in the context of ongoing political process. The CPI (M) and the LF constituents had convincingly won the Assembly election in 2006. The LF had garnered 50.12 per cent of votes winning 235 seats; whereas the divided opposition parties had received 49.88 per cent of valid votes cast. They won only 59 seats (TMC 30, Congress 23, SUC 2 and others 3). The difference of vote share between the LF and the opposition parties fighting separately was only 0.24 per cent. In the parliamentary election of 2004, the LF received 49.50 per cent of the valid votes cast, but secured 35 parliamentary seats.

It is not, therefore, the electoral calculus, but the changing political chemistry from time to time that determines the voters' preference. During these last many years spanning more than three decades, the opposition parties in West Bengal remained, as they were, when the 1st LF formed an invincible coalition government. The LF had been enjoying the fruits of the social coalitions of the upper class, middle class, the Schedule Castes, Schedule Tribes and, above all, the Muslims besides, teachers, professionals, service holders and business and small time industrial communities that consolidated for getting favour from the LF government. The political coalition of the left parties built upon the social groupings helped them survive for such a long period of time. Over the years, as stated above, the LF enjoyed the support of an overwhelming number of Schedule Castes, Schedule Tribes and Muslim voters. Their combined strength was 53.77 per cent (SC 23.02%, ST 5.50% and Muslims 25.25% as per the Census Report 2001); they constituted a majority in the state as always. The party or the coalition that would muster the support of this majority might hold the key to the power. Till the mid-1990s, the LF manipulated this social coalition in their favour as is reflected in the lower value of the Index of Opposition Unity (IOU). This social coalition began cracking in the mid-1990s. However, major opposition parties, for one reason or the other, failed to exploit this situation. The first UPA government at the Centre had to depend on the LF for its survival. Despite the same ideological orientation, the Bengal Congress found it difficult to align with the TMC. After the 2004 election, the TMC, as a silent partner of the NDA, made some sort of seat adjustment with the BJP. It fought the 2006 Assembly election with disastrous results. The Congress did not make any overture to the TMC because it was a partner of the NDA and had not snapped its tie with the BJP at the state level. Immediately after the 2006 Assembly election, Mamata Banerjee seriously began distancing herself and her party from the BJP, both at the national and state levels. After its split from the Congress in 1997, the Trinamool Congress ultimately emerged as the major opposition party in the state for its uncompromising political opposition against the CPI (M); other peripheral left parties like Progressive Democratic Socialism (PDS), Socialist Unity Centre (SUC), a faction of Communist Party of India-Marxist Leninist CPI (ML), etc., and other social groups with political objectives were absolutely localized, but collectively, they became a tangible force when they made some sort of an alliance with the TMC. The opportunity for the TMC to do the same came during the land grabbing movements of the CPI (M) in Bhangar, Singur and Nandigram. The 2009 parliamentary election was really a watershed in the electoral history of Bengal after 1977. After the murder of Indira Gandhi, sympathy wave as also the popular perceptions about the security of the country being in danger, helped the Congress to win 16 seats in 1984. But 2009 parliamentary election made history, as the opposition won 27 seats including one seat for the BJP.

This raises a question: Why and how did it happen? The policy of land reforms[65] over the years helped the LF consolidate itself and win support by the poor peasant communities. But it did not continue after 1987 so massively. Since the mid-1990s, a reverse process has been in operation. The LF government with the help of private entrepreneurs, promoters and anti-social elements, mafias and others, took over lands forcibly at different places from the lower middle class people and poor peasants under the direct patronage of CPI (M) higher ups. People were evicted and the Rajarhat and New township projects were built up on thousands of acres of agricultural and marshy lands. This directly affected the depressed classes, particularly the Muslims. They made up their mind to vote the LF out both in the *Panchayat* and then in parliamentary elections in 2009 as discussed earlier also.

As compared to other states, the West Bengal government appears to devise a model of its own in working the *Panchayat* system of rural governance. This process of running the system may be defined as a *centralizing decentralized model*. In the process, the CPI (M) has been, over the last several years, prone to develop a "partocracy"[66], obliterating the democratic distinctions between party, government and the state. By offering different types of opportunities to most sections of the people, the LF, particularly the CPI (M), earned trustworthiness among social groups for nearly three decades. The organizational strength of the CPI (M) increased from 25,000 in 1977 to more than 3,12,000 till October 2008.[67] Besides, there were equally powerful front organizations to help the CPI (M) throughout the year. All these organizations indirectly mobilized the people in favour of the party and the LF coalition. So long, the disgruntled people of the state could not find any coherent alterative political formation. The only opposition party, the Congress failed to throw any effective challenge before a differently oriented Mamata Banerjee and her party TMC stepped into the scene.

This signaled the beginning of the decline of the CPI (M). The remarkable political stability for which the LF coalition earned accolades quite handsomely by academics throughout began crashing when "saving agricultural land and life movement"[68] at Singur and Nandigram gathered momentum in the middle of 2006. Actually, Singur was the flash point of the ongoing politics of the opposition. The Chief Minister, Buddhadeb Bhattacharjee thought that the LF led by the CPI (M) became politically more powerful by winning 235 seats in the Legislative Assembly. His public outburst was "we are 235 and they are 30 only (meaning TMC). Let us see who dares to stand in our way."[69] The top most leaders like Binay Konar, Susanta Ghosh, Anil Basu, Shyamal Chakraborty and sometimes even Biman Basu, the Secretary of the State Committee of the CPI (M) and the Chairman of the LF Committee, used very offensive languages against Mamata Banerjee during this period of transition. They did not spare even the members of the Civil Society, like Medha Patekar, Saoli Mitra, Mahasweta Devi, Arundhati Roy and many others.

A secret agreement was finalized between the Chief Minister along with the minister of Industry Nirupam Sen and the representative of Ratan Tata of the Tata group of car industries. The proposed compensation to the owners for land acquisition under the Colonial Act of 1894 was a mere pittance. Immediately, a *Bhumi Raksha and Jiban Jibika Bachao Committee* (a committee to save land and living) was formed. Later, this type of committee was formed in different areas of the state by the peasants. Mamata Banerjee and her TMC actively supported the efforts; thousands of peasants and others affected by land acquisition move joined the movements. The Congress soft-pedaled the issue because of their fear that they might be misunderstood as anti-industry. Even the state Congress president, Pranab Mukherjee, opined, in one of his statements in his constituency at Jangipur in Murshidabad that industry could not be built in the air. The CPI (M) leaders often used this argument of Pranab Mukherjee during the peasants' movements at Singur, Nandigram, Nayachar and then at Lalgarh in west Midnapore.

More than 397 landowners at Singur in Hooghly district refused to accept the compensation. The government spent crores of rupees in fencing the entire area; the police had to open fire to the mob, which used to gather near the fencing areas to protest against the government policy. A few people including Rajkumar Bhul, a very young boy, and other activists died of bullet injuries. The local leaders of the CPI (M) let loose the party goons to rape and set on fire the body of Tapasi Malik, a teen aged girl, for allegedly assuming the leadership of woman activists at Singur. This actually angered the people all over the state. The civil society was split and highly respectable among them came out in the forefront to protest against the police atrocities at the behest of the CPI (M). After declaring 144 CrPc, the police arrested a large number of protesters and the leaders of the TMC including Mamata Banerjee. In the darkness (created by the CPI (M) as a sort of load shedding) of night, the police detained Banerjee along with her party members in the BDO office in the last week of September 2006. Not only had the leaders of the CPI (M), but also the so called intellectuals, the media persons, three TV channels namely 24 Ghanta, Aakash and the Star Anand and all the opportunity seekers of the cultural world branded the TMC as anti-industry, anti-development. Mamata Banerjee resorted to fasting for the cause of the peasants. The governor of the state, Gopalkrishna Gandhi and many national level political leaders including the Prime Minister, Dr. Manmohan Singh, requested Ms. Banerjee to give up her indefinite fast. A large number of eminent individuals and members of the civil society stood by her to save her life. On their request, after 26 days, she broke her fast, but during this period many smaller political parties like SUC, a section of the CPI (ML), PDS, SP and 14 other civil society groups came forward to form a politico-social coalition to evict the CPI (M) from the state through democratic methods. This proved to be a farsighted political decision. The state Congress unit was compelled to come closer to the TMC. The seat adjustment formula in West Bengal was finalized in Delhi sometimes in December 2008 by the Congress president, Smt. Sonia Gandhi, and Ms. Mamata Banerjee; possibly Pranab Mukherjee was a go between.

The LF partners, the RSP, FB and the CPI began advising the CPI (M) to desist from the suicidal path it started to traverse by taking over the fertile agricultural lands for the purposes of building industry in a Chemical hub in Nandigram. The "genocide"[70] at Nandigram took tolls of seven lives in the month of January 2007 and 14 lives in 14 March of the same year. Under the protection of police, the CPI (M)'s armed cadres "in police uniform" on 14 March 2007 raped quite a number of women. The raped victims of different villages in Nandigram intimately knew these CPI (M) men. The victims were mostly from Muslim and Scheduled Caste communities. On the request of the Trinamool lawyers, the Calcutta High Court ordered CBI inquiry. A large number of arms and men were hauled up in Janani Intbhata (a closed shade within the area of the Brickfield) at Khejuri, but the police administration did not take proper action. In a case filed before it, the Kolkata High Court expressed in its judgement that the police action on that day was "unconstitutional"; it ordered the government to pay compensation to the victims of police atrocities and take action against CPI (M)'s cadres in police uniform. Female victims have not yet received the compensation on the plea that an appeal by the government of West Bengal against the judgement was filed in the Supreme Court and was pending. When Singur and Nandigram incidents were taking place, the Governor, at the request of many, undertook to mediate between the TMC coalition led by Mamata Banerjee and the government led by Buddhadeb Bhattacharjee. They all agreed on a settlement; however, within a few days, the CPI (M) retracted on the plea of a secret agreement clause (which is regarded as a commercial clause as told to the present author privately by one of the lawyers of the Tatas) between the government and the Tatas. In the face of uncompromising opposition by the TMC coalition, the Tatas left the state for Gujarat to set up their small Nano car factory, which it had earlier intended to open in Singur. But at the point of time to leave Singur, it did not give up its land right at Singur and put an advertisement in the widely circulated language daily, *Ananda Bazar Patrika*, and the CPI (M)'s party daily newspaper appealing indirectly to the younger generations to vote in the next elections for the pro-industrial policy of the CPI (M). During the Singur and Nandigram days, the important leaders of the CPI (M) continuously made unparliamentary and uncharitable remarks against the Governor, Gopal Krishna Gandhi. They publicly expressed "let the Governor bear the party flag of the TMC". This was the comment of the leaders and members of the CPI (M)[71] throughout the period. It was not possible for any self-respecting men to tolerate such comments against a very well-meaning and statesmanlike head of the state; and all this went against the CPI (M). Moreover, The top CPI (M) leader's ugly and "indecent utterances" against the main opposition leader, Mamata Banerjee and the members of the civil society groups like Medha Patekar, Anuradha Talwar, Mahasweta Devi, Aparna Sen, Saoli Mitra and others, were not taken kindly by the people. Binay Konar said that the members of the CPI (M)'s woman organization would show their "buttocks"[72] to Medha Patekar and others if they continued their movement against the land acquisition programme in Singur and Nandigram. Encouraged by such comments, party men obstructed these celebrities to visit Nandigram, and used all sorts of "abusive languages."[73] Such rustic Konarish (Binay Konar) statements evoked severe reactions from all sections of people and even from important members of the ruling LF other than the CPI (M).

The land grabbing actions of the LF affected mostly the poor Muslim peasants, the Scheduled Caste groups, the Tribal groups and the marginal peasants and the day labourers. Till then, the Chief Minister and his party did not realize that they happened to stand on shifting sands. The Congress, on the other hand, kept quiet to appreciate the situation. The TMC was seeking to forge a broad-based coalition with the *Krishi Bachao and Jiban O Jibika Raksha* Committee, other smaller parties and a number of socio-political groups. This move helped by an overwhelming number of the Muslims and other caste-based communities to coalesce against the LF. But unfortunately, the Congress thought that without the support of the Trinamool Congress coalition, the Congress by itself would win many of the Local Government elections. Dipa Das Munshi, the wife of ailing Priya Ranjan Das Munshi of Uttar Dinajpur, Adhir Ranjan Chowdhury of Murshidabad, who used to lord over all the constituencies in the district of Murshidabad, did not go in for seat adjustment with the TMC in 2010 in 80 Corporations and Municipality elections. The Congress Party unit in West Bengal, being supported by the Union Cabinet Minister Pranab Mukherjee, wanted to establish its hold over the urban populace, decided to fight alone. The result of the Calcutta Corporation was absolutely demoralizing for the Party. It won only 10 seats out of 141. On the other hand, Trinamool won 95 seats. But the overall results of all the Municipal elections totally went against the LF. They won only 15 municipal bodies when in earlier elections, the LF had won 67 out of 80. The election at Mirik Municipality at Darjeeling district's hill areas was not held. Municipal bodies were like an eye opener to the Congress High Command. It also sent a signal to the state Congress Party about its future electoral survival in the state. At last, with perfect understanding unlike that of 2001, the TMC(+) and Congress coalition came into power 'The results were electrifying for this anti CPI (M) coalition that naturally may expect more in the near future if this coalition remains in place. The overwhelming electoral victory in the Assembly election in 2006 under the leadership of Buddhadeb Bhattacharjee made him "dizzy".[74] Without giving much thought to the land problems in the state, Buddhadeb babu, like his predecessor, went abroad and invited all sorts of investors (*Deshi and Bideshi*) to build modern industries in West Bengal at places they would choose. The Salem Group of Indonesia, Prasun Mukherjee, Ratan Tata and Jindal groups of the country were invited. A huge amount of land was necessary for the purposes. But no land map was available with the Ministry of Land Reforms. It was initially decided, without even consulting the LF committee and the core group of ministers that an amount of 41,000 acres of land would be given to the Salem group.[75] This group would use 120 acres for health and knowledge city. For Satellite Township, it would invest at the following places (a) Kukrahati: (5000 acres), Baruipur (3750 acres), Bhangar (1250 acres), for Chemical Hub at Haldia 10,000 acres, Special Economic Zone (SEZ) 12,500 acres, and others 825 acres. Most of the selected investors appeared to be realtors in this part of West Bengal, rather than industrialists. The idea of modern factory working with the latest technology, promising thousands of jobs to the younger people of the peasant families was unreal. Tata too wanted to build the Singur workshop as a centre for car assembling purposes only. He allotted more than 350 acres of land to the owners and the producers of car ancillaries. This infuriated the local peasants, small agricultural land holders, daily and marginal land labourers. Opposition parties, like the TMC, the other smaller parties and civil society groups, took up the cause of the farmers. It appeared that after Nandigram carnage, the CPI (M) led LF had lost its credibility. A large number of organizations and people stood against the government of the day. Other economic factors disillusioned the poorer sections of the people, who earlier appeared to stand by the LF in the state.

A look at the Human Development Index shown in an earlier chapter substantiates this observation. The Central government declared 200 districts as underdeveloped. Among them, 10 districts in West Bengal covering 4612 villages were earmarked for special development efforts. But the government did nothing during the last five years of its activities. These earmarked villages are located mostly in North Bengal and the western part of the state, that is, Jangal Mahal comprising of West Midnapur, Birbhum, Bankura and Purulia; the LF had won most seats in *panchayat* (2008) and parliamentary elections (2009) from these areas. With the help of its organizational strength and instilling fear about social boycott and political victimization in the minds of the poor, the CPI (M) won elections after elections. The amount the LF received from the Central government under different heads, like NREG schemes or 100 days' work, rural electrification programmes, *Indira Abas Yojona, Jawaharlal Nehru Urban Renewal Programme (JNURP),* could not be properly utilized; large amounts of central funds were partially spent with some being siphoned away by mostly the CPI (M) leaders. As compared to other large states, West Bengal's show in the management of the political economy of development was poor. This reflected laziness, inefficiency, lack of a sense of priority and rampant corruption at different levels of politics and administration.[76] It was really a matter of shame that given the "social capital" and human resources at their disposal, the LF led by the CPI (M) failed in most sectors of the economy to show at least a modicum of good governance during the last several years of their uninterrupted stay in the state.

It is quite legitimate to expect a certain level of good governance in a state that had the unique credit of political stability for more than three decades. Transparency in the system of communist rule is an anathema, but West Bengal is only a half-baked system within a liberal democratic framework and the element of good governance is conspicuously opaque here.

The question of good governance still remains unanswered. In the light of what had happened in Singur at Hooghly, Nandigram and Lalgarh in West Midnapur, these are the latest examples of the CPI (M)'s mismanagement of development strategy. People's movements backed by the Maoist grew from strength to strength. Buddhadeb Bhattacharjee went to Delhi to earnestly request the Home Minister, Chidambaram to send paramilitary forces to the state to contain the Maoist violence. The Home Minister asked the Chief Minister to go back and declare the Maoist groups banned, as done by the state of Andhra Pradeshin the last week of October 2007. Buddhadeb told the

Home Minister that the Center should immediately send the forces, otherwise the situations would go out of control. He also argued that as soon as he returned, he would convince his colleagues in the party and the partners of the Front to impose a ban on the Maoist organization in the state. Buddhadeb tried hard, but the LF because of their left ideological reasons, CPI (M) and the partners did not agree. The Home Minister found that without banning the Maoist Party, the deployment of the central forces might be legally questionable and would be of no avail. Accordingly, the Department of Home Affairs of the Central Government banned the CPI (Maoist) Party in its new incarnation. On November 5, 2007, central forces arrived in the Howrah Station. But the LF government did not immediately deploy the central forces along with the state forces in the Maoist infested places in Jangal Mahal, particularly in Lalgarh areas. The Central Forces sat idle for more than five days; the CPI (M) detained the Central forces at Howrah till November 11. On November 14, the CPI (M), along with some local police men and the party goons, applied brute forces against the people of Nandigram; They killed as many as possible opponents on the spot, then chased the fleeing women and raped and killed some of them. Then, they declared that after so many days, the CPI (M) was able to see the early morning sunrise or in other words, Nandigram became free from other forces, namely *the Bhumi and Jiban Jibika Raksha Committee* members. In the context of the cross fire between the joint forces and the Maoists at Lalgarh in West Midnapore, India's Human Development Report questioned the development perspective and deteriorating law and order situation in the state. The investment situation as compared is bleak; the state is placed at 18th position among 28 states and seven Union Territories; primary education stands at the 11th place. Development of infrastructure and marketing stands at 13th and 14th places, respectively with micro-economy at the 13th place.

All this does not augur well in a politically stabilized democratic system. In West Bengal, unlike its Kerala counterpart, there is some mismatch between occasional democratic change and the thrust of real politic to debar change by exercising organizational muscle. And lastly, the CPI (M) monolith began cracking. Factionalism in the CPI (M) had been growing unabated as never before. A large number of the members and supporters began leaving the sinking ship. The future was not so uncertain at this juncture. It would depend on the way the Congress and TMC (+) coalition outplayed the political games of the CPI (M) that it had been playing for the last several years. Apparently, fate was not on the side of the LF this time around. In the mist of great uncertainty, the parliamentary election was held in phases. The Congress and TMC+ coalition won 26 out of 42 seats in the state (see annexure below). Congress and TMC+ were far ahead of the LF with regard to the percentage points of vote share. The Congress and TMC+ were more than four per cent of the differences between the LF and the Congress and TMC (+) (SUCI included). Therefore, it was quite intelligible, the wind of change or the vote swing was against the LF [see the annexure of this chapter (below)]. Now it was quite clear after 34 years of almost unopposed LF regime, like the mysterious "Castle" as imagined by Kafka in his novel, *The Castle.* This castle or in Rabindranath Tagore's play *Achalayatan* was about to fall apart as a pack of cards. The immediate change of the old structure of power was in the offing. The LF front was really at a loss as to what would happen in the next Assembly election; particularly, it appeared to the general public to foresee the rising wave of protest against the misdeed and the political fate of the LF. The LF, particularly the CPI (M), appeared possibly to feel some sort of an existential crisis since the Panchayat election in 2008. They did not show it in public, but it almost became obvious to watch their public gatherings and meetings where most of the top leaders including Buddhadeb Bhattacharjee and the state party secretary, Biman Bose and Binay Konar used to speak in intemperate language. They even personally attacked Mamata Banerjee and mimicked her gesture, manner of speaking and her dress, the way she used to attire herself since she began her parliamentary political career during the mid-1980s (1984 to be exact). All this betrayed the nervousness of a party that always enjoyed surplus majority for a span of 34 years. As also, it dawned on the CPI (M) party circle that the party this time would fail to confront the louder voices of the protesting peasants, workers and groups of civil society. All this indicated meteoric rise of the popularity of the TMC supremo, Ms. Mamata Banerjee. The Congress broke the coalition with the TMC in the Municipal elections in 2010 to test their capacity to garner votes at Bidhan Bhawan (Congress Party Head Quarters in Kolkata). Four small time leaders like Nirbed Roy, Pradip Ghosh two others began fast unto death. The then state Congress president, Pranab Mukherjee got it okayed by the Congress High Command at Delhi. The four broke their farcical fast within one or two days. But the urban voters gave the Congress a good drubbing in Calcutta Corporation election. That compelled the state Congress Party to make seat adjustments with TMC in the ensuing Assembly elections. It was a remarkable election. The LF looked almost tattered. In the 2011 Assembly election, the Trinamool Congress Coalition alone won an absolute majority of 185 seats. The Congress won 42 seats. The largest party of the LF, CPI (M) garnered only 40 and the smaller partners like RSP, FB, and CPI together got 22 seats only. The vote share of the TMC (+) and Congress together was 49.75 per cent and the LF shared only 41.5 per cent, i.e., the differences between the TMC (+), Congress coalition and the LF were 8.25 per cent. It was a comprehensive defeat of the LF and the TMC Congress new coalition. It was really a severe blow to the politics of the CPI (M).

The party in the state was almost in disarray at that point of time, so also was the case of other smaller partners of the LF. The manner of adjustment between the Trinamool Congress and the Congress was on the even keel at that time. The TMC joined the Central Cabinet and was satisfied with one Cabinet and six State Ministerial portfolios. The parliamentary election of 2009 was really a watershed in the politics of West Bengal since 1977. The seat shares of the CPI (M) came down to nine from 26 after 2004 parliamentary election. The communists never thought out before and, began to realize that if they continued their politics like this, as they had behaved with the people, it would be next to impossible to come back in near future. In the central stage in parliament, the LF in general and CPI (M) in particular garnered 16 seats and LF partners nine seats. From West Bengal, the LF got only 15 seats [CPI (M) nine and smaller partners eight seats only]. In the all India scenario, they had to be satisfied with 25 seats only. What a fall from 62 seats to 25 only! This in short made the LF almost irrelevant in Indian politics at the moment during the second UPA government led by the Congress having 206 seats after a long gap of more than 11years from 1997 (at the end of Narasimha Rao regime).

A new Coalition after more than Three Decades: A new coalition government led by Ms. Mamata Banerjee replaced the almost invincible LF led by the CPI (M) on 20 May 2011. It was actually the rejection of the CPI (M) overwhelmingly by the poor rural peasantries across the spectrum of castes and communities. The social coalition that was forged by the LF in its long search for left unity over the decades gone by went tattered. The facades of their ideological background and people oriented promises gradually became a ghost of their past untiring struggle to dislodge the bourgeoisie and feudal elements represented by the Congress Party. For that reason, they were to break the Congress Coalition consisting of caste community and big landholders and others. The Leftist Parties got those indications from the percentage point of vote shares of the Congress and all the opposition taken together in each election after election. Mamata took oath as the new Chief Minister along with her other ministers in the council of ministers. After the ceremony was over, Mamata began walking from the Governor House to get to the Writers Building — the *Mahakaran,* the centre of power where most of the ministers' rooms were allotted. She found that hundreds of thousands of people thronged the entire way. But for the simple security cover, she would have been mobbed. The people saw the same scene years before when Jyoti Basu took over as the Chief Minister years back on June 21, 1977. Mamata Banerjee showed her mettle while taking over as the Minister in charge of Railway in the Congress led second UPA government. Her only motivation was to improve the lot of the ordinary people and as to how to improve the life and living conditions of the citizens living in Bengal. Taking the rein from the hand of the stagnating government led by the Leftist regime of more than 34 years, Mamata genuinely aimed at clearing the Augean stable as soon as possible. But it was really difficult within such a short period of two and a half years.

Going back to her Railway days, through a deft handling of the Railway portfolio, she wanted to lay down the foundation of Economic Development of the state, which was rapidly sliding down. Its political economy of development was shattered. The tribal areas were always under the threat of Maoists, mostly in Jangal Mahal comprising the western fringes in Midnapur, Birbhum, Bankura and Purulia. The Railway tracts also were not safe because of the presence of the Maoists. Just one day before the 80 Municipal elections throughout the state including Calcutta Municipal Corporations on May 30, 2010, the Maoists damaged the tract at the dead of night. This resulted in horrendous accident of Jnaneswari Express running at high speed from Mumbai to Howrah station. The accident took place near a very small station. It was pitch dark night and there was no arrangement for lighting system. Many bogies derailed and jumped up to another train coming by the second line. The villagers heard a terrific thud. Anticipating something terribly wrong, they began to run to the spot. They were the people, who arrived first and began helping the travelers, who were still alive. Next day in the morning, the Minister for Railways arrived at the place of accident and found the devastation. Through on the spot calculation, it was found that there were 170 dead bodies and many more seriously injured. She found to her surprise that the state government's minister, Susanta Ghosh holding the important portfolio of *Pachimanchal Unnayan Parishad* was there. It was surprising that how it was possible that Mr. Ghosh arrived at the spot much before the Railways Minister, who got the news in Kolkata and came to the place with top neck speed. This agitated the minds of many, particularly the civil society groups, who organized a press conference and urged upon the central government to unravel the mystery of a horrible accident just before the election of a large number of urban government local bodies (Municipal and Corporation) elections. An inquiry was ordered, but nothing came out till dates. It was concluded in most circles that the Maoists of that area caused the accident to the misery of many and to instill some sort of fear psychosis among the people. Therefore, it concluded that most probably the Maoists threw an open challenge to both the Central and the state government.

When Mamata Banerjee took the job seriously and was bringing many projects to West Bengal, allotting in her Railway Budget quite a large share of money, the MPs of the LF particularly the CPI (M) ridiculed her on the floor of the parliament shouting that she was no more than the Railway minister of West Bengal. She worked out a certain strategy. All the six ministers of State, which Mamata Banerjee wanted from the Prime Minister were Saugata

Roy, Sultan Ahmed, Sisir Adhikary, Dinesh Trivedi, Mukul Roy and C.M. Jatua. Sudip Bandyopadhyay was the leader and Chief Whip of the party in the Lok Sabha. These ministers of state, as they were not always attending to the files of their departmental office at Delhi, most of the time they took the opportunity to visit the length and breadth of the state to nurture different constituencies in the state. They were always busy to focus on the socio-economic problems of the state and as to how they would map the political economy of development of the state if the TMC led by Mamata Banerjee could replace the LF government. Possibly, this was a deliberate policy decision of Mamata. As a Railway Minister in the second UPA government till she and her party TMC remained with the UPA-II coalition led by the Congress Party, she pursued her policy of improving the railway system economically, socially and culturally. Simultaneously, the socio-economic development of West Bengal was the most important priority of her activities as the Central Minister in charge of the Railways. She introduced many high speed trains like *Durant* on different routes besides increasing the number of *Rajdhani* Express in different state's main stations to the capital, New Delhi. Many new trains would run all the days of the week. She increased the number of local trains and the number of bogies in each train. She introduced a type of local train named *ijjat (to be used by the subaltern women with dignity)* having lower train fare than ordinary local trains to give economic succor to the village women, who used to come daily by train to work as domestic helps in the town in the early morning and returned home in the evening. Her objectives were to improve the service sectors of the Railways. She gave serious thought as to how the vacant railway lands around the stations could be utilized and make viable economically through Public Private Partnership (PPP) model of initiative. After her stint as the Minister for Railways, when she became the Chief Minister, she recommended the name of Sri Dinesh Trivedi from the TMC quota to the Prime Minister to induct in his cabinet as the next Minister of Railways. Dinesh Trivedi, in his Railway Budget, was supposed to increase the passenger fare and enhance the freight rate. That irritated the TMC supremo Mamata Banerjee. She requested the prime minister to replace Trivedi by the minister in charge of Shipping, Shree Mukul Roy, a Member of Rajya Sabha. Mamata, also in her earlier stint as the Minister of Railways during the NDA regime in the late 1990s, was in favour of giving succor to the poor and middle class people. Still now, the Railways earned a huge amount of fare from the middle class and the poorer sections of society than the people belonging to the upper strata of society. Fare structure revision upward would be really burdensome for the middle class and the poor. At that point of time also, she was averse to increase the passenger fare. The Railway Budget failed to satisfy the corporate sectors. It did not matter to Mamata Banerjee because she knew well that the leaders of the corporate sectors cared less for the rate of Railways fare structure as the means of communications. Manmohan Singh and the Congress Party, as also some of the Railway Board members desired that for the better maintenance of the Railway systems, the passenger fare and the structure freight rate should be hiked. Mukul Roy, replacing Trivedi, placed the Railway Budget exactly the way Mamata wanted. The TMC led by Mamata Banerjee, though an ally of the UPA-2 government led by the Congress Party, while in Manmohan's cabinet objected to many policies of the government that appeared to be anti-people. But she continued to be in the governing structure that Manmohan Singh piloted. When Shree Pranab Mukherjee was elected as the President of India, Mamata Banerjee was not very happy. Hers was the second largest Party that was supporting the second UPA coalition. But she was not properly consulted about; rather she was misled by the Congress President, Sonia Gandhi. Mulyam Singh Yadav resorted to a double game with Mamata Banerjee. After initial hesitation, Mamata supported the candidature of Pranab Mukherjee. Mamata Banerjee's personal relation with Mukherjee was never vitiated. Therefore, Mukherjee was elected unopposed as the President of India. A few weeks later, Mamata arranged for a public felicitation to the newly elected President of India, Shree Pranab Mukherjee in the Netaji indoor stadium. In his public address, Pranab Babu spoke highly of Mamata Banerjee as the Chief Minister of Bengal as also their cordial relations for a long time. What the Congress was not able to do during the LF regime from 1977 till date, Mamata, because of her relentless fight against the LF, did it within a shorter period of time since she broke away from the Congress in January 1998. Mamata and the Congress combination won the election on May 13, 20011, but formed the government on 20th May. Before the election, the CPI (M), particularly its out spoken Muslim leader and a cabinet minister Abdul Rezzak Molla prophesied on 13th night that the whole state would be drowned with bloodshed in case either side won. But he was blissfully falsified. From the night of the victory, the TMC people asked by Mamata Banerjee, the CM elect, began playing the Rabindra Sangeet everywhere in the state wherever it was possible. No interparty quarrel and violence took place. The Congress was always vaunted, specifically after the TMC came out of the Central coalition that it would have not been possible for Mamata to win the election, but for the vote share of the Congress. This was the refrain of the Congress leaders as they might be suffering from a false ego. The lesser leaders of the Party always tried to belittle TMC for the transfer of the Congress vote in favour of the TMC. They forgot the parliamentary vote share of TMC and the Congress vote share separately, although they contested the 2009 Parliamentary and 2011 Assembly elections under a seat adjustment formula. Like in 2009, in the Assembly election, the TMC Congress collectively got more than 49.5 per cent of the total votes polled. After statistical disaggregation, it was found that the TMC had a share of 50.12 per cent and the Congress got 9.09 per cent resulting in TMC's 195 seats and the Congress had to be satisfied with 42 Assembly seats only. Later on, in every election, the percentage points of vote share of the Congress declined. The recent examples were the *Panchayat* elections of 2013 and the recently concluded five Municipal elections, which were held on November 22, 2013,

Observing the sustained attitude of the middle level leaders of the Congress, one can easily conclude that they are in a habit of deluding themselves. Or it may be a hidden calculation on the part of the state Congress that in the next parliamentary election (2014), the moribund Congress Party here may have aimed at some sort of seat adjustment with the LF, actually with the CPI (M). As the election scenario is sufficiently bleak for the Central Congress at present, the Congress supremo Sonia Gandhi is still in a dilemma what to do next. The state Congress president, Pradip Bhattacharjee, general secretaries and many others whatever they may utter against Mamata and her TMC, as the last resort, they have to depend upon the decision of the Congress supremo Smt. Sonia Gandhi at the Centre. In politics, anything is possible. To get rid of BJP under the banner of National Democratic Alliance, Sonia Gandhi may persuade Mamata Banerjee to side with the UPA in the next government making, as one can see that the top leadership at the Centre are not voicing against Mamata Banerjee. But indirectly, the minority UPA government is not financially helping the debt burdened state government as alleged by the Finance Minister of Bengal, Dr. Amit Mitra; the Chief Minister, Mamata Banerjee has also been reiterating the same in several of her official and public meetings. Mamata is to bear the legacy of the previous LF government. There is a huge fiscal deficit. The last LF government left behind a debt trap amounting to 2.6 lakh crore. The state leaders kept mum about the difficulty the government was facing here even while the Congress was in the government. Now in the present situation, seeing the execution of TMC's development programmes, many Congress men and even people belonging to the CPI (M) and other LF parties are joining hands with the TMC. Mass exodus is continuing from the Congress Party and even the members of the CPI (M) and its LF partners are joining now and then to "strengthen the development agenda pursued by the TMC government. That both the members of the opposition parties of the LF and the Congress are deserting their old folds are seen in the urban areas of the state. In the last five Corporation (Howrah) and Municipal elections, the CPI (M) lost both Howrah and Jhargram that the CPI (M) reigned for a period of more than 25 years at a stretch. Only the Congress Party in Murshidabad led by Adhir Chowdhury was in a position to retain its hold in Berhampur Municipality, but with less strength, losing two seats to the TMC and in other 24 seats, the TMC being the runner up, which never happened in the history of the last several elections. Mamata Banerjee had to struggle hard with a single minded devotion to overthrow the

CPI (M) regime entrenched in every nook and corner of the state, which seemed impossible to be dislodged in the life time of our generation. This was historically a marvelous feat of achievement for a frail lady whose party was not yet genuinely a structured one like the Marxist parties. She fought on the plank of all round development of the state whose "material resources as also the human capital"[77] were looted by the all-powerful so-called Communists for the last more than 34 years. After completing two years in power, she proclaimed, "We draw confidence from the fact that our government enjoys your (people) overwhelming support in this journey towards equality and justice".[78] The Chief Minister, Mamata Banerjee, after the end of two years of the TMC government, further reiterated, "We are happy to see these achievements as the first few milestones of a great journey."[79]

The economic performance of the new government led by Mamata is as follows:

West Bengal Achieved Higher Growth than the National Average in GSDP, Agriculture, Industry and Services

• India's GDP Growth in 2012-13	4.96%
• West Bengal's GSDP Growth Rate in 2012-13	7.6%
• India's Growth in Agriculture and Allied Sectors, 2012-13	1.79%
• West Bengal's Growth in Agriculture and Allied Sectors, 2012-13	2.56%
• India's Industrial Growth Rate, 2012-13	3.12%
• West Bengal's Industrial Growth Rate, 2012-13	6.24%
• India's Services Sector Growth Rate, 2012-13	6.59%
• West Bengal's Services Sector Growth Rate, 2012-13	9.48%

Source: *Powering Progress Empowering People* 2 years, Kolkata, Government of West Bengal, 2013. p. vi.

The present government led by Ms. Mamata Banerjee has been working since 20 May 2011 under several economic constraints. The success rate may not be remarkable, nonetheless it must be highlighted. Despite enormous debt burden within its limited areas, it is doing quite well. The state's yearly revenue earning has improved as compared with last several years of the previous LF government. The TMC government is always keen about different projects and their implemention on time. The state government has aimed at consistent increase in the state plan expenditure for the last two years: 2010-2011, 11837.85 crore, 2011-2012 1407.52 crore (more than 18% growth), plan expenditure (expected) in 2012-13 17600.00 crore. (25.28% growth). Despite financial constraints, 75 per cent of the state plan for 2012-13 was released to different departments in the first quarter of the financial year.[80] The TMC government led by Ms Banerjee initiated several measures to increase the revenue of the debt trapped state government; otherwise, the almost bankrupt government, a legacy that was left behind by the previous LF regime, the system of governance would have derailed altogether. The present government from the very beginning resorted to massive reforms of tax administration, mandatory online filing of VAT returns, increasing the tax base, excise reform during 2012-13. It took initiative to restructure the terminally sick PUSs and attempted in monetizing the surplus land assets. And finally, the introduction of transparent auction mechanism of land for commercial purposes.[81] The finance minister of the state, Dr. Amit Mitra formulated the above measures from the very beginning of the new regime under the dynamic leadership of the Chief Minister to augment the flagging financial health of the state. But unfortunately, out of Rs. 32,000 crores of revenue generated during the year, over 25,000 crores was cut off by the Reserve Bank of India for interest and repayment obligations, due to the debt of more than 2.6 crores left behind by LF government as the legacy to be met by the incoming government.

In comparison with the previous government, the present government appears to be much more vibrant. Despite financial crunch, the team of ministers has been trying their best to improve the administrative functions and the Chief Minister has been able to motivate the upper echelon of bureaucracy and the police administration. Mamata Banerjee has been working on the plank of all round development and trying her best to give social justice to the unfed and underdogs, particularly among the poor scheduled castes and the tribal people living at the peripheral areas of different districts. They are getting rice and wheat at a very cheap price. Her only objective is to improve their life and living conditions. It appears possible, taking a cue from Bihar (from 2005 to 2010), now headed by Nitish Kumar, Mamata Banerjee launched a programme of empowering the women in the rural backyard of the state. The *Panchayat* elections were held in 2013 on the basis of 50 per cent reservation of woman in all the three tiers. A new enthusiasm was found among the people in rural bodies. It inculcated a sense of involvement in policy making and actual participation in the process of development equally among the men and women. The Chief Minister herself is very energetic, hard working and mobile. She has been able to energize both her cabinet colleagues and the bureaucrats. She is determined to cause the bureaucracy to be always people oriented. She has always been trying to bring the administrative machineries to the grassroots level, i.e. to the door of the people. She visited all the 18 districts of the state several times. No other Chief Minister visited Darjeeling and Jangal Mahal as the new Chief Minister Mamata did. She is always in mood to see the real conditions of the people of Darjeeling hills; it helped her to understand the intractable problems of the fissiparous organizations of the Gorkha League Liberation and then Gorkha Janamukti Morcha. Whenever she visited any district, she went there with the retinue of the Chief Secretary,

Home Secretary and other selected Secretaries of the concerned department. Any meeting held at her auspices, she accompanied the higher bureaucracy and the DM, SDO, BDO and other important office bearers and members of the rural and urban bodies of that district. She always tried to understand the problems of the districts from very close quarters; then instructed the officials to do the job the people desired to be performed. To do away with Maoist menace in the Jangal Mahal, comprising the whole western belt, West Midnapur, Bankura and Purulia, etc., she understood the miserable life and living conditions of the tribal living on the forest resources, people living in the forest and the poorest of the poor living at the edge of the forest. Still they could not think of a minimum civilized living, i.e., *roti kapara aur makan* (food, clothes and a shelter with a roof above). Economic development was totally absent there. During the last lap of the LF regime, the government sent a few higher officials to gauge the problems of the people and as to how people used to live there under constant threats of the Maoists. But unfortunately, the government activities stopped there. They did nothing to concretize the government's idea of development. Rather the main partner of the LF, the CPI (M) wanted to manage the unbearable situation there by its own party cadres, which ultimately went haywire. Even the joint forces of the central paramilitary and state police were not properly utilized. When the central forces went ahead to the forest to fight or in some cases to contain the Maoists, the state police forces were to look after the party cadres, so that the CPI (M) backed families might safely come back to those areas behind the forest and maintain the vote bank of the CPI (M) and politically cleanse the opposition.

In the new dispensation, the ground situation at the Jangal Mahal appears to be in a new light. Still there are central forces in some critical areas; but the state police forces are not used in perverse manner as did the leaders of the CPI (M). The Maoist movements that instilled a sense of terror in the minds of the people during the previous regime are contained to the advantage of the tribal and other poor people around. Income, occupational uncertainty, nearly total absence of educational opportunities, even the problems of illiteracy and income consumption ratio were horribly low. The people, mostly the tribals, did not have a sustainable level of food. Now the condition of those areas has reached a satisfactory level. The families living by the side of the forest areas are not forced to allow their sons and daughters to Maoist dens in exchange for a pittance. Survival was the greatest problem for those underfed, half naked, illiterate people.

The present government has taken steps to cleanse the area of the Maoists as far as possible. Even many Maoist leaders and activists came round. And many of them surrendered to authorities and came back to the mainstream of the society. The present Chief Minister visited those areas again and again.

The poor people are made to dream a normal life and way of living. The government agencies are supplying rice and wheat at very cheap rate, i.e., rice at the rate of Rs. 2 per kg and wheat at Rs. 3. Garments and other useables are provided. To remove illiteracy, schools are opened nearby. Bicycles are given to the girl students to attend the schools that are at a distance from their houses. The present government led by Ms. Mamata Banerjee is seen to work hard for all round development and teach the rural people as to how they would participate in the development process. The aim of the state government is singularly to empower both the men and women of the state. In this connection, the present government brought out a Report that would list the achievements and the role of the government to tackle sagging political economy of development within two years. The very name of the Report is significant, i.e., *Powering the Progress and Empowering People.* Districts of North Bengal have been perennially underdeveloped. The ministers of previous regimes frequently visited the areas; Shree Asoke Bhattacharya of the CPI (M), a very powerful minister with more than two/three portfolios to look after, hailing from Siliguri, the most important district town of Darjeeling, substantially did not do anything to economically and socially ameliorate the industrial backwardness of North Bengal as a whole. There are many things that could have been done. The numerous tea gardens gradually became sick during the LF regime. Darjeeling tea is world famous and was used to be exported. But the government did not sufficiently take care of the gardens; and during the Gorkha National Liberation Front movements at Darjeeling Hills, led by Subhas Ghising, the effort of the government came to a standstill. Even the tea gardens situated in the lower part of Darjeeling and Terai were not taken care of. Most of the tea processing factories went red. The labourers used to live on boiled wild vegetables. The young children in those areas had been suffering from acute malnutrition. On the other hand, at the connivance of the government, the tea gardens were sold to the real estate promoters. Different businesses from drugs, illegal liquor, ISI money transaction via Nepal, to money laundering were carried on gleefully by the business community, mostly the non-Bengali businessmen. All this happened under the nose of the government and their ministers. There are several tourist sports in North Bengal apart from the beautiful hill stations in the upper reaches. Enormous amount of scope of revenue earning was there, had the sports been maintained and improved. There are several tourist destinations in Jalpaiguri, its forest resorts and Cooch Behar with its river system, hilly terrain, Boxsa forest overlooking the hills of Bhutan. This is the gateway of Bhutan also. Without any permit from the government of Bhutan, the tourists can follow the gateway to Bhutan through the last spot; Phultshilling itself is a beautiful tourists heaven. But the previous government was not as sensitive as it should have been to boost up government revenue.

The present government as seen in the activities of the CM and her ministers in charge of different Departments are working hard and trying seriously to bring about a change in the work culture as compared to the last lap of the previous LF government. The objectives to be achieved are many and multifaceted. Under the present cash deficit situation, it is really difficult in "powering the progress and empowering people".[82] Yet, it has taken the job seriously before the completion of two and a half years of the new dispensation. Most important of them is to aim at enriching capital in governance. Minute focuses are broadening in agriculture, industry and service sectors and when compared, all these three sectors are a bit ahead of the national average.[83]

The two largest intractable problems that the Chief Minister had to face were (1) the Maoist menace at Jangal Mahal, and (2) Gorkhaland problem in Darjeeling Hill and the adjacent areas of Terai and around. There is absolutely no denying the fact that the solution of the two problems has far reaching consequences for the state, one of them having international boundaries, are the most visible achievements of the presents government led by Mamata Banerjee. Earlier, the LF government mostly used force and Marxist party mobilization; for them, party decision rather than administrative political development process was the priority. The question of Gorkha identity, the localized Nepalis' ambition was really the cause of the disturbances in Darjeeling Hills. Subhas Ghising, a retired military man in the Gorkha regiment, earlier started the movement to gain a Gorkhaland state separate from West Bengal under the Indian federal scheme. After hot and cold dialogues with the LF government, Subhas Ghising did not back out. Even the CPI (M)'s arm tactics by the party cadres did not quell the frequent disturbances at the cost of the tourism industry. The central government was quite unhappy to watch the situation in Darjeeling, particularly at the time when other fissiparous groups in the Northeastern states became the hot bed of conflicts among the tribal groups. Rajiv Gandhi intervened at this juncture. A tripartite agreement among Subhas Ghising and his Gorkha National Liberation Front (GNLF), the West Bengal state government, the Central government led by the Prime Minister Rajiv Gandhi was singed at the Raj Bhawan in Calcutta and the Darjeeling Gorkhaland Hill Council (DGHC) was formed in 1988. Subhas Ghising took over as the chairman and singlehandedly began reigning the councils, giving almost no power to the members of the council. Enormous amount of money that were pumped into the council, some by the centre and mostly by the West Bengal state government for development purposes, was siphoned away. Only the window dressing was done by the chief of the council. He did not hold election as long as Subhas Ghising was the head of the council till early 2011. Supply of water, electricity and other amenities essential for the life and living of the ordinary people of the Hill areas were absolutely inadequate. The municipal and

Panchayat elections at this end of Darjeeling district were never held. Gradually, the people and many other members became restive. Subhas Ghising was in a habit of passing the buck to both the state and central government and claiming for more and more autonomy. The claim was not very realistic. A new state as claimed by Ghising within the territorial boundary of West Bengal were not, and still are not viable economically, socially geographically and demographically as well. The DGHC under Subhas Ghising did not have any development perspective in view. Rather the possibility of developing industrial scenario in hill areas was getting bleak. Water supply and the voltage of electricity were anything, but desirable. Peaceful interactions among social groups were sliding down. The tea industry that used to produce world famous tea was in the red.

Due to Ghising's personal attitude and leadership thrust to solve local problems vis-vis concentration of power in his own hand, his colleagues in the council became disenchanted. Without any development programme to improve the life and living of the hill people, public opinion was also gradually going against him. Ghising's recent alibi was that without complete autonomy, the DGHC could not work as it should in the contemporary realm of DGHC. It was a poor excuse that his once intimate colleagues, Bimal Gurung and others felt. They were trying to distance themselves from the "hoaxes" of Ghising. But still Subhas Ghising was trying to entrench his power; he advised his colleague to demand for Autonomous Gorkha Hill Council (AGHC). At that point of time, he went to Delhi to get the council to be entrenched in the 6th schedule of the Constitution. During those days, the colleagues of Ghising resorted to fasting in a makeshift tent in the Siliguri-Darjeeling road. Ghising returned from New Delhi, but was not allowed to proceed further to Darjeeling. He had to take shelter in a Bungalow (Pental cottage) in the plains of Siliguri.

Bimal Gurung took over. Gorkha people rallied round him and his lieutenants, like Roshan Giri, Chchatre Bahadur Subba, Harka Bahadur Gurug, Binay Tamang, P. Arjun and others began a second movement against both the centre and the state for their Gorkha self-determination. In the midst of severe controversies, Mamata Banerjee, her Trinamool Congress party and Congress Party, a coalition partner, TMC being the surplus majority party took over the reign in the state. After a prolonged negotiation with the central government and Gorkha Jana Mukti Morcha (GJMM) led by Bimal Gurung, a tripartite agreement, named Gorkhaland Territorial Administration (GTA) in the presence of the Indian Home Minister, Chidambaram, Chief Minister Mamata Banerjee and the Gorkha Jana Mukti Morcha was signed. On behalf GJMM Shree Rosan Giri the secretary of the GJMM signed the document. It was decided in the meeting after joyous fanfare that a committee would be formed to determine the areas and boundaries of the GTA. The signing in ceremony was over. Bimal Gurung addressed his constituencies saying that to achieve a state separate from West Bengal, the acceptance of the GTA was the first step.

Actually, the very name of GTA was illusive. Critics might have argued that the administration of the territories of the Gorkhas had the connotation of the formation of a federal state. The use of the word territory and administration in this context was not a very happy formulation. The territorial determination Committee led by Justice Shyamal Sen brought out the Report within three or four months. Bimal Gurung and his colleagues wanted that the committee should incorporate more than 350 *moujas* spreading over the Terai region, some areas of Jalpaiguri, Alipur Duars and Cooch Behar. They contended that these places had large concentrations of Nepalese. But when the Shyamal Sen Committee Report came out, Gurung, the chairman of the GTA found that the new incarnation of the previous DGHC led by Subhas Ghising, was allotted only three *moujas* to his utter disenchantment. To ally the fear of the Gorkha people and other inhabitants, the new Chief Minister Ms. Mamata Banerjee visited the Darjeeling hills and adjacent districts on more than 17 occasions. Every time Mamata visited the Hills, she attended to both administrative problems and political demands, but never did she allow the two distinct areas of activities to overlap. In an administrative meeting organized in Darjeeling, slogans were raised by some from the audience about Gorkhaland, while the GTA chairman, Bimal Gurung was on the dais, the Chief Minister immediately reacted reminding them that no political questions would be allowed in the ongoing administrative meet. But Bimal Gurung did not address the audience or tried to pacify the people in response to the political controversies raised. This was not taken by the Chief Minister kindly, who might have anticipated what would happen in the near future. It appeared that Gurung, to keep his promise to organize the Nepalese in a separate state, was hell bent to proceed in his own way as before. Most possibly, Bimal Gurung could not fathom the depth and strength of the politic of the present Chief Minister Mamata Banerjee. Bimal Gurung and his GJJM resorted again to their old strategy of continuous bundh, sit in strike, *hartal* again and again to the detriment of the life and living of ordinary people of Darjeeling. The tourist inflow, the main revenue earner, of the place came to a standstill. Other rational members of the GJJM realized the enormity of the financial problems. But that was of no avail. During this period, Mamata Banerjee went on a political visit to Kalimpong and then to Darjeeling. She declared immediately the formation of a Lepcha Development Council (LDC).

Originally, the Lepchas are the original inhabitants of Darjeeling Hills or, in other words, the sons of the soil; but they are far outnumbered by the Gorkhas. Actually, there are not more than five to seven per cent. There are other tribal communities, like Limbu, Bhutias, etc. Now Mamata Banerjee is thinking about giving these smaller tribal communities their due place.

The time is not yet ripe to comment on it. Coming back to the GJJM's movements with all its previous means even after the formation of GTA, the Chief Minister gave a master stroke. Bimal Gurung tendered his resignation from the chairmanship of GTA. Perhaps he might have thought that Mamata would negotiate to come to a settlement. Mamata did the opposite. She immediately accepted the resignation and ordered the district authorities to enforce law and order and got a few members having some criminal records arrested. The GTA elected another member chairman of the GTA; even then, this man was in jail. Bimal and Rosan visited Delhi to hobnob with the Home and Finance Ministers, so that their movements and demands should find immediate recognition. Bimal Gurung, to his surprise, found that the Trinamool Congress Party considerably got its foothold in the hill areas. It was almost unthinkable to Gurung and his colleague even a few months ago. By this time, the Telengana Movements started in Andhra Pradesh. The demand for a separate state of Telengana was longstanding, going back to the 1950s, when the State Reorganization Commission had begun working; but the commission and even after the Central government did not pay heed to it; because the problem, i.e., to bifurcate Andhra Pradesh beset with different problems common with Tamil Nadu was very tricky and almost intractable. By the start of 2013, the Telengana movement got momentum. The leaders of the Telengana Rashtriya Samiti led by Chandrasekhar Rao resigned from the Parliament. A few Congress MPs and MLAs of Andhra wanted to resign. From the very beginning, Andhra Bidhan Sabha was divided on the issue. In this context, the Central Congress Core Committee members took the decision to create a new state of Telengana, which was endorsed by the Congress Working Committee. But still now, the UPA (II) government could not take a final decision; or more appropriately, the Congress party was not in a position to open the Pandora's Box. From this decision of the Congress Committee, Bimal and Rosan Giri took a cue. If Andhra can be bifurcated by the central leadership in July 2013, then why not Bengal! The Gorkhas of Darjeeling showed their restiveness and resorted to their earlier tactics. They did not use the words bundhs and hartal. Instead, they asked the people to confine themselves in their houses for 48/72 hours and sometimes for days together. The CM Mamata Banerjee's tactics worked well. She visited Kalimpong and then Darjeeling to appeal to the people to follow her for their development purposes. She felt that Gurung was losing control not only over the people, but among a large chunk of the members belonging to the GJJM. Moreover, Mamata already declared the formation of a Lepcha Development Council and was even ready to form a Tamang Development Council. Watching the rising intransigence Gurung and company, Mamata Banerjee asked her party leaders to give a membership drive. The Trinamool Party General Secretary Mukul Roy acted accordingly that resulted in growing a large numbers of Trinamool Party members. That was a danger signal for GJJM. To gain back his control over the hill areas, Gurung Proposed to the CM that he would again call an election to be the Chief of GTA replacing Binay Tamang — the present Head of the GTA. Bimal also wanted the arrested members of the GTA to be released. Mamata agreed on condition that only those people would be released from jail against whom there were only petty charges of corruption. Bimal Gurung agreed and subsequently he was elected again the Executive Chief of the GTA. Harka Bahadur Chchetri — an important member of the GTA and an MLA from Kalimpong said that they no longer wanted a truncated Bengal. They now stood ready to share the development plank of the Chief Minister Ms Mamata Banerjee.

Really it is one of the greatest achievements of the new Chief Minister Ms Banerjee. Recently, the CM has brought back normalcy in the Hills of North Bengal after a period of three and a half decades. Darjeeling is the queen of hill stations and, naturally, a proud possession of the people of Bengal. The government of Bengal can never afford to sacrifice the Darjeeling Hills. This is also understood by all the tribal communities (Lepchas, Limbus and Tamang, etc.) both at the hills and the plains, particularly the largest community, i.e., the Gorkhas. To pursue several development programmes to finish, it is necessary that there should be a working Secretariat, a second one after Kolkata, in Darjeeling where the people of the areas concerned can approach for speedy movement of official files and directions to implement development programmes accordingly. To the satisfaction of people of North Bengal, the Chief Minister, as per her promise made earlier, opened a new Secretariat Building named "Üttarkanya" on January 20, 2014. To head the Secretariat, there is a provision for an additional chief secretary; the Chief Minister promises that she would certainly visit North Bengal frequently to attend to the needs of the people there. There are other outstanding problems, like Kamtapuris, demand for separate Cooch Bihar state and the conflicts between the Rabanshis and the Vatias (people who migrated from the then East Pakistan long back after the partition of undivided Bengal as also the problems and the national politics of the exchange of Enclaves on either side of Bengal, now Bangladesh). The Rajbangsi were agitating for the recognition of their Rajbangsi language for quite a long time. The problem is unresolved till date. Secessionists are not new in Cooch Behar district, because there is a history. Cooch Behar was a princely state. It was merged with the Indian Union after the partition in 1949. A section of Kamtapuris, i.e., Kamtapuris Liberation Organization (KLO) along with the Assamese ULFA and other terror groups, are still demanding separate state. There are occasional attacks against people and government properties, like railway compartment and blowing the railway tracks across the state of West Bengal and Assam. These types of terrorist movements, though occasional, have been going on unabated.

Immediately after she took over as the CM, the second most important problem that she confronted was to tackle the perennial ill-nourished tribal people in Jangal Mahal as also the massive Maoist presence in the entire western belt of the state. The Maoists had been taking advantages of the perennial problems of poverty among the tribal people and other lower caste people, who used to live on whatever they got from the forest. During their thirty four years of reign, the LF actually did nothing for the development of the areas and the poor people were almost starving to death. Amlasole was one of the many examples where more than seven people died. The LF made an alibi that the people died because of malnutrition and very skillfully avoided the urgent questions. Watching the situations as prevailing in marginal areas of West Midnapur, Bankura and Purulia, the Maoist exploited the demographic situation and began giving paltry amount of money to the families in exchange for young men and women and even adolescents to be trained as the members of the Maoist brigade. Every now and then, they attacked the police and armed personnel in their camps situated in different places in Jangal Mahal as found in the Northern Province of Sri Lanka and even in Myanmar. The LTTE (Liberation of Tamil Tigers Elam) continuously fought for a separate state of Tamil Elam. But ultimately, the Sri Lankan army carried out genocide on the LTTE at Jaffna in the northern part of Sri Lanka.

It was not that the LF government did not know the strategy of the Maoist. Because of the leftist ideology, the CPI (M) was unwilling or at best was circumscribed to ban the Maoist Organization in West Bengal in spite of heavy loss of lives of their cadres and others ordinary citizens at the hands of the extremists. Rather, they liked to get it done by the central forces which the Home Minister of India sent at the urgent request of the Chief minister Buddhadeb Bhattacharjee.

The Chief Minister Mamata Banerjee understood the real problems of the Mao infested areas. It was the problem of life and living of the people, which resulted from gross neglect of the people, who were not living at even the subsisting level. Mamata, even before taking over as the CM, used to visit these areas with a large contingent of the members of the civil society groups. She with some of the members of her party visited with great risk quite a number of Mao dominated areas including the most dreaded Lalgarh, Jhargram, Binpur, Ayodha Phahar and other places at Purulia. The TMC government very successfully contained the free play of the Maoists. Her line of thought followed a pattern, i.e., by offering them different ways so that ultimately they could come to the mainstream of politics. Later on, many of them gave up the arms and surrendered to the TMC government for a comparatively decent way of living.

The new CM, Ms. Mamata Banerjee, long before she came to power, knew the demography of all the 19 districts of the state and made a constant liaison with all classes of people as she always claimed. She understood the topsy-turvy conditions of the political economy of development of Bengal. In the process, she came to realize that unless a massive programme of development was undertaken, the marginal men of the state, particularly the poorest of the poor sections, be it the Schedule castes, Schedule tribes, the Muslims and the Adibasis all along the forest areas would remain the same.

The Chief Minister's focus, as she declares, in all the undeveloped districts including Darjeeling, particularly the hill areas like that of Jangal Mahal, massive all round, development programmes are to be undertaken[84]. She asks different departments of the government to undertake a number of schemes for the development of Jangal Mahal areas. In fact, a nodal department has been created to monitor the achievements of the administration continuously.[85]

Some of the achievements are as noted by the report: 10,000 appointments to National Volunteer Force, Home Guards in addition to 700 schedule tribe junior Constables were already appointed. Arrangement has been made for vocational training and skill development. Thousands of below poverty line people are getting rice at the price of Rs. two per kilo per week with vitamin contents for nutrition. New Colleges and a few Universities have been built up and this is a continuous process. Even a women University at Diamond Harbor has been set up recently. Arrangement has been provisioned for portable and piped water; irrigation facilities are gradually being increased. The government has made provision for water conservation, *Jal Dharo Jal Varo* projects. The government makes the people understand the advantages of watershed. For this purpose, 150 big and small water ponds, particularly in the dry areas[86] were dug in the state utilizing the funds set apart for hundred day's employment programmes.

Special emphasis is given on minority welfare, women welfare, to encourage self-help groups and backward classes' welfare. All this ongoing projects give enough encouragement to the rural people and that in the process has helped the new government earn popular confidence. The TMC government inherited almost a bankrupt economy, the debt burden was two lakh, six thousand crore. In each installment, the government has to clear up its debt to the central government by paying more than three fourth of the state revenue earning per year. Therefore, it is essential to look back to the health of the political economy of development of the state, which was in shambles. How to tackle the situation was the measure headache of the new government. The major initiatives of the new government as seen after two years of its governance are not too little. The TMC government introduced *Kanyashree* Scheme – targeting to stop early marriage and eradicate dropout rates among the girls; secondly, targeting unmarried girls between 13-18 years with family income less than Rs. 50,000 per annum; thirdly, scholarship of Rs. 500 per annum is to be given to girls studying between VIII and XII; and finally, for the girls Rs. 25,000 on completion of 18 years of age for attending formal or open school and recognized vocational training course or marriage whatsoever.[87] The achievements of the new government as stated in brief are as follow: growth in development expenditure, the state government's initiative for additional resource mobilization; enriching human capital in governance; agriculture and allied activities; large scale industries; micro and small scale industries; improvement of power generation capacity; to build up infrastructure and to utilize social capital as far as possible; serious attention and imaginative steps are to be undertaken to boost up tourism industries; Emphasis has been given on eight Public Private Partnership (PPP) project offers, to enhance tourism in different places in the state; rigorous attempt to improve health, education, minority welfare, women welfare sector of the state; to enlarge self-help groups and employment.

The present government feels that the women, particularly in the rural and urban hinterlands, have been neglected since long. Unless the government of the day makes specific schemes, the other half of the population cannot progress in a free and plural society. But, there are many obstructions on the way. To overcome these difficulties, multipronged strategies are to be taken. With these objectives in mind, the present Chief Minister has thought to change the mind-set of the people, both men and women. Therefore, she has started to bring the cultural bind and development strategy to a higher trajectory in the process. But it requires taking into account the political economy of development of the inherited government. Finally, the backward classes welfare is to be put on the priority list in the development trajectory of the economy.

The state ministers often allege that the LF government had made even more than an "outstanding borrowing to the tune of Rs. 1,98,195 crore in 2010-2011" The figure might be higher as per the statement of the Chief Minister immediately after she came to power (two lakh, six thousand crores). Whatever it may be; but now the interest sum is 22,000 crores annually and the sum has been gradually increasing to 28,000 crores; "To add to this, the state exchequer has been getting less than 425 crore from the Centre. In such a situation, the state government is not in favour of indulging in wasteful spending"[88] The new government had to face many odds, particularly after TMC led by Mamata Banerjee withdrew its support from the Congress led UPA II government. The immediate cause was that the Congress led central government was determined to increase the quantum of Foreign Direct Investment (FDI) in multi brand retails. Previously, many unpopular measures were introduced; but this was too much for the second largest party led by Mamata, supporting the UPA II to tolerate. She came out from the coalition.

Both the LF and the Congress conjointly have been opposing Mamata Banerjee in every issue. Despite the fact, the Chief Minister was able to manage the economy. The finance minister took into account every sector of the economy and made an encouraging report. According to the Report at hand, it has stated that West Bengal achieved higher growth than the national average in GSDP, Agriculture, Industry and Services: West Bengal's GSDP growth rate in 2012-13 was 7.60 per cent whereas India's GDP in the same period is 4.96 per cent. Second West Bengal growth in Agriculture and the allied sector was 2.56 per cent during the same period and India's was 1.79 per cent. West Bengal's growth rate in 2012-13 was 6.24 per cent. India's growth rate remained at 3.12 per cent. Finally West Bengal's the service sector growth rate during 2012-13 was 9.48 per cent, while India's rate during the same period was 6.59 per cent.[89]

These are, in fact, the economic scenario of West Bengal at present. In comparison with other developed states in the country, the scenario may not be outstanding, but it cannot be ignored away. The disheartened Congress Party and the demoralized CPI (M) are always on their toe to find fault with the government at every step for not doing the things, which the LF government failed to do during its 34 years rule. The opposition parties like the LF coalition, the Congress and even BJP are time and again crying hoarse about alleged 'deteriorating' law and order problems like inter and intra-party clashes, robbery occasionally though as also dishonouring the women in the state by molestation and rape here and there and highlighting many other issues and non-issues that were surprisingly unresolved during the LF's long period of stay in office. They are not making constructive suggestions, or anything keeping in mind that two and a half years of governance cannot bring about substantial socio-economic changes. These were the burning issues during the Congress rule for many years and the LF for three and a half decades from 1977 as also during the United Front (UF) regimes in 1967 and 1969. The history has already judged the system of governance of the Congress Party. In a plural democratic system, good governance as far as possible is what the people want. The democratic and electoral wishes of the people cannot be bottled in. A time will come when the oppressive cork of the bottle would be blown up. People wanted change when the political establishment became too entrenched and unresponsive, as people experienced during the previous LF government. This change is exactly what a large sections of people wished for, in the parliamentary elections in 2009 and the Assembly election in 2011 in Bengal. The much awaited change has come about. As change is permanent as it is ever changing. It depends upon the moods and want of people from time to time. The people of West Bengal must give sufficient time to the government led by Mamata Banerjee and her Trinamool Congress Party and then judge its capacity to really govern for the welfare of the people.

Annexure

Per cent of Votes Polled by Different Parties in Parliamentary Election 2009

Party	*CPI (M)*	*CPI*	*RSP*	*FB*	*INC*	*TMC*	*SUC*
(1)	(2)	(3)	(4)	(5)	(6)	(7)	(8)
Vote Share	33.10	3.60	3.56	3.04	13.45	31.18	1.65
Seat	(9)	(2)	(2)	(2)	(6)	(19)	(1)

Annexure (contd.)

Party	*BJP*	*SP*	*JMM*	*NCP*	*BSP*	*MUL*	*IND + Others*
(1)	(9)	(10)	(11)	(12)	(13)	(14)	(15)
Vote Share	6.14	0	0.26	0.09	1.002	0.07	2.7
Seat	(1)	(12)	–	–	–	–	–

Source: Reports (provisional) Election Commission of India.
Note: Figures in parenthesis indicate number of seats.
Total Number of Seats = 42.

Human Development Indices of District in West Bengal

Districts	*Health Index*	*Income Index*	*Education Index*	*Human Development Index (HDI)*	*HDI Rank*
Darjeeling	0.73	0.49	0.72	0.65	4
Jalpaiguri	0.61	0.38	0.60	0.53	10
Koch Bihar (Cooch Behar)	0.50	0.41	0.65	0.52	11
Dinajpur	0.62	0.39	0.53	0.51	13
Malda	0.49	0.36	0.48	0.44	17
Murshidabad	0.57	0.29	0.52	0.46	15
Birbhum	0.53	0.27	0.61	0.47	14
Bardhaman (Burdwan)	0.74	0.47	0.71	0.64	5
Nadia	0.65	0.41	0.66	0.57	9
North 24-Parganas	0.72	0.49	0.76	0.66	3
Hugli (Hooghly)	0.77	0.46	0.67	0.63	6
Bankura	0.67	0.26	0.62	0.52	11
Purulia	0.61	0.18	0.55	0.45	16
Medinipur (Midnapore-east and west together)	0.68	0.45	0.74	0.62	7
Haora (Howrah)	0.77	0.58	0.75	0.68	2
Kolkata	0.82	0.73	0.80	0.78	1
South 24-Parganas	0.71	0.40	0.68	0.60	8
West Bengal	0.70	0.41	0.69	0.61	8*

Source: *West Bengal Human Development Report 2004*, Government of West Bengal, Kolkata.

6
Conclusion

The decade 1937 to 1947 in Indian history, particularly the political activities of the province of Bengal is very important. It laid out a scenario that would never be eradicated from Bengali psyche. But it is to be remembered also that it was a culminating point for both Indian history in general and the history of Bengal in particular. The historical moments in all their ramifications encompass and their evolution and development are not linear as shown by some great minds. In contrast, the period was extremely tortuous and often meandering. The history for the last few centuries, more specifically the recent one or two, would bear out the fact, as indicated in the very beginning of this study. One example from the past is presented to substantiate the point. Incomplete and faulty planning of strategies to achieve or to mistime to carry out the missions may sometimes be disastrous for the cause in view. Here is an example from the 19th century. The French emperor Napoleon had to retreat from his Russian invasion at the heaviest cost with the loss of thousands of foot soldiers in the coldest winter in the Czarist Russia. In his heart of hearts, perhaps he realized for the first time that the word 'impossible' was still to be found in his dictionary. One of the greatest masters of the literary world, Tolstoy had to aim at justifying elements of determinism in the making of history in several of his masterpieces, particularly his magnum opus, *War and Peace*. He sought to find out the causal relationship of the great moments of history, failing of which, he talked about the design of nature that predetermined even the smallest events in the history of mankind.

They say history is made by man. But what happens if some unforeseen elements intrude in the process? The result is that in the making of history any indiscretion on the part of the makers of history is visited with nemesis in the successive generations. That was what happened to Napoleon in France after his abortive war effort in Russia. Was it not true of the makers of the history of India in general and Bengal in particular that has been unfolded in our study of the undivided Bengal and its subsequent development? Apart from larger issues in the ongoing process of history, even a small event in the life of people creates history. Let us think back of the colonial history in the Indian subcontinent and its great leaders like Gandhi, Jinnah and Jawaharlal Nehru Subhas Chandra Bose and others. Subhas had to leave Congress Party due to Gandhi's noncooperation in making the Working Committee of Congress (CWC) the main policy making body of the Congress. In the penultimate days of the Partition of India, the colonial power viciously bifurcated two of the larger Indian provinces — Punjab and Bengal was traumatic. The hangover still continues in Bengal and the flow of the Hindus from erstwhile East Pakistan and now Bangladesh trickles down to West Bengal after being tortured by the vicious Muslim fundamentalists backed by the ISI of Pakistan (as earlier West Pakistan).

There are no reasons to misunderstand the role played by Jawaharlal Nehru, Sardar Patel and other leaders of the Congress Working Committee including Gandhi — prisoner of the circumstances in those days of the mid-1940s. The reasons of their own as also because of the historic churning of Indian socio-political life in that point of time, the leaders could not or did not want to confront head on, with the messiah for his demand of Pakistan. The sad outpouring of the "Frontier Gandhi", Khan Abdul Ghaffar Khan to the Congress leaders against the vivisection of the secular India was a recorded fact in the history of the sub-continent.

The provinces of Bengal on the east and Punjab on the west have been still bearing the brunt of the Partition of India. Of course, the greatest impact was on Bengal for several reasons. West Bengal has been bearing the unbearable legacy of the Partition even today in the first decade of the 21st century. A very small unthinking comment or an eloquent silence on a very specific historic moment by the man in history or a simple gesture to wish away a possible solution may bring about situations that might have determined the fate of an entire generation or subsequent movements of history.

In retrospect, one may think of what transpired among the three leaders that Leonard Mosley narrated in his *Last Days of the British Raj*. In this connection, an earlier comment may be pointed out (www.channel4) the drama centres on the Viceroy's palace where Mountbatten, Jawaharlal Nehru, Mahatma Gandhi, Mohammed Ali Jinnah fought and squabbled over the future of India and where British officials were charged with creating a Muslim homeland on the basis of religion and to a small extent ethnicity. In his last effort to stall the division of the country, Gandhi was prepared to offer the Prime Ministerial chair of the undivided India to the Muslim League leader, Jinnah. Possibly, Jinnah was not unhesitant, but Nehru's eloquent silence and leaving the room, finally helped Jinnah charting out his next course of action. Jinnah had a political perspective and shrewd angle rather than his belief of a Two Nation theory that motivated him to create a state entirely at the final moments of his life and his chequered career all through. His skin deep faith in the theory of an exclusive Muslim homeland helped him in immensely mobilizing the elite sections of the Muslim communities in favour of a Sovereign Muslim State of Pakistan. A new history began to unfold that culminated in the vivisection of the country and its aftermath. And this was the final and lasting offer that the British political establishment of their imperial objectives was happy to leave behind as a painful legacy to the truncated Bengal.

To many a historians, the partition of Bengal was an inevitable fact of ongoing history of the subcontinent, as was Punjab on its western front. The problems of the West Punjabi refugees were fairly well tackled by the Indian leaders. The idea of the exchange of population to a large extent between the two nations and, division of properties appeared to be accepted. But these measures had not the chance to be effected perhaps for the misconceived notion of the Nehru-Liaquat Ali Pact, 1950. The refugees from the Pakistan dominated Punjab (Eastern part of Punjab) got all sorts of unhindered opportunities. But they were dispersed all over the country, although mostly around Delhi and the contiguous states. Because of their perseverance and the will to eke out a living with any job and capacity to face almost stoically any situation available to them was not a burning problem. As a result, the Sikh and the Punjabi Hindus were fairly well rehabilitated almost immediately after the Partition. But in case of the East Bengali Refugees, the exact opposite happened for various reasons that would come up in the present discussion of this study. In the last century (20th century), the Partition of Bengal occurred twice. The first one was in 1905. The second Partition was made in 1947. In both the cases, the British maneuver and bureaucratic machination in collaboration with the Muslim elites and their political organization, Muslim League, worked behind it. The British rulers, in order to exploit the Indian market as also to be politically present in proxy in Indian politico-economic space as also psyche of elites, wanted to communalize the country. In the first instance, the colonial master did not succeed. The Partition in 1905 was annulled within five years. But the communal seed between the two main communities – Hindu and Muslim, that they sowed eventually, came to fruition in the late 1930s and mid-1940s. The second Partition of Bengal was irreversible with severe impact on the subsequent history, geography, demography, political economy, party politics, electoral process and the popular culture in the Eastern part of Bengal, subsequently designated legally as West Bengal. In the ongoing processes of history, man always attempted to change its course wittingly or otherwise that helped in evolving politics in its varied manifestations. The processes were reciprocal that influenced the management of the economy of the state in a cultural perspective as seen in different developing countries in their development objectives and process.

Alongside, the study of political history, electoral process that sustained the democratic polity is a part of political history in West Bengal, which is starkly conspicuous by its absence in West Bengal's bordering state, be it the East Pakistan of the past or the present sovereign Bangladesh, at least till the Bangladesh Parliamentary Election in December 29, 2008.

East Bengal was renamed East Pakistan in 1956. Again, East Pakistan rebelled against Pakistani military rule when the democratic rights of the Bengalis of the eastern part were denied after 1970s election in Pakistan. But in the process of the birth of a new nation, Bangladesh, there came undesirable as well as unbearable demographic changes in West Bengal.

This trend has been still continuing, even long after the new entity Bangladesh — the bordering eastern neighbour of West Bengal came into being. The work on West Bengal since Partition in 1947 is not a theoretical discourse on history only. The focus is on its intertwining with the socio-cultural and political economy. Throughout our discussion in previous chapters, an attempt has been made to trace the politics of the state based on some of the historic moments and process and the electoral dynamics as well as the interplay of different political parties. It is the story of a truncated state that was economically deprived many a times for the last sixty years. The methodology followed is the same as it should be in such electro-history oriented political studies. It looked through various relevant governmental and legislative reports, newspaper stories of outstanding importance and personal memoirs and interviews as part of oral history. There is a number of older generation people scattered in different districts of West Bengal and nearer home at Kolkata, who themselves saw the redrawing of the map of Bengal in 1947 and felt the trauma, have narrated their stories. The comments and narratives of the participant observers are incorporated in different chapters of our discussions. As has been seen in the substantive part under discussion in the work, different strands of thought have been considered wherever it was necessary. To link electoral process in the historical perspective and interplay of the politics of important political parties in West Bengal since the first parliamentary and legislative election in 1952 and in the subsequent periods are shown in different chapters above. This study was intended to be normative substantially, but occasional empirical findings to substantiate the conclusions were taken into consideration as seen above in different Tables.

The study includes several phases of the evolution of politics in West Bengal. Many other factors are brought in to focus to appreciate the ongoing process of politics, society and economy. There are several elements determining the politics that are temporal and contemporary. The demography, geographical location, financial viability of the truncated state, the skill and capacity of the government of the day to manage the political economy, the part played by the opposition political parties in different point in time in securing the responses of the government, the cultural ambience and the attitude of the people, the influence of the popular culture on the evolving social movements, among others, constitute the core of a genuine and unbiased account of society and polity in the state. All these have been described as factually as possible in different chapters. We have been watching West Bengal in detail since Partition of Bengal in 1947. From this perspective, chapter one and chapter two as traced earlier are the starting ground.

Keeping in mind a modular representation in segments with a stitching thread within all through might have been better than a very simple narration of actual facts during the last sixty years or so have been made all through the five chapters in the work. That is why the scheme of the present study even in its totality has been divided into several phases as traced out in the following manner:

The partition of Bengal and its socio-economic and cultural fallouts are the greatest historic event in the eastern part of India. The coexistence of the two main communities — Hindu and Muslim was irretrievably disturbed by the "Great Calcutta killing" in 1946. In the penultimate stage, this incident determined the fate of the two communities, which lived peacefully in the past except certain transient conflicts with each other occasionally and particularly during the 1920s of the last century. The events, whether small or great during the early and mid-1940s, were so important that they left indelible print in the subsequent histories of the decades in the state, which became a truncated one, just one third of the undivided Bengal. But it had a population with insufficient economic resources, both agricultural and industrial for the people to live on. With it was added continuous influx of uprooted refugees from the border on the eastern side to this part of Bengal. It was a massive displacement of people not seen anywhere in the world. The British Barrister, Cyril Radcliff was possibly in a hurry by the official instructions of the British authorities, to divide the territory which earlier was economically complementing each other's' society and economy in Bengal. At that point of time, it was difficult for a cultural mix, as we have to experience today, between the original inhabitants of this part of Bengal and the incoming refugees in this part of the border over the years, even much beyond 1947.

The business communities were keen to take advantages of the fluid situations, both demographic and economic. They made their influence visibly felt in the political contents and even the structure. Dr. P.C. Ghosh — a Gandhian was chosen as the first Chief Minister just at the point of independence on August 15, 1947. He was a man of principle and was not ready to compromise. Within a few years, he had to resign for an alleged "irrational" letter to induct a man of Marwari community in the council of ministers, written by Gandhi to one of the Congress's cronies. Dr. Bidhan Chandra Roy became the next Chief Minister on January 1948. Earlier, Dr. Roy was offered the post of Indian Ambassador to the United States. Dr. Roy declined to accept the offer because of his professional compulsions side by side with his party and political attachment and ambition as well. However, Dr. Roy continued as the Chief Minister till his death in July 1, 1962. The Left politics was almost rudderless because it was carrying on a crusade against the Congress Party without any alternative policy orientation. Moreover, all the left political parties were at loggerhead with each other both ideologically and circumstantially till the end of the regime of Prafulla Sen, the Chief Minister after Dr. B.C. Roy. To them, without economic independence as understood through the prism, Marxist thought, political freedom as such was devoid of the contents of humanism. Therefore, to the Communists, it was a sham freedom that was achieved by the so-called Congress freedom fighters. The Congress Party, in their perception, was a party of the bourgeoisie and big landlords that could not be the proper instrument of change, upholding the cause of the poorer sections of society, which could best be served by the Communists.

Being inspired by the earlier *Tebhaga* movements on behalf of the peasant communities, the Communist Party became ambivalent about the Congress taking over the reign of the state. For it, the nature of the Indian state did not change with the change of the colonial rule. Again to begin with, to the Communist, the Indian Independence was a sham independence. They started resorting to slogan mongering, "*Ei azadi zhuta hai, bhulo mat bhulo mat(Independence is false, don't forget and is not to be forgotton).*" After the Constitution of India as Sovereign, Democratic Republic was adopted on January 26, 1950, the Communist Party of India were beset with their earlier position regarding the national bourgeoisie. By that time, the ban on the Communist Party in India was revoked. The Communists made up their mind to participate in the first democratic election in 1951-1952.

The Congress Party came to power with absolute majority under the leadership of Dr. Bidhan Chandra Roy, both in the Assembly elections 1952 and 1957. It was a decade of consolidation for the Congress Party, both nationally and regionally.

To tackle successfully the refugee problems, Dr. Roy took several steps. The leftist parties were in continuous conflict with the government with regard to the places of settlement of the refugees, and won the hearts of the pauperized displaced people from East Pakistan. The Communist Party's first salvo against the government was with regard to the "one paise increase in the tram fare in 1953." West Bengal became a chronic food shortage area. Industrial growth became insignificant due to insufficient raw materials that mostly fell within the territory of the East Pakistan. The opposition parties led by the Communists of different hues launched a severe food movement. The agricultural problems were aggravated by natural calamities, like the flood in 1959. Despite all, this was a decade of economic take off. Industrialization began after launching of the first and second Five Year Plans. The abolition of Zamindari system and its subsequent socio-economic impacts were remarkable.

The implementation of State Reorganization Commission was also important during this decade. Panchayat raj system, after the recommendations of Balbant Rao Mehta, was implemented. But the system did not work as desired and, ultimately, it became absolutely sick due to the lack of official encouragement, political corruptions and bureaucratic bungling. On the other hand, opposition's demand for annulling the suggestion of the Bengal-Bihar merger mooted by Dr. Roy and his counterpart Shreekrishna Singh, the Chief Minister of Bihar, was accepted. The anti-sentiment of the merger proposal was respected by Dr. Roy after a by-election defeat of the Congress candidate. It was as if some sort of a referendum through a by-election in the Northwest constituency in Calcutta. Not only the left parties, but by and large, the discerning people of the state were against the merger

Dr. Roy was conscious of and very concerned with the acute housing problems of the middle class people, particularly in the urban areas. By that time, smaller shanties and *busties* around Calcutta and the suburbs were coming up in an embarrassingly unplanned manner. To give moderately decent home to the middle and lower middle class people, the Salt Lake areas, till then marshy lands, were selected. After Roy, the Salt Lake area was really developed although Dr. Roy himself invited foreign experts to know as to how to lay the foundation of the project in a vastly marshy land and in perfect manner. Initially, the middle class people thought to get a right over the lands. But ultimately, the place became the hub of the richer sections of society and illegally the plots of lands and the houses built up there changed hands mostly to the novae rich and the Marwari business communities. Many of the families originally from East Pakistan by dint of their perseverance stood against many odds and established themselves and ultimately had the luck to settle themselves in Salt Lake. But their numbers were not large enough.

Now it is gorgeous and an aristocrat satellite city on the eastern part of Kolkata. Or in other words, it has become spectacular extension of the city of Kolkata. Almost at the end of the decade, the cultural mix between the people of original western part of Bengal and the incoming refugees from the East Bengal began taking a positive shape.

Factionalism is not new in politics of the Congress Party. In fact, leadership conflict and factionalism has been germane in Congress political party system since 1920s of the last century. The two Congress stalwarts, the successor Chief Minister Prafulla Chandra Sen after Dr. Bidhan Chandra Roy, and the State Congress President, Atulya Ghosh were of the same political wave length. But there arose occasional differences of opinion, particularly on administrative matters between Dr. Roy and the Congress Working Committee member, Atulya Ghosh. As regards the running of the party machineries, particularly at the block level and grassroots arena, Atulya Ghosh did not like the probing eyes of Dr. Roy in party matters. Sometimes, tension arose between the two. Ultimately, the problem was sorted out between them by the friendly intervention of Shree Bijay Singh Nahar (referred to in an earlier chapter). In case of Prafulla Chandra Sen, the successor of Dr. Roy, the running of the administration and the party under the control of Atulya Ghosh was not of any difficulty. But this time (1962-1967), the new Chief Minister did not have a smooth sailing. Food production in a food deficit state became abysmally low due to occasional drought and flood from mid 1950s to the entire period of the 1960s. Public distribution system was getting unmanageable despite stringent cordoning system in the districts throughout the state. But, it should be recognized that it was Shri P.C. Roy who brought back the ration system in the state to great relief of the lower middle class and poorer sections. The procurement policy and its actual implementation was not sufficient and the rationing system, particularly in urban and peri-urban areas, failed. Sporadic food riots were the order of the day and the left political parties capitalized the situations to their political advantage when police opened fire against people participating in food movements and sometimes food riots, this time in 1966. During this time, because of the factional fight between the two warring factions of the Congress units of Hooghly and Midnapur districts, the state Congress Party was almost vertically split. Ajay Mukherjee of Midnapore group left, to be exact, was driven out from the Congress under the leadership of the duo Atulya-Prafulla. Ajay Mukherjee and his comrade in arms, Sushil Dhara mentored by Satish Samanta, the most respected leader of the "Quit India Movement" fame in Midnapur formed his own party, the Bangla Congress. In spite of factionalism, the Congress system was open and liberal to the extent it was possible. The process of governance might not be up to the expected level to popular perceptions, but there was no democratic deficit that might be felt after several decades from 1970s to the recent times (till May, 2011). There was scarcity of politics, but not politics of scarcities as one experienced in the state from 1977); although a contemporary foreign scholar was of a view that the Congress government was unresponsive at that point in time, i.e., earlier Congress regime in West Bengal.

After the Indo-China border war in 1962, the Communist Party of India was split on ideological questions into two parties. The original, Communist Party of India (CPI) retained its old identity. A new Communist Party, coming out from its original form established its new and vigorous presence as the Communist Party of India (Marxist) or in short CPI (M). Both of these two Marxist parties were at daggers drawn with each other. But in the crucial election in 1967, the two groups of left parties formed two electoral fronts in the Fourth General election in 1967 under the leadership of Ajay Mukherjee and his newly formed Bangla Congress. For the first time in the history of the state, the Congress Party was defeated. In the defeat of the Congress government, the "radicalism" of the past found its new appearance in a different garb. A social transformation, as it were, was on the anvil. After that, several governments on the basis of electoral alliances among political parties of different hues came to power in the state. But none survived for a longer period of time except, the LF coalition and government. The first United Left Front (ULF), Progressive United Left Front (PULF) was formed and led by CPI and the second United Front was led by the CPI (M). Humayun Kabir was instrumental in coalescing the two groups and helped stitching the two fronts to form the First United Front (UF). The politics of the time made the First UF very short lived. The Second United Front in 1969 came with a thumping numbers, but could not stay in office as expected. After a spell of President Rule for the second time, a very fragile and short lived Democratic Alliance government led again by Ajay Mukherjee came up. After the first UF government came to hold power, another split occurred in the CPI (M). A new party, the Communist Party of India (Marxist-Leninist) or CPI (ML) was formed on 1 May 1967. This split was really a blow to the CPI (M). It did not believe in electoral and parliamentary politics. Immediately after its reincarnation, quite distinct from the objectives of the CPI (M), it launched a series of violent movements of individual annihilations. The main target was to attack the *Jotdars* in different rural areas of the state and their sympathizers. Different government establishments and police personnel were attacked every now and then in the state. Frequent violence was perpetrated by organized groups. The Naxalites, in the name of a political party, indulged in inter group and intra-group conflict, which were anathema to the very definition of politics itself. This vengeful group and the 'so-called instant' revolting parties could not be an alternative vehicle of politics. This period of West Bengal history might possibly be designated as the imported variety of 'Politics of violence in West Bengal.' The movement started at Naxalbari, very near to Siliguri in the district of Darjeeling, one of the six districts of North Bengal. It was actually a reaction of the extremist group of the CPI (M) against the UF's land reforms minister, Hare Krishna Konar's promise. He promised to the extremists within the party that to participate in election in bourgeois parliament is transient. Shree Konar was a fire-eating leader once the CPI (M) came to power. Being a heavy weight minister of the First UF government holding the most important portfolio of his choice in a peaceful parliamentary system, he ate his words and woke up from his revolutionary dreams to the reality of a parliamentary democratic system. He could not or did not keep his promise. The soft option to him at that point of time was simply to backtrack from his earlier position and promises to his colleague regarding the problems of land in a predominantly agricultural state and the land acquisition question for the government.

As already hinted above, the Naxalites further proliferated in different groups. They could not ignite the younger generations of the populace in the state with their revolutionary ideas and surreptitious activities. They wanted to preach cultural Maoist thesis, but failed. During this period, the education system was in disarray. The Vice-Chancellor of a Calcutta based University (Jadavpur University) was murdered and people of the street, though afraid of their life and property, began hating awful revolt and denounced the Naxalite violence. A cultural transformation indeed! The cultural activities and their various manifestations that were found earlier with rapidly expanding space in the state came almost to a halt. The already tattered economy of the state was in shambles during this period and even thereafter.

In the end of 1971, Bangladesh, which was known as East Pakistan earlier, was dominated ever since its inception by its western part, became independent from Pakistan after a gruesome genocide and historic fight by freedom fighters aroused by Sk. Mujibur Rahman. But during the Bangladesh war, the economy of West Bengal was shattered due to the Bangladeshi immigrants, both Hindus and Muslims coming to West Bengal. More than nine million people had to flee to West Bengal in India and the state of Tripura was also affected. The demographic map of West Bengal irretrievably changed for the worse. It went on for months together. India had no other alternative. Indira Gandhi appealed to the USA and other Western countries to come forward to give succor to the devastated country and the unfortunate people there. She campaigned to all those countries for recognizing the birth of this new Nation. Even Communist China played a different game. Except Soviet Russia, none of the big States was sympathetic to the cause of the newly born nation of Bangladesh. Before that, India signed a twenty year treaty with Soviet Russia on August 20, 1971. India had to depend upon Soviet Russia, and its anticipated help, even against the USA, with regard to Indo-Pak war on behalf of Bangladesh. Indira Gandhi had to retaliate against Pakistan for its undeclared war against India in its western part. She immediately recognized Bangladesh as a Nation State and won the war against Pakistan for Bangladesh on December 16, 1971. Otherwise, socio-economic and political scenario in India would have been worse. With her victorious image, Indira Gandhi went in for parliamentary election that won her nearly 2/3 seats of parliament. It was a psychological boost for the people of India, the consequences of which were many. In 1972, Siddhartha Shankar Ray by just utilizing three factors, namely, (1) Mrs. Gandhi's victory in Bangladesh war, (2) electorate's disillusion of the negative politics of the leftist parties, particularly the aggressive politics of the CPI (M) and, (3) depending upon the youth power, aggressively went in for West Bengal Assembly election. He won the electoral battle having 216 seats and another 35 seats by the CPI in loose alliance; but this election was perceived by many as unfair and rigged. Dr. Ashok Mitra publicly denounced the "results as having rigged"; and in the next Assembly election in 1977, when the Left Front took over, Dr. Mitra being a Finance Minister said on the floor of the House that the Assembly (1972-77) was "*Chorether Bidhan Sabha*", i.e., the house of the thieves. However, in 1972 election, the CPI (M) was badly mauled and won only 14 seats, which was really unnatural. It did not participate in the legislative business for the next five years in protest, but did not dare launching any popular movements in the state. With the help of the elite police establishment, Mr. Ray destroyed the Naxalite presence in the state and brought peace all around. He became infamous for his indiscretion, but really did what he wanted to. During his period as the Chief Minister, he encouraged his efficient and able ministers to enact certain notable legislations, like the *Panchayat Raj* Acts, the Land Reforms (Amendment) Acts, CMDA Acts, Comprehensive Area Development Projects (CADP) later renamed as (CADC) or a Corporation, which were not timely implemented, first because of factionalism among his younger colleagues and later, due to his involvement with the central leadership in implementing the infamous provisions of the Internal Emergency clause in the Constitution on June 25, 1975 in the dead of night. This continued till March 1977 parliamentary election. Freedom of speech and expressions were curtailed and press censorship enforced. As a consequence, the Congress's Assembly seats were reduced from 216 to 17 only. During the whole period, the CPI was always in tandem with the Congress, both nationally and regionally. In West Bengal, the Congress and the CPI formed a pre-election political coalition named as Progressive Democratic Alliance (PDA), but the CPI did not participate in the Cabinet making. It was an informal, but written understanding. They stood against the "fascist forces led by Jayprakash Narayana", as they vented their spleen, but they themselves acted likewise. Democratic values and argumentations were given a good bye. The government of Mrs. Gandhi and her collaborators in the states by resorting to changing democratic institutional ethos for the sake of "discipline" wanted to bring about a cultural reorientation, but failed miserably`. The Left Front (LF) is the combination of left parties or a political coalition (with a difference having surplus majority all the time 1977-2011, when the TMC came to power, except in 2001 under the leadership of Buddhadeb Bhattacharjee). The LF has been ruling the state uninterruptedly for the last three and a half decades. During Siddhartha Shankar regime, the CPI (M) had to go in hiding as the leaders of CPI (M) claimed. All its front organizations, like the Kisan Sabha, Student Front, Youth Organization and Trade Union were almost in hibernation. In the early 1977s, Jayprakash brought all the opposition political parties — left, right and the centrist under a common umbrella to fight out the misrule of the Congress both at the Centre and the states. The CPI (M) came out in the open and agreed to be included in the Janata Party Coalition during the parliamentary election in 1977. It was a grand victory for the rainbow coalition. But the coalition broke down because of over bearing attitude of Janata Party leader, Prafulla Chandra Sen. Immediately, the left parties except the CPI (initially though) formed the LF and as a political coalition fought the Assembly election 1977 and won handsomely. The Janata Party was in disarray and the Congress was decimated. From now on, there was no looking back for the LF. The first LF government and the left parties gave an indication that they would not go in for political vendetta. But one has to remember still now that the LF led by Jyoti Basu surreptitiously carried on the Marichjhapi massacres in January, 1979 and Bijan Setu murders of 17 Sanyasins of Ananda Margis (a religious community) on January April, in 1982. CPI (M)'s objectives were to entrench themselves in the rural areas to reach the people irrespective of their caste, creed and community. This was the first step of the LF to build up a "Social Coalition" in support for the subsequent Left Front regimes. Most possibly, this sort of social engineering helped the LF in coming back to power again and again till 2006. The last Assembly elections in the state were a novel experiment indeed. During this period, the LF took two historic decisions: (1) to complete the unfinished agenda of land reforms (enacted earlier by the Congress regime) and *Operation Barga,* (2) Implementation of the *Panchayat Raj* legislation enacted by the previous government and deciding for three tier *Panchayat* elections. In early 1980s, the LF went in for elections of all the urban governing bodies. These three measures brought about enormous dividends that helped the LF government to continue for such a long period of time. As a result of fragmented opposition parties and their insignificant presence in the rural hinterland, no significant social and political movements against the existing political establishment in the state grew up for the last several years, till the days of Singur and Nandigram in the late 2006s and early 2007s.

Uninterruptedly, the LF led by the CPI (M), the largest party in the state enjoying surplus majority in the LF coalition all through, has been ruling the state with all authority at its command. During this time, all the Assembly elections held in 1977, 1982, 1987, 1991, 1996, 2001 and 2006 took place. The LF in 2001 Assembly election, led again by the CPI (M) having only 143 seats, five seats below the benchmark, took over as it was. Buddhadeb Bhattacharjee took up the mettle as the Chief Minister after Jyoti Basu, just six months before the election of 2001. Therefore, the Chief Minister Buddhadeb babu was at the helm during this election. From 1982 to 1987 till the Bofors scam came to light, the Chief Minister raised the bogey that at any time, the Congress governments at the Centre, first led by Smt. Indira Gandhi and then Rajiv Gandhi might take over the reign of the state government. It might have been for alerting as well as mobilizing the LF supporters, CPI (M)'s frontal organizations that penetrated in most of the societal spaces in the state. During three parliamentary elections in 1984, 1998 and 1999, the opposition parties, the Congress, the Trinamool Congress and BJP combine made some dent in the social arena. An oligopolistic political coalition led by the CPI (M) ruled through all the years in West Bengal.

People wanted some sort of a change in the structure and contents of politics and ruling alignments of the left parties. But belying the calculations of many and even beyond the expectation of the CPI (M), the LF won the 2006 Assembly election with 235 seats. During this long period, some outstanding events, some of them negative, but mostly remarkable, came out in bolder focus. Jyoti Basu came to be regarded as the guardian angel during the politically volatile time at the federal stage. He was asked by different regional parties to be the Prime Minister to be supported by the Congress in 1997. But his party vetoed the proposition. Not only to Jyoti Babu, but to the discerning Bengali society at large, it was a "Himalayan Blunder." Secondly, the LF propped up the United Progressive Alliance (UPA-I) – a minority coalition government of the Congress Party from 2004 to the middle of 2008.

Some of the decisions of the successive LF government raised ripples of protest even within the front. The government ultimately had to retract. The social impact of many a decisions was enormous, some of them were not positive though. It was really a feat on the part of the single majority party CPI (M) to stitch the coalition partners together even in the face of grave provocation. In course of time, many of the important portfolios like Industry, Health, Housing, and *Panchayat* were taken over by the CPI (M) from the hands of influential partners like the Forward Bloc (FB) and the Revolutionary Socialist Party (RSP). The coalition partners made occasional noises, but could not get away. Same was the case when the Singur and Nandigram issues came in the forefront in the late 2006. The opposition parties and a considerable part of civil society groups and several intellectuals belonging to different professions launched socio-political and cultural movements against the "pro-industrial policy of Buddhadeb Bhattacharya."

Finally, many socio-cultural dimensions of the ongoing political process in the state over a period of many decades have been brought into proper focus in earlier chapters as the politico-historical discourse progressed. The socio-political space appeared to be a mosaic of many hues to the observers. In the course of discussion, special emphasis has also been laid on the political economy of development over the years in this "problem state" of West Bengal. Ultimately, a change has taken place in the end. The people of the state were restive. The huge amount of fertile land acquisition under 1894 Act in Bhangar, Rajarhat and then Singur, Nandigram and finally Nayachar was protested by the peasants' communities mostly belonging to the Scheduled Castes, Scheduled Tribes and above and above all the Muslim communities. The protest movements spread throughout the state. By and large, people were against the land policy of the CPI (M), invitation to the indigenous industrialists, like Tata and the foreign investor infamous Beni Santosha for almost peanut investment in the state in exchange for a huge amount of lands and other privileges given to them, was sufficient indications to the CPI (M) that this time the LF would have to go. The protest movements got booster from the able leadership of the opposition leader, Ms. Mamata Banerjee of the TMC. She was always active, daring and extremely energetic, who began her first salvo against the CPI (M) led LF government right in 1990. At that time, she was in the Congress Party. After that, she formed her TMC in January 1, 1998. During the late 2006, she got hints that the Trinamool coalition was getting genuine foothold in the electoral arenas at all levels of society after the three tier *Panchayat Raj* elections in 2008. Finally, she was able to garner support from a group of civil society people. Mamata Banerjee was actually the face of the change that the civil society groups perceived at that point of time. The 2009 parliamentary election was handsomely won by the Trinamool and Congress with seat adjustment that ultimately whitewashed the CPI (M) led LF in 2011 Assembly election in the state, removing 34 year old ageing CPI (M) led LF government. It was actually a victory for the ordinary working people and the poorer sections of the peasants in the state. Mamata Banerjee acted really as a catalytic agent. It is a victory for the alternative coalition that Mamata had the capacity to forge. The vote share between the TMC — Congress and the LF was more than eight per cent as shown in earlier chapter. It was really a conclusive victory for Mamata Banerjee. She took office in May 20, 2011. Against heavy odds, she began her saga for all round development of the state. Her outstanding performances were to bring back peace and harmony in the entire area of Jangal Mahal in the western part of the state and solve the problems of Darjeeling Hills. After two and a half decades, she was the first Chief Minister, who was able to contain the identity problems of the Gorkhas.

The Central Coalition government, to be exact the minority government, led by the Congress Party by adopting a dubious method, i.e., by flouting all the Rules of Business of the Houses, passed the Telengana Bill with haste that bifurcated Andhra Pradesh by voice votes only in the midst of unprecedented ruckuses in the Houses. After a lot of persuasion and positive communication, both political and administrative, the Chief Minister was quite able to contain the agitating Gorkha leaders by creating Gorkhaland Territorial Administration (GTA) within the state by a tripartite agreement. The new government led by Mamata Banerjee understood the miserable state of political economy of development left behind by the LF government. So she began her activities in every field of the economy on the overarching development plank. She overlooked nothing. Through her process of development in every aspect of economy proceeded by utilizing both human and social capital to achieve the goals that were underestimated by the CPI (M) to their utter dismay in 2009 and 2011.

The general public is really apprehensive. There is already an audible whisper among the leaders, who supported Gorkhaland as a separate state; they will still be happy when they find the bifurcation of Andhra Pradesh becoming a reality. If the Central Government can fulfill the demand for a Telengana state by bifurcating Andhra Pradesh before the 2014 election, then why the same government will not heed to the outstanding demand for a Gorkhaland. If the problem arises, the Chief Minister will have to confront the situations she faced time and again in the past two and a half years.

This is also to be noted that the administrative acumen of the new Chief Minister has brought her in this new height of power, because her political instinct and foresight are undeniable. She established herself and her party TMC, as it appears at present, at an all-time high position. The left parties, particularly, the CPI (M) seem to be demoralized and their grassroots workers seeing the development activities of Mamata, who is always trying to improve lot of people at large, are continuously coming into the fold of the TMC. The state Congress Party leaders are still unable to appreciate the potentialities of Mamata Banerjee as the Chief Minister and every now and then, they are jeering her. The Lok Sabha election is in the offing. The political position of the Congress is pitiable. Every now and then, the Congress party-men and workers are entering the Trinamool Congress Party. On the other hand, Mamata Banerjee, her own party and many others like Anna Hazare think three months before the election that Mamata is going to play a very important role in the national politics after the election of 2014.

Endnotes

CHAPTER 1

1. Leo Tolstoy, *War and Peace*, translated in English by Constance Garnett, published by Random House, The Modern Library of the World's Best Books, New York date of publication not mentioned.
2. *Ibid*
3. Annadasankar Roy, *Mukta Banger Smriti* (a Bengali autobiography), Mitra and Ghosh Publishers, Kolkata, 1405 (Bengali year).
4. Amalendu Dey, *Fazlul Haque O Pakistan Prastab*, Ratna Prakasan, Calcutta, 1970.
5. Interview, Amalendu Dey, September 21, 2004.
6. *Ibid*
7. Madhu Dandavate, told this author in his south Avenue Apartment sometimes in 1983 that he had heard Khan Abdul Gaffar Khan—the Frontier Gandhi referring to it while in India for a while in the !970s. This is also in the air and people either by conviction or wishful thinking like to believe that Jinnah understood his wrong step in the very critical stage of the deciding decade of British Indian history in dividing India into a Muslim Pakistan and a secular India with the vastness of its territory.
8. Stanley Wolpert, *Jinnah of Pakistan*, Oxford University Press (PB), 2002.
9. Frederick Burrows, Reports to Viceroy Wavell, 1946
10. Broomfield JH, *Elite Conflict in Plural Society Twentieth-Century Bengal*, Oxford University Press, Bombay, 1968.
11. Prasanto Kumar Chatterjee, *The Cripps Mission: An In-depth Study*, Minerva Associates, Kolkata 2004
12. Arther Herman, *Gandhi and Churchill: The Epic Rivalry that Destroyed an Empire and forged our Age*, Bantam, and New York 2008.
13. *http;//en.wikiquote.org/wiki/Winston_Churchill#disputed_quotations*
14. *Ibid.*
15. William L. Shirer, *Gandhi: A Memoir*, ABACUS, Great Britain, 1981, p. 211.
16. PK. Chatterjee, *The Cripps Mission*, *op. cit.*
17. V.P. Menon, *The Transfer of Power in India*, Orient Longman Limited, First Published in 1957; Reprint, Calcutta, 1957, p. 135.
18. R.J. Moore, *Churchill, Cripps, and India, 1939-45*, Oxford University Press, Oxford, 1979, pp. 114-32, as quoted by Ian Henderson Douglas, and edited by Gail Minault and Cristian W. Troll, *Abul Kalam Azad: An Intellectual and Religious Biography*, Oxford University Press, Delhi,1988, p. 294.

19. Sir Strafford Cripps as quoted by V.P. Menon, *Ibid*, p. 135
20. V.P. Menon, *op. cit.*
21. *Ibid*, p. 136.
22. Gandhi's statement as quoted by V.P. Menon, *The Transfer of Power in India*, *op. cit.,* and p. 136.
23. *Ibid*, p. 136.
24. Jajabar, *Dristipat* (a discourse on Cripps Mission in the context Japanese invasion by aerial bombing in different places in Bengal formatted in a Bengali novel), New age, Calcutta, First Edition, 1946.
25. V.P. Menon, The Transfer of Power in India, *op. cit.,* p. 140.
26. From, *Harijan* (Patrika used to be edited by MK. Gandhi), Weekly, as quoted by Menon, *Ibid*,
27. *Ibid*, pp. 140-41.
28. Maulana Abul Kalam Azad, India Wins Freedom, Orient Longman, Madras, 1988.
29. Nassim Yousaf, "Hidden facts behind British India's freedom: a scholarly look into Allama Mashrqi and Quaid-e-Azam's political conflict ", p. 137 as quoted in *http://en. Wikipedia.org/wiki/Quit_India_Movement* accessed on September 16, 2011.
30. V.P.Menon, *The Transfer of Power In India*, *op. cit.* p. 141.
31. Interview, Arun Banerjee, retired Professor of History, Calcutta University, September 7, 2011.
32. Interview, Jayanta Kumar Ray, Centenary Professor of International Relations, Department of History (retired), Calcutta University, September 21, 2011; see also his recent publication, *India's Foreign Relations,* Routledge, New Delhi 2011.
33. Quoted by Dhanjay Bhat, *The Tribune*, Chandigarh Sunday, February 12, 2006 Chandigarh; *see also* Sukha Ranjan Sengupta, *Bangasanghar Ebong*, Naya Uddyog, Kolkata, 2002; Shree Sengupta quoted frequently from A Campbell John, *Mission with Mount batten*, Paperback edition, New Age International Ltd, New Delhi, 1997.
34. *Ibid.*
35. R.C. Majumdar, *Three Phases of India's Struggle for Freedom*, Bharatiya Vidya Bhavan,. Bombay, 1967, pp. 58-59.
36. *Ibid.*
37. Informal discussions (part of oral history) with several intellectuals, (Prafulla Chandra Sen, Atulya Ghosh, Sushil Dhara, Ajoy Mukherjee, Hossanur Rahman, even Jayaprakash Narayana in March 1977, while this author was writing his *Legislative Control over Public Administration*), and Anisuzzaman Professor Chattogram University, in September 1971 we had regular meetings with Anisuzzaman and others in our office of Bangladesh Sahayak Samiti in Darbhanga Building, Calcutta University, and other political activists at different points of time.
38. This is the opinion held by many an intellectual of Dhaka and Rajshahi Universities who were nearing the age of 70 in their personal discussions while this author visited Bangladesh in the December of 2008; even old timer Indians both Hindu and Muslim still like to believe that Jinnah realized his short sightedness after a short stint at the highest office, while he was in his terminal stage completely at mercy of his trusted lieutenants. This was the opinion of a few senior journalists now retired. Mr. Jinnah the founder and first Governor General of Pakistan in the last few months till his death was incapacitated and had to depend upon his prime minister Liaquate Ali Khan and others was really a solitary man looked after by his sister Fatima Jinnah. It

was very difficult to know the utterances of Jinnah, which might be heard or noted by Fatima. Therefore, Jinnah's perceptions as voiced about Indo-Pak partition the dynamics that follow was not possibly recorded; it may even regard as hearsay. In unfolding the history of a certain period not only the published records and archival documents but certain stories, ongoing oral whispers and gossips might play a part.

39. Interview, Sushil Dhara was making a presentation in a conversational mood on October 2, 1996 (on the occasion of the birth day celebration of Gandhi) at the Gandhi Peace Foundation, Kolkata.
40. Hiteshranjan Sanyal, *Swarajer Pathe*, Papyrus, Kolkata, 1994, pp. 131-67.
41. Mahasweta Devi (ed), B*ortika*, the special number dedicated to the memory of Maitreyo Ghatak, July-December, 2003.
42. Shukhendu Sekhar Roy, a post edit about P.C. Joshi and the communist movement, Sambad Pratidin, November 16, 2011; P.C. Jhoshi was the General Secretary of the Communist Party of India from 1935 till he was replaced in the 1950; the Communist party was banned by the British Government; the ban was lifted in 1942 when it vowed that it would help the British Government in its war efforts; to this effect Joshi wrote a number of letters in 1942, 1943 and 1944 to Maxwell promising everything necessary for the British forces in India fighting against Japan; again some of them were even acted as police informers so that the police might apprehend the local leaders in the forefront of the 'Quit India' movements; the Communist Party was also instrumental to belittle the character of Subhas Chandra Bose as fascist and, accused him as 'quisling', and the running dog of the imperial forces fighting against allied powers now Soviet
43. As quoted by Amalesh Tripathi, *Swadhinata Sangrame Bharater Jatio Congress(1885-1947),* Ananda Publishers Ltd, Kolkata, first edition, 1397 (Bengali Year), pp. 333.
44. Amalesh Tripathi, *Ibid*, p. 333.
45. *Ibid*, a number of articles came out in the special number penned by Mahasweta Devi, documents gathered by Maitreyo Ghatak, Reporter Madhu, *1946-47 er Tebhaga Andolener kaekti dik and kichu prasna, Krishak Andolan o gathan samparke Medinipur;* Dr. Purnendu Ghosh, *Tebhaga and Ashok Bose; Tebhaga Andolan and Adibasi samaj; composition of three songs on the movement at Dinajpur.*
46. Bijon Bhattacharjee (a great theatre personality during 1940s and 50s), *Nabanna*, first staged this play of his on stage in 1944
47. Debabrata Biswas, *Bratyajaner Rudha Sangit*, Deys Publications (recent reprint) Kolkata, 2005; a remarkable stage drama based on this book depicting lives and times of these people directed by Bratya Basu is occasionally shown in different Kolkata theatre halls in recent times.
48. Oral History; Shri Hem Chandra Chattopadhyay, the Headmaster of the Baliakandi H.E. School during the pre-partition years. This was a remote but well developed village in Faridpur district that has been given the status of an Upa Zilla now in Bangladesh. Hem Babu left the school after Partition and any how managed to survive. After quite a time and with a lot of effort he joined a school at Sodepur near Kolkata as an ordinary teacher. Sometimes in 1960s while I was still a University student in coincident meet he told me the story and several other incidents that took place in 1940s and then on.
49. Interview, of Hem Chandra Chattopadhyay, *Ibid*.
50. Narayan Gangopadhyay, *Shilalipi,* Ananda, Kolkata, 1950; Tarasanka

Bandyopadhyay, Monoj Mitra and many others touched on the historic movements and their repercussions in Bengal in some of their novels.

51. Bishnu Basu, "Smiti Nie Dhaka" (a reprinted essay), Madhumoy Pal (ed), Deshbhag: *Binas o Binirman*, Gangchil, Kolkata, 2011, pp. 21-38.
52. Bankim Chandra Chattopadhyay, *Anandamath*, in *Bankim Rachanaboli* (2 volumes), published by Government of West Bengal, Calcutta, 1986.
53. *http://www.oldindianphotos.in/2009/12/bengal-famine-part-1.html*
54. Usha Rani Chaudhuri was telling the story of the Tatallisher Mantanttar (1943 or Banglar 1350 er Mannantar to her grand children when the price of the rice was soaring high during the early nineties, Kolkata, 1992.
55. Bimal Kar, *Deoyal*, Ananda Publishers, 1989.
56. Bibhuti Bhusan Bandyopadhyay, *Asani Sanket* a Satyajit Film,
57. Amartya Sen, *Poverty and Famines*: *An Essay on Entitlement and Deprivation*, Oxford University Press, Delhi, 1981, p. 82.
58. *Biplabi, Sankha* (issue) 45, May 15, 1943, translation mine.
59. *Ibid*, p. 159: quoted by Hiteshranjan Sanyal, *op. cit.*
60. http://en.wikipedia.org, *op. cit.,* accessed on November 20, 2011
61. Sankar Ghose, *Jawaharlal Nehru, a biography*, Allied Publishers, 1993, p. 111.
62. Bengal Famine of 1943-Wikipedia, the free encyclopedia, see http://en.wikipedea.org/ *op. cit.,* accessed on 25.11.2011.
63. Madhusree Mukherjee, *Churchill's Secret War*, Tranqueber, (an Indian imprint), Daryagunj, New Delhi, 2010.
64. *Ibid*, p. 207.
65. Amartya Sen, *Poverty and Famines: An Essay on Entitlement and Deprivations*, Clarendon Press, Oxford, 1981.
66. Abul Kasem Fazlul Huq, *Bengal Today*, Gupta and Rahaman, Calcutta, 1944; the original work was published by the University of California Press; a renowned journalist Sukharanjan Sengupta who were personally known to many of the Bengali politicians of those days gave a detailed and vivid account of the eventful period of Undivided Bengal in his book *Bangasanhar Ebong*, *op. cit.* pp. 31-36.
67. Sukharanjan Sengupta, *Bangasanhar Ebong* (Bengali), Naya uddog, Kolkata, 2002.
68. Nitish Sengupta, *Land of Two Rivers*, (A history of Bengal from Mahabharata to Mujib), Penguin Books India Pvt., Ltd., New Delhi, 2011, p. 422.
69. Ram Chandra Guha, A review as printed on the front cover of Madhusree Mukherjee's book, Churchill's *Secret War*, *op. cit.*
70. Dr. Jayanta Chaudhuri, "The Political and Journalistic Ideas of Subhas Chandra Bose", an unpublished Thesis submitted for a Degree of PhD to the Calcutta University in 2008.
71. Jayanta Chaudhuri, *Netaji Gelen Khothaye*, Pandulipi 1st edition, 1995.
72. Purabi Roy, *The Search for Netaji: New Findings*, Purple Peacock Books and Arts, Kolkata, 2011.
73. Patrick French, *Liberty or Death: India's Journey to Independence and Division*, Harper Collins Publishers India Pvt Ltd, New First Indian Edition, New Delhi 1998, p. 209.
74. Jayanta Chaudhuri, *op. cit.*
75. In course of the field work a large number of elderly refugees living in colonies like Bijoygarh, Bikramgarh Garia, Baranagar, Bonhooghly, Sodhpur, Ranaghat,

Barrackpur, Khardah, Asok Nagar, Nabadwip, Krishnanagar etc. in Kolkata, south Bengal districts and around as also the refugees now living in Coochbihar (in the language of the original inhabitants the East Bengal refugees are only 'Bhatias), Jalpaiguri, Siliguri, Uttar Dinajpur and Dakshin Dinajpur expressed their resentment frequently against Nehru and other Congress leaders. Even today they can not forgive the then Congress leaders; more so because of the Nehru-Liaquat Ali pact that negated the exchange of population and properties in the eastern side of India. This Pact failed to serve the interests of refugees in eastern India in any manner whatsoever. They were to eke out a living by absolutely insufficient government doles for many years. The colonies now look not at all what they did earlier. New buildings have come up in place of shanties in marshy lands with bushes here and there. The CPI (M) came to power with surplus majority along with other left parties being supported by the refugees in a big way. The LF promised that it would settle the refugees everywhere by giving them permanent land rights. But for reasons of their own political and electoral possibly, the CPI (M) and other left parties did not settle the problems intending to make the refugees dependant on the CPI (M) permanently. But the table appeared to be turned after many years in power in the three successive election; panchayat elections in 2008, parliamentary election in 2009 and finally West Bengal Assembly election in 2011.

76. Interview, Sunil Roy Chaudhuri, a Calcutta University Professor of Political Science and expert in the history of the Constitutional Development in India, August 15, 2008.
77. *Ibid.*
78. Cabinet Mission Plan, June 16, 1946; its just a summary form of the essentials of the original Programme culled out from various entries of the then Viceroy, Lord Wavell, *Wavell The Viceroy's Journal* (ed) Penderel Moon, Oxford University Press, Delhi, (first Indian impression), 1977.
79. Lord Wavell's Note for Cabinet mission, 25 June, 1946, Appendix VII, pp. 91-2, *The Viceroy's Journal*, Oxford University Press, Delhi, 1977.
80. *Ibid.*
81. Rajinder Puri, "A Failed Nation", *The Statesman*, Kolkata edition, January 11, 2011.
82. Patrick French, Dear or Liberty, *op. cit.* p. 256.
83. Wavell *The Viceroy's Journal*, *op. cit.,* Epilogue, p. 457.
84. Dilip Banerjee, *Election Recorder: An Analytical Reference, West Bengal (1862-2009),* Star Publishing House, Kolkata, Revised Edition, November 2009; surprisingly such a detailed statistical as well as analytical compendium has been worked out by the single handed effort of a scholarly but solitary individual.
85. Patrick French, *op. cit.* p. 322.
86. Sankar Ghosh, *Hastantar, (3 volumes in Bengali),* Ananda Publishers, Kolkata, 2001.
87. Prafulla Roy, *Sata Dharoye Bohejaye*, Karuna, Kolkata 2010: the book was serialized in *Saptahik* (weekly) *Bartaman*, for nearly one and half years during 2005-06.
88. Such stories were narrated to me by my maternal uncle while I was lower class student during 1950s. He used to go to the station to collect information about the relatives and familiar people from his own village in Kumarkhali, now in Bangladesh. My maternal uncle, to whom I was sent during the early age of my life to pursue my studies at Howrah, had to go to the Sealdah Station to receive my parents, as also occasionally to receive his people from his locality, during later part of 1950s.
89. Prafulla Roy, *Keya Patar Nauka, Karuna Prakashni,* Kolkata, 1969.

90. In course of our conversations during last several days, Kashinath Kar (the owner of a scholarly and quality book shop) who migrated to India in January 1949 had left behind his parents and other members in Dhaka to seek a living in India with the thought that once he was settled here others of his joint family would get a foothold here. But it never happened. Before the Passport system was introduced between the two the countries around mid 1950s Kasi Babu used to visit to East Pakistan every year. Even now he used to go to Bangladesh. When sitting in a corner of the coffee house in Jadavpur opposite Jadavpur University, in a very sad mood he used to tell the tales of the horrible experiences the Hindu families who were unable to cross over the border had been undergoing in Pakistan. Even the present situation was no better till the Jatiya Sansad was elected in December 29, 2008. Minorities had been persecuted after Sheik Mujib was assassinated in August 15, 1975.
91. Anthony Mascarenhas, *The Rape of Bangladesh*, Vikas Publications, Delhi, 1971.
92. Debajyoti Roy, *Keno Udbastu Hote Holo*, Publisher: Shri Syamaprasad De Pal, Ultadanga, 1st edition, Kolkata, 2001.
93. Tathagata Roy, *My People Uprooted*, Ratna Prakashan, Kolkata, 2002.
94. Prafulla Chakraborty, *The Marginalmen*, Naya Udyog, Calcutta, 1999.
95. Shri Hiranmoy Bandyopadhyay, *Udbasthu*, Sahitya Sansad, Kolkata, 1970.
96. *Ananda Bazaar Patrika,* February 16, 1957; the letter was written by Gandhi to the would be Chief Minister Dr. Ghosh some time in June 1947; in 1957 Dr. Ghosh joined a new party Praja Socialist Party (PSP) to become a Chief Ministerial candidate immediately at the time of Independence; In 1957 before the Assembly election Dr. Ghosh referred to the matter in a public meeting, but while challenged by the then Provincial Congress President Dr. Atulya Ghosh, in a press conference Dr. Prafulla Ghosh distributed the photo copy of the letter, which he was able to find out in the Museum Gandhi Smarak Nidhi in Delhi.
97. Interview, Sukharanjan Sengupta a retired Journalist from Ananda Bazaar group of Newspaper during the period under our consideration; January 20, 2012
98. Sankar Ghosh, *The Disinherited State*; *A study of West Bengal 1967-1971*, Orient Longman, Bombay, 1971.
99. *Ibid.*, pp. 15-51.
100. Ashok Mitra, *Apila Chapila*, Ananda Publisher, Kolkata, 2004.
101. Interview with the Congress leader Bijay Singh Nahar, as incorporated in *Legislative Control over Public Administration: India*, a revised edition, Willies, New York, 1998 by Amiya K. Chaudhuri.

CHAPTER 2

1. Kalyani Chaudhuri, When the Pendulum Stops: Death of Bengal Bureaucracy, Nachiketa Publications, The Statesman Publication, Kolkata, 2010.
2. Deputation to the Chief Election Commssion at Delhi by Mukul Roy and others, of TMC as also by Sitaram Yechury and his colleague of the CPI (M) on August 3, 2010: it is really surprising that the members of the ruling front (LF in West Bengal) for the last three decades are complaining against the TMC while CPI (M) cadres are still regarded as the manipulators of the voter list: news item as appeared in *The Times of India*, Delhi, August 4, 2010.
3. Myron Weiner, *Politics of Scarcity,*
4. Interview with Atulya Ghosh, May 15, 1980, in Amiya K. Chaudhuri, *Legislative*

Control over Public Administration: India (revised edition) Willies, New York, 1998, Chapter 2 *see also Saptaha* a Bengali Weekly January 4, 2013.

5. Jaya Chatterje, *The Spoils of Partition* (Indian edition), Cambridge University Press, New Delhi, 2008.
6. Interviews, Hashim Abdul Halim, the present Speaker of the WBLA, still believes that the law making body in a bourgeois parliamentary system is a weapon for the CPI (M) to achieve the goals of social revolution, August 17, 2004.
7. Ajit Naroyan Basu, *Paschimbanger Arthoniti O Rajniti*, (revised edition), Nagarik Mancha, Distributer: Sahitya Sansad, 2003, p. 148.
8. Interview, Dr. Sunil Rai Chaudhuri, Principal Presidency College, Calcutta, January 7, 2001
9. Interview, Prafulla Chandra Sen, the former Chief Minister (1962) 1967), August 16, 1982.
10. Interview, Bijay Singh Nahar, see, Amiya K. Chaudhuri, *Legislative Control over Public Administration*, Minerva, Calcutta, 1993, Chapter 8.
11. Asoke Chatterjee in conversation with the present author in the early 1990s.
12. Interview, Jyoti Basu, Amiya K. Chaudhuri, "Coalition Politics in West Bengal", A UPIASI project, New Delhi, to be published soon.
13. Barun Sengupta, *Palabadaler Pala*, Ananda Publisher, reprinted in *Barun Sengupta, Rachana Samagra*, 2nd edition, 2008; actually Mustak Murshed (a senior IAS of Bengal cadre) the then Secretary PWD used to draft the official letters unofficially to the chief minister and used to advise Shree Basu how to oppose the chief minister Ajoy Mukherjee.
14. *See*, detailed discussion, Amiya K. Chaudhuri, *Legislative Control over Public Administration,* Minerva, Calcutta 1993. There are several other works on this subject Barun Sengupta *Pala Badaler Pala,* Anand Publishers, Calcutta 1971, Prafulla Roy Chaudhuri, *West Bengal—A Decade (1965-1975),* Boipatra, Calcutta 1977, *Left Experiment in West Bengal*, Patriot, New Delhi, 1985.
15. *Ananda Bazar Patrika*, Calcutta, March 18-23, 1970.
16. Amalendu, Sengupta, *Joar Bantaya Shat Sattar*, Pearl Publishers, Ist edition, may 1997.
17. Interview, Arun Moitra, the then President of the state congress committee, August, 8, 2004.
18. WBLA Proceedings 1977, as quoted by A.K. Chaudhuri, chapter 2, *op. cit.*
19. Atul Kohli in many of his writings opined that actually the period of crisis of governance continued for more than a decade since 1966 to 1977 including the period of 1972 to 1977 during the re-emerging Congress regime with Siddhartha Sankar Ray as the Chief Minister. But many including the author would differ. The repression was there because of naxalite menace but governance of the State was not that bad as it was during 1967 to 1971.
20. Professor Dilip Chakravarty, the Secretary Bangladesh Sahayak Samiti, Calcutta University told this with other information which he had gathered during his visits to different refugee camps during late 1971 to the members of the samiti including the present writer.
21. David Butler, *Governing without a Majority, Dilemmas for Hung Parliaments in Britain*, Second edition, The Macmillan Press Ltd., London, 1986, Michael Laver and Norman Schofield, *Multiparty Government*: *The Politics of Coalition in Europe,*

University of Michigan Press, USA, 1998, Laver and Budge(eds), *Party Politics and Government Coalition,* St. Martin's Press, New York,1992.

22. The CPI (M) alone had absolute majority, continuing for long, up to 2001.Before that, it was an oversized coalition of surplus majority.
23. The Front partners are: Forward Bloc (FB), Forward Bloc (Marxists), Revolutionary Socialist Party (RSP), Revolutionary Communist Party of India (RCPI), Communist Party of India (CPI), Ashim Chatterjee's Naxalite Group; the non-Marxists parties: Biplabi Bangla Congress (BB Cong), Democratic Socialist Party (DSP) and West Bengal Socialist Party (WBSP), Rastriya Janata Dal (RJD), but not all are in the government.
24. *Ananda Bazar Patrika,* Kolkata, May 1, 2, 4, 5, 2001, report showing correspondence between CPI (M)'s Local Leaders and some Local leaders of the BJP was published by *ABP* during the days mentioned.
25. Interview, Mamata Banerjee at her Harish Chatterjee Road Residence on August 16, 2005.
26. Prafulla K. Chakraborti's *The Marginal Men,* Lumiere Books, Kalyani, West Bengal, 1990.
27. The following has been reported in the *Statesman, Calcutta,* May 29, 2000, "It may be recalled that all these years, it was mainly the UCRC (United Central Refugee Council) which used to do the spade-work in the refugee pockets on the CPI (M)'s behalf. According to a report prepared by the State Government's refugee rehabilitation committee in 1981 the total population of such refugees was about 80 lakhs. Now the figure stands above a crore. The CPI (M)'s state committee admits in a note that the new generations of these refugees are no longer swayed by the leftists."
28. Suman Chatterjee, Executive editor of *Ananda Bazaar Patrika*, coined the term during early Nineties, confirmed on February 9, 2013.
29. D. Bandyopadhyay, *Land Reforms in West Bengal,* former secretary, Board of Revenue, Govt. of West Bengal, Calcutta, 1980. *See also* N. Mukarji and D. Bandyopadhyay, *New Horizon for West Bengal's Panchayat,* Govt. of West Bengal, Deptt of Panchayats, Calcutta, 1993. *See also,* D. Bandyopadhyay, *Enduring Status Quo,* EPW, Vol. XXXVI No. 21, May 26 – June 1, 2001.
30. Arun Ghosh, *West Bengal Landscapes, op. cit., see also* D. Bandyopadhyay, *Enduring Status Quo,* EPW, *ibid.*
31. A Marxist Government is in power for more than two decades, twenty-four years to be exact. The Marxist-Leninist Party and other Left parties are by the compulsion of political circumstances always appeared to adjust themselves to the on-going socio-political realities. As a result they have to dilute their ideological rigidities. The Communists today, are therefore, regarded by its critics as "social democratic". *See* also, Atul Kohli, *op. cit.*, and to some extent Tom Nossiter, *op. cit.*
32. The term "New Class" was coined by Milovan Djilous, in Yugoslavia during the time of Marshal Tito about the Party apparatchik. Once before the Assembly election in 1996, the most respected CPI (M) leader (Late) Benoy Krishna Chowdhury in a very sad state of mind talked about this emerging `new class' in West Bengal saying that the Left Front Government had become a "Government of the contractors". Buddhadeb Bhattacharyya also left Basu Cabinet for a while wishing to dissociate from "some ministers with underground connections". He also wrote against the regime in a play "Dussamaya" (Worst of Time) and got it staged.
33. Manas Ghosh, Senior Writer, *The Statesman,* Kolkata, July 23, 2000.

34. Aditya Negam, "Logic of Failed Revolution", EPW, January 29, 2000.
35. *Field Survey and Interviews.* A cross section of elderly people without having fixed political party affiliations expressed the views in informal discussions during the intervening period between the two elections in 1998 and 1999.
36. Interview, Sunanda Sanyal and D. Bandyopadhyay, January 11, 2011 while we visited together the infamous Netaigram in West Midnapore to learn from the villagers the scale of the violence perpetrated by the hired goons of the CPI (M), on January 7, 20011.
37. Interview, Mahasweta Devi, February, 27, 2009.
38. Nirmal Basu Roy Chaudhuri, "Votex of Ideological Politics", in Iqbal Narain, (ed.) *State Politics in India,* Mennakshi Prakashan., Meerut, 1976, pp. 371-83,
39. D. Bandyopadhyay, "West Bengal Enduring Status Quo" *EPW* May 26, 2001, *op. cit.* pp. 1784-86.
40. A. Lijphart, "The Puzzle of Indian Democracy: A Consociational Interpretation", *American Political Science Review,* No. 2, June 1996.
41. Databank, Centre
42. John R. Wood (ed.), *State Politics in Contemporary India, Crisis or Continuity?* West View Press, London, 1984, pp. 81-102.
43. *The Statesman,* Calcutta, 13 June 2000. The postal ballots are served to the on-duty government officials and police forces. Several newspapers like *Ananda Bazar Patrika, Bartaman and the Statesman,* all published from Kolkata, on several occasions before the dates of election had the reports that the CPI (M)'s affiliated state government employees co-ordination committee and non-gazetted police associations' office-bearers often collected the ballots in favour of the government employees on election duties.
44. Atul Kohli, J, Wood (ed.), *State Politics in Contemporary India, op. cit.,* pp. 81-101.
45. Interview, Mamata Banerjee, December 30, 2001.
46. Interview, Robin Dev, chief whip, CPI (M) Legislature party, February 10, 2001.
47. Interview, Somnath Chatterjee, September 18, 1998.
48. Interview, Pradip Bhattacharjee, working president, Congress, March 4, 2004.
49. The reports carried by *Bartaman, Kolkata,* June 1, 2000; *Pratyahik Sambad Kolkata,* June 1, 2000.
50. *Election Manifesto,* 13th Lok Sabha, 1999, Communist Party of India (Marxists).
51. *Ibid,* (Bengali edition).
52. *Election Manifesto, 1999,* All India Trinamool Congress (AITC).
53. *Ibid.*
54. *Ganasakti,* Kolkata (CPI (M)'s party paper), September 29, 1999.
55. Besides, Bengali dailies, *Asian Age,* Kolkata, *Telegraph,* Kolkata, brought out occasional reports during September 14 – October 1, 1999.
56. Interview, the veteran Congress leader, who left Congress and joined the Janata Party, October 19, 2002.
57. *Frontline,* Chennai, December 10, 1999, pp. 38-3
58. Biman Basu, *Dainik Statesman*, Kolkata, May 9, 2006, in a press statement Basu said that CPI (M)'s seats in election 2006 would be more or less around 199 (as in 2001 election).
59. Amiya K. Chaudhuri, "Coalition Politics in West Bengal", A UPIASI project published by Academic Publisher, Delhi, 2014.

60. Buddhadeb Bhattacharjee *et al.,* (eds) *20 Years of LF government*, National Book Agency, Calcutta, 1997.
61. Jayati Ghosh (ed), West Bengal Human Development Report 2004, Development and Planning Department, Govt. of West Bengal, 2004.
62. *Bartaman,* (A Bengali daily) Kolkata, August 20, 2010
63. *The Statesman*, Kolkata, August 4, 2011.
64. Myron Weiner, *Politics of Scarcity,*
65. Amiya K. Chaudhuri, Legislative Control over Public Administration: India (revised edition) Willies, New York, 1998, Chapter 2.
66. Jaya Chatterje, *The Spoils of Partition* (Indian edition), Cambridge University Press, New Delhi, 2008.
67. Interviews, Hashim Abdul Halim, the present Speaker of the WBLA, still believes that the law making body in a bourgeois parliamentary system is a weapon for the CPI (M) to achieve the goals of social revolution, August 17, 2004.
68. Barun Sengupta, *Palabadaler Pala*, Ananda Publisher, reprinted in *Barun Sengupta, Rachana Samagra*, 2nd edition, 2008; actually Mustak Murshed the then Secretary PWD used to draft the official letters unofficially to the chief minister and used to advise Basu how to oppose the chief minister Ajoy Mukherjee.
69. *See*, detailed discussion, Amiya K.Chaudhuri, *Legislative Control over Public Administration,* Minerva, Calcutta 1993. There are several other works on this subject Barun Sengupta *Pala Badaler Pala,* Anand Publishers, Calcutta 1971, Prafulla Roy Chaudhuri, *West Bengal—A Decade (1965-1975),* Boipatra, Calcutta 1977, *Left Experiment in West Bengal*, Patriot, New Delhi, 1985.
70. *Ananda Bazar Patrika*, Calcutta, March 18-23, 1970.
71. Amalendu, Sengupta, *Joar Bantaya Shat Sattar,* Pearl Publishers, Ist edition, may 1997.
72. WBLA Proceedings 1977, as quoted by AK. Chaudhuri, chapter 2, *op. cit.*
73. Atul Kohli in many of his writings opined that actually the period of crisis of governance continued more than a decade since 1966 to 1977 including the period of 1972 to 1977 during the re-emerging Congress regime with Siddhartha Sankar Ray as the Chief Minister. But many including the author would differ. The repression was there because of naxalite menace but governance of the State was not that bad as it was during 1967 to 1971.
74. Professor Dilip Chakravarty, the Secretary Bangladesh Sahayak Samiti, Calcutta University told this with other information which he had gathered during his visits to different refugee camps during late 1971 to the members of the Samiti including the present writer.

CHAPTER 3

1. David Butler, *Government Without Majority,*
2. The CPI (M) alone had absolute majority, continuing for long, up to 2001. Before that, it was an oversized coalition of surplus majority.
3. The Front partners are: Forward Bloc (FB), Forward Bloc (Marxists), Revolutionary Socialist Party (RSP), Revolutionary Communist Party of India (RCPI), Communist Party of India (CPI), Ashim Chatterjee's Naxalite Group; the non-Marxists parties: Biplabi Bangla Congress (BB Cong), Democratic Socialist Party (DSP) and West Bengal Socialist Party (WBSP), Rastriya Janata Dal (RJD), but not all are in the government.

4. Prafulla K. Chakraborti's *The Marginal Men,* Lumiere Books, Kalyani, West Bengal, 1990.
5. The following has been reported in *The Statesman,* Calcutta, May 29, 2000, "It may be recalled that all these years, it was mainly the UCRC (United Central Refugee Council) which used to do the spade-\ work in the refugee pockets on the CPI (M)'s behalf. According to a report prepared by the State Government's refugee rehabilitation committee in 1981 the total population of such refugees was about 80 lakhs. Now the figure stands above a crore. The CPI (M)'s state committee admits in a note that the new generations of these refugees are no longer swayed by the Leftists."
6. Atul Kohli, *Democracy and Discontent, India's Growing Crisis of Governability,* Cambridge University Press, Cambridge, 1991.
7. Francine R. Frankel, *Dominance and State Power in Modern India,* Vol. I, Oxford University Press, Delhi, 1990. Atul Kohli, in John R. Wood edited *State Politics in Contemporary India,* West View Press, London, 1984. During the regime of two UF governments, the *Jotedar* class went against the CPI (M) due to the land grabbing movement let loose by the CPI (M) leader Shri Harekrishna Konar. But the same class of *Jotedar* had to fall in line with the CPI (M) and the LF when the later entrenched itself in the rural areas.
8. Occasional Reports, *The Statesman,* Calcutta, Jan-March 1998.
9. Myron, Weiner, *The Politics of Scarcity,* Asia Publishing House, Calcutta, 1963, p. 35.
10. See for a detailed discussion in Amiya K. Chaudhuri's *Legislative Control over Public Administration,* Minerva, Calcutta 1993. There are several other works on this subject Barun Sengupta's *Pala Badaler Pala,* Anand Publishers, Calcutta 1971, Prafulla Roy Chaudhuri, *West Bengal—A Decade (1965-1975),* Boipatra, Calcutta 1977, *Left Experiment in West Bengal*, Patriot, New Delhi, 1985.
11. Atul Kohli in many of his writings opined that actually the period of crisis of governance continued more than a decade since 1966 to 1977 including the period of 1972 to 1977 during the re-emerging Congress regime with Siddhartha Sankar Ray as the Chief Minister. But many including the author would differ. The repression was there because of naxalite menace but governance of the State was not that bad as it was during 1967 to 1971.
12. This was almost a common experience of many an intellectual who had the opportunity to study West Bengal situation from a close quarter from December 16, 1970 till the Simla Agreement between Smt. Indira Gandhi and Mr. Bhutto, the Prime Minister of a truncated Pakistan.
13. Atul Kohli, *op. cit.*, Dr. Asoke Mitra, the first Finance Minister vehemently criticised the government; Dr. Mitra's contention was that the government was formed on the strength of a "*Jal Bidhan Sabha*" i.e. the election of 1972 was based on electoral fraud. *See* also, T.J. Nossite, *Marxist State Governments in India,* Printer Publishers, London and New York, 1988.
14. *Interview.* Prafulla Chandra Sen (Late since), the former Chief Minister. Arun Ghosh, *West Bengal Landscapes,* K.P. Bagchi & Co., Calcutta, 1989, and Neil Webster, *Panchayati Raj and Decentralisation of Development Planning in West Bengal,* K.P. Bagchi & Company, Calcutta, 1992.
15. D. Bandyopadhyay, *Land Reforms in West Bengal,* former secretary, Board of Revenue, Govt. of West Bengal, Calcutta, 1980. *See also* N. Mukarji and D. Bandyopadhyay, *New Horizon for West Bengal's Panchayat,* Govt. of West Bengal,

Deptt of Panchayats, Calcutta, 1993. *See also,* D. Bandyopadhyay, *Enduring Status Quo,* EPW, Vol. XXXVI No. 21, May 26 – June 1, 2001.

16. Arun Ghosh, *West Bengal Landscapes, op. cit., see also* D. Bandyopadhyay, *Enduring Status Quo,* EPW, *ibid.*
17. A Marxist Government is in power for more than two decades, twenty-four years to be exact. The Marxist-Leninist Party and other Left parties are by the compulsion of political circumstances always appeared to adjust themselves to the on-going socio-political realities. As a result they have to dilute their ideological rigidities. The Communists today are, therefore, regarded by its critics as "social democratic". *See* also, Atul Kohli, *op. cit.*, and to some extent Tom Nossiter, *op. cit.*
18. The term "New Class" was coined by Milovan Djilous, in Yugoslavia during Marshal Tito about the Party apparatchik. Once before the Assembly election in 1996, the most respected CPI (M) leader (Late) Benoy Krishna Chowdhury in a very sad state of mind talked about this emerging 'new class' in West Bengal saying that the Left Front Government had become a "Government of the contractors". Buddhadeb Bhattacharyya also left Basu Cabinet for a while wishing to dissociate from "some ministers with underground connections". He also wrote against the regime in a play "Dusamaya" (Worst of Time) and got it staged.
19. Manas Ghosh, Senior Writer, *The Statesman,* Kolkata, July 23, 2000.
20. Aditya Negam, "Logic of Failed Revolution", *EPW*, January 29, 2000.
21. *Field Survey and Interviews.* A cross section of elderly people without having fixed political party affiliations expressed the views in informal discussions during the intervening period between the two elections in 1998 and 1999.
22. Nirmal Basu Roy Chaudhury, "Votex of Ideological Politics", in Iqbal Narain, (ed.) *State Politics in India,* Mennakshi Prakashan, Meerut, 1976, pp. 371-83.
23. D. Bandyopadhyay, "West Bengal Enduring Status Quo" *EPW* May 26, 2001, *op. cit.* pp. 1784-86.
24. A. Lijphart, "The Puzzle of Indian Democracy: A Consociational Interpretation", *American Political Science Review,* No. 2, June 1996.
25. John R. Wood (ed.), S*tate Politics in Contemporary India, Crisis or Continuity?* West View Press, London, 1984, pp. 81-102.
26. *Ananda Bazar Patrika,* Kolkata, May 1, 2, 4, 5, 2001, report showing correspondence between CPI (M)'s Local Leaders and some Local leaders of the BJP was published by *ABP* during the days mentioned.
27. *The Statesman,* Calcutta, 13 June 2000. The postal ballots are served to the on-duty government officials and police forces. Several newspapers like *Ananda Bazar Patrika, Bartaman and the Statesman,* all published from Kolkata, on several occasions before the dates of election had the reports that the CPI (M)'s affiliated state government employees co-ordination committee and non-gazetted police associations' office-bearers often collected the ballots in favour of the government employees on election duties.
28. During the months of Nov-Dec 1989, the walls of hundreds of buildings carried the cartoons in various colourful shapes and sizes.
29. *The leaflets and handbills,* circulated by different LF candidates, Dec' 1989.
30. Atul Kohli, J, Wood (ed.), *State Politics in Contemporary India, op. cit.,* pp. 81-101.
31. Interview, Mamata Banerjee, December 30, 2001.

32. Interview, Tathagata Roy, president state committee, BJP, August 2, 2004.
33. Interview, Robin Dev, chief whip, CPI (M) Legislature party, February 10, 2001.
34. Interview, Pradip Bhattacherjee, working president, Congress, March 4, 2004.
35. The reports carried by *Bartaman,* Kolkata, June 1, 2000; *Pratyahik Sambad,* Kolkata, June 1, 2000.
36. Partha Chatterjee, *State and Politics in India,* Oxford University Press, Kolkata, 1997.
37. *Frontline,* Chennai, December 10, 1999, pp. 38-39
38. *Parliamentary Elections in West Bengal* (1952-1999), *op. cit.*
39. *See, Parliamentary Elections in West Bengal (1952-1999), op. cit.*
40. C.R. Irani, Caveat, *The Statesman,* Calcutta, March 6, 2001.
41. Anil Biswas (deceased since), secretary, state committee of CPI (M), January 2, 2006.
42. *Report of the Election Commission,* (provisional), Assembly Election, 2001.
43. Biman Basu, *Dainik Statesman*, Kolkata, May 9, 2006, in a press statement Basu said that CPI (M)'s seats in election 2006 would be more or less around 199 (as in 2001 election).
44. Amiya K. Chaudhuri, "*Coalition Politics in West Bengal*", A UPIASI project (2004-2006), submitted on September 7-9, 2006.
45. Interview, Manas Ghosh senior political correspondent (presently Editor *Dainik Statesman*), *The Statesman,* Calcutta, June 14, 2000.
46. A series of newspapers articles written by economists like Avijit Vinayak Bandyopadhyay, Asok Sanjay Guha, Kausik Basu, Dilip Mukhopadhyay, Debraj Roy, Pranab Bardhan, Mukul Majumdar, Mrinal Dutta Chowdhury, Maitreyish Ghosal, *Ananda Bazar Patrika,* Kolkata, June 14-20, 2001.

CHAPTER 4

1. K.S. Subramanian, *Parliamentary Communism: Crisis in the Indian Communist Movement*, Ajanta Publications (India), Delhi, 1989.
2. UPIASI *Field Survey*, interview, Shymal Chakraborty, CITU, West Bengal, August 22, 2004.
3. *Interview*, Jyoti Basu, September 4, 2004.
4. *Interview,* Prabhas Ghosh, secretary, SUC, September 10, 2004
5. E. Shreedharan, "Principles, Power and Coalition Politics: Lessons from Theory, Comparison and Recent History", D.D. Khanna and Gert W. Kueck (eds), *Principles, Power and Politics*, Macmillan India, New Delhi, 1999, pp. 270-90.
6. Myron Weiner, *Politics of Scarcity: Public Pressure and Political responses in India*, Asia Publishing House, Calcutta, 1963
7. *Interview*, Jyoti Basu, *op. cit.*
8. Aktar Majeed, *Coalition Politics and Power Sharing*, Manak Publications Pvt. Ltd, New Delhi 2000, p. 3.
9. *Ibid*, p. 4.
10. David Butler, *Governing Without a Majority,* second edition, Macmillan Press, London 1986.
11. Michael Laver and Norman Schofield, *Multiparty Government: The Politics of Coalition in Europe,* University of Michigan Press, USA 1998. pp. 7-13.

12. Ian Budge and Hans Keman, *Parties and Democracy: Coalition Formation and Government Functioning in Twenty States,* Oxford University Press, New York 1990, p. 11.
13. William H. Riker, *The Theory of Political Coalition,* Oxford IBH Publishing Co. Calcutta, 1970, pp. 32-33.
14. Laver and Budge (eds), *Party Politics and Government Coalition,* St. Martin's Press, New York 1992.
15. A.K. Chaudhuri, "Minority Government: Coalition Politics an Indian Experiment", *Indian Journal of Political Science*, April-June 2005.
16. Ramakrishna Sithanen, "Coalition Politics under the Tropics: Office Seekers, Policy Makers, Nation Building: A case study of Mauritius", http://www.eisa.org.za/PDF/ppr-mauritius.pdf
17. Ian Budge and Hans Keman, *Parties and Democracy: Coalition Formation and Government Functioning in Twenty States, op. cit.,* p. 2.
18. *Census Report, 2011* (provisional).
19. Conceptually to trace localism and the regional politics of the Districts, as they are different from one region to another, the districts are put into five cluster: Cooch Behar, Jalpaiguri, Darjeeling, two Dinajpur districts in cluster one; Malda, Muirshidabad and Birbhum in cluster two; Purulia, Bankura and two Midnapore districts in cluster three; Nadia, 24 Parganas (North), 24 Parganas (South) and Kolkata in cluster four; Burdwan, Hooghly and Howrah in cluster five. Geographically there are some common features in each of the contiguous districts as well as the clusters. There are various considerations for making a five-fold clustering of the areas. Economic reasons such as "least development", "moderate" and "sufficient development", and, caste/ community considerations, cultural and ethno-political elements are some of the criteria. The FB and RSP had their pockets of influence primarily in scheduled caste and tribal areas of North Bengal districts, western belts of Purulia, Bankura, and a few pockets of Murshidabad, 24 Parganas and Hooghly.
20. *UPIASI field survey*, from June-September 2005.
21. *Dainik Statesman*, Kolkata, January 28, 2006.
22. Glyn Williams, "Rethinking West Bengal's Stability: From Party organization to Local Practices of Politics", John Zavos, *et al.,* (eds) *The Politics of Cultural Mobilization in India*, Oxford University Press, 2004, *see also*, Atul Kohli, *Democracy and Discontent: India's Growing Crisis of Governability*, Cambridge University Press, 1990, Rudolf and Rudolf, *In Pursuit of Lakshmi: The Political Economy of Indian State*, Orient Longman, Bombay, 1987.
23. Glyn Williams, *Ibid*, pp. 72-73.
24. Arild Engelsen Ruud, *Poetics of Village Politics: The Making of West Bengal Rural Communism*, Oxford University Press, New Delhi, 2003. *See also*, Ruud, "From Untouchable to Communist: Wealth Power and Status among Supporters of the Communist Party (Marxist) in Rural Bengal", Rogaly, *et al.*, *Sonar Bangla*, *op. cit.,* pp. 253-78.
25. 73rd and 74th Amendment of the Constitution of India.
26. Neil Webster, *Panchayati Raj and the Decentralization of Development Planning in West Bengal*, K.P. Bagchi & Co. 1992; G.K. Lieten, *Development, Devolution and Democracy: Village Discourse in West Bengal*, Sage Publications, New Delhi, 1996.

27. Pranab Bardhan and Dilip Mookherjee "Political Economy of Land Reforms in West Bengal", people.bw.edu/dilipm/wkpap/wbpelref17.pdf
28. *Ananda Bazar Patrika*, Kolkata, July 27, 2005.
29. *Dainik Statesman*, November 25, 2005; *The Statesman* Kolkata, January 26, 2006; It is reported in the newspapers that the LF government intended to issue 1 crore 53 lac BPL—ration cards in the wake of Assembly Election 2006. 2006; *Ananda Bazar Patrika*, January 17, 2006, the Minister, Department. of Food, Naren Dey himself admitted. The Central minister Sharad Pawar admitted in a Press Conference in Kolkata that there were 85 lac additional ration cards while the CAG Report pointed out earlier that the number of unaccounted ration cards are 65 lac, *Ananda Bazar Patrika*, January 4, 2006.
30. *Dainik Statesman*, Kolkata, July 30, 2005.
31. *Ananda Bazar Patrika*, Kolkata, August 8, 2005, *See also, West Bengal Human Development Report 2004*, Development and Planning, Government of West Bengal, 2004.
32. *India Development Report 2004-04*, Indira Gandhi Institute of Development, Oxford University Press, New Delhi, 2005, p. 4.
33. *Ananda Bazar Patrika*, Kolkata, August 21, 2005, See *also*, Abhirup Sarkar, "Political Economy of West Bengal: A Puzzle and a Hypothesis", *Economic and Political Weekly*, January 28, 2006, pp. 341-48. Industrial scenario as reported by *Annual Review of West Bengal Economy 2004-05,* Centre for Monitoring India Economy Pvt. Ltd., Kolkata, 2006.
34. *CSDS Survey: Parliamentary election, West Bengal 1999 and Assembly Election, 2001; UPIASI Project Finding* – 2004-05.
35. *Census of India 2001*: the Muslims population is 25.25 per cent. The figure (28.62%) in *West Bengal Human Development Report 2004 reported (28.62)* as per *National Sample Survey Organization (NSSO).*
36. *Interview,* Prabhas Ghosh, secretary of the SUC, July 7, 2005.
37. *Field Surveys, CSDS*, 1999 parliamentary and 2001 WB Assembly elections, *UPIASI Survey 2004-2005.*
38. Prafulla K. Chakrabarti, *The Marginal men,* Lumier Books, Kalyani, West Bengal, 1990, *see also* Tathagata Roy, *My People Uprooted: A Saga of the Hindus of Eastern Bengal,* Ratna Prakasan, Kolkata, 2001.
39. Ranajit Roy, *The Agony of West Bengal,* The New Age Publishers, Calcutta, 1972.
40. *Interview*, Asok Ghosh, secretary FB, November 5, 2004.
41. R. Chatterji (ed), *Politics in West Bengal: Institution, Process and Problems*, "Introduction", World Press, Calcutta 1985.
42. Nirmal Basu Roy Chowdhury, "West Bengal: Vortex of Ideological Politics", Iqbal Narain (ed) *State Politics in India*, Meenakshi Prakashan, 1976, pp. 370-403.
43. Source: CPI (M) Central Party office, Kolkata: In 1977 the CPI (M) had a membership of 25 thousand only. In December 2005, the full time members were 2 lac 66 thousand; Front organizations: Student Federation of India (SFI): 13 lac 2 thousand 542; Democratic Youth Federation of India (DYFI): 41 lac 93 thousand. *Krisan Sabha* (Peasant Organization): 1 crore 32 lac 78 thousand and 998; *Mahila Samity* (Women Organization): 41 lac 93 thousand; Centre of Indian Trade Unions (CITU): 12 lac 74 thousand.
44. *Interview,* Jyoti Basu, *op. cit.*

45. Myron Weiner, *The Politics of Scarcity*, Asia Publishing House, Calcutta, 1963: *Party Politics in India*. Princeton University Press, NJ, 1957;

Marcus F. Franda, *Radical Politics in West Bengal*, Cambridge, Mass, MIT Press, 1971; ———*Political Development and Political Decay in West Bengal, Firma K.L. Mukhopadhyay, Calcutta 1971; Paul Brass, Ethnicity and Nationalism, Sage Publications, New Delhi, 1991;*

Atul Kohli, *The State and Poverty in India*, Cambridge University Press, 1987; *Democracy and Discontent*, Cambridge University Press, 1991,

Atul Kohli (ed), *The Success of India's Democracy*, Cambridge University Press, 2001;

Biplab Das Gupta, *The Naxalite Movement*, Allied Publishers, Bombay, 1975;

Profulla Roy Choudhury, *The Left Experiment in West Bengal*, Patriot Publishers, New Delhi 1984; Sankar Ghosh, *The Disinherited State: A Study of West Bengal 1967-70*, Orient Long man, Calcutta, 1971.

46. Ross Mallick, *Development Policy of Communist Government: West Bengal since 1977*, Cambridge University Press, 1993; *The Statesman*, Calcutta, February 10, 1998.
47. *Interviews,* Dr. Amiya K. Samanta (Retd. DGP), Aug 17, 2005.
48. *The Statesman,* Calcutta, May 25, 1980, Shree Jyoti Basu told" the state government had decided to give them the right to strike".
49. Prafulla Roy Choudhury, *Left experiment in West Bengal, op. cit.,* p. 141.
50. Glyn Williams, "Panchayatiraj and the changing Micro-Politics of West Bengal", Ben Rogaly *et el. Sonar Bangla: Agricultural Growth and Agrarian Change in West Bengal and Bangladesh*, Sage Publications, New Delhi, 1999.
51. Arild Engelsen Ruud, "From Untouchable to Communist: Wealth Power and Status among Supporters of the Communist Party (Marxist) in Rural West Bengal", Beng Rogaly, et el, *Sonar Bangla*, *Ibid*, p. 254.
52. *Interview,* Jyoti Basu, *op. cit.*
53. Endnotes 26, loc cit.
54. Tom J. Nossiter, *Marxist State Governments in India: Politics Economics and Society*, Printer Publisher, London, New York, 1988, pp. 138-39.
55. *Organizations of Parties*: The structures and organizations of the left parties follow the principle of Communist organization; Maurice Duverger, *Political Parties,* Wiley, New York, 1954; David Apter, *Introduction to Political System*, Hall of India, New Delhi, 1981, p. 158.
56. Bidyut Chakraborty, *Forging Power: Coalition Politics in India*, Oxford University Press, New Delhi, 2006; D Sundar Ram (ed), *Coalition Politics in India: Search for Political Stability*, National Publishing House, Jaipur, New Delhi; 200; Lakshi Krishnamurti, R. Hariharan and Gert W. Kueck (eds), *Making a Success of Coalition*, East West (Madras) Pvt. Ltd., Chennai, 2000; Paranjoy Guha Thakurta, Sankar Raghuraman (eds), *A time of Coalitions Divided We Stand,* Sage Publications, New Delhi 2004; N. Jose Chander, *Coalition Politics: The Indian Experience*, Concept publishing company, New Delhi 2004, Chapter 5; Akhtar, Majeed (ed), *Coalition Politics and Power Sharing,* Manak Publications, New Delhi, 2000.
57. Jan-Erik Lane and Svante D. Ersson, *European Politics: An Introduction,* Sage Publications, London, Reprint, 2001, pp. 133-43.
58. Asoke Kumar Mukhopadhyay, *The Panchayat Administration in West Bengal,* 3rd edition, World Press, Calcutta, 1991.

59. Myron Weiner, *The Politics of Scarcity*, *op. cit.*, p. 35.
60. Sankar Ghosh, *The Disiinherited State*, *op. cit.*, p. 156.
61. Sankar Ghosh, *Ibid*, p. 157.
62. Barun Sengupta, *Pala Badaler Pala* (Bengali), Ananda Publishers Private Limited, Calcutta, 1971.
63. Prafulla Kumar Ghosh, *The Left politics in West Bengal*, Calcutta, 1982 and see also A.K. Chaudhuri, *Legislative Control over Public Administration*, Minerva Associates, 1993, p. 27.
64. Atul Kohli, *Democracy and Discontent*: *India's growing Crisis of Governability,* Cambridge University Press, Cambridge, 1991.
65. Anjali Ghosh, *peaceful transition to power*, Firma KLM Pvt. Ltd., Calcutta, 1981.
66. Barun Sengupta, *Pala Badaler Pala op. cit.,* p. 139.
67. *Ibid*, appendix, pp. 249-78.
68. *The Statesman*, Calcutta, November 10, 1969.
69. *West Bengal Legislative Assembly Proceedings*, Vol. 50, No. 1, February '05,1973, p. 524.
70. *The Statesman*, Kolkata, March 23, 1970.
71. *Interview*, Arun Moitra—the then Pradesh Congress President, August 20, 2005; Siddhartha Sankar Roy, former chief Minister, August 10, 2005.
72. *Interview*, Buddhadeb Bhattacharya, Chief Minister, West Bengal, September 5, 2005, Biman Basu, chairman, left front committee January 18, 2005.
73. *Interview,* Kamal Guha (FB), Minister, Department of Agriculture, October 26, 2005.
74. Interview, Prof. Satya Sadhan Chakraborty, former Education Minister (1991-2006), April 28, 2006; Nilotpal Basu, former MP(CPI (M)) in an interview with the author on May 8,2006.
75. Jyoti Basu (chief Editor), Buddhadeb Bhattacharya, Biman Basu Anil Biswas (ed), *People's Power in Practice 20 Years of Left Front in West Bengal,* National Book agency, Calcutta, 1997, p. vi.
76. Data based on personal interviews (2004-05) with most of the ministers.
77. *The Statesman*, September 24, 1998; *The Statesman*, October 4, 1988.
78. *Dainik statesman*, referring "Ganabarta-RSP paper, September 15, 2005; Ashok Ghosh, FB, *Dainik Statesman, October 15, 2005.*
79. Amiya K. Chaudhuri, "Coalition Politics in West Bengal", project funded by the University of Pennsylvania Institute of Advanced Studies in India (UPAISI), New Delhi, submitted in January 2007.
80. Anil Biswas, press conference, October 21, 2005 as reported in *Ganasakti*, October 22, 05.

CHAPTER 5

1. *West Bengal: An Analytical Study, sponsored* by the Bengal Chamber of Commerce & Industry, Calcutta, Oxford & IBH Publishing Co, Calcutta, 1971, An Empirical study—the first of its kind, was made by Professor S.N. Sen and his team of investigators in this regard during the late 1950s. He gave an account of the refugees that crossed over the border, almost forcibly acquired the lands much of which were left behind by the Muslims migrating to East Pakistan and many of the marshy plot of lands around Calcutta and its suburbs, settled as masses of impoverished and

pauperized lots. The Communist and other left political parties stood behind them and in the process earned their solid support politically and socially.

2. Amiya K. Chaudhuri, "Electoral Politics in West Bengal: A predominant Party in Government", in Suchandana Chatterjee edited *Asia Annual 2006*, Standard Publishers (India), New Delhi, 2007.
3. Leon Trotsky, *General consideration of the United Front*, 1924; In this connection the Marxists focused on the contribution of Georgi Dimitrov's concept of "united and popular fronts directed against the rising tide of fascism", Vijay Singh, "Georgi Dimitrov and the United National Front in China 1936-1944", *http://www.revolutionary democracy.org/rdv5n2/drimitrov.htm*; *see also* E.N. Sivadasan, "A comparative Study of the CPI (M) and CPI led Coalition Government in Kerala: Politics and Policy Implementation" (unpublished Paper), Department of Political Science, St. Thomas College, Palai, Mahatma Gandhi university, June, 1971.
4. Interview, Jyoti Basu, August 4, 2004; this author, interviewed Jyoti Babu, in connection with the UPIASI project on "Coalition Politics in West Bengal"; Shree Basu expressed this forthright opinion in this private discussion.
5. During a few LF rallies in the Kolkata Maidan after the UPA coalition taking over the CM made this comment, The Statesman, Kolkata, July 12 2008.
6. Marcus F. Franda, Radical Politics in West Bengal, MIT Press Cambridge, Mass, 1971; Atul Kohli (ed), India's Democracy: An Analysis of Changing State Society Relations, Princeton, N.J., Princeton University Press, 1988.
7. John. Broomfield, Elite Conflict in a Plural Society, Berkeley, University of California Press, 1968. This categorization of Bengal society in the 1920s among the political leadership still holds good in the present day West Bengal society and political classes.
8. Ross Mallick, *Development policy of a Communist government: West Bengal since 1977*, Cambridge University Press, New York, 1993.
9. *Ibid*, p. 214.
10. *Sambad Pratidin*, Kolkata, July 5, 2009, it is a very well circulated language daily that carries the story, the "RSP's Central Committee comes to the conclusion that the CPI (M) has gradually been detached from the people for their land and industrial policies".
11. Kshiti Goswami, PWD minister of the LF government told the author in a Television (DD, Kolkata centre) interview on May 16, 2009.
12. The statesman, Calcutta, March, 18, 1970.
13. Udayan Nambudri, *Bengal's Night Without End*, India First Foundation, New Delhi, 2006.
14. Jagadish Chandra Mondal, *Marichjhapi: Naishabder Antarale (Gana hatyar ek Kalo Itihas)* in Bengali people's Book Society Kolkata 2002.
15. Udayan Nambudri, *Bengal's Night Without End, op. cit.; see also* the book written by Amitava Ghosh, *The Hungry Tide,* Ravi Dayal, Publisher, New Delhi, 2004.
16. Niranjan Halder, former assistant editor of Ananda Bazar Patrika who lived near the place of this gruesome incident described the scene most vividly in his occasional writings and told the author recently in an interview on April, 12, 2009; see also Udayan Nambudri *West Bengal's Night never Ends* in greater detail, *op. cit.*
17. The Statesman, Calcutta, May 18, 1990.
18. Udayan Nambudri, *Bengal's Night without End*, *op. cit.*, p. 393.
19. *Ibid*, p. 85.

20. Barun Sen Gupta, editor, *Bartaman* Patrika a language Daily in post edit wrote extensively about the electoral malpractices of the CPI (M) after most of the Assembly and Parliamentary elections in West Bengal particularly since 1987; he even investigated every panchayat and municipal elections and printed pictures to show as to how all those happened during the days of elections; see also Prabir Ghosal, *CPIM-er rigging,* (Bengali), Mukherjee Publishing, 2005 and a number of researched Bengali publications on the subject.
21. Udayan Nambudri, West Bengal's Night Never End, *op. cit.,*
22. *Ibid*, pp. 27-35.
23. D. Bandyapadhyay and N. Mukerji, New Horizon for West Bengal Panchayats 1993, a report, the government of West Bengal commissioned in 1992 but the published report was withheld for circulation.
24. Glyn Williams, "Rethinking West Bengal's Stability From Party Organization to Local Practices of Politics" in John Zavos, *et al.,* edited, The Politic of Cultural Mobilization in India, OUP, Kolkata, 2004: Arild Engelsen Ruud, Poetics of Village Politics The making of West Bengal Rural Communism, OUP, New Delhi, 2003; Neil Webster, Panchayati Raj and the Decentralization of Development Planning in West Bengal, KP Bagchi & Co, 1992; O.k. Lieten, Development, Devolution and Democracy: village Discourse in West Bengal, Sage Publications, New Delhi, 1996, and a few others among them, Nossiter, Marxist State Government in India: Politics, Economics and Society, Printer Publishers, London, 1988.
25. D. Bandyapadhyay and Nirmal Mukerji, *op. cit.*
26. Pranab Bardhan and Dilip Mukherjee, "Political Economy of Land Reforms in West Bengal. People.bw.edu/dilipm/wkpap/wbpelref17.pdf
27. Interview, Jawahar Sarkar, joined as the secretary of Industry being transferred from the post of the CEO of West Bengal, November 6, 2001
28. Debabrata Bandyapadhyay, the present state General Secretary of the RSP, used the same term while the CPI (M) led by Jyoti Basu took away the Panchayat port folio from him and his party after 1987 Assembly election in West Bengal; Shri Bandyapadhyay expressed the same opinion while talking to the present author while writing on "The Coalition Politics in West Bengal" in an interview in August 8, 2006.
29. Mahasweta Devi, *Dainik Statesman* (the Bengali edition of *The Statesman*, Kolkata), July 20, 2009.
30. Tusar Talukdar, this former Calcutta police Commissioner assessed Mamata Banerjee's rise to the political height that Mamata Banerjee achieved, August, 2, 2009.
31. Interviews, this is only one of the interactions with Mamata Banerjee (among several beginning from January-March 2005), May 20, 2009.
32. The Governor, Shri Gopal Gandhi issued the statement in the night of 14th March and published in all the leading Newspaper, March 15, 2007
33. Mahasweta Devi, Amitava Chaudhuri (ShreeNirapeksha), Saoli Mitra, Bivas Chakraborty, Kaushik Sen, Kabir Suman (singer), Nachiketa (singer) and many others took up the causes and wrote several pieces in different Newspaper, particularly the *Dainik Statesman*, Kolkata from the very beginning of the Nandigram incident on March 14,2007
34. Just before the 2009 General Election in India, hoardings conceptualized, devised by Shuvaprasanna—the renowned Bengali artiste. Several faces of eminent Bengali

intellectuals, writers, poets, social activists, Professors, cinema directors, stage actors, and directors, artistes and singers were seen in several different places in each of the 42 parliamentary constituencies; the theme was "We want Change"; it appeared to be a surrealistic painting to the discerning viewers; there were only a dozen faces on the hoarding; on the faces and the ambience created on the canvas one can imagine more than 5 crore voters who might be desiring for a change after a span of 32 years of a cartel of political oligopolies. This hoarding might have a tremendous influence on the people of the state; the LF particularly the CPI (M) became shaky and began making wide allegations that American imperialistic forces and the foreign money of the NGOs had been playing the most significant roles to destabilize a "very well governed Marxist government," as claimed by the CPI (M) leaders in the state; but the bad logic and the knee-jerk reactions of the CPI (M) did not cut much ice this time around; the people made up their minds and exercised their options in West Bengal election that was unique after 1984 when the opposition Congress Party was able to garner only 16 seats.

35. Interviews, with several rational leaders, including University teachers, once holding the post of Vice-chancellors, of the CPI (M), on different days, 20th, 25th May, and July 22, 2009.
36. Quoting the much earlier document the two commentators dilated the phrase; Gene D. Overstreet and Marshall Wind Miller, *Communism in India*, The Perennial Press, Bombay, 1960
37. Atin Sarkar, a member of the undivided Communist Party, "Shameless False Propaganda is the forte of the CPI (M)," Dainik Statesman, Kolkata, August 12, 2009.
38. *Istehar, Panchadash Lok Sabha Nirbachan, 2009, Bharater Communist Party,(Marxbadi*), [tran, Manifesto, 15th Lok Sabha Election, 2009, Communist Party of India (Marxist)],
39. Survey Findings, July, 2004; undertaken for writing a chapter on "Coalition Politics in West Bengal" for UPIASI, New Delhi, to be published from OUP in the end of 2009;
40. Survey Findings, July, 2008, *Ibid*, a large number of sample (3800) was chosen with a structured Questionnaire and interesting feedback was recorded.
41. Field Survey, *Ibid.*
42. A B Bardhan, The Statesman, Kolkata, July 7, 2009; the other national dailies carried the stories circulated by the LF partners in their central party meeting during the first week of July, 2009.
43. Shyamal Chakraborty, vice-president CITU, told in an interview taken by Kathkali Chanda, now a sub-editor, *The Times of India*, Bombay for a project undertaken by the present author for UPIAS, New Delhi, August 4, 2006.
44. Dainik Statesman, Kolkata, May 2-May 5, 2005.
45. Interview, D. Bandyapadhyay, May 4, 2009; Shree D. Bandyapadhyay (retd. IAS), Professor Sunanda Sanyal and a few others of the world of Theater and culture went to have an idea as to what happened in Keshpur, Garbeta and other places during the past several elections; they were not allowed to enter the areas and asked by the CPI (M) cadres "to live the village people undisturbed."
46. *Ibid.*
47. The State Election Commission, West Bengal; the data put into the website of the

Commission were incomplete; therefore the data given in the text had to be compiled from different newspaper of the time and news magazine.

48. Aparna Sen, Saoli Mitra, Bratya Basu, Shuvaprasanna, Shirsendu Mukhapadhyay and others were continuously expressing the opinion after what happened at Nandigram in March 14 and November 10, 2007.
49. *Dainik Statesman*, Kolkata, March 16, 2006; other languages dailies also made the same assessment about the party and its local leaders and hired goons and cadres after the Singur and Nandigram incidents in 2006 and 2007 in the state.
50. *India Social Development Report, 2008*, Council for social Development, Oxford University Press, New Delhi, 2008.
51. Pre-Budget, *Economic Survey 2006-07*, West Bengal Legislative Assembly, Kolkata, 2007.
52. Dwaipayan Bhattacharya, Partha Chatterjee, *et al.*, *Strengthening Decentralization*: a report, Centre for the Studies in Social Sciences, Kolkata, 2006
53. K.S. Subramaniam, Parliamentary Communism: Crisis in the Indian Communist Movement, Ajanta Publications, Delhi, 1989.
54. *Singur: ekti unnayan Santras, Samiksha* May 1, 2009 Kolkata; and an Interview with Jyoti Basu, August 4, 2004 and July 6 2006; Jyoti Babu gave an elaborate interview to the present author for a project undertaken for the UPIASI, New Delhi.
55. Asoke Ghosh, general secretary of the AIFB expressed his views after the Singur imbroglio after an All Party Meeting at Mahajati Sadan in 2007 where the main opposition leader Ms. Mamata Banerjee was present but left in huff when the proposal was opposed by Subhas Chakraborty (CPI (M)) the Transport Minister; Bartaman, Kolkata, February 2007, Kshiti Goswami (RSP), Minister for PWD Bartaman, February 26, 2008.
56. Rezzak Molla, Land Reforms and Revenue Minister, LF government, The Statesman, Kolkata, September, 2009: Mr. Molla expressed the same opinion to the displeasure of his chief minister and the minister for Industry, earlier also during the land grabbing operation at Bhangar, South 24 Parganas and Rajarhat at North 24 Parganas
57. Arindam Ghosh-dostidar, the Statesman, Kolkata, September 14, 2009.
58. Buddhadeb Bhattacharjee, September 3, 2009 as quoted by Arindam Ghosh-dostidar, in the Statesman, edit page, *ibid.*
59. Dipak Kumar Ghosh, "A monster takes on its creator", Perspective, *The Statesman*, Kolkata, August 27, 2009.
60. Soumen Nag, *Prasanga: Gorkhaland, Saptarshi Prakasan*, Shreerampur Hooghly, 2005"; series of post edit pieces in *Uttarbanga Sambad*, Siliguri, from May to August, 2009.
61. Saoli Mitra, *Anyaya Je kore Ar Anyaya Je Sahe*, Ubudosh, Kolkata, 2009; Saoli is a famous theatre director, dramatist and an accomplished actress; she extensively visited many tea garden areas and other undeveloped places of North Bengal. The title of the book is a quote from Rabindranath Tagore's one of the bold pieces of poem. She is an essayist and authored a few books; she is a newspaper columnist; she writes frequently in the Dainik Statesman and language dailies, Kolkata; She took a leading role in the civil society movements against the CPI (M) and LF government against its land grab policy at Singur and Nandigram and Lalgarh as also the government's implementation of the Special Economic Zone (SEZ) projects.
62. *Ibid.*

63. Ashok Bhattacharya, minister for urban affairs, *Uttarbanga Sambad*, Siliguri, September 9, 2009; the chief minister Buddhdeb Bhattacharjee in an election meeting declared electoral sops to the audience and reiterated the same theme Ashok Bhattacharya referred to, in most of his election campaign; the opposition parties made a reference to the state election commission that the chief minister violated the election conduct rules after the campaign period was over for the election to be held on September 13, 2009;
64. Biman Basu, secretary state committee of the CPI (M) told it in a press conference as reported in the Statesman, September 17, 2009.
65. D. Bandapadhyay, the Land Reforms Commissioner and Secretary revenue department, wrote a booklet on *Land Reforms through Operation Barga,* Government of West Bengal, 1980, to celebrate the third year of the LF government (the booklet was withdrawn since)
66. Dmitri Volkogonov, The Rise and Fall of the Soviet Empire, Harper Collins Publishers, Great Britain, 1998.
67. Syamapada Pal, member of the control commission CPI (M) quoting from a Party Document placed in the Coimbatore Party conference in October 2007 gave the figure.
68. Amit Bhattacharyya, *Singur to Lalgarh via Nandigram*: *Rising Flames of People's Anger against Displacement, Destitution and State Terror*, Bisthapan Virodhi Jan Vikass Andolan, Ranchi, Jharkhand, 2009.
69. *Singur Theke Nandigram; ekti parjalochana*, People's Book Society Kolkata, 2006; *Nandigram - What really happened*, May 26-28, Report of the people's Tribunal on Nandigram, Danish Books, Delhi, 2007; *Nandigram; ganahatya*, A report published by APDR and PBKMS (*Paschimbanger Khet Mazur Samiti*), 2007;
70. Mahasweta Devi, Saoli Mitra, Shuvaprasanna, Bibhas Chakraborty, Shirshendu Mukharjee and many others of the Civil Society Group expressed the term which was published in the Statesman, Kolkata, Bartaman and Sambad Pratidin, continuously brought out the news items, after March 14, 2007.
71. Leaders like Biman Bose, Binay Konar and others, Dainik Statesman and most of the language dailies since March 15 and even after March 14, 2007.
72. Binay Konar, Daily Statesman, Kolkata, March 7-8, 2007; Buddhadeb Bhattacharya also continuously made a distinction between "we" and "they" particularly in a party rally in the Kolkata Maidan; he also made the comments frequently that the opposition party to the policy of industrialization by the Trinamool Congress would be dealt with severely; quoted by several language dailies, like *Daily statesman*, *Bartaman, Sambad Pratidin* and the March 8-11, 2009; national Daily *The Statesman*, Kolkata march 11, 2009.
73. Interview, Aparna Sen, December 20, 2008.
74. Manoj Bhattacharya, RSP, former MP (Rajya Sabha), September 2, 2009.
75. Sajal Rai Chaudhuri an Anup Bandyapadhyay, *Singur Theke Nandigram: A survey*, Ganaudyog, Kolkata, 2009; *Unnyan Singur Nandigram Tatwa, Tathya, Dalil Sankalan* (tran, Development Singur, Nandigram: A collection of Theories, Facts and Documents) in collaboration with the forum of Artistes, Cultural workers and intellectuals, *Durbar Kalam*, Kolkata, March 2008; Dipankar Chakraborty, *Prasanga Sez, Aneek granthmala/3* Aneek, People's Book Society, Kolkata.
76. Bibek DebRoy and Laveesh Bhandari, *Transforming West Bengal: Changing the Agenda for an Agenda for Change*, Indicus White Paper, February, 2009.

77. Quotes from the several speeches of Mamata Banerjee in different places of the state particularly in Lalgarh and Jhargram in West Midnapur, June in 2013 a few days before the 8th Panchayat elections and Belpahari on September 22, 2013, September 24, in Shildah, Bagmundi and Barikul and Jhargram in the first week of November before the 5 Municipal elections in 2013.
78. *Powering Progress and Empowering People*, Mamata Banerjee, on Foreword Government of West Bengal, a Report on performance, significant achievements and pipeline projects during the period from May 2011 to March, 2012.
79. *Powering Progress and Empowering People, ibid* page, v.
80. *ibid*, p. VII.
81. *ibid.*
82. *Ibid.*
83. Government of West Bengal, Documents, 2013.
84. Interview, the Chief Minister, Ms. Mamata Banerjee, July 25, 2011.
85. *Hope to Reality: one year of working together*, A report card, Government of West Bengal, Kolkata, p. 99.
86. As declared by the chief minister Mamata Banerjee in recent public meetings in different districts in January, 2014 and earlier also she emphasized the importance of these programmes.
87. Powering Progress and empowering people, *op. cit.*, p. X
88. The Statesman, Kolkata, February 7, 2014.
89. *Powering Progress and empowering people*, *op. cit.,* p. VI.

Select Bibliography

Apter, D. (1981). *Introduction to Political System.* New Delhi: Hall of India.

Azad, M.A. (1988). *India Wins Freedom.* Madras: Orient Longman.

Bandyopadhyay, D. (1980). *Land Reforms in West Bengal.* Calcutta.

Bandyopadhyay, D. (2001). *West Bengal Enduring Status Quo.* Kolkata: EPW.

Bandyopadhyay, N.M. (1993). *New Horizon for West Bengal's Panchayat.* Calcutta: EPW.

Bandyopadhyay, S.H. (1970). *Udbasthu.* Kolkata: Sahitya Sansad.

Basu, B. (2011). *Smiti Nie Dhaka.* Kolkata: Gangchil.

Bhandari, B.D. (2009). *Transforming west Bengal charging the Agenda for an Agenda for change.* Indieus white paper.

Bhattacharjee, B. (1997). *20 Years of LF government.* Calcutta: National Book Agency.

Biswas, D. (2005). *Bratyajaner Rudha Sangit.* Kolkata: Deys Publications.

Broomfield, J. (1968). *Elite Conflict in a Plural society.* Berkeley: University of California Press.

Budge, L. a. (1992). *Party Politics and Government Coalition.* New York: St. Martin's Press.

Butler, D. (1986). *Governing without a Majority.* London: The Macmillan Press Ltd.

Chakraborti, P.K. (1990). *The Marginal Men.* West Bengal: Kalyani.

Chakraborty, B. (2006). *Forging Power: Coalition Politics in India.* New Delhi: Oxford University Press.

Chakraborty, P. (1999). *The Marginalmen.* Calcutta: Naya Udyog.

Chander, N.J. (2004). *Coalition Politics: The Indian Experience.* New Delhi: Concept Publishing company.

chatterje, J. (2008). *The Spoils of Partition.* New Delhi: Cambridge University Press.

Chatterje, J. (2008). *The Spoils of Partition.* New Delhi: Cambridge University Press.

Chatterjee, P.K. (2004). *The Cripps Mission: An in-depth study.* Kolkata: Minerva Associates.

Chatterjee, P. (1997). *State and Politics in India.* Kolkata: Oxford University Press.

Chatterji, R. (1985). *Politics in West Bengal: Institution, Process and Problems.* Calcutta: World Press.

Chattopadhyay, B.C. (1986). *Anandamath.* Calcutta: Government of West Bengal.

Chaudhuri, A.K. (2007). *Electoral Politics in West Bengal: A predominant Party in government.* Delhi: Stander Publishers.

Chaudhuri, A.K. (1998). *Legislative Control over Public Administration: India Willies.* New York: Ananda Publishers.

Chaudhuri, A.K. (2005). *Minority Government: Coalition Politics an Indian Experiment.* Indian Journal of Political Science.

Chaudhuri, J. (1995). *Netaji Gelen Khothaye.* Pandulipi.

Chaudhuri, K. (2010). *When the Pendulum Stops: Death of Bengal Bureaucracy.* Nachiketa Publications.

Chaudhury, N.B. (1976). *Votex of Ideological Politics.* Meerut: Mennakshi Prakashan.

Choudhury, P.R. (1984). *The Left Experiment in West Bengal.* New Delhi: Patriot Publishers.

Dey, A. (1970). *Fazlul Haque O Pakistan Prastab.* Calcutta: Ratna Prakashan.

el, B.R. (1999). *Sonar Bangla: Agricultural Growth and Agrarian Change in West bengal and Bangladesh.* New Delhi: Sage Publications.

Ersson, J.-F.L. (2001). *European Politics: An Introduction.* London: Sage Publications.

Frankel, F.R. (1990). *Dominance and State Power in Modern India.* Delhi: Oxford University Press.

French, P. (1998). *Liberty or Death: India's Journey to Independence and Division.* New Delhi: Harper Collins Publishers India Pvt. Ltd.

G.K. Lieten. (1996). *Development, Devolution and Democracy: Village Discourse in West Bengal.* New Delhi: Sage Publications.

gangopadhyay, N. (1950). *Shilalipi.* Kolkata: Ananda Publishers.

Ghose, S. (1993). *Jawaharlal Nehru, a biography.* New Delhi: Allied Publishers.

Ghosh, A. (1981). *Peaceful transition to power.* Calcutta: Firma KLM Pvt. Ltd.

Ghosh, A. (2004). *The Hungry Tide.* New Delhi: Dayal Publishers.

ghosh, S. (2001). *Hastantar.* Kolkata: Ananda Publishers.

ghosh, S. (1971). *The Disinherited State; A study of West Bengal 1967-1971.* Bombay: Orient Longman.

Gupta, B.D. (1975). *The Naxalite Movement.* Bombay: Allied Publishers.

Herman, A. (2008). *Gandhi and Churchill: The Epic Rivalry that DestRoyed an Empire and forged our Age, Bantam.* New York.

Huq, A.K. (1944). *Bengal Today.* Calcutta: Gupta and Rahaman.

Industry, B. c. (1971). *West Bengal: An Analytical Study.* New Delhi: Oxford and IBH Publishing Co.

Jajabar. (1946). *Dristipat.* Calcutta: New Age Publishers.

JH, B. (1968). *Elite Conflict in Plural Society Twentieth-Century Bengal.* Bombay: Oxford University Press.

John, C. (1997). *Mission with Mountbatten.* New Delhi: New Age International Ltd.

Kar, B. (1989). *Deoyal.* Ananda Publishers.

Keman, I.B. (1990). *Parties and Democracy: Coalition Formation and Government Functioning in Twenty States.* New York: Oxford University Press.

Kohli, A. (1991). *Democracy and Discontent, India's Growing Crisis of Governability.* Cambridge: Cambridge University Press.

kohli, A. (1988). *India's Democracy: An Analysis of Changing State Society Relations.* Princeton: Princeton University Press.

Kohli, A. (2001). *The Success of India's Democracy.* Cambridge University Press.

Kueck, D.D. (1999). *Principles, Power and Politics.* New Delhi: Maclillan India.

Lakshi Krishnamurti, R.H. (2000). *Making a Success of Coalition.* Chennai: East West Pvt. Ltd.

Majeed, A. (2000). *Coalition Politics and Power Sharing.* New Delhi: Manak Publications.

Mallick, R. (1993). *Development Policy of Communist Government: West Bengal since 1977.* New York: Cambridge University Press.

Mascarenhas, A. (1971). *The Rape of Bangladesh.* Delhi: Vikas Publications.

Menon, V.P. (1957). *The Transfer of Power in India.* Calcutta: Orient Longman Limited.

Miller, G.D. (1960). *Communism.* Bombay: The Perennial Press.

Mitra, A. (2004). *Apila Chapola.* Kolkata: Ananda Publishers.

Mondal, J.C. (2002). *Marichihapi: Naishabder Antarale.* Kolkata: Bengali People's Book Society.

Moore, R.J. (1979). *Churchill, Cripps, and India, 1939-45.* USA: Oxford University Press.

Mukherjee, M. (2010). *Churchill's Secret War.*

Myron, W. (1963). *The Politics of Scarcity.* Calcutta: Asia Publishing House.

Nambudri, U. (2006). *Bengal's Night Without End,.* New Delhi: India First Foundation.

Negam, A. (2000). *Logic of Failed Revolution.* Kolkata: EPW.

Nossiter, T.J. (1988). *Marxist State Governments in India: Politics Economics and Society.* New York: Printer Publishers.

Pal, M. (2011). *Deshbhag: Binas O Binirman.* Kolkata: Gangchil Publication.

R.C. Majumder. (1967). *Three Phases of India's Struggle for Freedom.* Bombay: Bharatiya Vidya Bhavan.

Raghuraman, P.G. (2004). *A Time of Coalitions: Divided We Stand.* New Delhi: Sage Publications.

Ram, D.S. (2009). *Coalition Politics in India: Search for Political Stability.* New Delhi: National Publishing House.

Roy, J.K. (2011). *India's Foreign Relations.* New Delhi: Routledge.

Riker, W.H. (1970). *The Theory of Political Coalition.* Calcutta: Oxford IBH Publishing Co.

Roy, A. (1405). *Mukta Banger Smriti.* Kolkata: Mitra and Ghosh Publihsers.

Roy, D. (2001). *Keno Udbastu Hote Holo.* Kolkata: Ultadanga (Shri Syamaprasad De Pal).

Roy, P. (1969). *Keya Patar Nauka.* Kolkata: Karuna Prakashni.

Roy, P. (2010). *Sata DhaRoye Bohejaye.* Kolkata: Karuna Prakashni.

Roy, P. (2011). *The Search for Netaji: New Findings.* Kolkata: Purple Peacock Books and Arts.

Roy, R. (1972). *The Agony of West Bengal.* Calcutta: The New Age Publishers.

Roy, T. (202). *My People Uprooted: A Saga of the Hindus of Eastern Bengal.* Kolkata: Ratna Prakashan.

Rudolf, R.A. (1987). *In Pursuit of Lakshmi: The Political Economy of Indian State.* Bombay: Orient Longman.

Ruud, A.E. (2003). *Poetics of Village Politics: The Making of West Bengal Rural Communism.* New Delhi: Oxford University Press.

Sanyal, H. (1994). *Swarajer Pathe.* Kolkata: Papyrus Publications.

Schofield, M.L. (1998). *Multiparty Government: The Politics of Coalition in Europe.* USA: University of Michigan Press.

Sen, A. (1981). *Poverty and Famines: An Essay on Entitlement and Deprivation.* Delhi: Oxford University Press.

Sen, S.N. (1960). *The City of Calcutta.* Calcutta: Bookland Private Ltd.
Sengupta, A. (1997). *Joar bantaya Shat Sattar.* Pearl Publishers.
Sengupta, B. (2008). *Palabadaler Pala.* Ananda Publishers.
Sengupta, B. (2008). *Palabadaler Pala.* Ananda Publishers.
Sengupta, N. (2011). *Land of Two Rivers.* New Delhi: Penguin Books India Pvt. Ltd.
Sengupta, S. (2002). *Bangasanhar Ebong.* Kolkata: Naya Uddog.
Shirer, W.L. (1981). *Gandhi: A Memoir.* London: Abacus.
Subramanian, K.S. (1989). *Parliamentary Communism: Crisis in the India Communist Movement,.* Delhi: Ajanta Publications.
T.J. Nossite. (1988). *Marxist State Governments in India.* London and New York: Printer Publishers.
Tolstoy, L. *War and Peace.* New Yord: Random House.
Troll, G.M. (1988). *Abul Kalam Azad: An Intellectual and Religious Biography.* Delhi: Oxford University Press.
Wavell, L. (1977). *Wavell The ViceRoy's Journal Penderel Moon.* Delhi: Oxford University Press.
Webster, N. (1992). *Panchayati Raj and the Decentralization of Development Planning in West Bengal.* K.P. Bagchi & CO.
Weiner, M. (1963). *Politics of Scarcity: Public Pressure and Political responses in India.* Calcutta: Asia Publishing House.
Wolpert, S. (202). *Jinnah of Pakistan.* Oxford university Press.
Wood, J.R. (1984). *State Politics in Contemporary India, Crisis or Continuity.* London: West View Press.

Index

Sen, S.N. (1960). *The City of Calcutta.* Calcutta: Bookland Private Ltd.

Sengupta, A. (1997). *Joar bantaya Shat Sattar.* Pearl Publishers.

Sengupta, B. (2008). *Palabadaler Pala.* Ananda Publishers.

Sengupta, B. (2008). *Palabadaler Pala.* Ananda Publishers.

Sengupta, N. (2011). *Land of Two Rivers.* New Delhi: Penguin Books India Pvt. Ltd.

Sengupta, S. (2002). *Bangasanhar Ebong.* Kolkata: Naya Uddog.

Shirer, W.L. (1981). *Gandhi: A Memoir.* London: Abacus.

Subramanian, K.S. (1989). *Parliamentary Communism: Crisis in the India Communist Movement,.* Delhi: Ajanta Publications.

T.J. Nossite. (1988). *Marxist State Governments in India.* London and New York: Printer Publishers.

Tolstoy, L. *War and Peace.* New Yord: Random House.

Troll, G.M. (1988). *Abul Kalam Azad: An Intellectual and Religious Biography.* Delhi: Oxford University Press.

Wavell, L. (1977). *Wavell The ViceRoy's Journal Penderel Moon.* Delhi: Oxford University Press.

Webster, N. (1992). *Panchayati Raj and the Decentralization of Development Planning in West Bengal.* K.P. Bagchi & CO.

Weiner, M. (1963). *Politics of Scarcity: Public Pressure and Political responses in India.* Calcutta: Asia Publishing House.

Wolpert, S. (202). *Jinnah of Pakistan.* Oxford university Press.

Wood, J.R. (1984). *State Politics in Contemporary India, Crisis or Continuity.* London: West View Press.

Index